Botticelli *and Treasures from the Hamilton Collection*

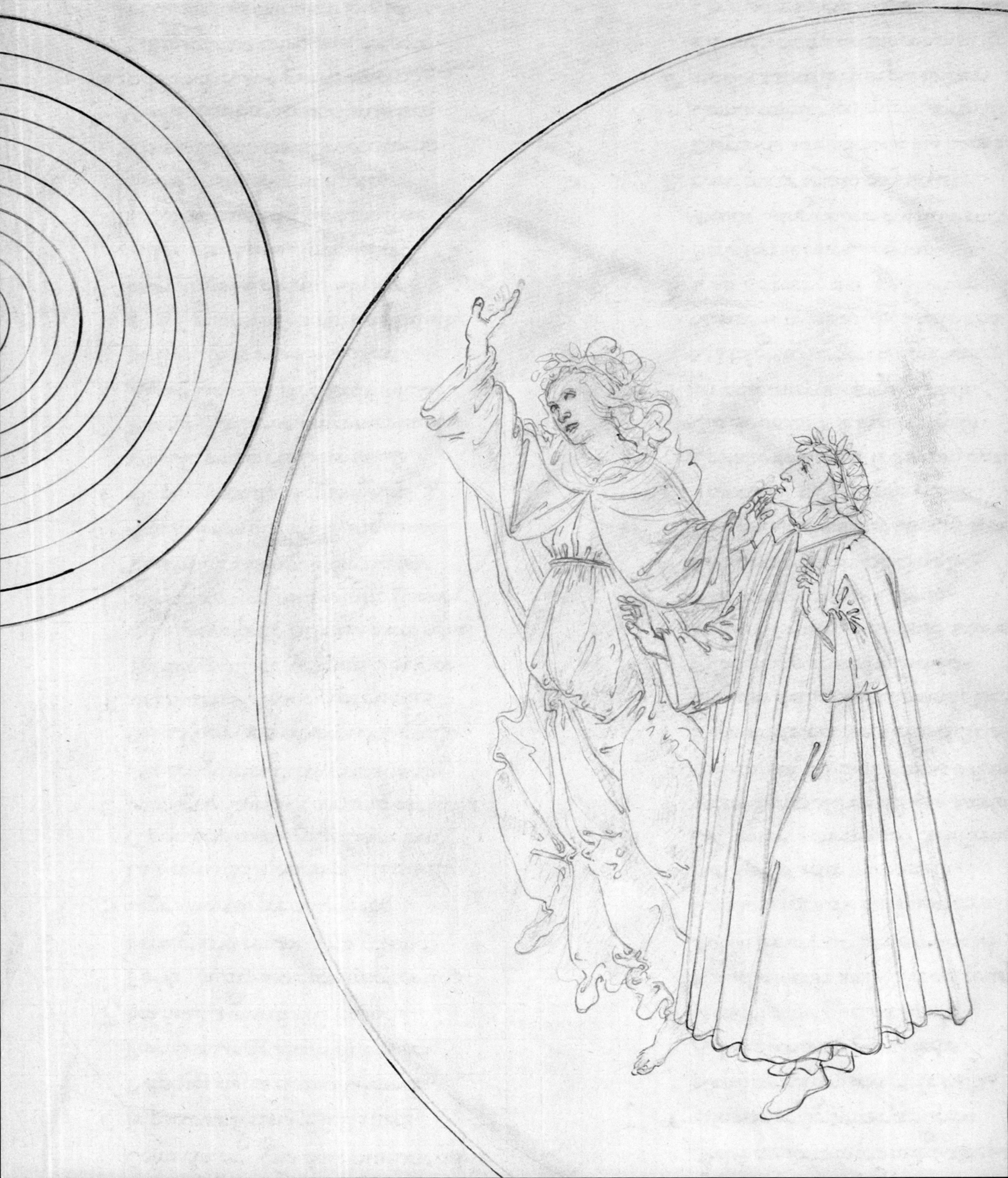

Botticelli *and Treasures from the Hamilton Collection*

EDITED BY
Dagmar Korbacher

WITH CONTRIBUTIONS BY
Stephanie Buck, Dagmar Korbacher, and Frauke Steenbock with Beatrice Alai and Georg Josef Dietz

THE COURTAULD Gallery

Kupferstichkabinett
Staatliche Museen zu Berlin

IN ASSOCIATION WITH
Paul Holberton publishing

First published to accompany the exhibition

Botticelli and Treasures from the Hamilton Collection

The Courtauld Gallery, London
18 February – 15 May 2016

The exhibition was first shown at the Kupferstichkabinett, Berlin, as
Der Botticelli-Coup. Schätze der Sammlung Hamilton im Kupferstichkabinett,
16 October 2015 – 24 January 2016

The Courtauld Gallery is supported by the Higher Education Funding Council for England (HEFCE)

HIGHER EDUCATION FUNDING COUNCIL FOR ENGLAND hefce

ISBN 978 1 907372 92 6

British Library Cataloguing in Publication Data

A catalogue record for this book is available from the British Library

Produced by Paul Holberton publishing
89 Borough High Street, London SE1 1NL
www.paul-holberton.net

Designed by Laura Parker

Translated from the German by Büro LS Anderson, Berlin
(Graham Fallowes: essays; Isabel Aitken: manuscripts;
Joel Scott, Lance Anderson and Orla Ambrose: Dante drawings)

English versions of Dante's poem derived from the translation by John Dickson Sinclair (published in numerous editions)

Origination by Wienand and printing by B.O.S.S Medien GmbH

FRONT COVER Botticelli, *Paradiso* VI, cat. no. 41 (detail)
BACK COVER Northern France, *Histoire du bon roi Alexandre*, fol. 67r, cat. no. 5 (detail)
FRONTISPIECE Botticelli, *Paradiso* II, cat. no. 38 (detail)
PAGE 6 Botticelli, *Inferno* XXII, cat. no. 20 (detail)
PAGE 9 Botticelli, *Paradiso* I, cat. no. 37 (detail)

Contents

6 *Foreword*

8 *Exhibition benefactors*

10 *The Hamilton Collection*
FRAUKE STEENBOCK

14 *"I am very, very happy that we have it": Botticelli's Dante and the Hamilton collection at the Kupferstichkabinett*
DAGMAR KORBACHER

24 *Botticelli's "Dante on vellum": Unfinished but Works of Art in Their Own Right*
STEPHANIE BUCK

36 *Catalogue*

38 *The Manuscripts of the Hamilton Collection*

72 *The Jewel of the Hamilton Collection: Sandro Botticelli's drawings for Dante's Divine Comedy*

154 *The Divine Comedy: Early illustrations in printed editions*

162 *Bibliography*

Foreword

In the museum world of late nineteenth-century London and Berlin, few events caused as much of a stir as the sale, in 1882, of the Duke of Hamilton's collection of rare manuscripts. The event sparked a discussion that involved the public on both sides of the English Channel as to the value and importance that such private collections carry for nation states – a discussion that remains highly relevant to this day. The prospect of the sale resulted in feverish attempts to keep these masterpieces of manuscript illumination and illustration – and Botticelli's drawings of Dante's *Divine Comedy* in particular – firmly on British soil. From a curatorial perspective, the idea has always greatly appealed to us of presenting an exhibition in both our capitals on the sale, or conversely the acquisition, of the Hamilton Collection. For us, it is an opportunity to highlight, in spite of their fragility, the works' enormous importance, especially as it was felt that such a display would follow on perfectly from the exhibition of all Botticelli's Dante drawings in 2000–01.

The Berlin Kupferstichkabinett is the largest collection of graphic art in Germany. What is extremely unusual, perhaps even unique for a museum of the graphic arts is that, in addition to drawings and prints dating from all epochs, illuminated manuscripts and individual miniatures from the Middle Ages and Renaissance were, from the outset, also the subject of its collecting activities. Its manuscripts department boasts some of the most beautiful and most important examples of manuscript illumination anywhere in the world – thanks not least to the rich accession that the Hamilton manuscripts represented. This aspect of the collection is inextricably linked to the fact that the museum has its origins in the court library of the House of Brandenburg. In 1652, Friedrich Wilhelm von Brandenburg, dubbed 'the Great Elector', acquired more than 2500 drawings and watercolours collected by Johan Maurits of Nassau, who had been governor of the Dutch West India Company in Brazil from 1637 to 1644. By doing so, the Great Elector established a diverse and superb collection of works on paper, which was bestowed on the Kupferstichkabinett upon its founding, in 1831.

The act of collecting beautiful manuscripts has its roots in the Renaissance and specifically in the artistic spirit and learning of that age. Our two institutions, the Berlin Kupferstichkabinett and the Courtauld, share a rich history of scholarship that makes them ideal partners in the present exhibition. The Courtauld Institute of Art, one of the leading institutions for the research and study of the fine arts, founded in 1932, was the first place in Britain to teach art history as an academic discipline and to seek to do so by applying the rigorous methods that had been established in Germany and Austria in the late nineteenth century. The art of the Middle Ages and the Renaissance has occupied a central position in the curriculum since the Courtauld Institute of Art's founding. As a public art museum, The Courtauld Gallery plays an important role in British cultural life, and Botticelli's large altarpiece *The Trinity with Saints* is one of the many masterpieces in its outstanding collection.

Especially in recent years, The Courtauld Gallery has emerged as a crucial centre for the scholarly investigation and presentation of drawings. Against this backdrop it is with great pleasure that we can now show, along with the manuscripts, a great number of Botticelli's drawings for Dante's *Divine Comedy*. The exhibition is the latest expression of a fruitful collaboration between the curators and conservators of our two institutions, though the most significant to date.

We extend our heartfelt thanks to the two curators: the project's initiator, Dagmar Korbacher (Berlin Kupferstichkabinett) and her London counterpart, Stephanie Buck (now director of Dresden's Kupferstichkabinett). Special thanks also go to Hanka Gerhold, the manuscripts expert at the Kupferstichkabinett's conservation and restoration department, for devising such an appealing display format for the codices. We are also indebted to the contributors, Frauke Steenbock, Beatrice Alai and Georg Josef Dietz, who have applied their extensive knowledge and wealth of experience in their respective fields each to make a fundamental contribution to the re-evaluation of the acquisition of the Hamilton Collection, the Dante drawings and the historical role of the Berlin Kupferstichkabinett.

HEINRICH SCHULZE ALTCAPPENBERG
Director of the Kupferstichkabinett,
Staatliche Museen zu Berlin

ERNST VEGELIN VAN CLAERBERGEN
Head of The Courtauld Gallery, London

Exhibition Benefactors

The Courtauld Gallery wishes to thank the following generous benefactors of the exhibition:

Anonymous in memory of Melvin R. Seiden

The International Music and Art Foundation

Friends of The Courtauld

This exhibition has been made possible by the provision of insurance through the Government Indemnity Scheme. The Courtauld Gallery would like to thank HM Government for providing indemnity and extends its thanks to the Department for Culture, Media and Sport, and to Arts Council England for administering the scheme.

IMAF
INTERNATIONAL MUSIC & ART FOUNDATION

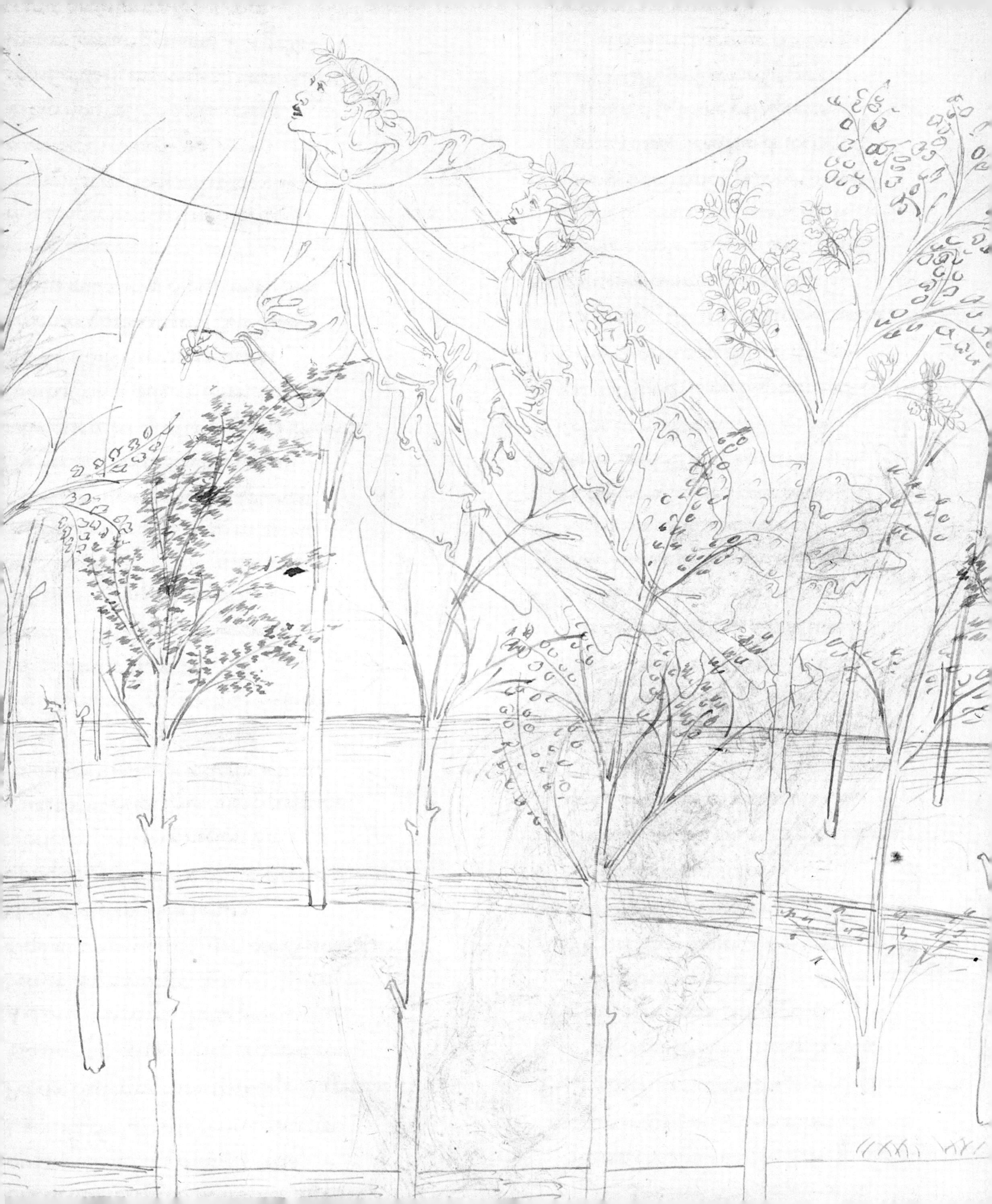

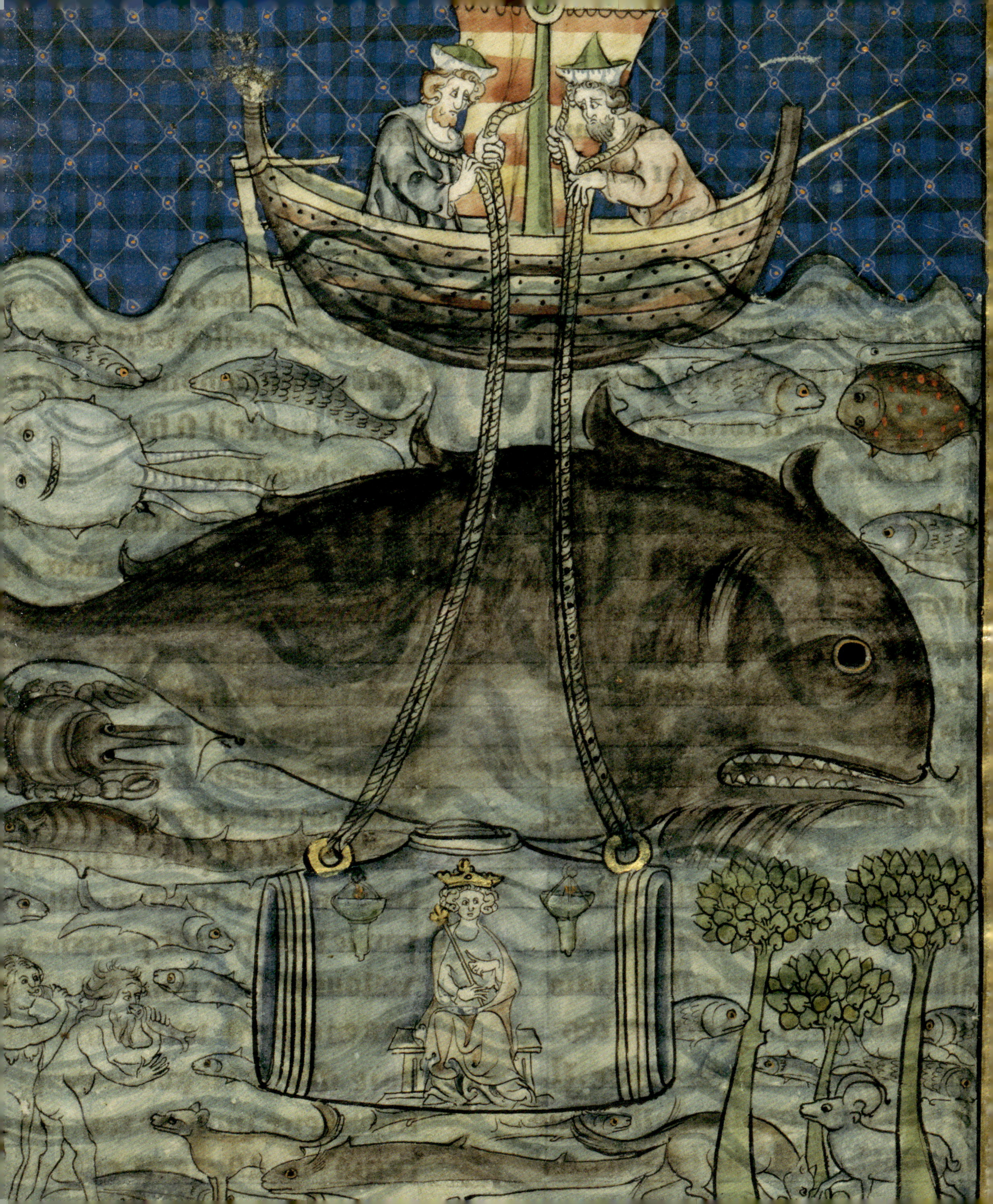

The Hamilton Collection

FRAUKE STEENBOCK

The Marquess of Douglas and Clydesdale (1767–1852), 10th Duke of Hamilton (from 1819), belonged to an ancient Scottish family that traced its origins back to the early Middle Ages through a long line of powerful and wealthy landowners (fig. 1). Like other young noblemen of the period, Alexander Douglas embarked on the customary Grand Tour. However, his travels were not limited to Italy, instead taking him to all parts of Europe (partly for diplomatic purposes) and even as far as Russia. During this tour he was already acquiring books for his collection, including – as befitted his classical education – costly early printed editions of texts by Greek and Roman authors and illuminated manuscripts, typically of Italian provenance. A selection of the works is listed in a book edited by William Clarke and published in 1819, entitled *Repertorium Bibliographicum or Some Account of the Most Celebrated British Libraries*.[1] It includes (on p. 260) a reference to "Dante Alighieri, La Commedia, MS. on vellum, oblong folio. Saec. XV. This fine MS., written about the year 1450 contains the entire poem, with the exception of some Cantos of the 'Inferno'. It is ornamented with eighty-eight original designs supposed to be executed by the hand of Sandro Botticelli, or some other eminent Florentine artist."[2]

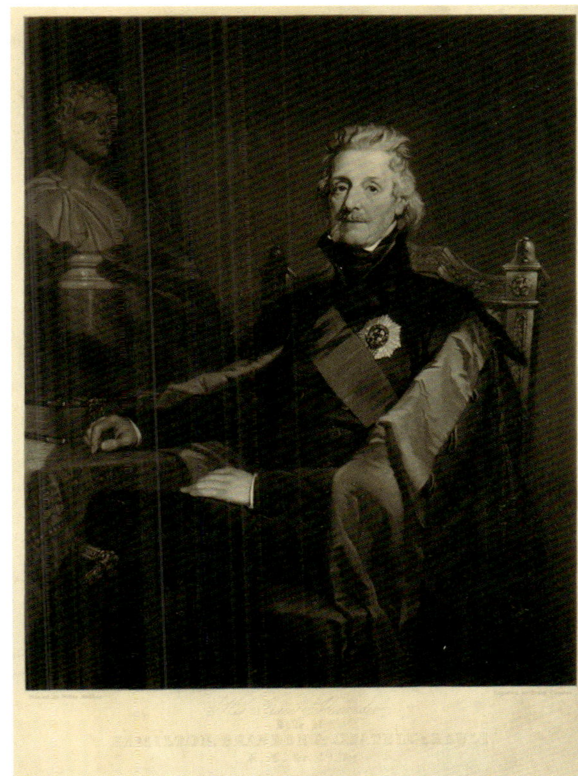

FIG. 1
Henry Cousins after Willis Maddox, *His Grace Alexander Duke of Hamilton*, c. 1850, mezzotint and mixed media, London, British Museum, inv. no. 2010,7081.4059

With his varied literary interests, his scholarship of impressive scope, and considerable financial wherewithal, the Duke was able to expand his library over the course of the years through an impressive series of acquisitions at auctions and booksellers (fig. 2). Having first dealt with William Clarke (until 1830) and his son George Clarke (until 1835), the Duke's primary agent and supplier from 1831 was the young and upcoming bookseller Henry G. Bohn. When Bohn later learned of the forthcoming sale of the library, he wrote a letter to *The Times* in which he gave an account of his prominent client.[3] He recalled that, in the early years, the Duke would regularly meet up with his father-in-law, William Beckford,[4] and choose from the books acquired by Bohn during his extensive trips to the Continent. Hamilton's selections continued to favour books with Italian provenances, which included both illuminated

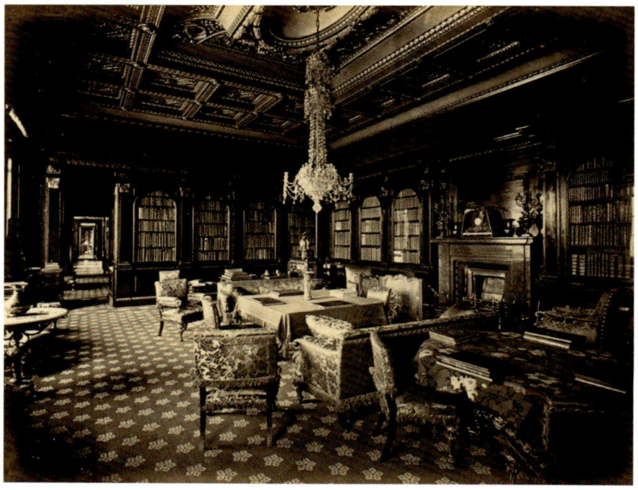

FIG. 2
Hamilton Palace Library, photograph, Glasgow, University of Glasgow, photo B10/11

manuscripts and early illustrated editions. Upon William Beckford's death in 1844, his daughter inherited his library in his villa near Bath, which Henry Bohn was then given the task of valuing – and since the Duchess did not wish for the books to be sold, he was also entrusted with transporting them to Hamilton Palace. He was invited to set up and organise the library in the Duchess's own specially prepared rooms. The Duke participated enthusiastically in the project and proved to be a generous host. Bohn was particularly impressed by the aristocratic lifestyle he encountered, which included formal evening dinners at which liveried servants would stand behind the chair of every guest.

Gustav Friedrich Waagen gave a similar account of Hamilton Palace following his visit in 1850. He was, however, disappointed that he was only given a short time to look at the Botticelli manuscript, which is why his description of the work was limited to just a few words.[5]

Under the stewardship of the 11th Duke of Hamilton, William Alexander Douglas (1811–1863), in the decades that followed, the collection was looked after with appropriate care, albeit without a significant number of additional acquisitions. The 10th Duke's grandson, by contrast, squandered the family inheritance with his costly and extravagant lifestyle, accruing such enormous debts that he was forced to sell parts of the collection and put the library up for auction. The manuscripts of the Hamilton and Beckford libraries were to be auctioned at the same sale. A catalogue was compiled, although, instead of being put on general release, it was distributed exclusively to potential buyers. The Dante manuscript is listed as lot number 201.[6]

The forthcoming auction not only attracted a good deal of attention in Great Britain, it also provoked a flurry of interest among Continental collectors and connoisseurs. News of the planned sale soon reached Friedrich Lippmann (1838–1903), the acting director of the Berlin Kupferstichkabinett (Museum of Prints and Drawings) from 1876 (he was formally appointed in 1878). His interest in the collection was centred primarily on the Dante manuscript. In a letter to the director-general of the Königliche Museen (Royal Museums) of Berlin, Richard Schöne (1840–1922), he described the manuscript illustrated by Botticelli as "one of the most important landmarks in Renaissance art to be found anywhere in the world".[7] However, the chances of acquiring this artistic gem on its own were slim indeed, and the idea of leaving its fate to the luck of the auction held little appeal. Thus the idea came about to purchase the complete collection of manuscripts. A commission was then sent to London with the task of assessing the collection's scholarly and artistic value. As well as Lippmann, the group included Wilhelm Bode (1845–1929), then employed by the Berlin Gemäldegalerie, Adolf von Beckerath (1834–1915), a silk manufacturer from Krefeld and himself an important collector, primarily of Italian drawings (his collection was acquired by the Kupferstichkabinett in 1902), and Alfred Schöne (1836–1908), a classical scholar at the Academy of Sciences in Paris. Initial reservations about the proposed purchase led the commission to recommend bidding on only the most important manuscripts at the auction. Yet this approach seemed just as unlikely to yield a successful outcome. A subsequent appraisal, by contrast, concluded that the museum was presented with an unparallelled opportunity to obtain a number of unique treasures for Berlin. In a letter to his brother Richard, the director-general of the Königliche Museen of Berlin, Alfred Schöne highlighted the good state of preservation both of the codices and of their bindings (some of which were original), as well as their potential value for academic research. In the light of additional appraisals and consultations, a recommendation was made to proceed with the acquisition.

However, there were also a number of dissenting voices in Great Britain who sought to prevent the manuscripts from being sold to foreign buyers. The painter John Ruskin wrote a pamphlet appealing for donations to ensure the collection remained in Great Britain, although the campaign met with little success.[8] Even Queen Victoria and her daughter Victoria, Crown Princess of Prussia and wife of the heir to the German throne, expressed in their correspondence the view that such a valuable piece of cultural heritage, and particularly the Dante manuscript, should remain in Great Britain.[9]

In the meantime, Friedrich Lippmann had used his extraordinary negotiating skills to finalise the sales contract. The agreement stipulated that any documents relating specifically to England and/or Scotland should be removed from the collection, and that these should remain in the country.[10] The sale price remained confidential, although estimates varied between £70,000 and £88,000.[11] Among documents relating to the Hamilton manuscripts held at the manuscripts department of the Staatsbibliothek (Potsdamer Straße), there is a statement of account issued by Ellis & White, 29 New Bond Street, and signed on 8 December 1882. It gives the figure of £82,000 for a total of 692 manuscripts. From this, £8,000 was to be deducted to take into account those works considered to be of British interest. This left a total amount owing of £74,000 – equivalent to 1,480,000 gold marks.[12] Since this sum could not be covered by the two institutions' collective annual budget, they were faced with serious difficulties. An intervention by the Minister of Culture, Gustav von Gossler, secured a concession from his counterpart at the Ministry of Finance, which authorised the release of the required sum from the Kaiser's general revenue fund – although the money would eventually have to be paid back. In order to balance the accounts, it was agreed that a portion of the manuscripts would be re-sold. By the end of October, the booksellers Ellis & White had packed the manuscripts into eighteen zinc containers, which were then loaded on to four ships; the items arrived in Berlin between 30 October and 1 November 1882. The containers were unpacked in the exhibition rooms of the Kupferstichkabinett and the manuscripts laid out on tables. Initially, only a small number of experts and members of the press were given the opportunity to examine the manuscripts.

In a letter dated 17 November, von Gossler wrote to the Königliche Bibliothek's chief librarian, Karl Richard Lepsius, that the Kaiser "[wished] to inspect a selection of manuscripts from the Hamilton Collection this coming Sunday, 19 November, at around 11:30 a.m. in His Majesty's Palace". The sources are, however, silent as to whether the Kaiser was impressed by what he saw.

Reports of the purchase had already appeared in the press. On Sunday 5 November and Tuesday 7 November, the supplement of *Die Post* (nos. 302, 304) featured articles by Alfred Rosenberg, including one entitled 'On the Circumstances Surrounding the Acquisition of the Hamilton Collection of Manuscripts' ('Über die Vorgänge beim Ankauf der Hamilton'schen Manuskripten-sammlung'), a column with the headline 'The Acquisition of Hamilton Collection of Miniatures and Manuscripts' ('Der Ankauf der Hamiltonschen Sammlung von Miniaturen und Manuskripten'), and a piece published over the course of two issues, 'The Hamilton Manuscript Collection in the Royal Kupferstichkabinett' ('Die Hamiltonsche Manuskripten-Sammlung im Königlichen Kupferstich-Kabinet'). The articles provided a detailed account of the acquisition and devoted particular attention to the collection's main point of interest, the Dante manuscript with its drawings by Botticelli. They also included an informative overview of a number of other manuscripts. Friedrich Lippmann immediately announced the acquisition in the *Jahrbuch der Königlich Preußischen Kunstsammlungen*.[13] A catalogue compiled by Paul Wescher, *Beschreibendes Verzeichnis der Miniaturen, Handschriften und Einzelblätter des Kupferstichkabinetts der Staatlichen Museen Berlin*, was published in 1931. A more recent catalogue appeared in 1966: compiled by Helmut Boese, *Die lateinischen Handschriften der Sammlung Hamilton* listed the items as meticulously as the division of Berlin would allow, and included a history of the collection in its detailed introduction.[14]

The loss of this important collection attracted limited further comment in Great Britain, where the press appeared more concerned with the Duke of Hamilton's scandalous behaviour. However, in December 1882 a lengthy article appeared in *The Bibliographer – A Journal of Book-Lore*,[15] which referred to information given in *The Times* and gave a detailed description of the most important manuscripts: "Above all others in the first class must be mentioned the manuscript of Dante's 'Divina Commedia', written in the fifteenth century, and illustrated with upwards of eighty drawings by the hand of Sandro Botticelli. This priceless volume may, without exaggeration, be described as the most valuable manuscript in existence for its artistic interest, for it stands alone as an example of a literary work of the first order illustrated by an artist of the highest rank."

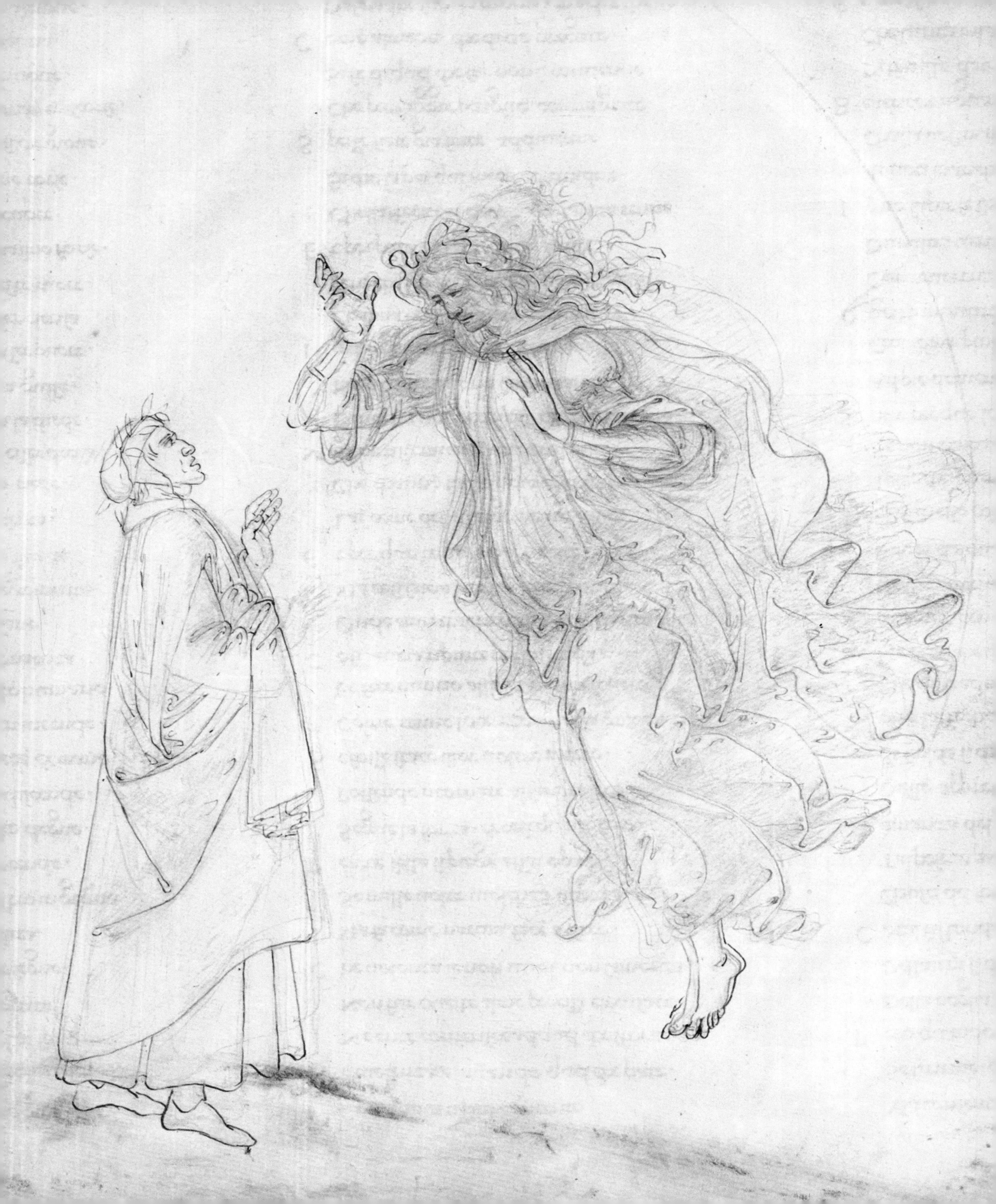

"I am very, very happy that we have it": Botticelli's Dante and the Hamilton collection at the Kupferstichkabinett

DAGMAR KORBACHER

In 1882, the Königliche Museen (Royal Museums) of Berlin pulled off an unprecedented coup when they successfully acquired *en bloc* the near-complete library of the Duke of Hamilton, comprising over 700 valuable manuscripts, before an auction in which the works were due to be sold could take place.

The event is unique in the annals of art collecting, art history, and the museums' own acquisitions policy. But what could possibly have induced the Prussian government to raise the enormous sum of 1.5 million gold marks? Why would an art museum – the Kupferstichkabinett (Museum of Prints and Drawings) – have invested so much energy into initiating and pushing through the acquisition of the library? And of all the world-class manuscript collections coming on to the market in Great Britain during this period, what was it about the Hamilton Collection in particular that made it so coveted? The answer to all these questions is simple, and appears as lot 201 on page 31 of a catalogue that, though printed, was never widely distributed. For here is listed a single codex ('Dante Alighieri, *Commedia*') which, according to the description, contained "88 exquisitely beautiful Designs by SANDRO BOTTICELLI" (fig. 3).[1]

By the time he became the 10th Duke of Hamilton in 1819, Alexander Douglas, Marquess of Douglas and Clydesdale (see fig. 1, p. 11), had already acquired numerous bibliographic treasures and accumulated a sizeable library. The first reference to the Dante volume appeared that same year in William Clarke's *Repertorium Bibliographicum or Some Account of the Most Celebrated British Libraries*,[2] where it is noted as one of the highlights of the Hamilton Collection. Since Clarke's visit to Hamilton Palace had taken place some three years previously, the Marquess must have acquired the codex before 1816 or 1817.

From the contents description pasted into the front of the volume in which the drawings were bound until they were brought to Berlin (fig. 4), we can trace the trail of Botticelli's *Commedia* drawings back to Giovanni Claudio Molini (1724–1812). Molini wrote the description on 17 April 1803 in Paris, where the Florence-born bookseller had

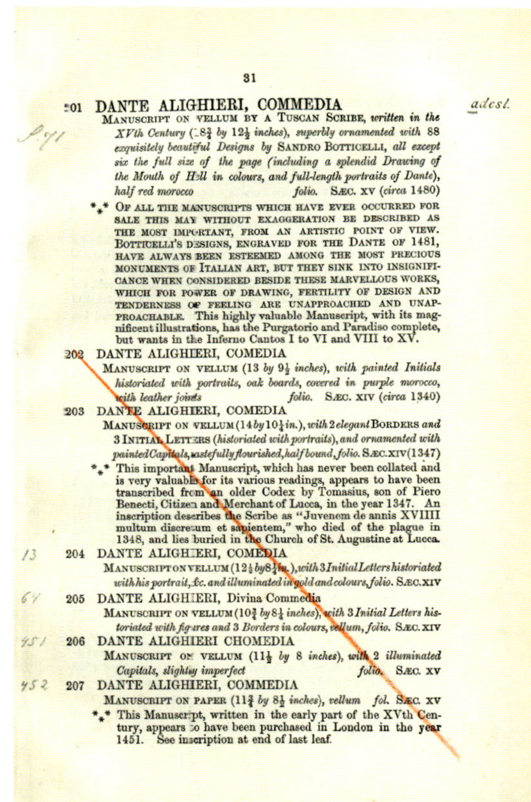

31

201 DANTE ALIGHIERI, COMMEDIA adest.
MANUSCRIPT ON VELLUM BY A TUSCAN SCRIBE, *written in the XVth Century* ($8\frac{3}{4}$ *by* $12\frac{1}{2}$ *inches*), *superbly ornamented with* 88 *exquisitely beautiful Designs by* SANDRO BOTTICELLI, *all except six the full size of the page (including a splendid Drawing of the Mouth of Hell in colours, and full-length portraits of Dante), half red morocco* *folio.* SÆC. XV (*circa* 1480)

*** OF ALL THE MANUSCRIPTS WHICH HAVE EVER OCCURRED FOR SALE THIS MAY WITHOUT EXAGGERATION BE DESCRIBED AS THE MOST IMPORTANT, FROM AN ARTISTIC POINT OF VIEW. BOTTICELLI'S DESIGNS, ENGRAVED FOR THE DANTE OF 1481, HAVE ALWAYS BEEN ESTEEMED AMONG THE MOST PRECIOUS MONUMENTS OF ITALIAN ART, BUT THEY SINK INTO INSIGNIFICANCE WHEN CONSIDERED BESIDE THESE MARVELLOUS WORKS, WHICH FOR POWER OF DRAWING, FERTILITY OF DESIGN AND TENDERNESS OF FEELING ARE UNAPPROACHED AND UNAPPROACHABLE. This highly valuable Manuscript, with its magnificent illustrations, has the Purgatorio and Paradiso complete, but wants in the Inferno Cantos I to VI and VIII to XV.

202 DANTE ALIGHIERI, COMEDIA
MANUSCRIPT ON VELLUM (13 *by* $9\frac{1}{2}$ *inches*), *with painted Initials historiated with portraits, oak boards, covered in purple morocco, with leather joints* *folio.* SÆC. XIV (*circa* 1340)

203 DANTE ALIGHIERI, COMEDIA
MANUSCRIPT ON VELLUM (14 *by* $10\frac{1}{4}$ *in.*), *with 2 elegant* BORDERS *and* 3 INITIAL LETTERS (*historiated with portraits*), *and ornamented with painted Capitals, tastefully flourished, half bound, folio.* SÆC. XIV (1347)

*** This important Manuscript, which has never been collated and is very valuable for its various readings, appears to have been transcribed from an older Codex by Tomasius, son of Piero Benecti, Citizen and Merchant of Lucca, in the year 1347. An inscription describes the Scribe as "Juvenem de annis XVIIII multum discretum et sapientem," who died of the plague in 1348, and lies buried in the Church of St. Augustine at Lucca.

13 204 DANTE ALIGHIERI, COMEDIA
MANUSCRIPT ON VELLUM ($12\frac{1}{2}$ *by* $8\frac{1}{4}$ *in.*), *with 3 Initial Letters historiated with his portrait, &c. and illuminated in gold and colours, folio.* SÆC. XIV

64 205 DANTE ALIGHIERI, Divina Commedia
MANUSCRIPT ON VELLUM ($10\frac{3}{4}$ *by* $8\frac{1}{4}$ *inches*), *with 3 Initial Letters historiated with figures and 3 Borders in colours, vellum, folio.* SÆC. XIV

451 206 DANTE ALIGHIERI CHOMEDIA
MANUSCRIPT ON VELLUM ($11\frac{1}{2}$ *by* 8 *inches*), *with 2 illuminated Capitals, slightly imperfect* *folio.* SÆC. XV

452 207 DANTE ALIGHIERI, COMMEDIA
MANUSCRIPT ON PAPER ($11\frac{3}{4}$ *by* $8\frac{1}{2}$ *inches*), *vellum* *fol.* SÆC. XV

*** This Manuscript, written in the early part of the XVth Century, appears to have been purchased in London in the year 1451. See inscription at end of last leaf.

FIG. 3
Annotated sale catalogue, *The Hamilton Palace Libraries. The Hamilton Collection of Manuscripts*, Sotheby, Wilkinson & Hodge, London, page with lot 201, Berlin, Kupferstichkabinett, Staatliche Museen zu Berlin

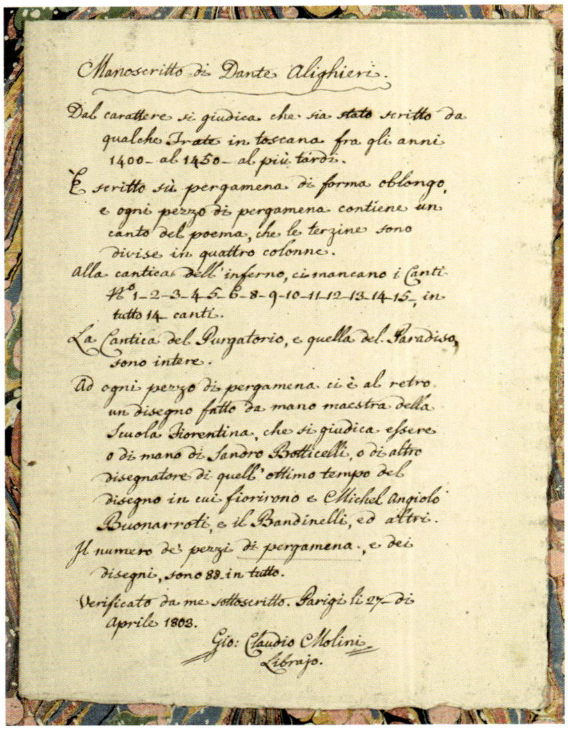
Manoscritto di Dante Alighieri.

Dal carattere si giudica che sia stato scritto da qualche Frate in toscana fra gli anni 1400 al 1450 al più tardi.

È scritto sù pergamena di forma oblongo, e ogni pezzo di pergamena contiene un canto del poema, che le terzine sono divise in quattro colonne.

Alla cantica dell'inferno, ci mancano i Canti N.o 1-2-3-4-5-6-8-9-10-11-12-13-14-15, in tutto 14 canti.

La Cantica del Purgatorio, e quella del Paradiso, sono intere.

Ad ogni pezzo di pergamena ci è al retro un disegno fatto da mano maestra della Scuola Fiorentina, che si giudica essere o di mano di Sandro Botticelli, o di altro disegnatore di quell'ottimo tempo del disegno in cui fiorirono e Michel Angiolo Buonarroti, e il Bandinelli, ed altri.

Il numero dei pezzi di pergamena, e dei disegni, sono 88 in tutto.

Verificato da me sottoscritto. Parigi li 27 di Aprile 1803.

Gio: Claudio Molini
Librajo.

FIG. 4
Contents description of Codex Hamilton 201, compiled by Giovanni Claudio Molini, Paris, 27 April 1803, Berlin, Kupferstichkabinett, Staatliche Museen zu Berlin, Cim. 33

worked since 1765 as an independent *imprimeur-libraire*. We can only assume that the Marquess purchased the volume containing the drawings directly from him, perhaps also in 1803 – the description subsequently pasted into the volume looks to all intents and purposes like a certificate – although there is no supporting evidence for this. Despite Giovanni Claudio Molini having a commercial contact in London – his brother Pietro Molini, who had made the city his home – it is just as likely that the Marquess acquired the volume directly in Paris. Molini's shop, which from 1784 to 1801 was situated on the rue Mignon, and then from 1803 to 1812 on the rue de Touraine, would have been a likely destination for a diplomat and collector with a passion for books.[3] As a bookseller and publisher, Molini specialised exclusively in printing and distributing Italian literature. He imported large numbers of books, including manuscripts and incunabula, from all regions of Italy.[4] There is, however, nothing to indicate where he might have obtained the volume containing the Botticelli drawings, which was possibly in his possession only for a relatively short period. As Georg Josef Dietz shows (cat. no. 47), the volume was most likely (re-)bound in France towards the end of the eighteenth century.[5] This suggests that Molini did not import the codex from Italy, but rather that it was already in France. However, we do not know whose hands the drawings passed through after leaving Botticelli's possession until they were catalogued by Molini some three hundred years later. In 1986 Peter Dreyer suggested that the drawings had been sent as a diplomatic gift to the French court as early as the turn of the sixteenth century.[6] What is certain is that the original cycle of drawings comprised 102 leaves, from which at some point seven drawings were separated, which in 1632 formed part of Alexandre Petau's library in Paris, and from 1658 were in the possession of Queen Christina of Sweden.[7] These then passed into the hands of Cardinals Decio and Pompeo Azzolini and of Pope Alexander VIII, and thence into the Vatican Library, where they were re-discovered in 1885 after their counterparts from the larger section of the suite had come to light.[8]

Potentially there may be evidence regarding the whereabouts of the drawings after Botticelli's death in works of art bearing a formal resemblance to some of them, and it might be inferred that the volume was still in Florence in the sixteenth century, when a small number of artists were able to study the drawings, either individually or as a series.[9] This group may have included Michelangelo,[10] Giovanni Stradano (Jan van der Straet)[11] and, in particular, Federico Zuccari, whose *Commedia* drawings (1585–88) appear to echo Botticelli's compositions in some ways.[12] Similarly it has been suggested, although not convincingly, that in the eighteenth century Johann Heinrich Füssli (Fuseli) might have seen and been influenced by the drawings while he was in Italy.[13] The first clear instance of the drawings' influence dates from the 1840s. The Scottish painter William Dyce likely saw the drawings on a visit to Hamilton Palace. His unfinished painting of Beatrice and Dante in Aberdeen (fig. 5) bears an unmistakable similarity to the drawing of Paradise I (cat. no. 37).[14]

With the discovery of the drawings came the task of confirming that they were indeed by Botticelli. A late eighteenth-century inscription on the cover of the codex already made this claim, although in a somewhat qualified manner (and with a spelling error in the artist's name):

FIG. 5
William Dyce, *Dante and Beatrice*, c. 1840–50, oil on canvas, Aberdeen, Aberdeen Art Gallery, inv. ABDAG003202

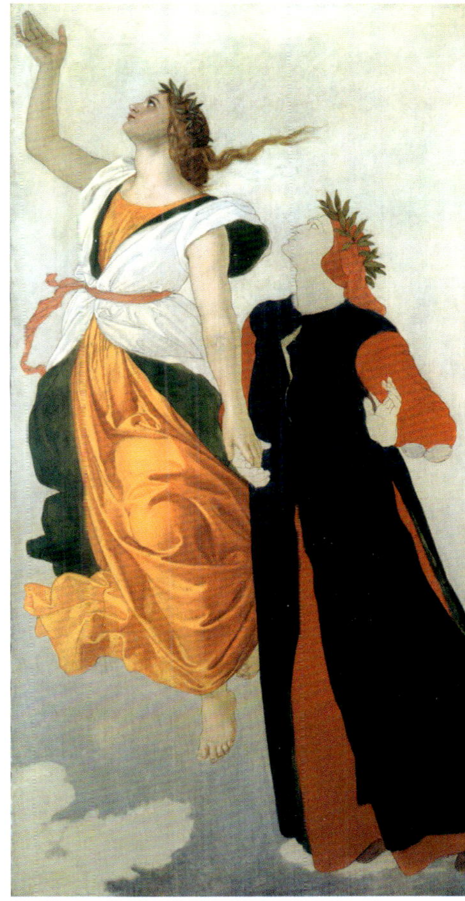

"... by Botirelli [sic] or another artist of the Florentine school".[15] The contents description mentioned previously, written by Molini and affixed in the volume, indicates that the Dante text had been illustrated by a Florentine artist – either Botticelli or some other artist from this golden age of drawing ("*o di mano di Sandro Botticelli, o di altro disegnatore di quell'ottimo tempo del disegno*"). This view informed Clarke's reference to the volume, as is clear from comments he wrote in 1819.[16] It seems rather unlikely, however, that either of these notices were based on any real expertise or critical analysis of the drawings' style. Well into the nineteenth century, works of art that looked in some way Florentine or simply out of the ordinary were attributed to Botticelli.[17] Furthermore it is striking that neither Molini nor Clarke picked up on the comments made by Vasari regarding Botticelli's work on Dante, or to the engravings from the 1481 edition of the *Commedia* that were believed to be by Baccio Baldini and based on Botticelli's drawings. The engravings remained well known in the centuries that followed their creation, and were routinely cited in association with Botticelli.[18] Gustav Friedrich Waagen, director of the Berlin Gemäldegalerie, was the first to establish the link with Vasari and the engravings during a visit to Hamilton Palace in 1850 or 1851.[19] Amending the vague description hitherto prevailing, Waagen declared that the work was the product of more than one hand, with Botticelli's contribution standing out from the others: "... various hands of various artistic skill are discernible; that of Sandro Botticelli is very obvious".[20] It was only with the compilation of the catalogue for the Hamilton manuscript sale that the drawings were all attributed – without qualification, reservation or hesitation – to Botticelli alone.[21] This rather slow and cautious approach to identifying the artist was both consistent with and a product of the growing critical appreciation for Botticelli's work, which had grown in intensity over the course of the century. Initially this critical attention was directed towards his paintings (and paintings attributed to him). However, in 1868 the poet Algernon Charles Swinburne referred to Botticelli's drawings in his 'Notes on Designs of the Old Masters at Florence'.[22] Walter Pater wrote an extensive article about him in 1870,[23] while John Ruskin devoted two lectures to him at Oxford in 1872 and 1873 respectively.[24] While focusing on different aspects of the artist, both critics demonstrated Botticelli's profound affinity to the poet, recognising him as the embodiment of the poetic painter and a peerless illustrator of Dante. Moreover this association with Dante raised Botticelli's status within just a few years from that of a "secondary painter"[25] to that of an "artist of the highest rank".[26] Hence by the time the auction scheduled for 1882 brought the codex and the Dante drawings to the attention of the wider public, they were considered Botticelli's crowning achievement and the Hamilton library's finest gem.[27] That the rediscovery of the artist and drawings should have coincided, following centuries of neglect by art historians and collectors alike, appears in hindsight to have been something of a stroke of luck. Had the admiration for the artist's work remained consistent and undimmed, then the album might have shared a fate similar, for example, to the drawings of Raphael, and the volume been split up or individual pages dispersed or even cut out.[28]

Given the background of Botticelli's rediscovery as a significant Renaissance artist, it is hardly surprising that an art museum such as the Kupferstichkabinett should take a special interest in this treasure of the Hamilton library and be the "driving force"[29] behind its purchase. Indeed, during the negotiations for the purchase, the codex was already regarded less as a manuscript than as a unique collection of drawings by Botticelli. On 16 August 1882, when the likelihood of Great Britain losing this treasure to Berlin was already becoming apparent, the Prime Minister William Gladstone wrote in a letter to Sir Henry Ponsonby, private secretary to Queen Victoria, that the value of the codex was mainly due to it containing a collection of works by the famous artist: "... it derives its value I imagine almost entirely from its being in fact a collection of paintings by Botticelli; a great artist without doubt; but I can conceive a question whether in this view it is altogether an appropriate purchase for a National Library".[30] Having thus advised against an acquisition by the British Library, he went on to write that an attempt should nevertheless be made to purchase the drawings for a museum – a task that would, however, fall under the remit of the Museum Trust. Figures on the Prussian side of negotiations took a similar view of the proposed purchase of the Dante codex: on 30 September the Minister of Culture, Gustav von Gossler, wrote in a memorandum to the Ministry of Finance that the codex was "a unique collection of drawings by one of the foremost artists of the early Renaissance".[31]

Some forty years earlier, the Berlin museums had missed out on acquiring a unique collection of drawings by some of the foremost artists of the Renaissance. In around 1840, an unsuccessful attempt had been made to acquire the collection of Sir Thomas Lawrence and Samuel Woodburn, which famously included an extraordinarily fine and diverse range of drawings by Raphael and Michelangelo (now in the Ashmolean Museum in Oxford).[32] Although the Berlin museums in 1843 managed a successful acquisition of a collection comprising over 9000 drawings belonging to the Roman sculptor Vincenzo Pacetti (c. 1746–1820) – a shift in emphasis that would help establish the international reputation of the Kupferstichkabinett's Italian collection – works by the great names of the Renaissance nonetheless remained conspicuous by their absence.[33] The pressure to ensure that this latest opportunity should not be lost was therefore all the more keenly felt.

Friedrich Lippmann, director of the Kupferstichkabinett, was firmly committed to securing the Botticelli drawings for his museum (fig. 6). He first viewed them on 9 June 1882 at Ellis & White in London, writing the following day to Richard Schöne, director-general of the Königliche Museen of Berlin, to confirm that they were indeed the illustrations to the *Commedia* described by Vasari.[34] Although Lippmann was not a Botticelli specialist in the strictest sense of the term, he was a great admirer of Renaissance art, in both a professional and technical capacity and personally. The "interest closest to his heart was, however, the Renaissance era: he ... compiled a very fine collection of illustrated books from the fifteenth century".[35] At the beginning of the 1880s, Lippmann wrote a series of essays on late fifteenth-century Italian woodcuts. Over the course of these essays, he also discussed book illustrations and early Florentine engravings, including the Dante illustrations attributed to Balidini and based on originals by Botticelli.[36] In addition to his specialist knowledge and his ambition as director to undertake a high-profile expansion of the collection, Lippmann also possessed diplomatic skills that were to play a crucial role during negotiations, particularly his ability to foster useful links with British society.[37] He was extremely well connected in Great Britain, "a well-known figure in artistic and literary society, not only in Berlin, but also in London, where an English marriage and many English friendships made him a frequent visitor".[38] After the first viewing, Lippmann remained in London and

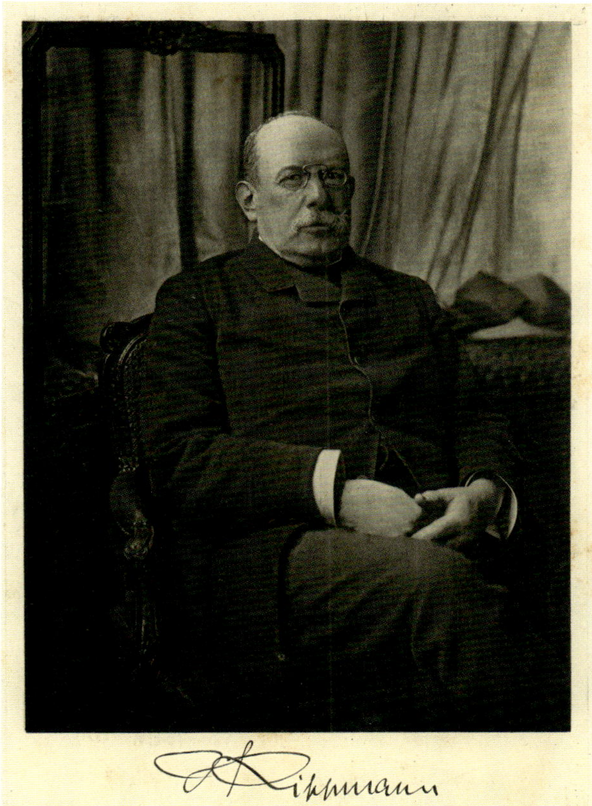

FIG. 5
Friedrich Lippmann, director of the Berlin Kupferstichkabinett (1876–1903), c. 1900
Berlin, Staatliche Museen zu Berlin, Zentralarchiv

set about negotiating the purchase, during which time it quickly became apparent that only an offer for the manuscript collection in its entirety would be considered by the seller, the 12th Duke of Hamilton, who had been brought into severe financial difficulties by his passion for dog and horse racing.[39] The Königliche Museen of Berlin then dispatched a commission to London, tasked with investigating whether a purchase of this kind should even be considered.[40] A preliminary investigation initially advised that the astronomical asking price of nearly £80,000 sterling, equivalent to around 1.5 million marks,[41] was much too high for the collection, and that efforts should instead be put into acquiring the more valuable titles, particularly given that interest was primarily focused on the Dante codex. This approach, of course, carried the risk of losing the works entirely. A closer examination of the manuscripts, as well as further consultations with a number of experts, including Karl Richard Lepsius, the director of the Königliche Bibliothek of Berlin, resulted in modifications to the conclusions of the preliminary investigation.[42] The individual manuscripts were judged to be so valuable that the decision was made to proceed and attempt the acquisition of the entire collection. In Prussia, the proposal sparked wide-ranging deliberations followed by frantic attempts to pull together resources and raise enough money for the purchase,[43] whereas in Great Britain it triggered a debate on the national significance of collections of this kind. By the end of May, the art historian Claude Phillips had, in a letter to *The Times*, voiced concerns that Great Britain would not be able to secure for its national museums artistic treasures such as the paintings of the Hamilton Collection, which were also at the time about to be sold off at auction. He feared that Great Britain would suffer a “lasting disgrace”.[44] His fears were not realised at the auction, for after a fierce bidding war with a representative from the Louvre a painting, attributed to Botticelli, of *The Assumption of the Virgin* was successfully secured for the National Gallery.[45] Despite a number of concerns and misgivings, the British government began granting generous sums of money on a case-by-case basis to ensure that important works of art remained in the country.[46] Since it was at this stage still unclear whether the policy would also apply to the sale of the Hamilton manuscripts, John Ruskin, who had previously seen them on a visit to Hamilton Palace in 1853, had by February launched an appeal to raise enough money to purchase the most important pieces for a national museum.[47] However, his project failed singularly to bear fruit, possibly because prior to the publication of the catalogue, scheduled for November 1882, the public had no clear understanding of what the library and hence the sale contained. When the auction was announced in *The Times* on 5 January 1882, only ‘the Dante’ and the Hamilton Bible (cat. no. 1) were referred to in any sort of detail (the description of both masterpieces clearly drew from Waagen’s comments), whereas everything else was listed in a short and uninformative inventory of manuscripts.[48]

Ten months separated the announcement of the planned sale from the report of its completion. On 2 November, *The Times*’s German correspondent broke the news that it was

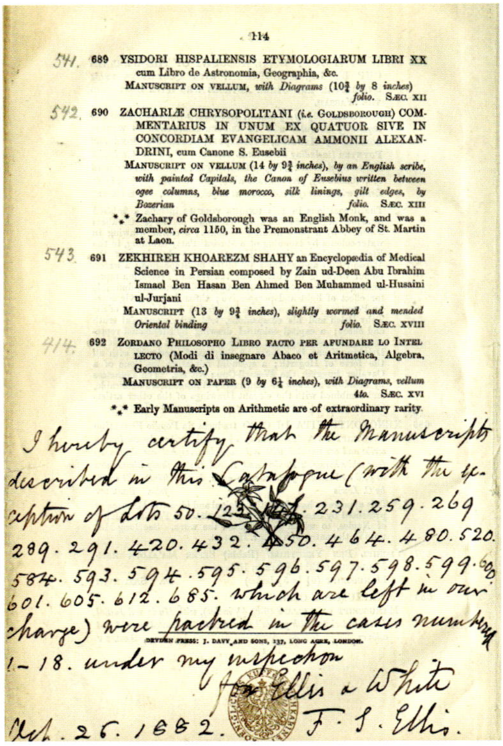

114

541\. 689 YSIDORI HISPALIENSIS ETYMOLOGIARUM LIBRI XX cum Libro de Astronomia, Geographia, &c.
MANUSCRIPT ON VELLUM, *with Diagrams* (10¾ *by* 8 *inches*) *folio.* SÆC. XII

542\. 690 ZACHARIÆ CHRYSOPOLITANI (*i.e.* GOLDSBOROUGH) COMMENTARIUS IN UNUM EX QUATUOR SIVE IN CONCORDIAM EVANGELICAM AMMONII ALEXANDRINI, cum Canone S. Eusebii
MANUSCRIPT ON VELLUM (14 *by* 9¾ *inches*), *by an English scribe, with painted Capitals, the Canon of Eusebius written between ogee columns, blue morocco, silk linings, gilt edges, by Bozerian* *folio.* SÆC. XIII
*** Zachary of Goldsborough was an English Monk, and was a member, *circa* 1150, in the Premonstrant Abbey of St. Martin at Laon.

543\. 691 ZEKHIREH KHOAREZM SHAHY an Encyclopædia of Medical Science in Persian composed by Zain ud-Deen Abu Ibrahim Ismael Ben Hasan Ben Ahmed Ben Muhammed ul-Husaini ul-Jurjani
MANUSCRIPT (13 *by* 9¾ *inches*), *slightly wormed and mended Oriental binding* *folio.* SÆC. XVIII

414\. 692 ZORDANO PHILOSOPHO LIBRO FACTO PER AFUNDARE LO INTELLECTO (Modi di insegnare Abaco et Aritmetica, Algebra, Geometria, &c.)
MANUSCRIPT ON PAPER (9 *by* 6¼ *inches*), *with Diagrams, vellum* *4to.* SÆC. XVI
*** Early Manuscripts on Arithmetic are of extraordinary rarity.

I hereby certify that the Manuscripts described in this Catalogue (with the exception of lots 50. 123. [illegible]. 231. 259. 269 289. 291. 420. 432. 450. 464. 480. 520. 584. 593. 594. 595. 596. 597. 598. 599. 600. 601. 605. 612. 685. which are left in our charge) were packed in the cases numbered 1–18. under my inspection
for Ellis & White
Oct. 26. 1882. F. S. Ellis.

DRYDEN PRESS: J. DAVY AND SONS, 137, LONG ACRE, LONDON.

FIG. 7
Handwritten list of the lots that remained in England (signed for Ellis & White by F.S. Ellis on 26 October 1882) in an annotated sale catalogue *The Hamilton Palace Libraries. The Hamilton Collection of Manuscripts*, Sotheby, Wilkinson & Hodge, Berlin, Staatliche Museen zu Berlin, Kupferstichkabinett

now too late: the Hamilton manuscripts had been brought to Germany, where museum staff were "rubbing their hands in glee".[49] The British art world reacted with shock to the news, for just as the successful purchase of the painting of *The Assumption of the Virgin* had been feted as a national triumph, so the loss of the Hamilton manuscripts and 'the Dante', precisely when contemporary tastes in art had shifted towards venerating Botticelli, was seen as a tragedy – indeed, a national scandal.[50] In addition to the often emotionally charged debate in the pages of the national press, a sale that had brought objects from the private into the public realm, from Great Britain to Germany, inevitably raised questions about the national significance of cultural assets and heritage.[51]

Since at the time there were no export controls in place in Great Britain, Friedrich Lippmann was in October 1883 at last able to conclude the purchase in London,[52] supervise the packing of the works into eighteen boxes at Ellis & White, and organise their dispatch in four separate ships.[53] He then wrote to Wilhelm Bode in Berlin: "Our Hamilton items are now for the most part packed and being kept in that familiar room on Fleet Street. The Dante really is extraordinarily wonderful! I am very, very happy that we have it. Hopefully everything will arrive home safely."[54] A copy of the 1882 sale catalogue, which in the light of the sale of the entire collection was now surplus to most requirements, served as the completion certificate; the catalogue is still kept by the Kupferstichkabinett as proof of the purchase. Volumes that were of particular national interest to the British remained in London at Ellis & White's premises (fig. 7).[55]

From the moment the decision was made to pursue the sale, it was clear that the larger portion of the works were destined for Berlin's Königliche Bibliothek. However, decisions relating to the allocation of individual books proved difficult and were discussed and eventually resolved in November 1883 in meetings chaired by the Culture Minister, von Gossler.[56] In retrospect, some of the decisions they reached might appear unwise.[57] Of the works brought to Berlin, 633 volumes ultimately came into the possession of the Königliche Bibliothek.[58] The works from the Hamilton Collection are today held by the Staatsbibliothek's manuscript department, where they are listed under the shelf mark prefix 'Manuscripta Hamiltoniana' (Ms. Ham.) and by the lot numbers allocated in the 1882 catalogue.[59] In terms of literary value, the most important of these include autograph texts of Giovanni Boccaccio's *Decamerone* (Ms. Ham. 90) and Francesco Petrarch's *De sui ipsius et multorum ignorantia* (Ms. Ham. 493).[60]

Nevertheless a certain number of manuscripts were always intended for the Kupferstichkabinett's own collection. From its foundation in 1831, and particularly during the decades that followed, the Kupferstichkabinett had distinguished itself from other museums of prints and drawings by building up a collection of manuscripts and book illuminations – a policy that was due at least in part to the personal interests of the Prussian King, Friedrich Wilhelm IV.[61] In August 1881 the Kupferstichkabinett held an exhibition of its finest manuscript illuminations, and then in the first half of 1882 "put a great many resources into, and nearly completed, [a catalogue] listing both illuminated manuscripts and individual

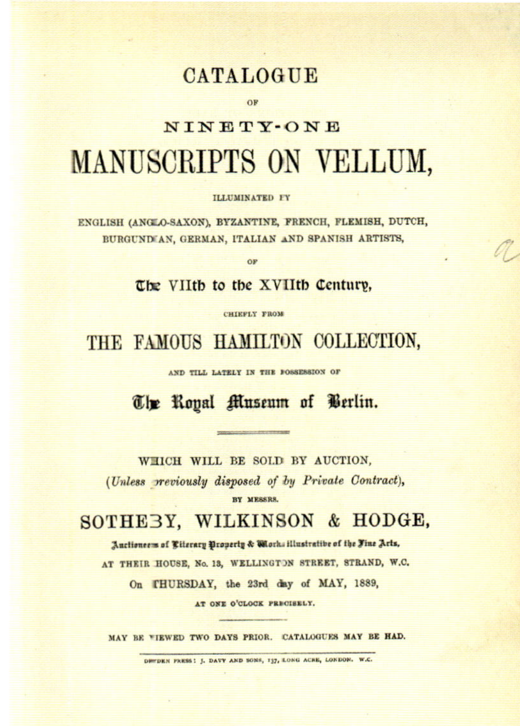
CATALOGUE
OF
NINETY-ONE
MANUSCRIPTS ON VELLUM,
ILLUMINATED BY
ENGLISH (ANGLO-SAXON), BYZANTINE, FRENCH, FLEMISH, DUTCH, BURGUNDIAN, GERMAN, ITALIAN AND SPANISH ARTISTS,
OF
The VIIth to the XVIIth Century,
CHIEFLY FROM
THE FAMOUS HAMILTON COLLECTION,
AND TILL LATELY IN THE POSSESSION OF
The Royal Museum of Berlin.

WHICH WILL BE SOLD BY AUCTION,
(*Unless previously disposed of by Private Contract*),
BY MESSRS.
SOTHEBY, WILKINSON & HODGE,
Auctioneers of Literary Property & Works illustrative of the Fine Arts,
AT THEIR HOUSE, No. 13, WELLINGTON STREET, STRAND, W.C.
On THURSDAY, the 23rd day of MAY, 1889,
AT ONE O'CLOCK PRECISELY.

MAY BE VIEWED TWO DAYS PRIOR. CATALOGUES MAY BE HAD.

FIG. 8
Title page of the sale catalogue *Catalogue of Ninety-one Manuscripts on Velum … chiefly from the Famous Hamilton Collection, and till lately in the possession of The Royal Museum of Berlin*, Sotheby, Wilkinson & Hodge, 23 May 1889, Berlin, Staatliche Museen zu Berlin, Kupferstichkabinett

pages of manuscripts".[62] This project was put on hold probably when it was confirmed that the manuscript collection was to undergo a significant expansion, since it would be necessary to ensure these additional works were included in the catalogue. Thus 158 manuscripts remained at the Königliche Museen and in 1884 were added to the Kupferstichkabinett's inventory catalogue. Despite being listed in the inventory (the 'Acquisitions Journal'), it was decided not even to stamp the works with the Kupferstichkabinett's stamp, since a re-allocation was to take place: anything considered to be outside the institution's area of collecting, namely the 24 non-European works, were transferred in 1891 to the Indian Department of the Völkerkundemuseum (Ethnological Museum). Today they are kept at the Museum für Asiatische Kunst and Museum für Islamische Kunst, respectively.

The acquisition of the collection was undertaken not only on the understanding that the works would subsequently be divided between the museums and library, but also with provision for recouping some of the costs by selling off any unwanted manuscripts.[63] This took place over two stages: in 1887, twenty manuscripts were sold through art dealers, while in 1889 a further sixty-one, including some high-profile works, were auctioned at Sotheby's in London, along with a number of others that had not been part of the Hamilton Collection (fig. 8).[64] The catalogue to this sale included a preface in which the authors wrote a short commentary on the events of 1882. They explained that at no stage during the acquisition had there been any intention whatsoever of incorporating the entire Hamilton library into the Königliche Museen and Königliche Bibliothek. The priority had always been to acquire the Dante and a select number of manuscripts, leaving bibliophiles and institutions at liberty to purchase the remaining works. To support this claim, the author cited the fact that the Kupferstichkabinett had yet to put its stamp on any of the books.

Seven years after the Kupferstichkabinett's spectacular coup, this effectively dispelled whatever residual resentment was still felt. Initially, however, it had been the manner in which the Kupferstichkabinett made its newly acquired treasures accessible to experts and public alike that succeeded in winning back the esteem even of the British art world. Following their delivery between 30 October and 1 November 1882, the treasures were first laid out on tables at the Kupferstichkabinett. Specialists were able to undertake detailed studies of individual works, which were then put on public display for an exhibition that lasted from early December 1882 until the end of May 1883: "The masterpieces selected from the collection were each accompanied by the pertinent explanatory text, and were kept either in sealed flat glass boxes or in solid, glass-covered frames".[65] We can assume that those latter, framed works are the Botticelli drawings, as they were apparently removed from the codex straight after their arrival in Berlin and mounted on passepartouts.[66]

In the years following the acquisition, individual pieces as well as groups of works from the collection were the subject of numerous essays and articles in newspapers, periodicals and specialist journals.[67] However, it was Lippmann himself who wrote about 'the Dante'. The 1883 issue of the museum yearbook contained the first extensive

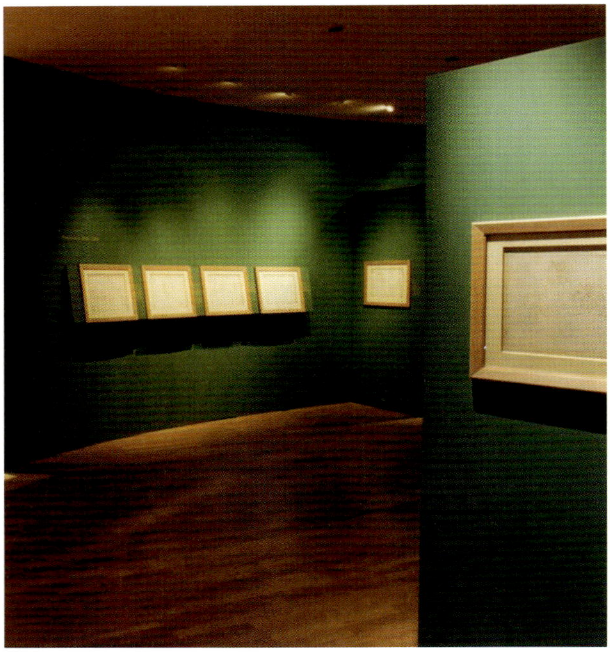

FIG. 9
View of the exhibition *Sandro Botticelli. Der Bilderzyklus zu Dantes Göttlicher Komödie*, curated by Hein-Th. Schulze Altcappenberg, in the Kupferstichkabinett, Staatliche Museen zu Berlin, April–June 2000

appraisal of the drawings, and featured an accompanying collotype plate (see cat. no. 39).[68] Four years later, Lippmann was able to produce a facsimile edition of the complete cycle, featuring actual-size collotype plates.[69] This allowed him on the one hand to respond to the public's desire to see the treasures at the earliest opportunity. On the other, he was able to realise a precocious suggestion made by Waagen during his visit to Hamilton Palace: "The publication of fac-similes of a selection of them, in woodcuts or lithography, now so easily accomplished, would be highly welcome equally to the lovers of Dante and of Italian art".[70] This development was followed with great interest by the British public, who greeted news of the facsimiles with enthusiasm and commended the speed with which the task had been accomplished.[71]

In 2000, Botticelli's *Commedia* drawings all returned for several months to Great Britain for a major exhibition held at the Royal Academy of Arts, entitled *Sandro Botticelli: The Drawings for Dante's Divine Comedy*. This exhibition, which in addition to London was also held in Berlin and Rome, brought together all 92 pages that survive of the *Commedia* cycle (fig. 9). It constituted something of a key moment in the reception history of a collection that had been split up and relocated during the Second World War, remained divided during the partition of Germany, and was eventually reunited in 1994 with the opening of the Kupferstichkabinett's new building at the Kulturforum.[72]

This current exhibition, by contrast, features a selection of approximately thirty of the finest and most representative of Botticelli's drawings from the *Commedia* cycle, surrounded by rare and magnificent manuscripts from the library of Alexander Douglas, 10th Duke of Hamilton. The aim is not to reconstruct the Hamilton library or to showcase its highlights in Berlin, particularly since the exhibition only features works from the Kupferstichkabinett's own holdings, and not those from the Staatsbibliothek's much more extensive Hamilton collection. Instead we aim to illustrate the significance of books as works of art within the context of a museum of European fine arts. With illuminated manuscripts, illustrated incunabula, prints and drawings all kept in the same museum, the various media and artistic genres transcend their formal differences to shed light on one another, their shared context helping to reveal the works' interconnections, common features and idiosyncrasies.[73] In this respect, Botticelli's drawings for Dante's *Commedia* here represent – in a manner consistent with their role at the time of the purchase of the Hamilton Collection – the primary and central focus of the selected manuscripts. Their origins, just like their rediscovery and subsequent reception, are closely related to the illustrations in the earliest printed edition of the work (see cat. nos. 48–50), a link that must have been foremost in Friedrich Lippmann's mind. In turn, the early printed and illustrated books bear close similarities to the illuminated manuscript, since each bring text and imagery together into a state of mutual elucidation that enhances the overall experience. Many of the magnificent codices shown here were produced in full knowledge of this other new medium, at a time when printed and even illustrated books were already extremely widespread. Botticelli's drawings for the *Commedia* are not only an outstanding example of art's capacity to bring a literary universe into the visual realm, they also bear testimony to the considerable overlap during this period between drawing and book illustration – as much from the artist's perspective as from that of the patrons who commissioned the work.[74] In addition to works praising great rulers, written and illustrated using the very finest materials, our selection incorporates a range of themes, from the journey into the afterlife, through heroic novels and love poetry, to allegory, science and history. The interrelationships between the works are diverse and operate on a variety of levels, bespeaking their place within the history of art, literature and art collecting. Thus, while the aim underlying Cecco d'Ascoli's scientific drawings (cat. no. 7) was to offer an alternative to Dante's poetic vision of the universe, Huon d'Auvergne's journey through the afterlife (cat. no. 3) faithfully replicates the path described in the poet's verse – a world we may also glimpse in the works of Francesc Eiximenis (cat. no. 4). In a vein similar to these voyages through the afterlife, Alexander the Great's adventures here on Earth also feature fantastical worlds and strange creatures (cat. no. 5). Amidst all this, a tiny booklet attempts to record the history of the Roman world (cat. no. 11). Dante's devotion to Beatrice in the *Commedia* serves as a literary emblem for love, a theme which is also explored through poetry and art in the story of Paolo and Daria (cat. no. 12), and in Petrarch's sonnets about his beloved Laura (cat. no. 8). Botticelli, moreover, lifts a number of allegorical motifs from works of poetry (cat. nos. 6, 9). The majority of these books, like Botticelli's drawings, were produced for princes and owned by popes, kings and dukes – ending up, fittingly, in the library of the Duke of Hamilton. The exhibition seeks to highlight the countless ways of seeing the world, the myriad imaginative possibilities that inhabit the exquisite objects from the Hamilton Collection, which continue to enrich the Kupferstichkabinett and uphold its status as a treasure house of visual art.

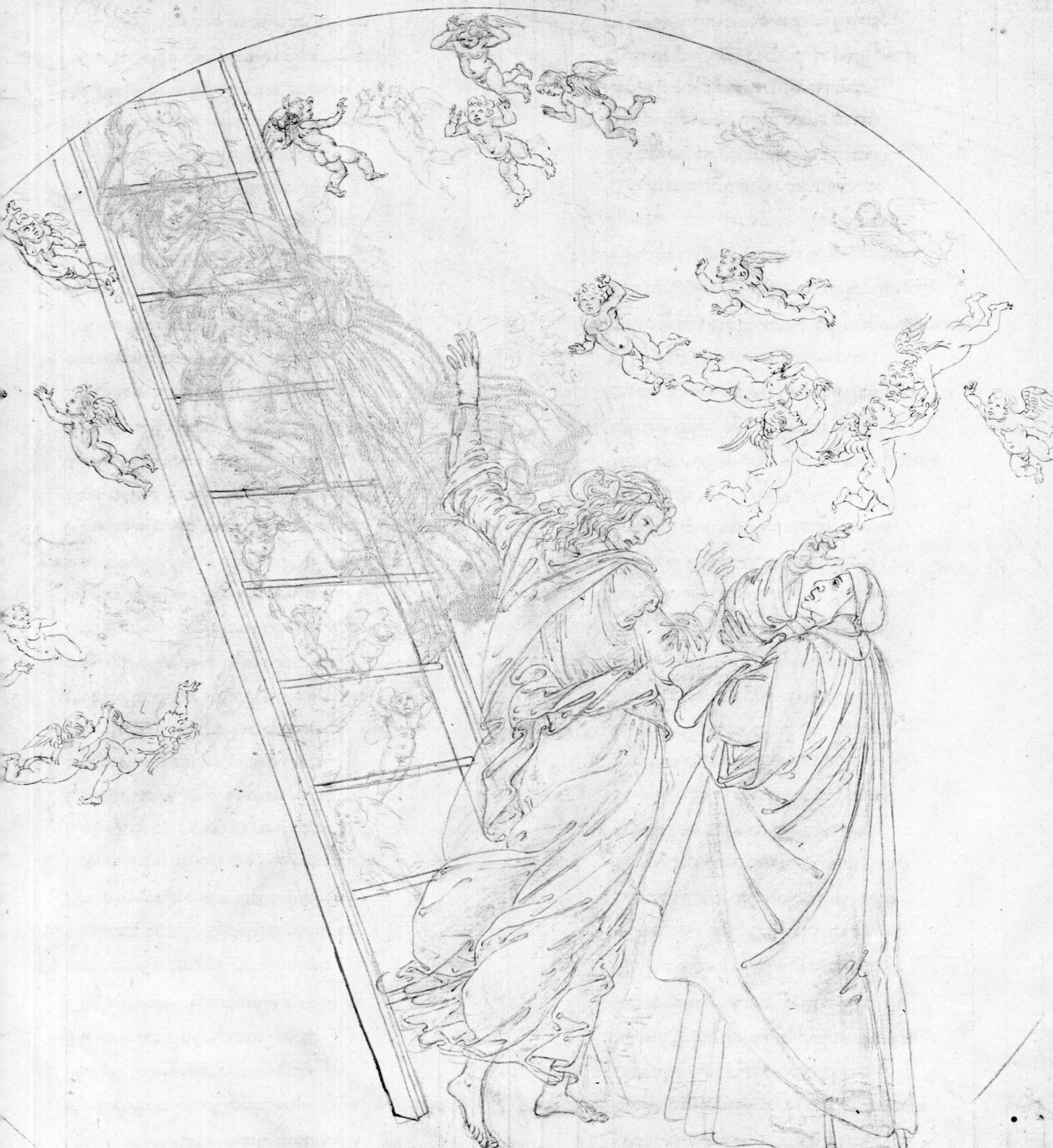

Botticelli's "Dante on vellum": Unfinished but Works of Art in Their Own Right

STEPHANIE BUCK

"*Il che fu cosa maravigliosa tenuto*" – Botticelli's Dante illustrations were highly acclaimed as a "marvellous thing" according to the much-cited Codice Magliabechiano,[1] an extensive collection of notes compiled in the 1540s in Florence constituting the nucleus of a projected series of artists' biographies. The codex also tells us that Botticelli painted and illustrated ("*dipinse et storiò*") a "Dante on vellum" for Lorenzo di Pierfrancesco de' Medici. Although it has not yet been possible to identify its author, this earliest surviving appraisal of the *Commedia* illustrations certainly seems credible.[2] His praise for the "Dante on vellum" is understandable, considering the fame Botticelli had achieved in his lifetime, not to mention the sheer scale of the enterprise, which is remarkable in itself, for Botticelli sought to illustrate every single canto from the *Divine Comedy* on more than one hundred large sheets.

Aside from the praise, it is notable that the author makes no mention of the obviously unfinished state of the work: strong linear pen drawings are often found alongside faint outlines in metalpoint (for example, cat. nos. 24, 26, 29, 30, 31, 45); at other times lone figures appear with no other context (cat. no. 46); colour has been added sporadically and unsystematically;[3] aesthetically, the character of the work is fragmented, as it fails to create the illusion of a visual continuum. The fact that the contours of the figures are often overlaid with numerous construction lines, drawn with a ruler and compass, would indicate that it was not Botticelli's intention to create highly finished drawings in the customary sense (irrespective of the colouring issue), and that he regarded his Dante illustrations as sketches or underdrawings. The thickness of the circles drawn with the compass is often inconsistent and there are frequent 'careless' gaps, especially in the *Paradiso* scenes (see, for example, cat. nos. 42, 43). The use of different shades of inks – at times a tone lighter or darker – shows that Botticelli was not attempting to create an end product with a unified pictorial scheme, even if the choice of ink does support Botticelli's visualisation of the content in some scenes, as Dagmar Korbacher observes.[4] The focus is much more on the creativity of drawing – on the process – and that is what captivates later commentators.

The praise from the Anonimo Magliabechiano (as the author of the codex is known) touches on the question of the increased appreciation of drawing as a medium in the first half of the sixteenth century in two respects. The first of these is the notion or term *disegno* ('drawing' or 'design'), which became more widely known after Giorgio Vasari's publication of his *Lives of Artists*, both the first edition of 1550 and, more importantly, the expanded edition of 1568. The notion of drawing as being almost the essence of the visual arts can be traced back even earlier to Leon Battista Alberti and Lorenzo Ghiberti,[5] for example, but at this time the medium was being propagated more forcefully as the concept that formed the intellectual foundation uniting the three arts of painting, sculpture and architecture.[6] As purely linear drawings that translate Dante's great literary work into visual images without trying to concretise it or make it tangible through the mimetic representation of descriptive surface details, Botticelli's Dante drawings embody, like few other examples, the true meaning of *disegno* as an intellectual principle. The Anonimo Magliabechiano must have come from similar circles to Vasari and he would certainly have been known to him. Taking this into account, his early review of Botticelli's unfinished drawings should be read in this theoretical context, even if it is not explicitly mentioned.

Secondly, the growing interest in drawings as collectors' items in the mid sixteenth century, especially in Florence, as exemplified for instance by Vasari's renowned *Libro de' Disegni*,[7] led to greater recognition of the autonomy of earlier drawings, too, even when they had not originally been planned as independent end products by their authors, but merely marked stages in the work process. When attributed to master craftsmen who were known by name, however, such drawings served as a document of the artists' individual styles and gave substance to their creative ideas. In this sense, drawings were also of interest

FACING Detail of cat. no. 40

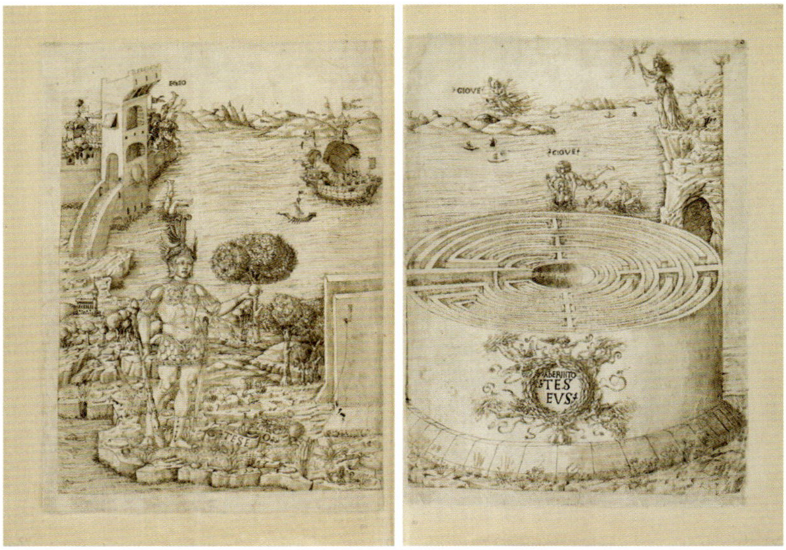

FIG. 10
Unknown Florentine artist,
Theseus and *The Labyrinth*, from the 'Florentine Picture Chronicle', c. 1470–75, pen and brown ink, brown wash, over black chalk, London, British Museum, inv. nos. 1889,0527.42 and 1889,0527.43

as actual objects and not just for their ability to express the theoretical and cultural concept of *disegno*.

More recent scholarly discourse on Botticelli's drawings takes place implicitly against this background. A crucial topic is the question whether the works should properly be regarded as unfinished coloured illuminations (i.e. paintings) or as 'pure drawings'.[8] A striking expression of a prevailing modern view can be found in Kenneth Clark's statement: "Three of the sheets are coloured. Most critics have rejected the idea that they were coloured by Botticelli himself, but I am inclined to agree with Mr Berenson that they were. For example, the draperies in Inferno XXIV are characteristic of Botticelli's colour. But even he, in his state of obsession, must have realised that to colour the whole series would have been an impossible task. And, thank God, he abandoned it."[9]

Like most authors in more recent times, Clark approaches the drawings as a connoisseur, and views them in the light of the (autonomous) artist. His proposal that Botticelli added colour to some of his drawings but then decided that it would be too time-consuming to complete is, however, an ahistorical notion that depends on the idea of the freedom of the creative artist. If the Dante drawings were made for Lorenzo di Piero Francesco de' Medici, then he most probably, as the patron, insisted on using high-quality and thus expensive vellum and would have expected colourful compositions of the kind known from miniature painting at the time.[10] We can only speculate on the reasons why the series was not finished in colour. The fact that Botticelli was preoccupied with the subject of Dante for so many years, as Vasari reports, and the works were executed over such a long period of time, no doubt played a role.[11] Nothing is known about the relationship between Botticelli and Lorenzo di Pierfrancesco de' Medici with regard to the Dante drawings. If it really took the artist from the early 1480s to the mid 1490s to execute the cycle, as is commonly assumed in the literature, it is highly likely that the patron made enquiries about the progress of the work at some stage. The inconsistencies in the production of the multi-part work, which have been analysed by Doris Oltrogge, Robert Fuchs and Oliver Hahn and summarised in the introduction to the catalogue section by Dagmar Korbacher,[12] could be explained as the result of the long drawn-out process behind its creation. At the beginning of the commission, Botticelli would have received a hundred leaves of superior-quality vellum with the job of illustrating the entire *Commedia*. The sheets would have been loose or gathered in quires even if – as we can assume – it was planned from the outset to present the Dante illustrations in a lavish codex. A book of one hundred leaves would have been cumbersome in a workshop and as one turned the pages the vellum would not have lain flat but have been bent back, making it difficult to draw near the gutter[13] or to add the text and the ruling on the verso of the leaves.

It is extremely likely that the addition of the text was intended at the beginning. While there are significant examples of large-format albums of drawings from the Italian Quattrocento that were designed as books in their

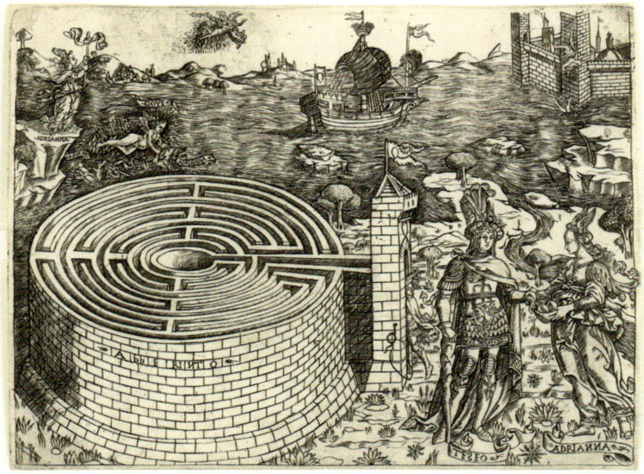

FIG. 11
Attributed to Baccio Baldini, *Theseus and Ariadne before the Labyrinth*, c. 1460–70, engraving, London, British Museum, inv. no. 1845,0825.487

own right and not later assembled by collectors, there are noticeable differences between them and Botticelli's illustrations – for instance, that both sides of their leaves are always drawn on whereas Botticelli only used the fine flesh side of the vellum. The drawings in such albums are of quite a different type and do not illustrate a continuous narrative, yet they provide compelling evidence that uncoloured illustrations were already prized as collectors' items in the fifteenth century – in other words a context existed in which Botticelli's 'Dante' could be placed, even though his drawings were not finished. All of the examples discussed here date from the second to third quarter of the fifteenth century and have the character of independent artworks that were produced with collectors in mind or were intended as demonstrations of the draughtsman's inventiveness.

Two impressive albums of drawings in folio format from the mid century, both originally containing 102 sheets, have survived from the workshop of Jacopo Bellini – a sketchbook with drawings in metalpoint and ink on vellum, today at the Louvre,[14] and another album drawn exclusively with metalpoint on paper, now at the British Museum.[15] The Louvre album has different compositions on each leaf, nearly all of which are meticulously finished, complete pictures in themselves.[16] The orientation of the sheets varies, with some positioned vertically, others horizontally, clearly placing it in the tradition of the pattern books that supplied workshops with numerous examples of compositions. Less eclectic and completed at greater speed, the sketches of the London album in contrast mostly comprise scenes spread over two leaves. Marcel Röthlisberger was able to demonstrate in the 1950s[17] that Bellini usually began with the right-hand leaf (the recto) and only added the composition on the left in a second step.[18] By extending the drawing in this way, he created horizontally orientated compositions of monumental dimensions. The reason for this highly unusual method is not known. It may be related to the function of the album, which, according to the convincing arguments put forward by Hugo Chapman, was meant to be perused in its entirety. The intention was to impress the reader with the book as a whole, with its numerous compositions linked through the comparatively skilful execution that lends the work a homogenous appearance.[19] The book's function was thus further removed from the immediate workshop context than the Louvre album.[20]

Almost half the size, at just 21.8 × 15.8 cm per leaf, are the highly finished and partly washed pen-and-ink drawings by Marco Zoppo that adorn the 26 leaves of the slender Rosebery Album.[21] It was created around the same time as Bellini's London album, in the mid fifteenth century, but was presumably made for a specific, albeit unknown patron, as indicated by several scenes that make humorous allusions to the subject of homosexuality.[22] Like Bellini, Zoppo does not provide a cohesive narrative context. A workshop context is entirely absent; the book was made as an independent work of art.

While these Northern Italian drawing books provide general evidence of the growing autonomy of drawing as a medium as early as the mid fifteenth century, the so-called 'Florentine Picture Chronicle' is important as a practical context for Botticelli's 'Dante' (figs. 10, 11).[23] Comprising 55 sheets of paper, it was illustrated in the 1470s by several artists following in the tradition of Maso Finiguerra. Measuring 32.6 × 23 cm per leaf, i.e. a quarto or half a folio, the format is half the size of the Botticelli drawings; a double folio was used for several drawings – quite closely corresponding to the dimensions of the Dante illustrations. The pictures from the 'Chronicle' are similarly finished in pen over preparatory sketches, although these are primarily drawn in black chalk. Unlike Botticelli's, however, these

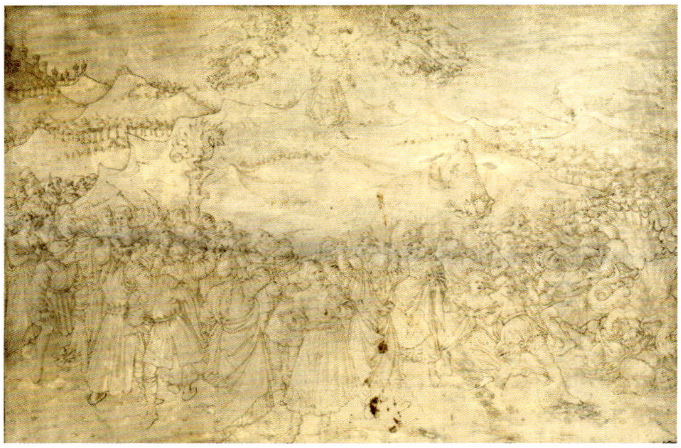

FIG. 12
Maso Finiguerra, *Moses on Mount Sinai and the Brazen Serpent*, c. 1455–64, pen and brown ink, brown wash, on vellum, London, British Museum, inv. no. 1898,1123.4

works are meticulously finished. Moreover, there is no continuous narrative and the text is limited to inscriptions that help to identify the main characters in various scenes.

Despite their differences, the 'Chronicle', conceived as a deluxe volume, is also of importance to the Dante drawings because both cycles have a close connection to the series of Florentine engravings traditionally attributed to Baccio Baldini: the 20.1 × 26.4 cm engraving *Theseus and Ariadne by the Labyrinth* (fig. 11)[24] from the 1460s was executed before the corresponding drawing in the 'Chronicle', for example. Similarly, while the scenes may not be identical, the motifs of the copper engravings from the *Commedia* edition with Landino's commentary of 1481 (cat. no. 48)[25] and Botticelli's lavish illustrations of "Dante on vellum" are closely related.

Three carefully finished large pen drawings on vellum by Maso Finiguerra have also survived from this period (fig. 12),[26] all in landscape formats which not only share this feature with Botticelli's Dante illustrations but also present themselves in a highly ambitious fashion with multi-figure compositions (depicting scenes from the Old Testament). Such is their degree of completion, they are generally regarded by scholars as autonomous drawings. The backs of the sheets are bare. The original context of the drawings, datable to c. 1455–64, is unknown. They may have been seen as stand-alone works of art or it may have been intended that the corresponding text from the Bible should be inscribed on the verso of the leaves, as in Botticelli's Dante, and the leaves then bound as a codex. In any case, Finiguerra's drawings, just like the 'Florentine Picture Chronicle', demonstrate that exquisite pen-and-ink drawings were collected in Florence around the time that Botticelli was commissioned to illustrate "Dante on vellum" and therefore his works could have been regarded as autonomous despite their *de facto* unfinished state.

Not all doubts have been dispelled about the original presentation of the Dante drawings and the question whether they were intended for a superb codex, whose leaves would have been bound on the long side,[27] as Lippmann first assumed and Dreyer postulated in 1986 with his facsimile reconstruction (fig. 13). Hein-Th. Schulze Altcappenberg rightly emphasises irregularities in, for example, the distribution of the text and the dual representation of Lucifer – once as a half figure in a landscape format (cat. no. 24) and again as a full figure on a double leaf that would have folded out from the book (cat. no. 25).[28] Through the extraordinary accuracy of Botticelli's interpretation of the text, the image gains "autonomy from the text .... Anyone with only a rough grasp of the *storia* could retell the great poem in its entirety on the basis solely of Botticelli's representations, quasi a '*commedia pauperum*', a self-explanatory cycle of images."[29] This confident attitude towards the text is seen as a sign that Botticelli has overturned the fundamental law of book illustration – the primacy of word over image. While this principle may have existed in theory, the autonomy given to the image in Botticelli's 'Dante' would by no means have been an isolated event in the evolution of book illumination in the late fifteenth century. Rather, the art of book illumination was, at this time, reinventing itself in a myriad of ways from within, thematising the relationship between image and support (the written page), and emerging supremely emancipated, for instance, in trompe-l'oeil paintings (see cat. no. 13). Dürer's *Apocalypse* (fig. 14), first published in 1498, is probably the most powerful example of a book in which the graphic image of the artist-entrepreneur is placed confidently alongside the text as its equal. Dante's *Commedia* with Botticelli's compositions is also comparable to Dürer's *Apocalypse* in terms of content: like Saint John the Evangelist, the poet Dante affords his readers insight into matters that remain closed to them in their lifetimes and, like Botticelli, Dürer's

FIG. 13
Facsimile edition of Dante's *Divina Commedia* with illustrations by Sandro Botticelli, edited by Peter Dreyer, 1986, open at *Purgatorio* X

FIG. 14
Albrecht Dürer, *The Four Horsemen of the Apocalypse*, from 'The Three Great Books' (*The Life of the Virgin, The Large Passion, The Apocalypse*), Nuremberg, 1511, woodcut, Berlin, Kupferstichkabinett, Staatliche Museen zu Berlin, Sign. 2550a

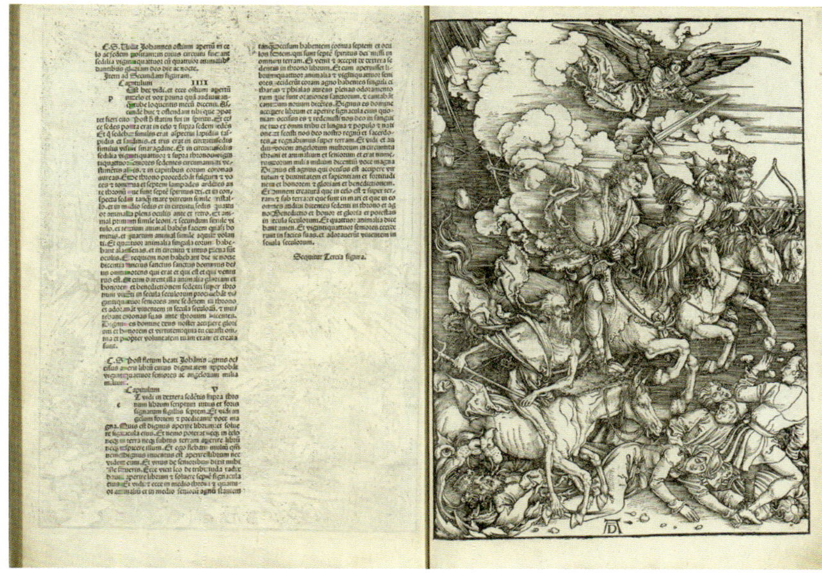

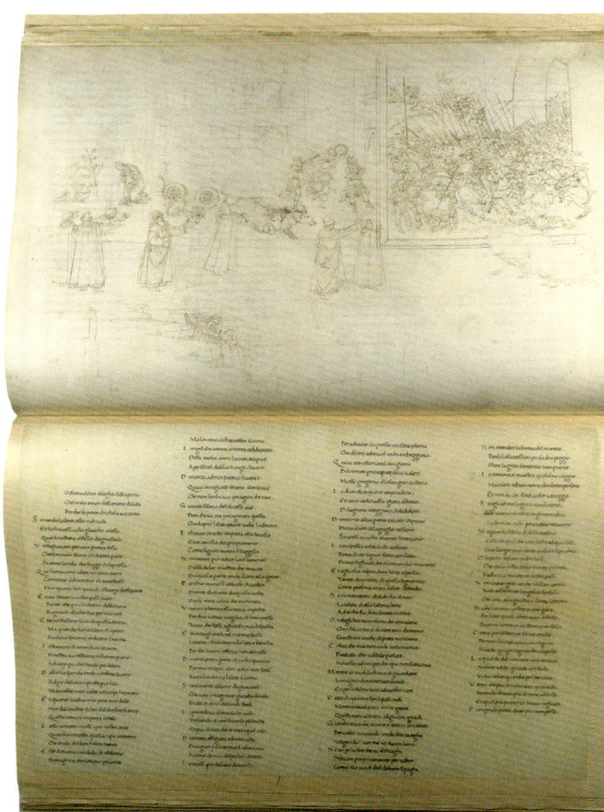

visionary images illustrate each chapter in an autonomous pictorial narrative.

Dürer's *Apocalypse* is in the common format of a codex, printed on upright pages. Nonetheless, there clearly was a tradition in fifteenth-century manuscript illustration, as Dreyer suggests, for the unusual landscape or oblong format. This was already noted by Oltrogge, Fuchs and Hahn when they convincingly reconstructed the historical process of the juxtaposition of image and text and surmised that it "developed in Flemish chronicles of the fifteenth century as a permutation of genealogical scrolls in codex form".[30] One of the best known and most magnificent examples of such chronicles is the *Chroniques de Jérusalem abrégées* (fig. 15) commissioned by Philip the Good, Duke of Burgundy.[31] This splendid manuscript illuminated by the Master of Girart de Roussillon after 1455 relates the story of the First Crusade and the three Crusader states. The genealogies of the rulers form the guiding thread, and this perhaps encouraged the arrangement of the text in four columns perpendicular to the spine – in a manner directly comparable with Botticelli's Dante. In a testamentary inventory of 1467 the codex is described as "*Un livre imparfait tournant de manière de rôle*".[32] Another example of such a hybrid between codex and scroll is the *Chronologie Universelle* probably created around 1480 in Bruges, which contains a family tree from Adam up to Christ and begins with God's creation of the world (fig. 16).[33]

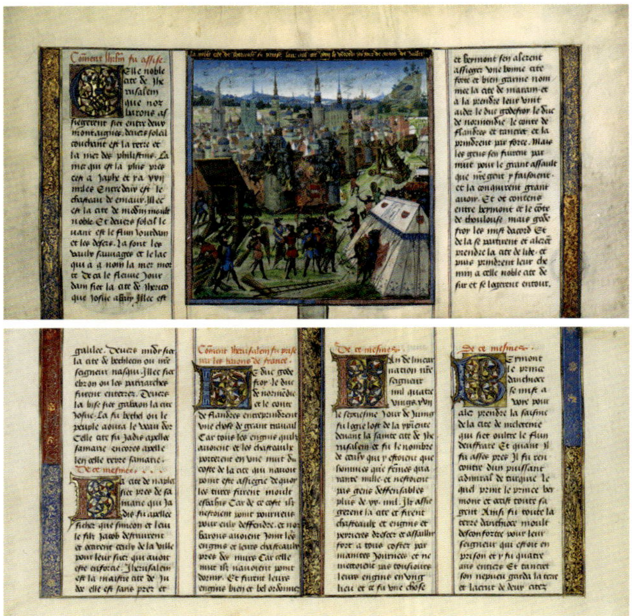

FIG. 15
The Conquest of Jerusalem by the Crusaders with two columns of text, fol. 7v, and page of text in four columns, fol. 8r, from *Les Chroniques de Jérusalem abrégées*, after 1455 (Flanders, Girart de Roussillon), illuminated manuscript on vellum, Vienna, Österreichische Nationalbibliothek, cod. 2533

It is not clear whether these splendid Netherlandish codices were known in Italy. They might not necessarily have been the sources for the choice of format, whose oblong shape conjures up the image of the ancient scroll, but it can hardly be accidental that precisely this codex form was chosen for the Dante illustrations. As in the *Chronologie Universelle*, the 'Dante' is concerned with the presentation in successive steps of a spiritual and transcendental journey, continually unfurling, the ultimate aim being the attainment of a higher knowledge. The continuity of the stages of the journey is reflected by Botticelli in his drawings by including figures from the preceding or following cantos at the edge of the image as references to earlier or later passages (see cat. nos. 15, 19, 20, 23, 26, 30, 37, 38). Thus it would seem that the connection between image and text postulated today was planned from the outset. The fact that Botticelli handed the illustrations over to the scribe Niccolò Mangona – presumably in quires[34] – before completing them would suggest that his patron was impatient with the project's progress. According to Oltrogge, Fuchs and Hahn's reconstruction of the working process of manufacturing a manuscript,[35] the sheets were returned to Botticelli with the text and rulings. It is possible that he added colour at the end, along with other members of the workshop; however, it remains unclear whether Botticelli, inexperienced in illumination, would have been given this task or whether the workshop of a Florentine artist trained in miniature painting would have been commissioned for the job – as would have been more appropriate and seems more likely.[36] The fluctuations in quality and the differences in execution between the four surviving illuminated leaves certainly suggest the work of at least two hands.[37] The fact that the colouring was soon abandoned (its forlorn, fragmentary state in the drawings for *Inferno* X and XV points to a hasty decision) implies that the client was not so utterly convinced by the result that he insisted on its completion. Instead, Botticelli's drawings were bound as unfinished masterpieces into a codex, and possibly served as an ambassadorial gift if, as is presumed, Lorenzo di Piero Francesco really did present it to the French court.[38] Thus accorded the status of completed representations, Botticelli's "Dante on vellum" sounded out the terrain in which drawing in the late fifteenth century established itself – between the poles of dependency on other works and true artistic autonomy.

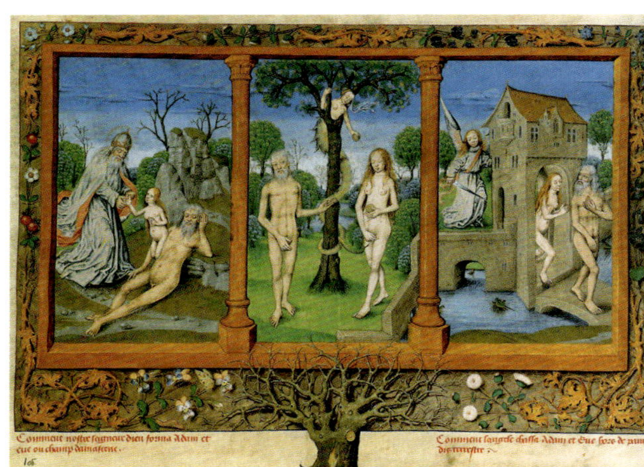

FIG. 16
The Creation of Eve, the Fall, the Expulsion from Paradise, fol. 1v from *Chronologie Universelle*, Bruges, 1480, illuminated manuscript on vellum, St Petersburg, Hermitage, inv. no. Fr. F. v. IV, 12

Notes

The Hamilton Collection

FRAUKE STEENBOCK

1 Reproduction of the original in the Staatsbibliothek zu Berlin, located in the manuscript reading room with the shelf mark RLS Dh 5100-1 and -2. William Clarke was a bookseller and publisher.

2 It is still not known for certain when and where Alexander Douglas acquired the Dante manuscript. In 1803 it was in the hands of an antiquarian bookseller in Paris, Giovanni Claudio Molini. See Dreyer 1986, pp. 20–3.

3 Henry G. Bohn to the editor of *The Times*, letter dated 19 January 1882.

4 William Beckford (1760–1844) was by this time living in a villa outside Bath. The Duke of Hamilton married Beckford's second daughter, Susanne Euphemia, in 1810.

5 See Waagen 1854 a, vol. 3, p. 306–07.

6 See sale catalogue 1882, cat. no. (= Ms Hamilton) 201, p. 31.

7 "[*Eines*] *der bedeutendsten Kunstdenkmäler der Renaissance, das die Welt besitzt*": quoted Pallat 1959, p. 172.

8 'The Hamilton Manuscripts', *The Bibliographer – A Journal of Book-Lore*, No. 13, December 1882, pp. 4–8, at p. 8.

9 See Fulford 1981, pp. 126–28. See also Dreyer 1986, p. 21.

10 These lots are listed on the final page of the Berlin copy of the sale catalogue (see fig. 5). They were subsequently sold to the British Museum.

11 See Steenbock 1998, p. 158, note 12.

12 See Staatsbibliothek zu Berlin, Acta, vol. III C 48.

13 See Lippmann 1883.

14 See Wescher 1931; Boese 1966. See also Havely 2014, specifically: 'From neglected to reverential guardians. The Hamilton Collection in Britain and Berlin', pp. 243–59.

15 'The Hamilton Manuscripts', cited note 8 above.

"I am very, very happy that we have it"

DAGMAR KORBACHER

1 See sale catalogue 1882, lot 201 (= MS Hamilton), p. 31.

2 See Clarke 1819, p. 260.

3 Figures such as Thomas Jefferson numbered among Molini's customers: see Hayes 2008, p. 282. Information on the location of Molini's shops can be found on the database of the Bibliothèque nationale de France: http://catalogue.bnf.fr/ark:/12148/cb12230833k/PUBLIC (accessed 27 July 2015).

4 Greco 1990, p. 266. The items listed in Molini's sales catalogues are almost exclusively editions of printed books (for example Molini 1774; Molini 1785).

5 See the research undertaken by Georg Josef Dietz, under cat. no. 47. We do not know how the drawings were kept beforehand. Presumably they were bound as a codex, and rebound when the binding had grown tired and unattractive. It is also unclear whether the new binding was commissioned by Molini.

6 Dreyer 1986, pp. 62, 141–42, note 152. This proposed sequence of events is given in Schulze Altcappenberg 2000, p. 23.

7 See Schulze Altcappenberg 2000, p. 22.

8 See Strzygowski 1885–86; Strzygowski 1887.

9 It is conceivable that contemporary drawings were made of the originals within the setting of the artist's workshop. There exist a small number of drawings which, like the originals, were made on vellum, but which differ slightly from them in size and significantly in their more laboured quality of drawing and use of underdrawings in red chalk (in the original these are in metalpoint): Bonham's, London, *Old Master Drawings* (sale 10511), 9 July 2003, lot 21 (pen and brown ink over red chalk on vellum, 31.1 × 46.9 cm); Reggio Emilia, Musei Civici (Collezione Villani; pen and brown ink on vellum, 26.5 × 48.7 cm); see Reggio Emilia 2000–01, no. IDV 68, p. 133. At least the latter of these appears to be a twentieth-century copy, drawn from the original. I am grateful to Georg Josef Dietz for examining the drawing in Reggio and offering the assessment upon which my comment is based.

10 See Dombrowski 1992, p. 24, note 1.

11 Florence, Biblioteca Medicea Laurenziana, Ms. Mediceo Palatino 75. In particular, Stradano's illustrations to *Inferno* XVII–XVIII, *Inferno* XXI–XXIII, *Inferno* XXVIII, *Inferno* XXXI–XXXII and *Inferno* XXXIV show similarities to Botticelli's drawings. See Brunner 1999, pp. 308–26.

12 Florence, Gabinetto Disegni e Stampe degli Uffizi, inv. no. 3474F; see Stoltz 2011, esp. pp. 65–68 (with older literature); Brunner 1999, pp. 52, 169; and Zgraja 2015, p. 430.

13 See Pescara 1985, p. 156 (regarding Füssli's drawing *Dante and Virgil on the Ice of the Kocythos*, Kunsthaus Zürich, inv. no. 1916/13, drawn in Rome in August 1874). John Flaxman was clearly unaware of Botticelli's *Commedia* drawings: see Büttner 2006, p. 102.

14 See Havely 2014, pp. 175–77, 246. The drawings' influence upon art continues to even today. In Andreas Siekmann's digital images, Dante and Virgil come face to face with problems of the modern world; see Cologne 2011–12, pp. 112–21. The small flames in Botticelli's illustration of *Paradiso* feature in the background of Heiko Blankenstein's lightbox work *Lorenz Attractor Tree* (2004). Martin Noll makes reference to individual motifs, such as the Earthly Paradise or the figures of Dante and Beatrice, in a number of works from his 'Botticelli' and 'fugit' series (both oil and tempera on paper, 2008 and 2011 respectively). Works by other artists such as Jorinde Voigt (see Voigt 2014) and Nick Fox also engage with Botticelli's drawings for Dante's *Commedia*.

15 The text reads: *LA COMEDIA/ DI/ DANTE ALIGHIERI/ MANOSCRITTO SU PERGAMENA/ DELL ANNO 1400 AL1450/CON DISEGNI ORIGINALI/ FATTI DA SANDRO BOTIREL/ LI* [sic]*/ OD ALTRO DI QUEL TEMPO DELLA SEUOLA* [sic] *FIORENTINA*.

16 See Clarke 1819, p. 260: "... supposed to be executed by the hand of Sandro Botticelli, or some other eminent Florentine artist".

17 See Watts 1995 a, p. 83: "For most of the century, virtually anything that looked 'strange' might attributed to Botticelli".

18 See Heinecken 1771, pp. 141–43; Heinecken 1778–90, pp. 208–12; Ottley 1816, pp. 404–25; 'Engraving' 1853, p. 293; Bartsch 1866, pp. 158–63, 175; Duplessis 1869, p. 19; Duplessis 1880, p. 41; Delaborde 1882, pp. 68–70.

19 For Waagen's visit and the year in which it took place, see Watts 1995 a, p. 93 (where it is given as 1850); Tait 1983, p. 396 (given as 1851).
20 Waagen 1854 a, vol. 3, p. 307.
21 See sale catalogue 1882, lot (= MS Hamilton) 201, p. 31.
22 Swinburne (1868) 1901, p. 326; see Levey 1960, p. 302.
23 Walter Pater, 'A fragment on Botticelli'; see Pater (1870) 1986, pp. 33–40.
24 John Ruskin, 'Design in the Florentine School of Engraving (Sandro Botticelli)'; see Ruskin 1903–12, vol. 22, pp. 422–62; and 'Lecture VIII: Sandro Botticelli'; see Ruskin 1903–12, vol. 23, pp. 265–79.
25 Pater (1870) 1986, p. 40. See also Fowler 1883, p. 32: "Botticelli was a merely second-rate painter" and, subsequently, "Botticelli is brought forth from his long neglect and announced to the world as one of the most earnest messengers that more ever passed ... between the world of the real and that of the ideal".
26 *The Times,* 4 November 1882, p. 5.
27 See Watts 1995 a, p. 83: "The high estimation accorded the Botticelli Dante reflected the artist's new status as a luminary of the Early-Italian schools, which Pater and Ruskin had brought about".
28 See, for instance, De La Chapelle 2015.
29 Boese 1966, pp. XVII–XVIII. The purchase is described in these terms in the detailed study by Nicholas Havely (Havely 2014, pp. 243–59).
30 H. [Henry] C.G. Matthew (ed.), *Gladstone Diaries. With Cabinet Minutes and Prime Ministerial Correspondence*, vol. 10, Oxford 1990, pp. 313–14, quoted by Watts 1995 a, p. 83.
31 "*Eine Sammlung von Zeichnungen eines der ersten Künstler der Frührenaissance, wie sie nicht wieder existiert*": Geheimes Staatsarchiv, I HA Rep. 151 Finanzministerium, I C No. 7156 (July 1880 until end of 1885), p. 7, quoted by Havely 2014, p. 248.
32 See Möhle 1963, p. 87.
33 A view supported by a critical survey of the Old Master drawings towards the end of the 1870s. See *Festschrift* 1880, pp. 103–04.
34 Friedrich Lippmann, London, to Richard Schöne, letter dated 10 July 1882 (Staatsbibliothek zu Berlin, Nachlass 248, Kasten 6, Umschlag II); see Havely 2014, p. 247.
35 "[*Seine*] *eigenste Liebhaberei aber war die Zeit der Renaissance: er ... brachte eine vortreffliche Sammlung illustrierter Bücher des 15. Jahrhunderts zusammen*": Bode 1903, col. 83. The illustrated books from the Lippmann collection are now in the possession of the Kupferstichkabinett and are identifiable by their ex-libris (see cat. no. 50). These and an additional Dante edition acquired directly for the Kupferstichkabinett were purchased from Ellis & White, the booksellers where Lippmann first saw the volumes of the Hamilton library (see cat. nos. 49, 50).
36 See Lippmann 1882, pp. 168–69; also Lippmann 1884, p. 22, note 1: "When the second of the present series of essays appeared, I was not aware of the drawings by Sandro Botticelli for the Divine Comedy or of the relationship between the engravings attributed to Baldini and the 1482s [sic] edition of Dante" ("*Als der zweite der vorliegenden Reihe von Aufsätzen erschien, waren mir die Zeichnungen des Sandro Botticelli zur Göttlichen Komödie und das Verhältniss, in welchem die dem Baccio Baldini zugeschriebenen Stiche der 1482er* [sic] *Dante-Ausgabe zu ihnen stehen, unbekannt*"). Straight after the acquisition of Botticelli's Dante drawings, it seems that Lippmann made efforts to purchase these engravings (from Ellis & White; see note 35). The Kupferstichkabinett's committee of experts agreed unanimously at a meeting held on 7 March 1883 to purchase eighteen prints of Baccio Baldini's illustrations of Dante's *Inferno* for a total price of £17,000. See the minutes of the Kupferstichkabinett's committee of experts (Zentralarchiv, Staatliche Museen zu Berlin, SMB-ZA, I/KK 22). However, it seems that the purchase never went through, since there is no mention of it either in the acquisition records of the Kupferstichkabinett or in the card index of the print collection.
37 Bode 1903, col. 87: "... however, he felt most at home in England" ("*am heimischsten aber fühlte er sich in England*").
38 C.D. 1904, p. 8. Another obituary from a British newspaper, published on 3 October 1903, is kept at the Zentralarchiv of the Staatliche Museen zu Berlin. This clipping, listed as 'Obituary. Privy councillor Friedrich Lippmann' and held in a file dedicated to Lippmann, describes at length his close relationship to England: "England commanded his sympathies and his lifelong admiration. He had a perfect command of the English language, and never missed his annual visit to London, of which his wife ... was a native. He had a large circle of friends in the British capital .... For a long series of years his hospitable house in Berlin was frequented by a succession of English visitors, many of whom were men of distinguished reputation in their own walks of life, and all of whom enjoyed the genial and illuminating conversation of their gifted host."
39 It is unclear as to whether negotiations took place directly with the vendor, the 12th Duke of Hamilton. It seems likely that seller and buyer never met in person or negotiated directly with one another (see Havely 2014, p. 246). By contrast, see Watts 1995 a, p. 95: "Lippmann ... travelled to Scotland to negotiate privately with the Duke". What is certain is that the final settlement was drawn up solely with one of the Duke's agents, as is attested by adminstrative account no. 703 (Zentralarchiv, Staatliche Museen zu Berlin. SMB-ZA, I/GV 518).
40 As well as Lippmann himself, the commission included Wilhelm Bode from the Königliche Museen and Adolf von Beckerath (an esteemed collector, primarily of Italian drawings, who was also a member of the committee responsible for authorising the Kupferstichkabinett's acquisitions), who both acted as expert advisors, together with Alfred Schöne, brother of the director-general of the Königliche Museen, who was a specialist in manuscripts. For an account of the sale, see Frauke Steenbock's essay in this catalogue, pp. 11–13.
41 For the exact purchase amount see Steenbock's essay, p. 13.
42 See Pallat 1959, pp. 172–73; Breslau 2003, p. 6. It seems that Lepsius tended initially towards opposing the acquisition, while the Königliche Bibliothek's manuscript experts were outright supporters.
43 For the financing model, see again Pallat 1959 and Breslau 2003.
44 Claude Phillips, 'To the editor of the Times', *The Times,* 30 May 1882, p. 5.
45 Today the painting is thought to be the work of Francesco Botticini (London, National Gallery, inv. no. NG1126); see also Watts 1995 a, p. 93.
46 See Watts 1995 a, p. 93; *The Times,* 16 June 1882, p. 10: "It is well known that the wish of the Trustees of the National Gallery had been met with a liberal and substantial grant".
47 See Watts 1995 a, p. 99, note 70 (regarding the visit to Hamilton Palace); Ruskin 1903–12, vol. 12, pp. LXVII–LXVIII; for Ruskin's campaign, see Ruskin 1903–12, vol. 30, p. XXXII; see also the 'General Statement explaining the Nature and Purposes of St. George's Guild', Ruskin 1903–12, vol. 30, pp. 43, 57, 58.
48 See *The Times,* 5 January 1882, p. 6. See also Watts 1995 a, p. 94.

49 *The Times,* 4 November 1882, p. 5. A more detailed description of the Hamilton manuscripts followed two days later (6 November 1882, p. 4).

50 See Bertram 1950, p. 483; see also Havely 2014, pp. 244–59 and passim.

51 See Harvey 2014, p. 243.

52 Lippmann remained in London from 7 to 27 October, where he was assisted by the law firm Fielder & Sumner. See receipt # 699–703 (Zentralarchiv, Staatliche Museen zu Berlin, SMB-ZA, I/GV 518). I am very grateful to Beate Ebelt-Borchert (Zentralarchiv) for her kind assistance in drawing my attention to this file.

53 Molini's note inside the cover of the Botticelli drawings was used by Lippmann as the completion certificate. His own note on the number and completeness of the vellums is dated 20 October 1882. F.S. Ellis's comment on the location of twenty-seven lots from the catalogue, held by his company in London for safekeeping, is dated 26 October (annotated copy in the Kupferstichkabinett).

54 "*Unsere Hamilton-Sachen stehen nun zum großen Theile verpackt in dem wohl bekannten Zimmer in Fleet-Street. Der Dante ist doch über alle Maßen herrlich! Ich bin sehr sehr glücklich daß wir ihn haben. Hoffentlich kommt alles gut nach Hause*": Friedrich Lippmann, London, to Wilhelm Bode, letter dated 21 October 1882 (Zentralarchiv, Staatliche Museen zu Berlin, Bode Bequest 3346); see also Havely 2014, p. 249.

55 This applied to lots 50, 123, 147, 231, 259, 269, 289, 291, 420, 432, 450, 464, 480, 520, 584, 593–601, 605, 612, 685.

56 See *Handbuch* 1994, p. 45 (Frauke Steenbock).

57 See Boese 1966, p. XIX, note 14. This view relates specifically to manuscript 78 C 11.

58 This corresponds to 506 lots, some of which were allocated to more than one volume. For the total number of volumes, see Breslau 2003, pp. 6–7.

59 The 42 Persian and Arabic manuscripts are today kept in the Orient-abteilung.

60 The view expressed by dissenting critics, who in December 1882 complained that the Hamilton manuscripts were of purely artistic value, and that "in the entire costly collection [there was not] a single work with any kind of 'pure literary' merit that had not already been known about for some time from manuscripts of either better or worse quality" ("*in der ganzen teuren Sammlung kein einziges Werk, welches 'reinliterarisch' von irgendwelchem Werte und nicht bereits in besseren oder schlechteren Handschriften längst bekannt gewesen wäre*"), has not been shared by scholars for some time. See Engel 1882, p. 72.

61 See *Festschrift* 1880, p. 100. For miniatures and manuscripts acquired in 1835 with the Nagler collection, see p. 96. After its move to the Neues Museum, the Kupferstichkabinett opened to the public under the name of *Abtheilung für Handzeichnungen Miniaturen und Kunstdrucke*: ibid, pp. 100–01.

62 "*… der mit Miniaturen gezierten Handschriften und der Einzelblätter der Handschriften … wesentlich gefördert und der Beendigung nahe gebracht.*" See Lippmann's brief report in 'Amtlichen Berichten aus den Königlichen Kunstsammlungen Berlin', *Jahrbuch der Königlich Preußischen Kunstsammlungen,* vol. 3, 1882, col. X (from 1 January 1882) and col. LVIII (from 1 July 1882). The manuscript catalogue was eventually published in 1931, edited by Paul Wescher, and remains today the most important reference work for illuminated manuscripts kept at the Kupferstichkabinett.

63 See Wehry 2013, p. 49.

64 In a meeting held on the 10 November 1888, the Kupferstichkabinett's committee of experts had come to the decision to sell 27 manuscripts from the museum's existing holdings in order to be able to retain the Hamilton Bible (cat. no. 1). See their minutes (Zentralarchiv, Staatliche Museen zu Berlin, SMB-ZA, I/KK 22). One manuscript, the Murano Gradual (78 F 1), was sold in 1889 and re-purchased in 1903, the year of Lippmann's death.

65 "*Die dazu ausgewählten und mit sachgemäßen Erläuterungen versehenen Prachtstücke der Sammlung befanden sich theils in verschlossenen flachen Glaskasten, theils in festen, mit Glas bedeckten Rahmen*": *Archiv für Post und Telegraphie*, no. 15, August 1884, p. 450.

66 See also Georg Josef Dietz's recent findings, under cat. no. 47.

67 For example, Seidlitz 1883–85; Biadene 1887.

68 Lippmann 1883.

69 See Lippmann 1887. Remarkably, Lippmann had made a habit of purchasing photographs of drawings and miniatures from other collections on behalf of the Kupferstichkabinett in order to build up a specialist research resource. See the acquisition records of the Kupferstichkabinett and the minutes of the Kupferstichkabinett's committee of experts (Zentralarchiv, Staatliche Museen zu Berlin, SMB-ZA, I/KK 22).

70 See Waagen 1854 a, vol. 3, p. 307.

71 See *The Times,* 9 March 1883 and 7 January 1885.

72 See Berlin/Rome/London 2000–01. For a precise inventory listing which pages were located in East and West Berlin respectively, see Dreyer 1986, pp. 119–21.

73 See also the introduction the manuscript portion of the catalogue, pp. 38–39, and Waagen's account of the significance of illuminated manuscripts: Waagen 1854 b, p. 10.

74 See Stephanie Buck's essay in this catalogue, pp. 25–30.

1 Florence, Biblioteca Nazionale di Firenze, Cod. Magliabechiano, XVII, 17, fol. 84r: "*Dipinse et storio un Dante in carta pecora a Lorenzo di Piero Francesco de' Medici, il che fu cosa maravigliosa tenuto*"; see Stapleford 1995, p. 408; earlier Frey 1892.

2 Summary of opinions in Wierda 2009, p. 157, which reject Stapleford's (1995, p. 397) identification of the author as Vincenzo Borghini (1515–1580), a scholar promoted by Cosimo de' Medici and known to Vasari, proposing instead the Florentine humanist Bernardo Vecchietti (1514–1590). This identification is also doubtful.

3 Only *The Chart of Hell* (see fig. 20, p. 75) is complete; the three other coloured leaves – *Inferno* XX, XV, XVIII (cat. no. 17) are incomplete.

4 See *Purgatorio* III (cat. no. 27).

5 Barkan 1999, p. 307; Mendelsohn 1982, pp. 79–80, 165–67.

6 Williams 1997, ch. 1, 'Vasari's Concept of Disegno', pp. 29–72.

7 Monbeig Goguel 1987, pp. 25–31; Ragghianti Collobi 1996; Bjurström 2001.

8 For more on the discussion, see the introduction to the Botticelli drawings in the catalogue section by Dagmar Korbacher, here pp. 72–76.

9 Clark 1976, p. 11.

10 For an example of a well-documented contract, see the Leonello d'Este Breviary (also known as the Llangattock Breviary), Ferrara, 1441–48: Mariani Canova 1998, pp. 19–20; Medica 1998, pp. 76–77; Avril/Reynaud/Cordellier 2011, no. 45. My thanks to Mara Hofmann for the reference.

11 For Vasari's description in Botticelli's *Vita*, see Vasari (1550/1568) 1987, pp. 516–17.

12 See the introduction to the Botticelli drawings in the catalogue section by Dagmar Korbacher, pp. 72–76.

13 Elen 1995, p. 449, makes a similar argument when discussing the Bellini albums; see also London/Florence 2010–11, no. 16, pp. 122–29, at p. 122 (Hugo Chapman).

14 Paris, Musée du Louvre, 42.2/42.7 × 28.5/29.2 cm, inv. nos. RF 147 5-1556 and RF 425, 427, 428; for further discussion, see Bernhard Degenhart and Annegrit Schmitt: *Jacopo Bellini – L'album dei disegni del Louvre*, New York 1984, pp. 30, 119; Elen 1995, no. 22, pp. 218–22 and 427–54.

15 London, British Museum, 41.5 × 33.6 cm, inv. no. 1855-8-11-1/98; see Elen 1995, no. 21, pp. 213–17; London /Florence 2010–11, no. 16, pp. 122–29, here p. 129 (Hugo Chapman).

16 Elen 1995, pp. 219–20.

17 Röthlisberger 1956, p. 360.

18 See Chapman's excellent summary in London/Florence 2010–11, no. 16, pp. 122–29 (with discussion of the chronology between the Paris and London albums and opinions in the literature).

19 London/Florence 2010–11, no. 16, pp. 122–29, at pp. 128–29 (Hugo Chapman).

20 In contrast, see Elen 1995, p. 449, who assumes for both that "The purpose of these drawing-books was both didactic and conservative, as a thesaurus of traditional motifs and 'modern' compositions for members of the workshop to study and copy. In them he intended to record the artistic tradition of the workshop, to be passed on to subsequent generations."

21 London, British Museum, inv. no. 1920,0214.1/26; Elen 1995, no. 29, pp. 236–40.

22 See London/Florence 2010–11, no. 25, pp. 146–49, dated c. 1455–65 (Hugo Chapman). For discussion of the function, see ibid., pp. 148–49. Elen 1995, p. 236, dates it to c. 1460–76 and considers it possible that the book was made for a client or to sell (p. 238).

23 London, British Museum, inv. nos. 1889,0527.1-95; 1890,0314.1-4; 1900,0226.1-8; Elen 1995, no. 31, pp. 242–47; London/Florence 2010–11, no. 34, pp. 166–71 (Hugo Chapman).

24 London, British Museum, inv. no. 1845,0825.487; see London/Florence 2010–11, no. 34, pp. 166–71 (Hugo Chapman), at p. 171, fig. 6.

25 Keller 2000, pp. 326–33 (with illustrations).

26 This refers to *Moses on Mount Sinai and the Brazen Serpent* (fig. 12); see London/Florence 2010–11, no. 28, pp. 154–55, 161 (Hugo Chapman); *The Flood*, 28.4 × 41.3 cm, Hamburg Kunsthalle, inv. no. 21080; see Klemm 2009, vol. 1, no. 233); and *Five Scenes from Genesis* (28.4 × 40.9 cm; Frankfurt am Main, Städelmuseum; see Jacoby 2014, no. 3, pp. 27–29), all in pen and brown ink, and wash, on vellum.

27 See Schulze Altcappenberg 2000, p. 28 (on its function with a review of pertinent literature).

28 For a thorough discussion of the relationship between text and image, see Oltrogge/Fuchs/Hahn 2000, pp. 338–41.

29 Schulze Altcappenberg 2000, p. 29: "*zu einer Autonomie gegenüber dem Text auf .... Jeder, der die Storia auch nur ungefähr kennt, könnte das große Gedicht allein anhand der Darstellungen Botticellis in seiner Gänze kontinuierlich nachbuchstabieren, quasi wie eine 'Commedia pauperum', ein sich selbst erklärender Bilderzyklus.*"

30 Oltrogge/Fuchs/Hahn 2000, p. 341, note 18: "*in flämischen Chroniken des 15. Jahrhunderts als Umsetzung genealogischer Rotuli in Codexform entwickelt worden*".

31 Vienna, Österreichische Nationalbibliothek, cod. 2533; Thoss 1987, no. 4, pp. 34–37.

32 Thoss 1987, p. 35.

33 St Petersburg, Hermitage, inv. no. Fr. F. v. IV, 12; see Voronova/Sterligov 1996, pp. 278–83.

34 See Schulze Altcappenberg 2000, p. 30. On Mangona, see the introduction to the Botticelli drawings in the catalogue section by Dagmar Korbacher, pp. 72–76.

35 Oltrogge/Fuchs/Hahn 2000, p. 340.

36 For a prominent example of the way two artists took on different aspects of making a magnificent manuscript, see the large-format 'Genealogy of the Royal Family of Spain and Portugal', datable to 1530–34 (London, The British Library, Add. Ms. 12531). The preparatory drawings were supplied by António de Holanda from Lisbon and then coloured by Simon Bening from Bruges. Of the thirteen surviving sheets, Bening completed only five, Holanda painted another seven, and one remained unfinished as a pen-and-ink drawing. See London/Los Angeles 2003, no. 147, pp. 460–63 (Thomas Kren). My thanks to Joris Corin Heyder for the reference.

37 Oltrogge/Fuchs/Hahn 2000, p. 338.

38 See Dreyer 1986, p. 62, pp. 141–42, note 152, and Schulze Altcappenberg 2000, p. 23, who suggest that Lorenzo di Pierfrancesco de' Medici may have presented the exquisite codex to the King of France Charles VIII in 1495 or Louis XII in 1501. Cox-Rearick 1994, p. 241, on the other hand, observes that none of the diplomatic gifts that were sent from Florence to France at the beginning of the sixteenth century seems to have been intended for the king himself.

FACING Detail of cat. no. 21

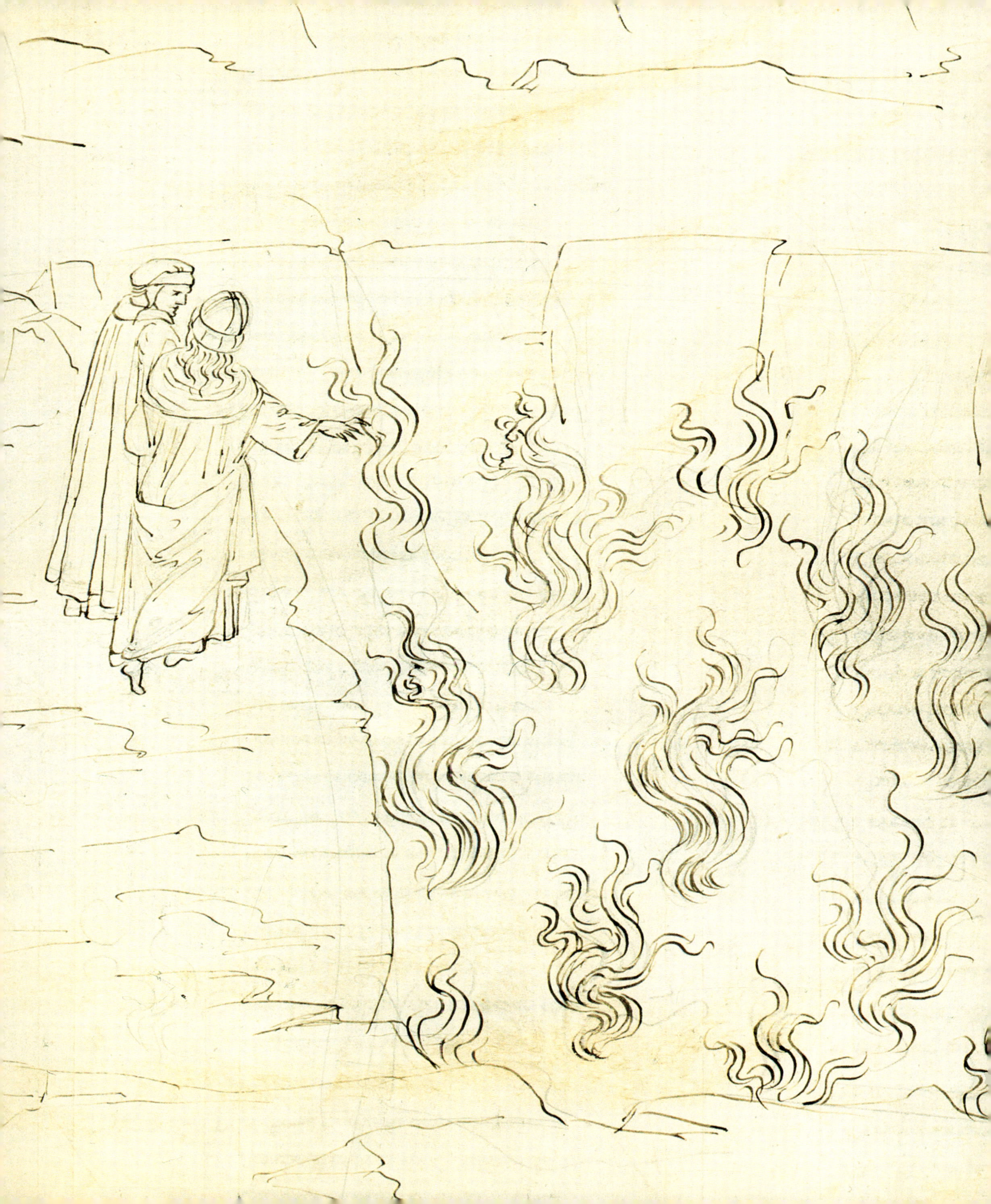

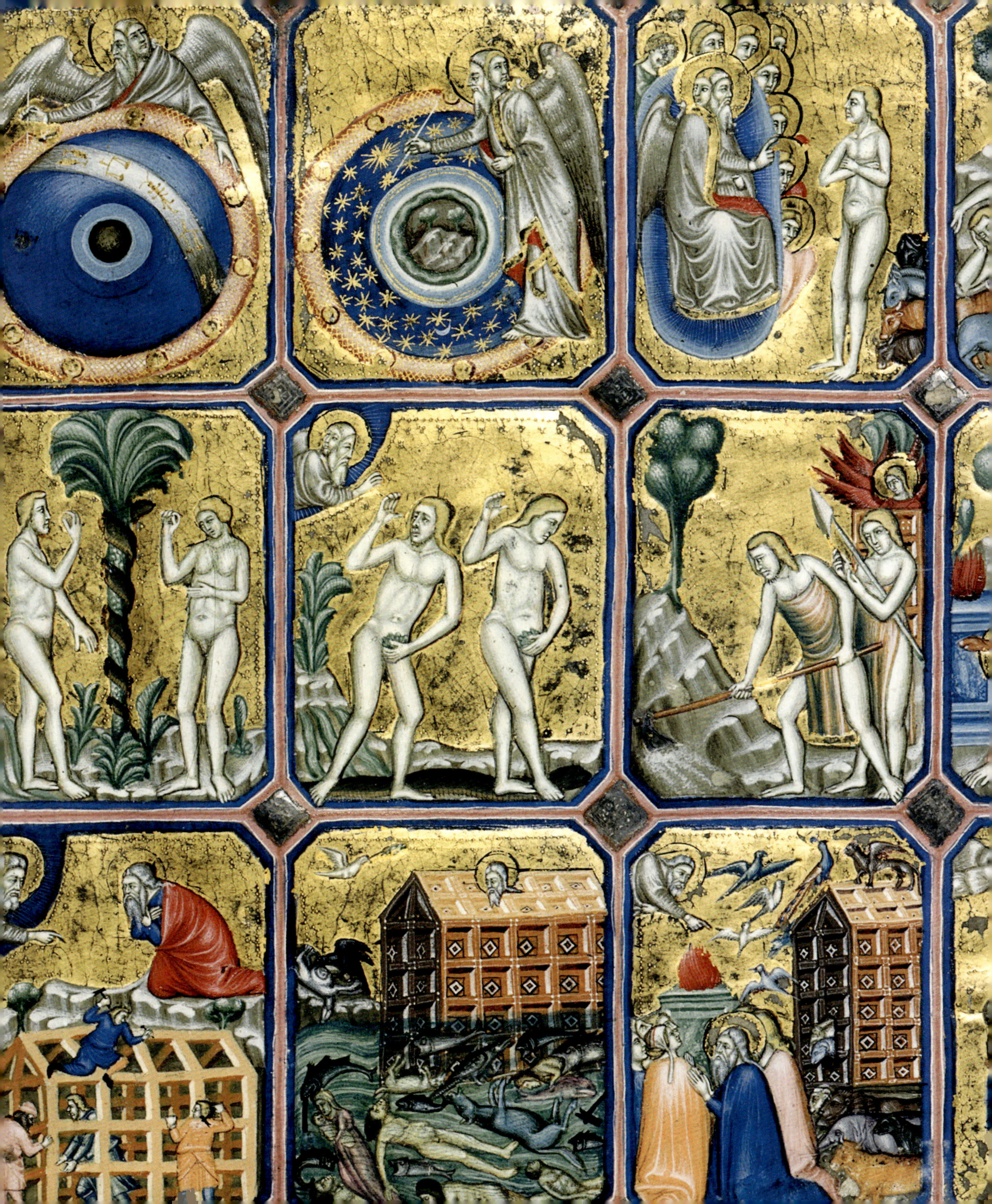

Catalogue

NOTES TO THE READER

All catalogue entries were written by Dagmar Korbacher, except the following:

Beatrice Alai (cat. nos. 1, 3, 4, 6–14)

Georg Josef Dietz (cat. no. 47)

The Kupferstichkabinett does not list its manuscripts and incunabula by inventory number, but instead uses shelf numbers that are a vestige of an earlier reference system. Similarly, no inventory numbers are used for the Botticelli drawings, since these are listed by reference to the relevant canto from the *Divine Comedy* (for example, Botticelli, *Inferno* XVIII).

Bibliographical details are not exhaustive and serve only to provide certain key pieces of information. Entries relating to specific examples of the Botticelli drawings only cite publications that are directly relevant to those drawings. Full details of publications can be found in the bibliography at the end of the catalogue.

The Manuscripts of the Hamilton Collection

With their sumptuous colours, great imaginative sweep, spectacular trompe l'œil, and – above all – their sheer splendour, the manuscripts of the late fifteenth and early sixteenth centuries still have the power to enthral. They were created at a time when book illumination experienced a great flowering, thanks to, rather than despite, the invention of the printing press. Printing meant, of course, that from the middle of the fifteenth century books could be produced more quickly and cheaply, but these advantages were of no interest to wealthy and aristocratic patrons. Their requirements, on the contrary, were for the unique and the costly. Only a handwritten book, magnificently illuminated at great expense for their exclusive use, befitted their status. Such books were not just for personal edification or the private enjoyment of the connoisseur; they were the status symbols of rulers. Most of the works selected for this exhibition (including Botticelli's illustrated Dante) were commissioned by secular or ecclesiastical princes. Whether this made them especially attractive in the eyes of their collector, Alexander Douglas, a man who, as 10th Duke of Hamilton and one of Scotland's foremost aristocrats, was very conscious of his noble descent and superior social standing, we can only speculate. We do know, however, that he was a bibliophile of the first order, and one with a positive passion for illuminated manuscripts and a burning desire to possess them.[1] Various sources indicate that he had already acquired some of the most important works in his collection as a young man, before he became Duke in 1819,[2] while travelling in Italy, France, Germany and elsewhere on the Continent. An early reference to his library, also dating to 1819, was made by William Clarke in his *Repertorium Bibliographicum*. Clarke had visited the library three years earlier and noted with admiration the great age of the manuscripts, their special rarity and their good condition. A short list of the most important works is prefaced by his remark that some are superior to many in the best private and public collections in the land. Among the manuscripts he specifically mentions are the Alexander romance (cat. no. 5), the *Odes* of Horace (cat. no. 10) and the chivalric romance *Huon d'Auvergne* (cat. no. 3), along with the Cecco d'Ascoli (cat. no. 7) and the missal of Cardinal Giulio de' Medici (cat. no. 14), which he describes in more detail, and, of course, the *Commedia*, illustrated with Botticelli's drawings (cat. nos. 15–47).[3] Gustav Friedrich Waagen, the director of the Berlin Gemäldegalerie, gives a report of a visit to Hamilton Palace. Made in the year 1850 or 1851, the visit very nearly did not take place, since the Duke had recently fallen off his horse and broken his arm. His Grace, however, arm in a sling and accompanied by his wife, did not let this prevent him from personally conducting Waagen on a tour of the greatest treasures of his library's manuscript collection. Waagen bemoans the fact that there was hardly time to admire the individual works or take a closer look at them, let alone make notes. Between the viewing and supper, he managed to write a few notes from memory, including one on Botticelli's Dante cycle,[4] and another on the Hamilton Bible (cat. no. 1), which he describes as being among the most beautiful Italian works of art of the period. His hosts also accompanied him on a tour of the library which the Duchess had inherited from her father, William Beckford. United with the Hamilton library through marriage and inheritance, this collection also contained some very valuable manuscripts (see cat. nos. 2–4, 7–13).[5] Only a few years later, in several of his writings, Waagen drew attention to the enormous art-historical value of illuminated manuscripts, maintaining that the very best of these magnificent works could give us a deeper insight into the painting of a period as a whole and the work of its greatest artists. Moreover, he argued, they possessed a treasury of themes and forms now preserved only in this medium.[6] The insight behind this defence of the value of illuminated manuscripts, and hence of the value of collecting them, certainly explains, at least in part, the decision by the Königliche Museen of Berlin to keep the most important Hamilton manuscripts (from an art-historical perspective) in an art museum, despite the fact that they had always hitherto formed part of a library. It was a decision further supported by the fact that the Berlin Kupferstichkabinett already held other valuable illuminated manuscripts.

Today, the Kupferstichkabinett possesses 52 illuminated manuscripts from the Hamilton Collection.[7] The current exhibition displays a selection of the most magnificent and interesting from the Italian and French schools. Besides manuscripts made for popes, cardinals and princes, the selection features works that best reflect, in the broadest sense, the themes of Dante's *Divine Comedy* – classical poetry, travel, the descent into Hell and the vision of Heaven. From all these diverse and splendid works "the smile of the pages" – to use Dante's metaphor from *Purgatorio* – radiates.

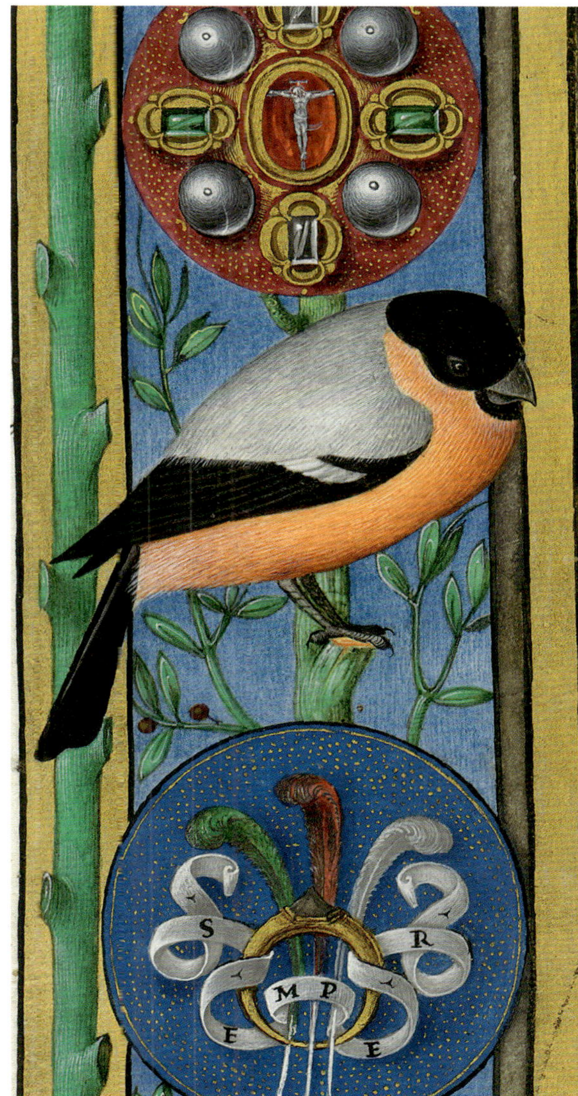

Detail of cat. no. 14

NOTES

1 Henry G. Bohn, 'Hamilton Palace Library', *The Times,* 19 January 1882: "... the Duke going ardently for illuminated manuscripts".
2 See ibid. and 'Death of the Duke of Hamilton', *The Times,* 20 August 1852. William Clarke notes that he acquired some of the Greek and Latin manuscripts ("unrivalled specimens of early art") while he was ambassador to Russia in 1806–07, Clarke 1819, p. 257.
3 Clarke 1819, pp. 257–64.
4 Waagen 1854 a, p. 307, ill. 3.
5 At an unknown point, the manuscripts of the Beckford Collection were integrated into the catalogue of the Hamilton Collection. Incunabula and other printed books, however, were kept separately, and also auctioned separately in 1882: see Boese 1966, p. XVI; Ricci (1930) 1960, p. 84, note 1.
6 Waagen 1854 b, p. 10.
7 The most important reference works for this part of the collection remain, above all, Wescher 1931 and Boese 1966.

1

The Hamilton Bible

Naples, 14th century (1350s)

Parchment codex, 37.5 × 26.5 cm; 497 ff.
Cloth binding, red velvet, with gilded silver clasps, 41.0 × 29.5 × 13.0 cm

PROVENANCE Beaufort family, Avignon; Pope Leo X, Rome; Queen Christina of Sweden (?); Hamilton Collection, Hamilton Palace (Ms. 85); acquired in 1882 for the Kupferstichkabinett, Berlin (78 E 3)

SELECT BIBLIOGRAPHY Erbach-Fürstenau 1905; Wescher 1931, pp. 54–61; Boese 1966, pp. 45–47; Bologna 1969, pp. 275–80, 305–10; Leone de Castris 1986, pp. 376–84; Perriccioli Saggese 2002, pp. 661–65; Bräm 2007, pp. 14, 24, 403–04; Perriccioli Saggese 2010, pp. 118–20

The Hamilton Bible is one of the best-known examples of Neapolitan manuscript illumination from the mid fourteenth century. It was written by the copyist known as Master Johannes de Ravenna, who signed his name on folio 497v. Various leaves bear the coat of arms of the Beaufort family, whose most famous progeny, Pierre Roger, reigned as Pope Clement VI (1342–52) at the time the work was made. It was traditionally thought that the Bible was a gift from Queen Joanna I of Naples to Clement VI, on account of her connection to the Beauforts, who were granted dominion over the city of Avignon by her. However, the heraldic devices in the codex make no reference to the pontificate or cardinalate of Beaufort, which leads us to assume that the manuscript was commissioned for the Beaufort family in general. When the papacy returned to Rome from Avignon in 1376, the Bible probably also made its way there with Bertrand Beaufort, the brother of Clement VI. The Bible was in the possession of Pope Leo X in the sixteenth century, as the famous portrait of him by Raphael shows (fig. 17). He is portrayed in the company of Cardinals Giulio de' Medici and Luigi de' Rossi and the Bible is also depicted in the painting, opened at folio 400v at the beginning of the Gospel of Saint John. What makes this Bible truly unique are its opulent and lavish illustrations: it is decorated with numerous historiated initials, four full-page miniatures and another 36 that take up three-quarters of a leaf, arranged in a series of miniature of panels, for example the page divided into sixteen scenes depicting the Creation (folio 4r). From the complex layout of the leaves, in which script and image come together in a balanced and harmonious interplay, we can surmise that the scribe and illuminator worked closely together. The latter would also have had to incorporate the ideas of the patron, for whom the Bible was intended both as a form of self-praise and a political manifesto. The frontispiece demonstrates this clearly, with its depictions of the coat of arms of the Beaufort family on each of its four corners and the upper margin, while Saint Ambrose is portrayed in prayer together with bishops and monks in the initial F, beneath which we see the Virgin with angels and Prophets. It thus declares a connection between the papal family and the Church, as sanctioned by God. As such, the Bible, the Holy Scriptures, carried a symbolic significance intended to underline the power of its owner. The illuminations are the work of the Neapolitan painter Cristoforo Orimina, whose name appears in the Anjou Bible (on folio 308v; Leuven, Universiteits-bibliotheek, Maurits Sabbebibliotheek, Ms. 1). About 40 illuminated manuscripts dating

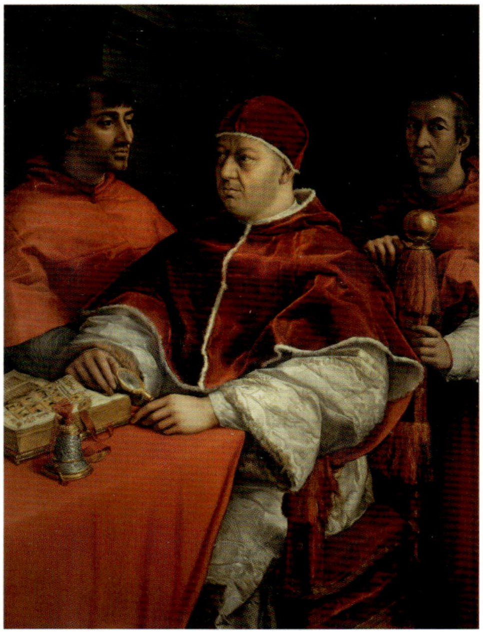

FIG. 17
Raphael, *Pope Leo X*, 1518–19, oil on panel, 154 cm × 119 cm, Florence, Galleria degli Uffizi

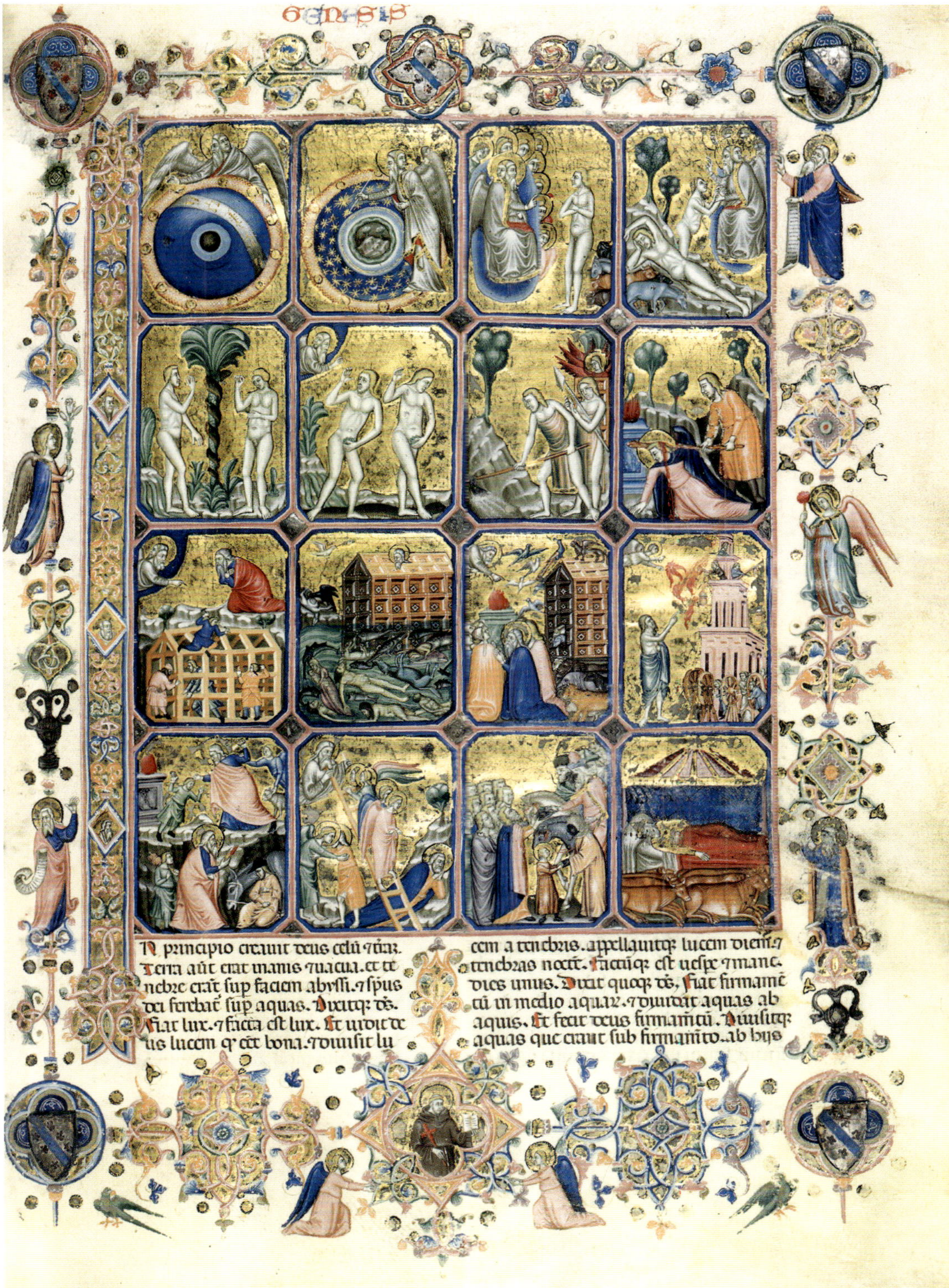
GENESIS
N principio creauit deus celū 7 terr.
Terra aūt erat inanis 7 uacua. et te
nebre erāt sup faciem abyssi. 7 spūs
dei ferebat' sup aquas. Dixitq; ds.
Fiat lux. 7 facta est lux. Et uidit de
us lucem q' eēt bona. 7 diuisit lu
cem a tenebris. appellauitq; lucem diem. 7
tenebras noctē. Factūq; est uespe 7 manē.
dies unus. Dixit quoq; ds. Fiat firmamē
tū in medio aquar. 7 diuidat aquas ab
aquis. Et fecit deus firmamētū. Diuisitq;
aquas que erant sub firmamēto. ab hys

Folio 4r

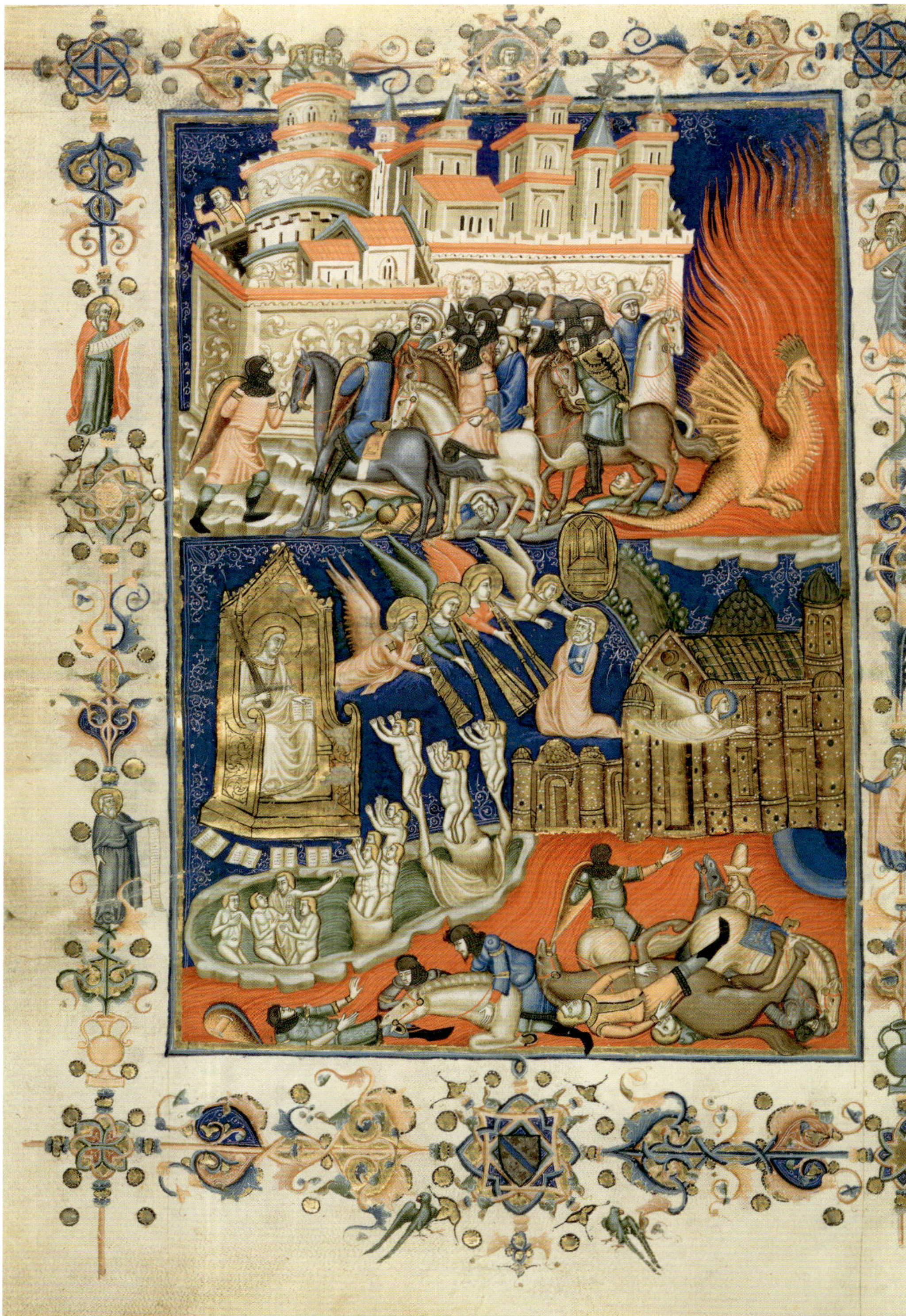

Folio 464v

from the 1340s to late 1350s have been attributed to this artist, who, from 1335, was the court painter of Robert of Anjou, King of Naples. Considering the large number of codices that he produced, it is likely that Orimina ran a workshop of illuminators who would have worked to his designs. From a Neapolitan aristocratic family, he was trained in the tradition of the painter and illuminator Pietro Cavallini, who was prominent in Naples before the arrival there of Giotto. Giotto resided in Naples between 1328 and 1333 and was involved in projects including the painting of the church of Santa Chiara and of the royal palace, the Castel Nuovo. The great Tuscan master's presence prompted a change in Orimina's art, especially with regard to his iconography. The scenes of the Sacrifice of Isaac (folio 4r), the stories of Moses (21v) and of Samson (83r), share many similarities with the New and Old Testament scenes of Giotto's frescoes in the Cappella Palatina of the Castel Nuovo. The other iconographic subject in which Orimina emulated Giotto was that of the Apocalypse (folios 455v–464v). In view of the relationship between these illustrations and the panels of the Apocalypse attributed to Giotto or one of his followers in the Staatsgalerie in Stuttgart, scholars have supposed that there must have been a cycle of frescoes by Giotto, now lost, that depicted scenes of the Apocalypse, perhaps in the church of Santa Chiara. Giotto's influence is probably also responsible for the narrative realism that can be admired on closer inspection of the urban views, seascapes, mountains and fauna and flora, as well as the human figures, their garments and hairstyles typical of the period, creating a pictorial testament to courtly life at the time. Orimina's decoration indicates that he was also schooled in French manuscript illumination, from which he borrowed the ornamental devices of arabesque patterns, fretwork and gilded bosses, and drolleries of animal and human figures. The costly use of gold leaf and ultramarine blue to embellish the scenes reflects the original purpose of this outstanding manuscript as a luxurious item intended for the royal court, making it one of the greatest treasures at the Kupferstichkabinett today.

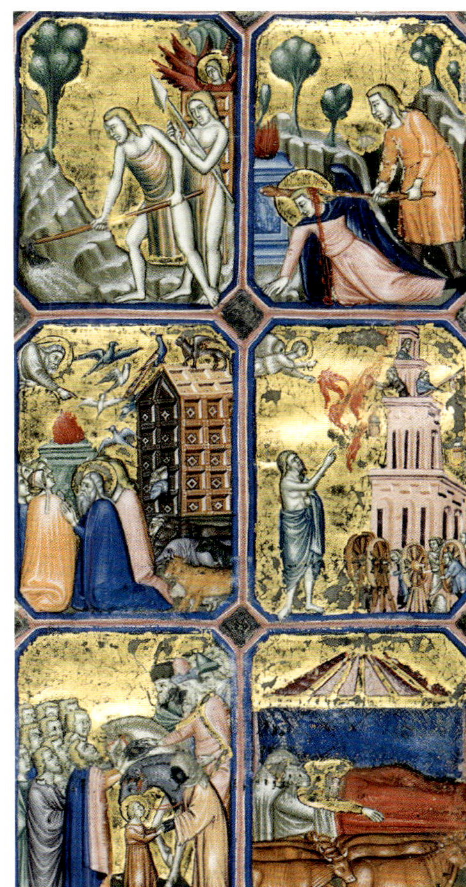

Folio 4r, detail

2

The Latin Hamilton Psalter

Tuscany or northern Italy, 12th century (around 1175)

Manuscript on vellum, 27.2 × 18.5 cm; 138 leaves
Leather binding, purple calfskin, purple velvet, 28.2 × 20.0 × 3.6 cm

PROVENANCE William Beckford collection, Fonthill/Lansdown Tower, Bath (Ms. 512); from 1844 Hamilton Collection, Hamilton Palace (Ms. 549); acquired 1882 for the Kupferstichkabinett (78 A 5)

SELECT BIBLIOGRAPHY Wescher 1931, pp. 21–24; Boese 1966, pp. 266–67; Augustyn 1989; Augustyn 1996

Like the large Cristoforo Orimina Bible (cat. no. 1) and a second Psalter (78 A 9) held by the Kupferstichkabinett, this codex is still associated with the name of its previous owner, the Duke of Hamilton. The Psalter is unusually richly decorated with pen-and-ink drawings, hand-coloured in both watercolour and body colour. Around two hundred drawings, representing human figures, animals and entire scenes, are distributed through the manuscript, each one positioned exactly at the point in the text to which it refers. Such an abundance of images is seldom found in a Psalter of this period. The two images shown here, although associated with different Psalms, are both devoted to the same theme, the so-called Harrowing of Hell. In the story of the New Testament, this event comes between the death of Jesus on the cross and his resurrection; it is referred to in the Apocrypha and again in the Creed ("He descended into Hell"). On folio 24v, illustrating Psalm 24, verse 7 ("Lift up your heads, O ye gates; and be ye lifted up ye everlasting doors; and the King of glory shall come in") we find a depiction of Christ, recognisable from his cruciform nimbus and his staff surmounted by a cross, approaching from the left and accompanied by an angel. As suggested by the words of the Psalm, the angel knocks on the gates of Hell, which promptly give way. Inside we can see the head of a lion-like monster; it is guarding the occupants, who are chained together and being attacked by snakes. The second scene, on folio 93v, accompanies Psalm 107, v. 16 ("For he hath broken the gates of brass and cut the bars of iron in sunder"). This also refers to the collapse of the gates of Hell, but the illustration this time shows what happens next: Christ frees Adam and Eve, the original progenitors of mankind, from Hell, along with other unbaptised figures from the Bible such as David, Solomon and John the Baptist. In this image, the monsters are no longer merely animal-like; they have assumed more human form. The theme of the Harrowing of Hell spread beyond the context of the Psalms to become an important motif of Christian art in general. In addition to the pictures, this Psalter is also remarkable for its carefully sustained system of rubrication for different categories of text: the incipits of the Psalms appear in red and those of the associated prayers in blue, while preambles and commentaries, including commentaries on the illustrations, are given in red. The Psalter was obviously written in Florence or its immediate environs, probably for a monastery of the Vallumbrosan Order, while the illuminator clearly learned his craft in Northern Italy.

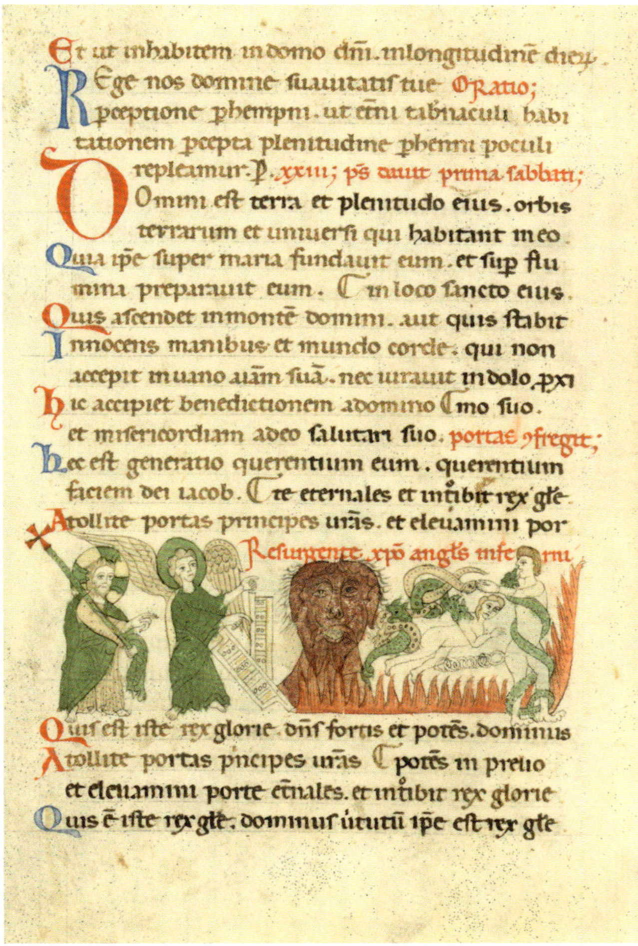

Et ut inhabitem in domo dn̄i. in longitudine dier̄.
Rege nos domine suauitatis tue. Oratio;
perceptione [illegible]. ut et̄ni tabnaculi habi
tationem percepta plenitudine [illegible] poculi
repleamur. P̄. xxiii; ps dauit prima sabbati;
Domini est terra et plenitudo eius. orbis
terrarum et uniuersi qui habitant in eo.
Quia ip̄e super maria fundauit eum. et sup flu
mina preparauit eum. [illegible] in loco sancto eius.
Quis ascendet in montē domini. aut quis stabit
Innocens manibus et mundo corde. qui non
accepit in uano aīam suā. nec iurauit in dolo pxi
hic accipiet benedictionem a domino [illegible] suo.
et misericordiam a deo salutari suo. portas cōfregit;
hec est generatio querentium eum. querentium
faciem dei iacob. [illegible] eternales et intrabit rex glē.
Attollite portas principes urās. et eleuamini por
Resurgente xp̄o angl's inferni
Quis est iste rex glorie. dn̄s fortis et potēs. dominus
Attollite portas pncipes urās [illegible] potēs in prelio
et eleuamini porte ētnales. et intrabit rex glorie
Quis ē iste rex glē. dominus uirtutū ip̄e est rex glē

Folio 24v

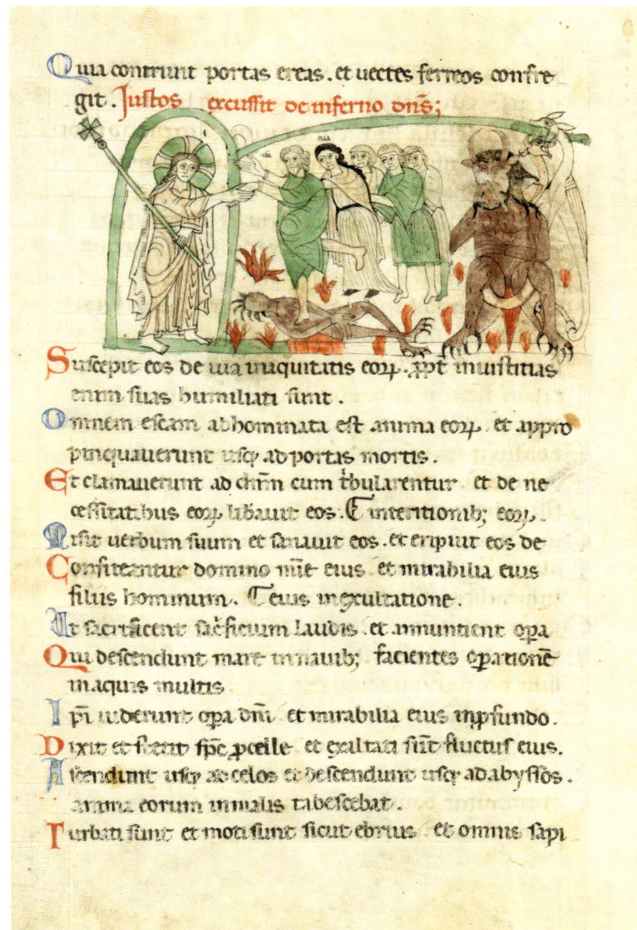

Quia contriuit portas ereas. et uectes ferreos confre
git. Iustos eruit de inferno dn̄s;
Suscepit eos de uia iniquitatis eor̄. ppt iniustitias
enim suas humiliati sunt.
Omnem escam abhominata est anima eor̄. et appro
pinquauerunt usq; ad portas mortis.
Et clamauerunt ad dn̄m cum tribularentur. et de ne
cessitatibus eor̄ liberauit eos. [illegible] interitionib; eor̄.
Misit uerbum suum et sanauit eos. et eripuit eos de
Confiteantur domino mīe eius. et mirabilia eius
filiis hominum. [illegible] eius in exultatione.
Et sacrificent sacrificium laudis. et annuntient opa
Qui descendunt mare in nauib; facientes opationē
in aquis multis.
Ipi uiderunt opa dn̄i. et mirabilia eius in profundo.
Dixit et stetit sps pcelle. et exaltati sunt fluctus eius.
Ascendunt usq; ad celos et descendunt usq; ad abyssos.
anima eorum in malis tabescebat.
Turbati sunt et moti sunt sicut ebrius. et omnis sapi

Folio 93v

3

Nicolas Trombeor, *Huon d'Auvergne*

Northern Italy, 14th century (1341), illuminated by a Venetian illuminator

Manuscript on vellum, 38.0 × 27.0 cm; 85 leaves
Leather binding, 39.6 × 27.9 × 3.8 cm

PROVENANCE 1407 Francescoa Gonzaga, Mantua; 1708 Bernardo Trevisan and Francesco Trevisan, Venice; 1732 Jacopo Soranzo, Venice; William Beckford collection, Fonthill/Lansdown Tower, Bath (Ms. 172); from 1844 Hamilton Collection, Hamilton Palace (Ms. 337); acquired 1882 for the Kupferstichkabinett (78 D 8)

SELECT BIBLIOGRAPHY Wescher 1931, pp. 68–70; Boese 1966, p. 164; Morgan 2003, pp. 67–85, 425–62; Scattolini 2012

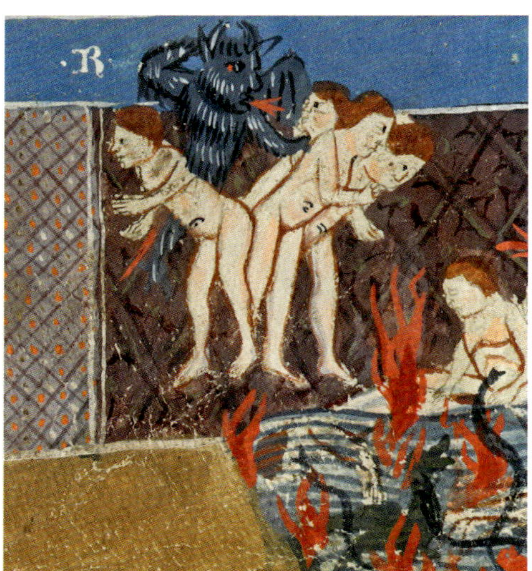

Detail of folio 72r

The manuscript relates, in verse, the heroic deeds of Huon d'Auvergne. As a note in the colophon informs us (folio 84v), the poem was composed in 1341 by the singer and poet Nicolas Trombeor. Its protagonist has to make a journey to Hell, at the behest of Charles Martel, to demand a tribute from Lucifer. Charles, himself, meanwhile, plans to seduce Huon's wife, Nida. Huon's journey is divided into three stages: first he makes pilgrimages to Rome and holy sites in the Near East and Spain; next he visits various mythical places, including the Kingdom of Prester John, the garden of Noah's Ark and the Promised Land; finally, accompanied by Aeneas and Guillaume d'Orange, he reaches Hell, where he meets Lucifer, who gives him what he demands – a litter (with magical powers) and a ring. After this, Huon can finally return to the Auvergne. From a literary perspective, this text belongs to the genre of Franco-Italian epic poetry and is of great significance because it proves the dissemination of the *Divine Comedy* within Northern Italy. In fact, there are innumerable parallels with, and often direct quotations from, Dante's work, both linguistically and in terms of narrative. The author skilfully combines the French chivalric model of the *chanson de geste* with that of Dante's *Inferno*, the latter providing the inspiration for Huon's descent to the realm of Lucifer. Its influence can be seen, among many possible examples, in Huon's two guides, reminiscent of Virgil and Beatrice, as well as in the introduction of several Dantean categories of sinners, such as the traitors (see cat. nos. 23, 24). As well as this close affinity with Dante, the composition of *Huon d'Auvergne* shares some similarity with courtly romance (for example, the protagonists' romantic entanglements), with works in the classical tradition, such as the *Histoire du bon roi Alexandre* (cat. no. 5), and with religious texts: Huon turns from warrior to penitent, he encounters hermits, and he experiences quite astonishing visions of the afterlife. The dissemination of *Huon d'Auverne* throughout the Italian peninsula between the fourteenth and fifteenth centuries is attested by three other manuscripts containing the text (Padua, Biblioteca del Seminario Vescovile, cod. 32; Turin, Biblioteca Nazionale Universitaria, N.III.19; Bologna, Biblioteca dell'Archiginnasio, B 3489). Of the four, the Berlin manuscript is the earliest and the Turin manuscript (dated 1441) the latest. They provide an overview of the development of the Franco-Italian language over the course of a century. Besides these codices, others, though now lost, are listed in the library inventories of three of the most important princely dynasties of Northern Italy – the Este of Ferrara, the Visconti of Pavia and the Gonzaga of Manua. The Gonzaga were also owners of the Berlin manuscript; it is mentioned as no. 21 in the *Capitulum librorum in lingua francigena* of 1407, a list of the French books at the court of Mantua.
In terms of decoration, the manuscript is extremely richly endowed: it has 76 miniatures, set in rectangular frames at the bottom of the page, as well as three large illuminated capitals. The illuminator, who was

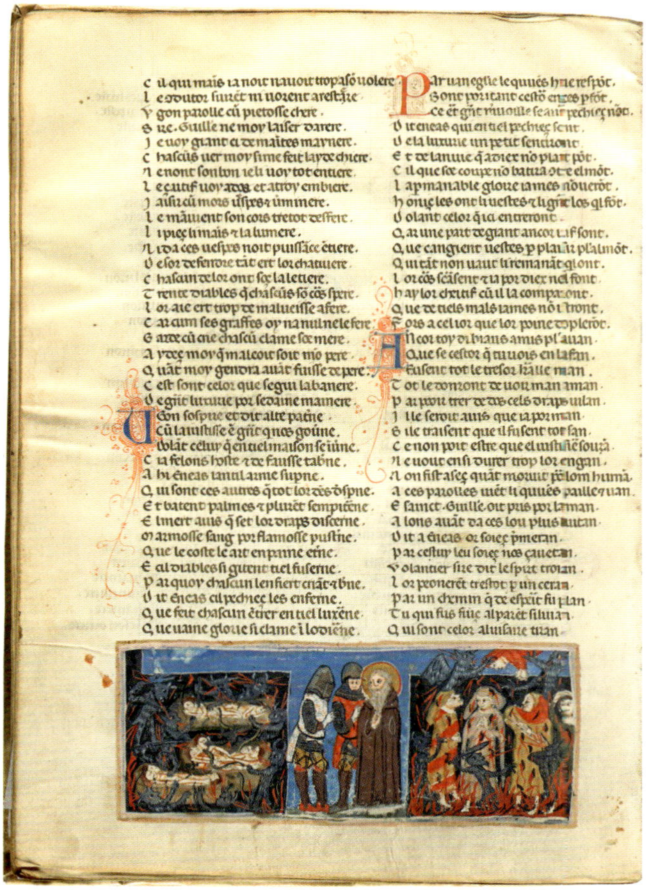

Folio 65v

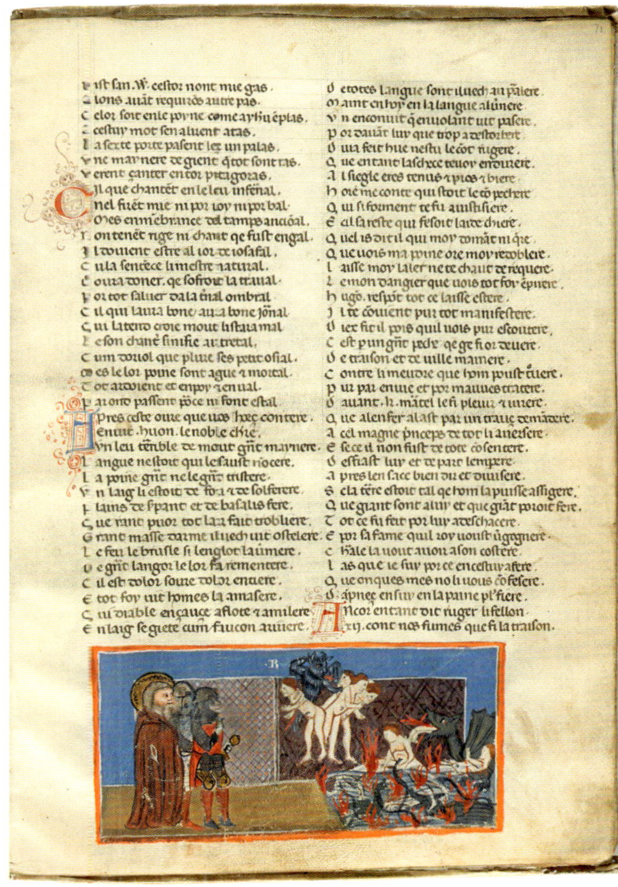

Folio 72r

probably from the Veneto, creates scenes of great narrative vivacity, skilfully reflecting the content of the text, as can be seen, for example, in the illustrations to the episodes related on folio 65v (Huon, Aeneas and William arriving in Hell, and the souls of the damned) and folio 72r (the same three protagonists). The artist's delight in the detailed depiction of costumes, architectural elements and animals and his preference for intense hues and flamboyant colour combinations are evident.

4

Francesc Eiximenis, *Livre des Anges*

France, 15th century (1430s)

Manuscript on vellum, 32.5 × 22.5 cm; 131 leaves
French binding, red morocco leather, 33.4 × 24.4 × 4.1 cm

PROVENANCE Admiral Louis Malet de Graville (1438–1516), Chateau Marcoussis (?); Anne de Graville (1490–c. 1540), Chateau Marcoussis (?); William Beckford collection, Fonthill/Lansdown Tower, Bath (Ms. 386); from 1844 Hamilton Collection, Hamilton Palace (Ms. 255); acquired 1882 for the Kupferstichkabinett (78 D 9)

SELECT BIBLIOGRAPHY Wescher 1931, p. 145; Boese 1966, p. 130; Berlin 1975, no. 123, pp. 188–89; Elbern 1990, p. 15; Eichberg 1998, pp. 25, 45, 58, 156, 160, 185

This codex contains a French translation of the *Libre dels Àngels*, written by Francesc Eiximenis (died 1409). The author, a native of Catalonia and a prominent member of the Franciscan Order, was the most important Catalan theologian of the Middle Ages. He wrote various works, including an encyclopaedia and numerous moral, didactic, devotional and ascetic treatises. Among the most famous is the *Libre dels Àngels*, written in 1392 in Valencia and dedicated, as the Prologue informs us, to the nobleman, Pere d'Artés, chamberlain to King John I of Aragon. Consisting of 201 chapters divided into five books, the work is essentially a treatise on angelology, that is, the study of angels. The angels are introduced, arranged into hierarchies and associated with particular characteristics. The fifth book is devoted to the Archangel Michael, who was particularly venerated by the town of Valencia and the House of Aragon. The work is not only a spiritual treatise, however; it is also a vehicle for Eiximenis's political views, in which he sets out his ideal of government in a clear prose style which could be readily understood by the laity. The *Libre dels Àngels* enjoyed great international success in the fifteenth and sixteenth centuries. It was translated into Latin, French, the Langue d'oïl and even Dutch, and in 1478 became the first book to be printed in Geneva. The Berlin manuscript is one of over two hundred copies of works by Eiximenis and probably once belonged to Anne de Graville (1490–c. 1540), daughter of the French admiral Louis Malet, a collector of manuscripts and printed books. The fact that the codex was intended for a member of high society is reflected in its exquisite workmanship and the elegant cursive script in which it is written. In terms of decoration, the volume has two large miniatures, one at the beginning of the text (folio 3r) and one at the end (folio 98v). The first shows the three hierarchies of angels (see also Botticelli, *Paradiso* XXVIII, XXIX), with the Holy Trinity above and Hell below, personified by a monster with gaping jaws. The second miniature shows the Archangel Michael in combat with the Devil; the scene appears to be set in the interior of a church: a church wall and various ecclesiastical hangings can be seen. The illuminator uses brilliant colours and a lively, almost comic-like narrative style to create a very effective commentary on the text. Both the background, composed of small squares, and the dense foliate tendrils are typical of French manuscript illumination and lend the decorated folios a tone of elegance which must have suited the educated taste of the patron who commissioned the work.

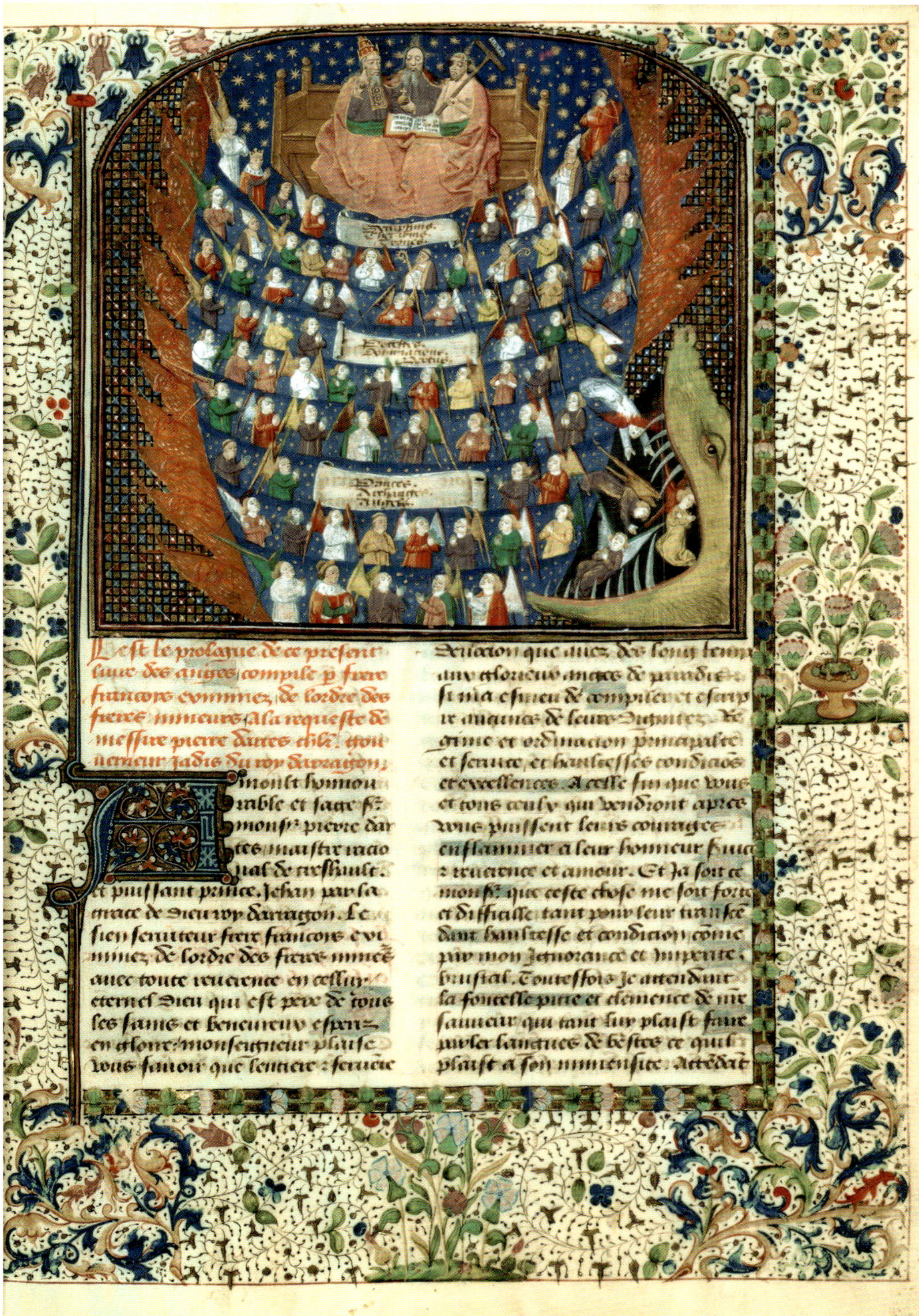
Cest le prologue de ce present
liure des anges compile p frere
francois eximinez de lordre des
freres mineurs a la requeste de
messire pierre dartes cheu'. gou
uerneur jadis du roy darragon.
[T]resnoble honnou
rable et saige s'
monss' pierre dar
tes maistre raco
nal de tres hault
et puissant prince. Jehan par la
grace de dieu roy darragon. Le
sien seruiteur frere francois exi
minez de lordre des freres mineu's
auec toute reuerence en celluy
eternel dieu qui est pere de tous
les sains et beneureux espris
en gloire. monseigneur plaise
vous sauoir que lentiere seruitu
deuocion que auez des tres beni
cux glorieux anges de paradis
si ma esmeu de compiler et escrip
re aucunes de leurs dignitez. re
gime et ordinacion principalle
et seruice. et haultesses condicions
et excellences. A celle fin que vous
et tous ceulx qui vendront apres
vous puissent leurs courages
enflammer a leur honneur sin[illegible]
z reuerence et amour. Et ja soit ce
monss' que ceste chose me soit forte
et difficille tant pour leur transce
dant haultesse et condicion comme
pour mon ignorance et imperitie
bestial. Toutesfois je attendant
la doulceur pitie et clemence de me
sauueur qui tant luy plaist faire
parler [illegible] de bestes ce quil
plaist a son immensite. attendant

Folio 3r

5

Histoire du bon roi Alexandre

Northern France (Théouranne, Saint-Omer or Reims), 13th century (c. 1290–1300)

Manuscript on vellum, 26.0 × 18.8 cm; 82 leaves
French binding, blue morocco leather, 27.5 × 20.3 × 3.8 cm

PROVENANCE possibly Foucaud de Rochechouart, Bishop of Noyon (1317–1331) or Robert de Fouilloy, Canon of Noyon, later Bishop of Amiens (1308–1321); before 1819 Hamilton Collection, Hamilton Palace (Ms. 19); acquired 1882 for the Kupferstichkabinett (78 C 1)

SELECT BIBLIOGRAPHY Wescher 1931, pp. 36–39; Berlin 1975, no. 122, pp. 187–88; *Handbuch* 1994, no. 1.4, p. 51 (Frauke Steenbock); Rieger 2002; Rieger 2006; Los Angeles 2010–11, no. 8, pp. 114–17 (Anne D. Hedeman)

Alexander the Great, king of the small state of Macedonia in northern Greece, became a legend in his own lifetime (356–323 BC). Myths abounded concerning his divine birth and unparalleled deeds of heroism. As a general he fought many battles, defeated Greeks and Persians and led victorious military campaigns as far afield as India, an unimaginably distant country, before dying in Babylon at the age of 33. It was not long before the imaginations of poets were fired by the fantastic wonders he had encountered among strange peoples in exotic lands.

Behind these tales of fabulous adventure, the historical figure of Alexander the Great receded. The idealised ruler of antiquity became the contemporary hero of chivalric romance, the knight who converted 'heathen' races to Christianity. He was integrated into the Christian world view and given a place among the Nine Worthies, thus becoming a model for contemporary rulers. After the Bible, the history of the life of Alexander – handed down in all manner of versions and traditions, in prose and in verse, in Latin and almost every European language – was the most widely disseminated book of the Middle Ages. The text of the Alexander romance from the Hamilton Collection is based on a free translation of the Latin *Historia de preliis Alexandri Magni*. Although this Old French version is imbued with the moral purpose of chivalric literature, the text's illumination, with its delightful representations of fantastic creatures and amazing feats of heroism, must have ensured that it also had considerable entertainment value. The only clue as to who originally commissioned the work are depictions of a coat of arms which can now no longer be clearly deciphered; however, the patron was probably a member of the senior clergy at Noyon, an episcopal see in Picardy from where three other early and related manuscripts of the *Histoire du bon roi Alexandre* are known to have come (London, British Library, Harley Ms. 4979; Brussels, Bibliothèque royale de Belgique, Ms. 11040; private collection). The market for luxurious editions of literature of this type – lofty adventure with pretentions to historical *gravitas* and a moral and didactic purpose – included both clerics with ambitions to high office and young noblemen, including the sons of princely houses. Of all the tales of Alexander's heroic deeds, it would seem that his flight up to Heaven and his underwater journey particularly enthralled the mediaeval reading public. Both these episodes are given the distinction of a full-page miniature in the Berlin *Romance of Alexander*. As these tales relate, reaching the edges of the known world did not satisfy the general-king; he also wished to explore the expanse of Heaven and the depths of the ocean. For his reconnaissance of Heaven, it was said that Alexander had himself carried up in a wooden litter borne by griffins, whom he enticed aloft with baits of meat skewered on a long spear (folio 66r). Immediately thereafter he set off to explore the underwater world. An enormous grey whale dominates the picture, while fish of all

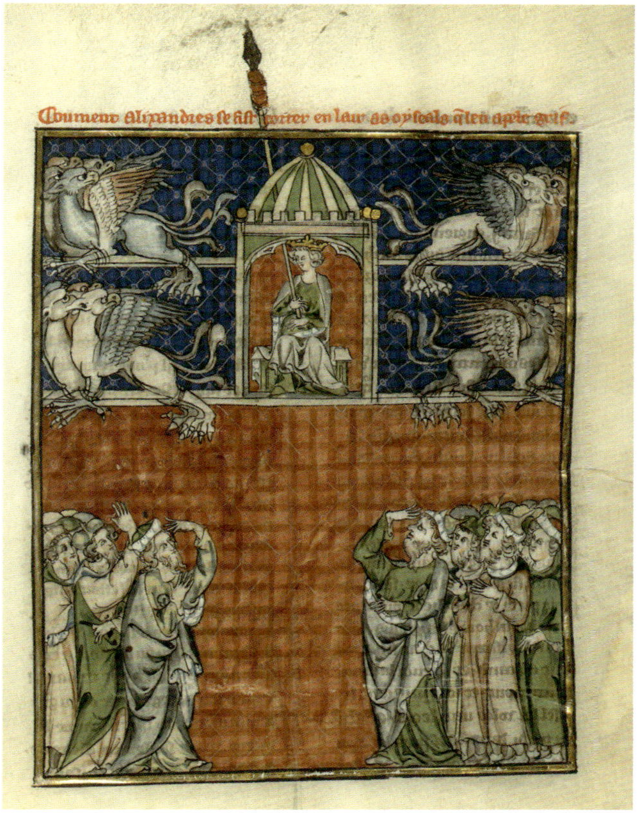

Folio 66r

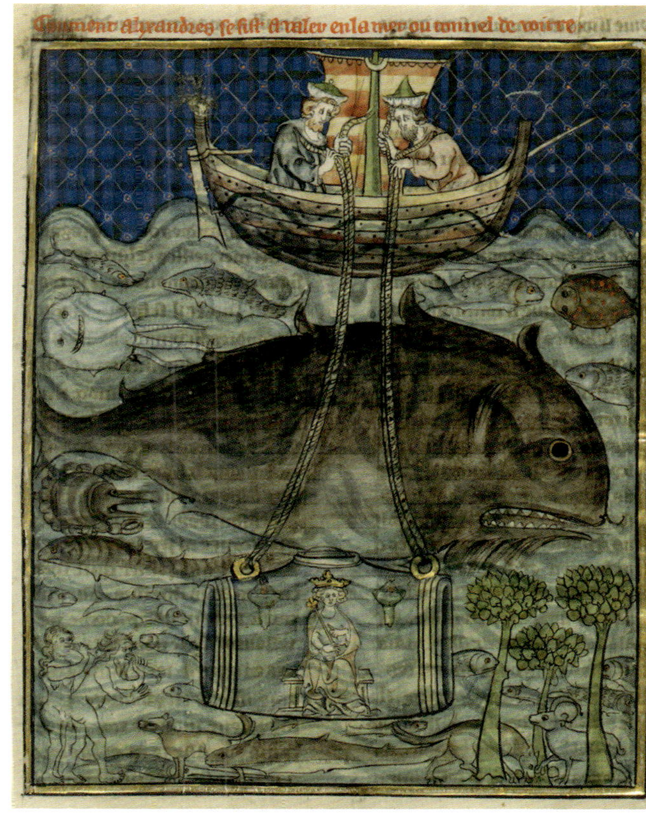

Folio 67r

sorts, including swordfish, skate and a crab, along with others shaped like men, foxes and sheep, disport themselves amongst huge seaweed trees. The illuminator imagines Alexander's transparent diving vessel, lowered into the depths from his boat, as resembling a glass wine-barrel lit by two oil lamps (folio 67r). Both pictures are characterised by a strange tension between the flat, ornamental, almost tapestry-like style of the depiction and the measureless breadth and depth of the celestial and underwater worlds they illustrate. Nineteenth-century century taste apparently did not greatly appreciate the aesthetic qualities of these "curious Paintings in vivid colours" (1882 sale catalogue, p. 4). Accorded no special place among the many sumptuous treasures of the Hamilton Collection, the manuscript is today one of the most famous highlights of the Berlin Kupferstichkabinett.

6

Lucian's 'Calumny', translated by Bartolomeo Fonzio

Northern Italy (Ferrara?), 15th century (1472), with an illustration by Bartolomeo Fonzio

Manuscript on vellum, 20.6 × 13.9 cm; 32 leaves
French binding, red goatskin and brown sheepskin, 21.5 × 14.6 × 2.2 cm

PROVENANCE Duke Ercole I d'Este, Ferrara; Hamilton Collection, Hamilton Palace (Ms. 416); acquired 1882 for the Kupferstichkabinett (78 C 26)

SELECT BIBLIOGRAPHY Wescher 1931, pp. 95–96; Berlin 1975, no. 165, pp. 253–54

This manuscript contains an Italian vernacular translation of the essay on Apelles's *Calumny* (or slander') by Lucian of Samosata (2nd century AD). The translation was made in 1472 by the Florentine humanist Bartolomeo Fonzio, and dedicated to the ruler of Ferrara, Ercole I d'Este. The story tells how the Greek painter Apelles (4th century BC) fell victim to slander and created a painting to illustrate the unhappy fate which had befallen him. The text of 'Calumny' had been translated into Latin by the humanist Guarino da Verona at the beginning of the fifteenth century, and had very quickly won popularity due to its moral and didactic appeal. It was, in fact, an admonition to rulers against heeding false accusations and succumbing to the flattery of slanderers. This vernacular version from Ferrara is embellished with an illustration by the translator, Fonzio himself, the earliest pictorial interpretation we have of Lucian's text. The picture is drawn on the frontispiece in black chalk, pen and ink, and watercolour and body colour, and is divided into two registers. The lower part resembles a stone tablet, with a circular medallion bearing the title, *Apellis pictura de Calumnia* (Apelles's painting of Calumny) in capital letters. Above is the scene itself. The priest or judge is depicted with ass's ears (as in the iconography of the mythical King Midas) and is accompanied by personifications of Ignorance and Suspicion. Calumny comes hurrying in, dragging her victim behind her, accompanied by Envy, Deceit and Treachery. Repentance and naked Truth bring up the rear of the procession. Fonzio relies for his composition on indications given in the text, taking up its three-part articulation of the scene: a first group of figures is formed by the judge and his false counsellors, a second by Calumny, her victim and the three negative personifications, and a third by the positive personifications. The humanist also gives a pictorial rendering of the actions, demeanours and attributes of the various figures described in the text. There are, nevertheless, some elements in the drawing which break with the original; Fonzio renounces the two-dimensional linearity it suggests in favour of a three-dimensional composition where Ignorance, seated on the steps, occupies a different spatial plane from that of the procession. The gestures of the figures also depart from those described: Calumny's victim is shown here with clasped hands, turning in a gesture of entreaty towards Truth. This has the effect of reversing the narrative progression with respect to the text, so that it runs from left to right, whereas Lucian's description begins with the figure on the right and proceeds towards the left. By obeying the principle of mimesis and the maxim *Ut pictura poesis* (as in painting, so in poetry), as epitomised by Horace, Fonzio creates the indissoluble link between painting and poetry which formed one of the pillars of the humanistic Renaissance aesthetic. The theme of *Calumnia* was taken up by many artists in the second half of the fifteenth century, including Sandro Botticelli, who made a small panel painting of the subject in 1494–95 (fig. 18).

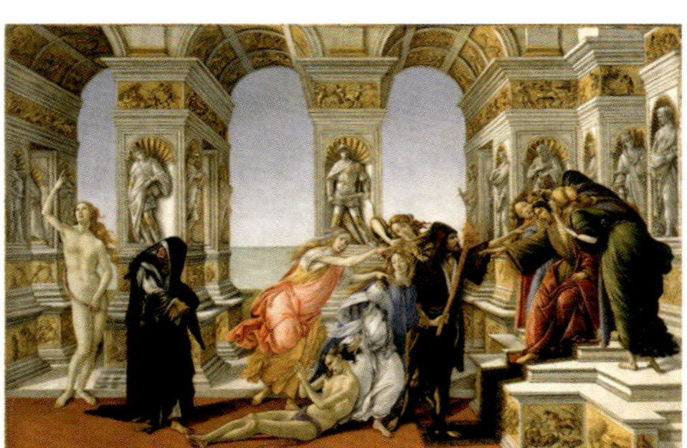

FIG. 18
Sandro Botticelli, *The Calumny of Apelles*, 1494, tempera on panel, 62 cm × 91 cm, Florence, Galleria degli Uffizi

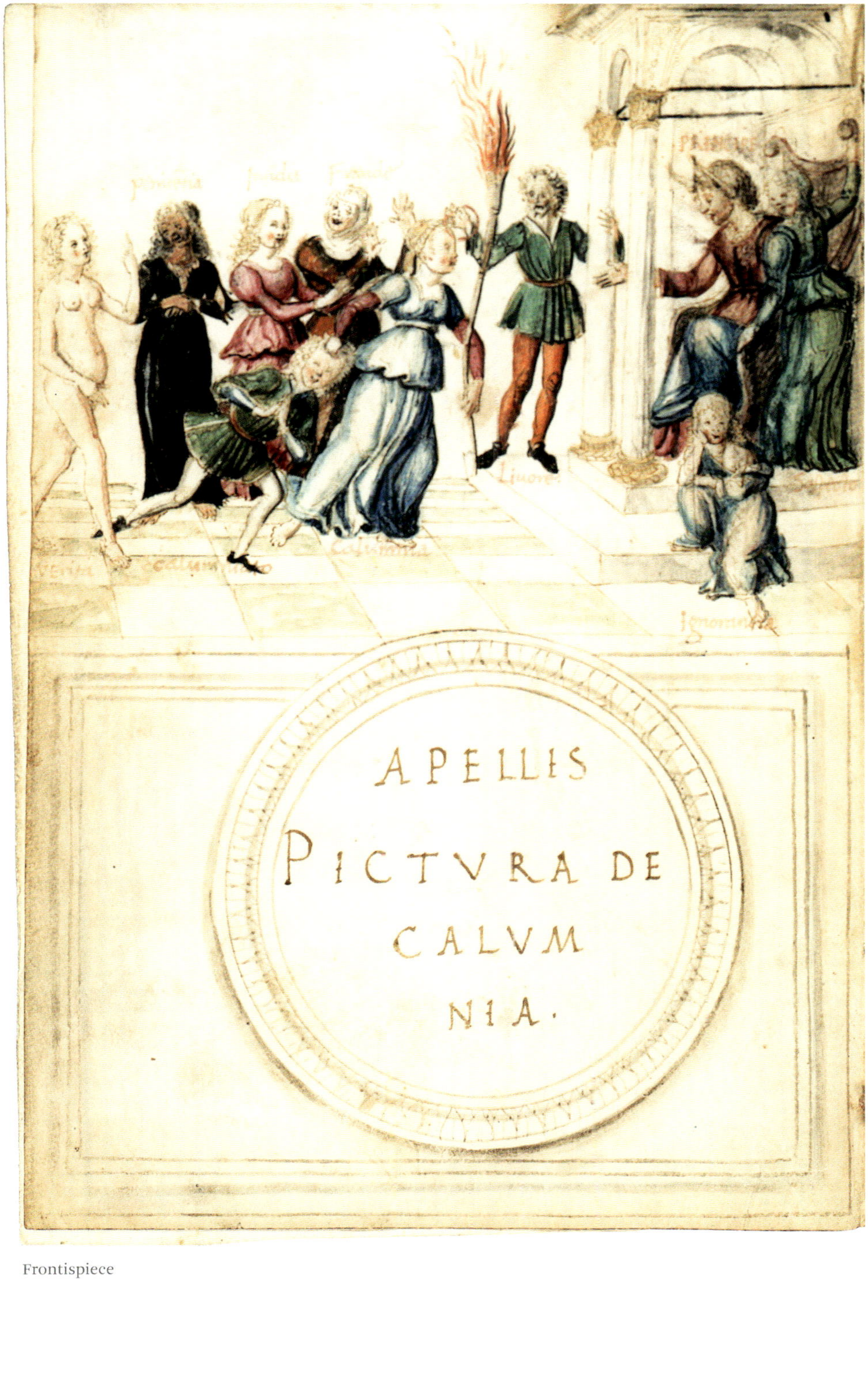

Frontispiece

7

Cecco d'Ascoli, *Libro dicto L'Acerba*

Northern Italy (Lombardy?), 15th century (1475)

Manuscript on vellum, 25.6 × 16.5 cm; 75 leaves
French binding, blue morocco leather,
27.3 × 18.4 × 4.0 cm

PROVENANCE Bianca Maria d'Este, Ferrara (?); William Beckford collection, Fonthill/Lansdown Tower, Bath (Ms. 79); from 1844 Hamilton Collection, Hamilton Palace (Ms. 138); acquired in 1882 for the Kupferstichkabinett (78 C 25)

SELECT BIBLIOGRAPHY D'Ancona 1920; Wescher 1931, pp. 124–26; Berlin 1975, p. 201, note 139; Cogliati Arano 1985, p. 243, Rao 2007

This manuscript, dated 1475, contains the *Acerba*, an allegorical-didactic treatise written by Francesco Stabili (1269–1327), better known as Cecco d'Ascoli. There have been various attempts to interpret the title. On the one hand, '*acerba*' could refer to the contents, which may be seen as dry and difficult, or to the great variety of themes discussed, since the Latin word *acervus* means a 'heap' or 'multitude'. On the other hand, it could also be read as *La Cerba* (the hind). Since the hind personified wisdom in the Middle Ages, this would have conveyed the didactic quality of a compendium. Finally, several lines which open the fifth book "*Io voglio qui che 'l quare trovi 'l quia/ levando l'ale de l'acerba mente/ seguendo del philosopho la via*" (I want the why to find the because/ stretching the wings of the unripe mind/ following the way of the philosopher) appear to be a reference to adolescence, a difficult stage in the mind's development and one in which the tutelage of philosophy is required. Composed in the Italian vernacular between 1324 and 1327, this epic poem represents one of the most complete encyclopaedias which the Middle Ages produced, and has clear popular-scientific appeal. It is divided into five books, comprising a total of 4867 lines. The first book deals with cosmology and astronomy; the second describes the influence of the constellations on the individual and his sins and virtues; the third is a bestiary, with moral interpretations of the behaviour of various birds, fish, reptiles and quadrupeds; the fourth returns to astronomy-related problems and uses a dialogue format to discuss questions of biology, alchemy and ethics. The fifth book, finally, remained unfinished when the author was condemned to death in 1327; it is a discussion of the Holy Trinity and the soul. As a synopsis, the work is both impressive and bewildering; it has no logical scheme of development, and is made more difficult to read by an excessive use of metaphor. *L'Acerba* is the best-known work by Cecco d'Ascoli, a doctor, astrologer and lecturer at the medical faculty of the University of Bologna. After being charged with heresy in 1324, he moved to Florence, where he became personal physician to Charles of Anjou, the son of Robert of Naples. Following further convictions for heresy, he was burned at the stake and his works were banned by the Church. Numerous copies of the *Acerba* nevertheless survived, including the Berlin copy and another in Florence (Biblioteca Medicea Laurenziana, Plut. XL. 52). One of the main reasons for the wide reputation of the *Acerba* is its attack on Dante Alighieri and the "*cose vane*" (vain things) extolled in his *Divine Comedy*. Cecco's work was even called the *Anti-Comedy*, since its intention, as the author explains in Book 4, was to offer the reader the truths of science instead of the Dante's "*fabulle*" (fables). Underlining his aversion to Dante, Cecco employed a *sestina* instead of the *terza rima* rhyming form. In the initial U on folio 1r of the Berlin codex we see a portrait of Cecco as he prepares to write. Both watercolour and body colour are used in the decoration of the manuscript. The verses are illustrated with elegant vignettes which provide a visual commentary to

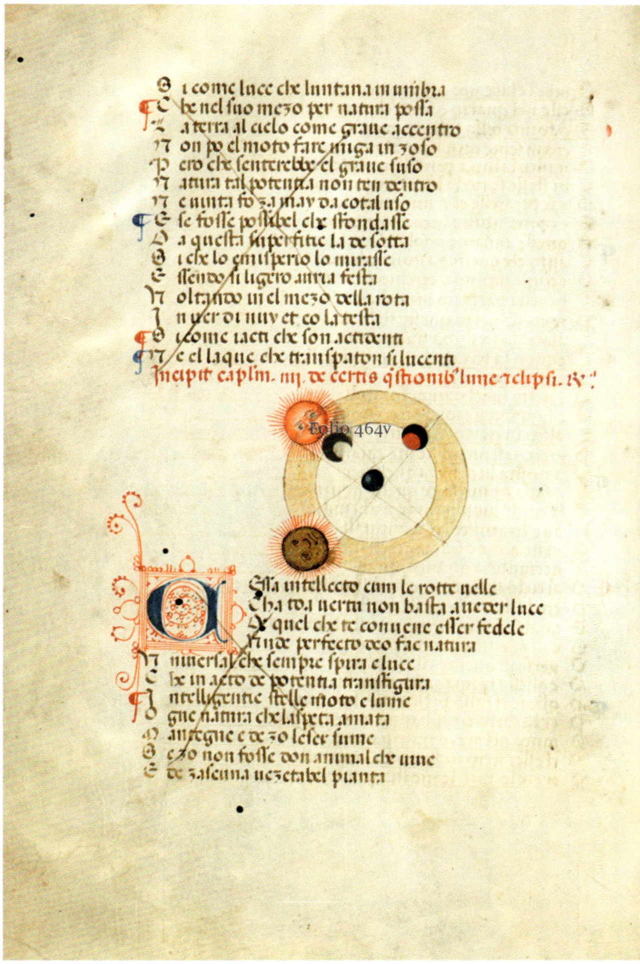

Folio 5v

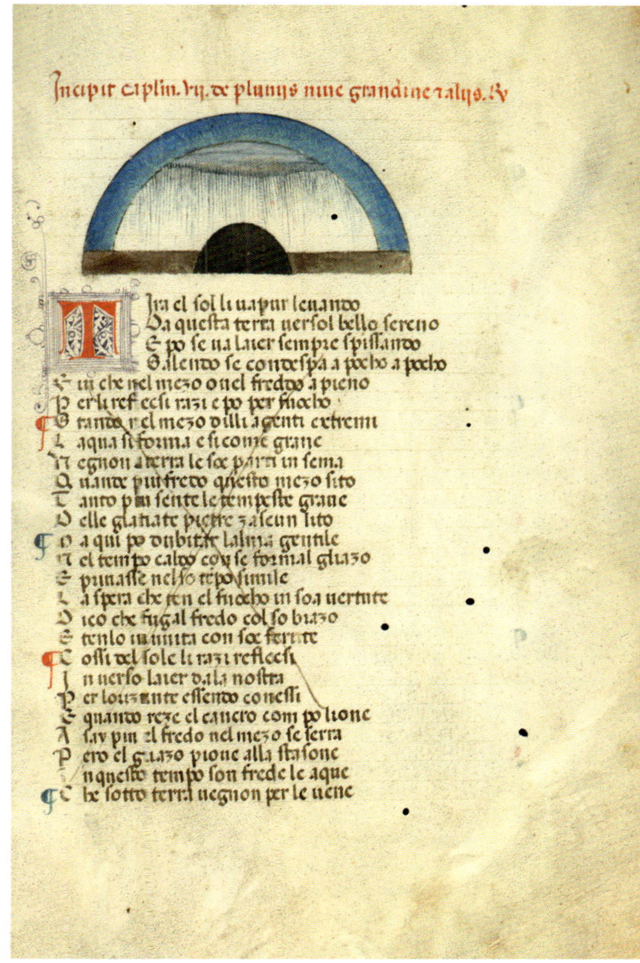

Folio 8r

the text, like the illustrations of the solar system and the solar eclipse on folio 5v, or the meteorological phenomena of rain, snow and hail on folio 8r. The concise but effective style favoured by the artist places him in the tradition of the late Gothic Lombard illuminators who decorated copies of the *Tacuinum sanitatis* with images of animals, plants and natural phenomena. The exquisite workmanship of the manuscript suggests that it was made for a member of the aristocracy; further confirmation is the motto of Bianca Maria d'Este on folio 1r: "*Nul bien sans poin*" (No gain without pain), giving rise to the possibility that this codex may originally have been in the library of the Dukes of Ferrara.

8

Petrarch, *Libro di Sonetti e Cançioni col expositione di Francesco Philelfo*

Northern Italy (Milan?), 15th century (before 1459)

Manuscript on vellum, 25.5 × 18.2 cm; 269 leaves
French binding, purple morocco leather, 27.6 × 21.1 × 6.4 cm

PROVENANCE Corrado da Fogliano, Milan; William Beckford collection, Fonthill/Lansdown Tower, Bath (Ms. 123); from 1844 Hamilton Collection, Hamilton Palace (Ms. 496); acquired 1882 for the Kupferstichkabinett (78 C 22)

SELECT BIBLIOGRAPHY Wescher 1931, p. 128; Boese 1966, p. 236; Sottili 1974, pp. 1–3

Not exhibited in London

This manuscript contains Petrarch's *Canzoniere*, a collection of 366 poems, composed after 1348, in which the poet extols his love for Laura and laments her death. As we are told by the text on the first leaf, the text is provided with a commentary by Francesco Filelfo. In all probability the manuscript was created in 1458 on the occasion of the marriage of Corrado da Fogliano, *condottiere* at the court of Francesco Sforza in Milan, to Gabriella Gonzaga, daughter of the Marquis of Mantua. The name and emblem of Corrado also appear on folio 1r, while the illuminated capital U (or V of *Voi che ascoltate* – You who listen ...) encloses an image of the bridal couple, rendered in profile in the style of antique coins and attired in the fashion of the day. On the last folio, a later hand has noted the years of birth of their two children, Ludovico, born 1459, and Constanza, born 1461. Corrado da Fogliano was not only a man of war, but also one of learning. Our codex is probably the *Canzoniere petrarchesco* from the Fogliano collection which is listed in the inventories of the Sforza library. The connection with the Sforza court is further confirmed by the style of the illumination. The work can be attributed to a Lombard artist of the mid fifteenth century who was also familiar with French book illumination. The French influence can be seen in the elegant tendril decoration and the tiny squares which make up the background of the initial on folio 1r. The commentary on this work of Petrarch also originated within Milanese circles, having been composed by Francesco Filelfo (1398–1481) at the behest of Filippo Maria Visconti, Duke of Milan, between 1444 and 1447. Filelfo had studied Greek in Constantinople and was an outstanding classical scholar and a leading humanist. His commentary enjoyed a certain amount of success, despite being left unfinished at sonnet no. 136. It was copied in several manuscripts, including another example formerly in the Hamilton Collection and now in the Berlin Kupferstichkabinett (cat. no. 9), and was printed in 1476 by Annibale Malpighi in Bologna.

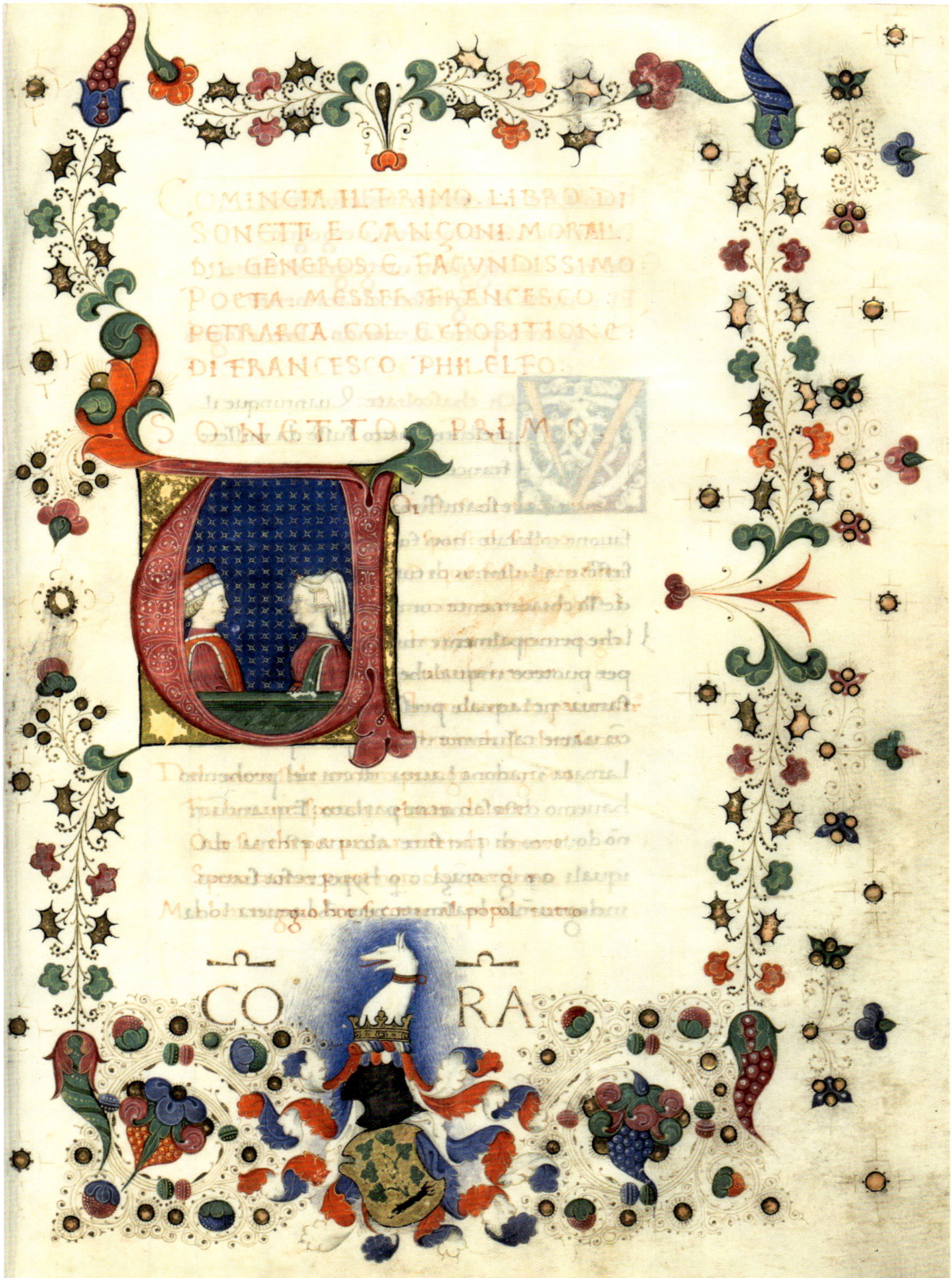
COMINCIA IL PRIMO LIBRO DI
SONETTI E CANÇONI MORALI
DEL GENEROSO E FACVNDISSIMO
POETA MESSER FRANCESCO
PETRARCA COL EXPOSITIONE
DI FRANCESCO PHILELFO
SONETTO PRIMO

Folio 1r

9

Petrarch, *Libro de Sonetti et Cancione col comento di Francesco Philelfo*

Naples, 2nd half 15th century

Manuscript on vellum, 34.3 × 23.0 cm; 218 leaves
Textile binding, yellow moiré silk, 35.7 × 25.5 × 5.1 cm

PROVENANCE Ruffo di Calabria family; William Beckford collection, Fonthill/Lansdown Tower, Bath (Ms. 166); from 1844 Hamilton Collection, Hamilton Palace (Ms. 501); acquired 1882 for the Kupferstichkabinett (78 D 11)

SELECT BIBLIOGRAPHY Wescher 1931, pp. 84–86; Boese 1966, p. 237; Sottili 1974, pp. 3–5; Berlin 1975, no. 135, p. 198

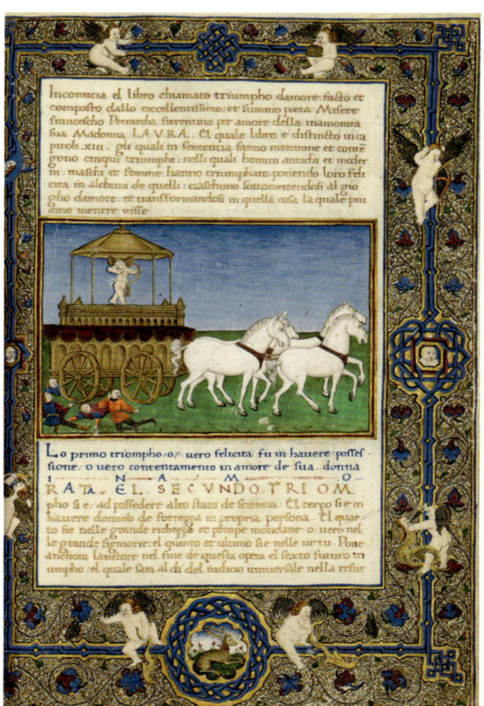

Folio 89r

Of all the works by the great Italian poet, Petrarch's *Canzoniere* and *Trionfi* were the most frequently copied and most often the subject of commentaries by fifteenth-century humanists. The two works were usually combined into a single codex, with the *Canzoniere* placed first. In this copy, the sonnets of the *Canzoniere* occupy folios 1r to 83r and are introduced by a miniature in the initial V (*Voi ch'ascoltate* – You who listen ...) portraying the poet and his beloved Laura. Folios 84r–87r contain the *Life* of Petrarch written by the humanist Leonardo Bruni, while folios 89r–218r have the *Commento ai Trionfi*, the commentary on the *Trionfi* by Francesco Filelfo (1398–1481). The *Trionfi* were written at some time after 1352. Divided into six chapters, they are devoted to descriptions of six visions, in the form of allegorical triumphal processions or 'triumphs', which appeared to the author in a dream. The triumphs of Love, Chastity, Death, Fame, Time and Eternity follow one another in a sequence which mirrors, in idealised form, the path of redemption from sin to salvation. Folio 89r shows the Triumph of Love (or Amor). Several figures are crushed beneath the wheels of the triumphal chariot driven by the personification of Love, and are thus 'conquered'. On Folio 110r we see Chastity, embodied in the figures of the mythical Astraea and the Roman general Scipio, who was regarded as a model of continence. Powerless here against triumphant Chastity, Love falls from the carriage. The iconography of the triumph is borrowed from the ancient world. To celebrate a military triumph, a victorious general would be drawn in his chariot in triumphal procession beneath a *porta triumphalis*, in an event which carried great religious and political significance. While some of its essential elements, including a background of classical architecture and figures in antique costume, were constants in illustrations of Petrarch's *Trionfi*, new and ever more subtle interpretations were devised by the book illuminators who worked for learned patrons. The present codex is a typical example. Once owned by the noble Ruffo family, as we know from the emblem on folio 1r, it was decorated by an unknown illuminator of the Neapolitan school. Depictions of triumphs of this type may have been amongst the inspirations for Botticelli's illustration of Beatrice's triumphal car (see cat. no. 36).

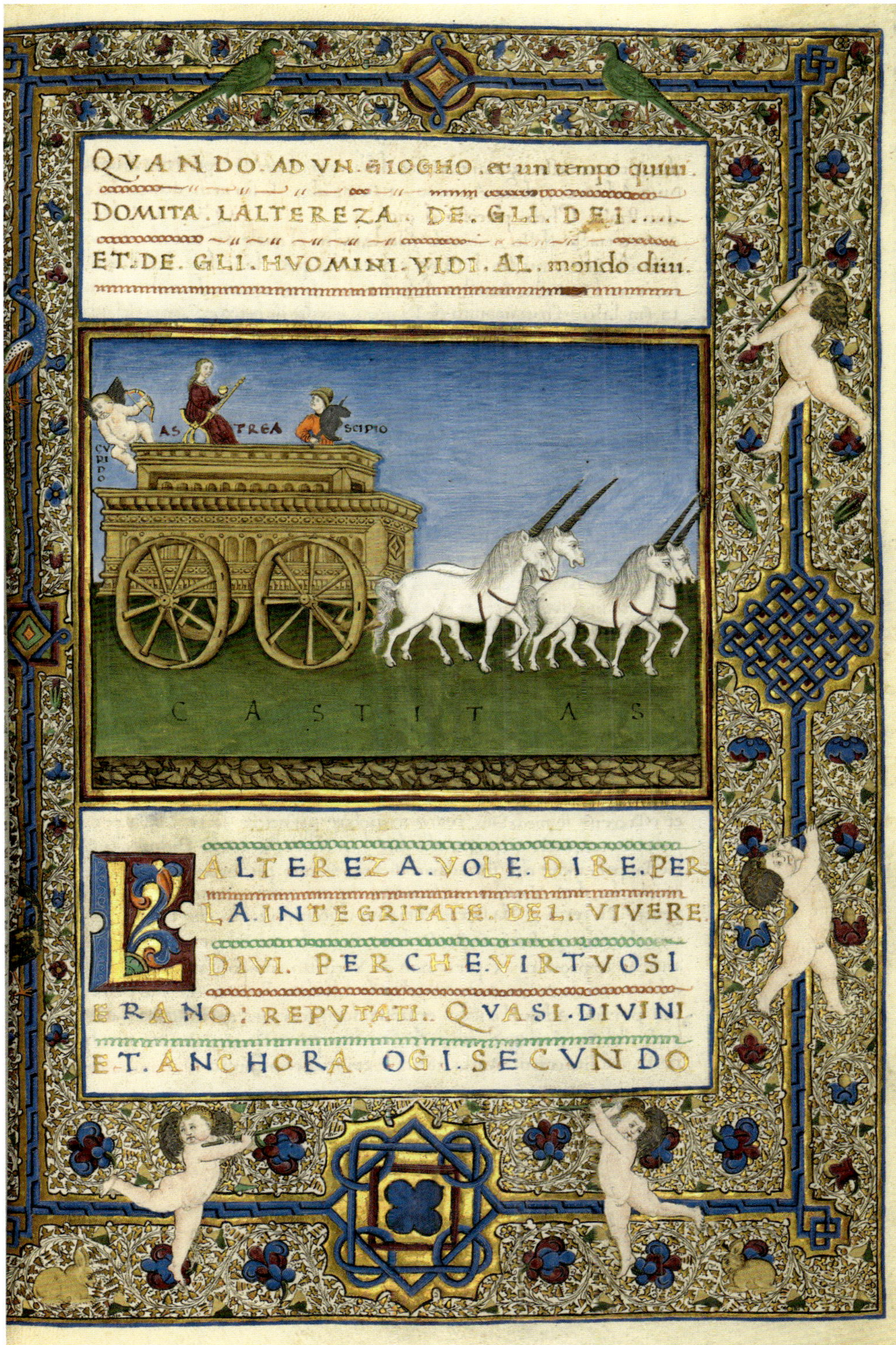
QVANDO. AD VN. GIOGHO. et un tempo quivi.
DOMITA. LALTEREZA. DE. GLI. DEI.....
ET. DE. GLI. HVOMINI. VIDI. AL. mondo divi.
CVPIDO
ASTREA
SCIPIO
CASTITAS
LALTEREZA. VOLE. DIRE. PER
LA. INTEGRITATE. DEL. VIVERE
DIVI. PERCHE. VIRTVOSI
ERANO: REPVTATI. QVASI. DIVINI
ET. ANCHORA OGI. SECVNDO

Folio 110r

10

Horace, *Carmina*

Naples, 15th century (1490–1495), transcribed by Gianrinaldo Mennio, illuminated by Giovanni Todeschino

Manuscript on vellum, 40.0 × 25.8 cm; 135 leaves
French binding, red morocco leather, 41.8 × 27.6 × 4.4 cm

PROVENANCE Alfonso II, King of Naples (1448–1495, reg. 1494–1495); James Edwards, London (1757–1816); William Beckford collection, Fonthill/Lansdown Tower, Bath (Ms. 163); from 1844 Hamilton Collection, Hamilton Palace (Ms. 334); acquired 1882 for the Kupferstichkabinett (78 D 14)

SELECT BIBLIOGRAPHY Wescher 1931, pp. 113–14; Boese 1966, pp. 163–64; Toscano 1993, p. 280; London/New York 1994, no. 45, pp. 112–14 (Jonathan J.G. Alexander); D'Urso 2007, pp. 166–71, 326

This manuscript contains the one hundred and three Latin *Odes* (*carmina*) by the Roman poet Horace. The *Odes* were among the classical works most prized by the humanists and princely patrons of the Renaissance, who commissioned illuminated copies not only for their literary merit but also for their moral, social and political significance. To impart a classical aura appropriate to the verses, the codex is embellished *all'antica*, and the text was written in *littera antiqua*, a script derived from Roman lettering. It opens on folio 2r with majuscule letters in four lines of alternating gold and blue. An architectonic façade, adorned with garlands, rubies, pearls and cameo portrait reliefs *all'antica*, frames the text. On the left, a pedestal, inscribed with the words *Saluti Reipublicae* (For the welfare of the state), supports the allegorical figures of *Caritas* (Charity) and two children. A second pedestal on the right, inscribed *Divus Augustus Pater* (Augustus, god and father), supports a soldier attired in the breastplate of a Roman legionary. Between the two pedestals, the view opens out on to a green landscape with a village and a river. In the foreground stands a peasant, his spade poised to dig. Next to him is a figure whose red robe and cap suggest the academic garb of a scholar. Since the introduction begins by describing mankind's most important activities (athletics, war, trade and relaxation) and ends with the 'apology' (justification) of the poet, this red-robed figure would appear to be a personification of the poet, representing the *vita contemplativa* (contemplative life), as opposed to the *vita activa* (active life) of the man who tills the soil. Finally, in the top left-hand corner of the text field, below the initial M, the three Graces are depicted in monochrome on gold. The lavish decoration of the folio suggests that the owner of the work must have been a person of high rank, and, since the codex bears the coat of arms of the Kings of Naples, probably those of Alfonso II, we may assume that this was a princely commission. This hypothesis is supported by the illumination, which was executed by Giovanni Todeschino, working in Naples in the last quarter of the fifteenth century as "*miniatore del senyor Rey*" (illuminator to his Majesty the King). His pictorial language betrays both his training in the new Venetian style of book illumination, known as *garbo antiquo* (the antique manner), and clear traits of the traditional Neapolitan painting style. The suggestion that the copyist of the codex may have been Gianrinaldo Mennio from Sorrento, also in the employ of Alfonso II, is further confirmation of the important and refined circles within which these *Carmina* were produced.

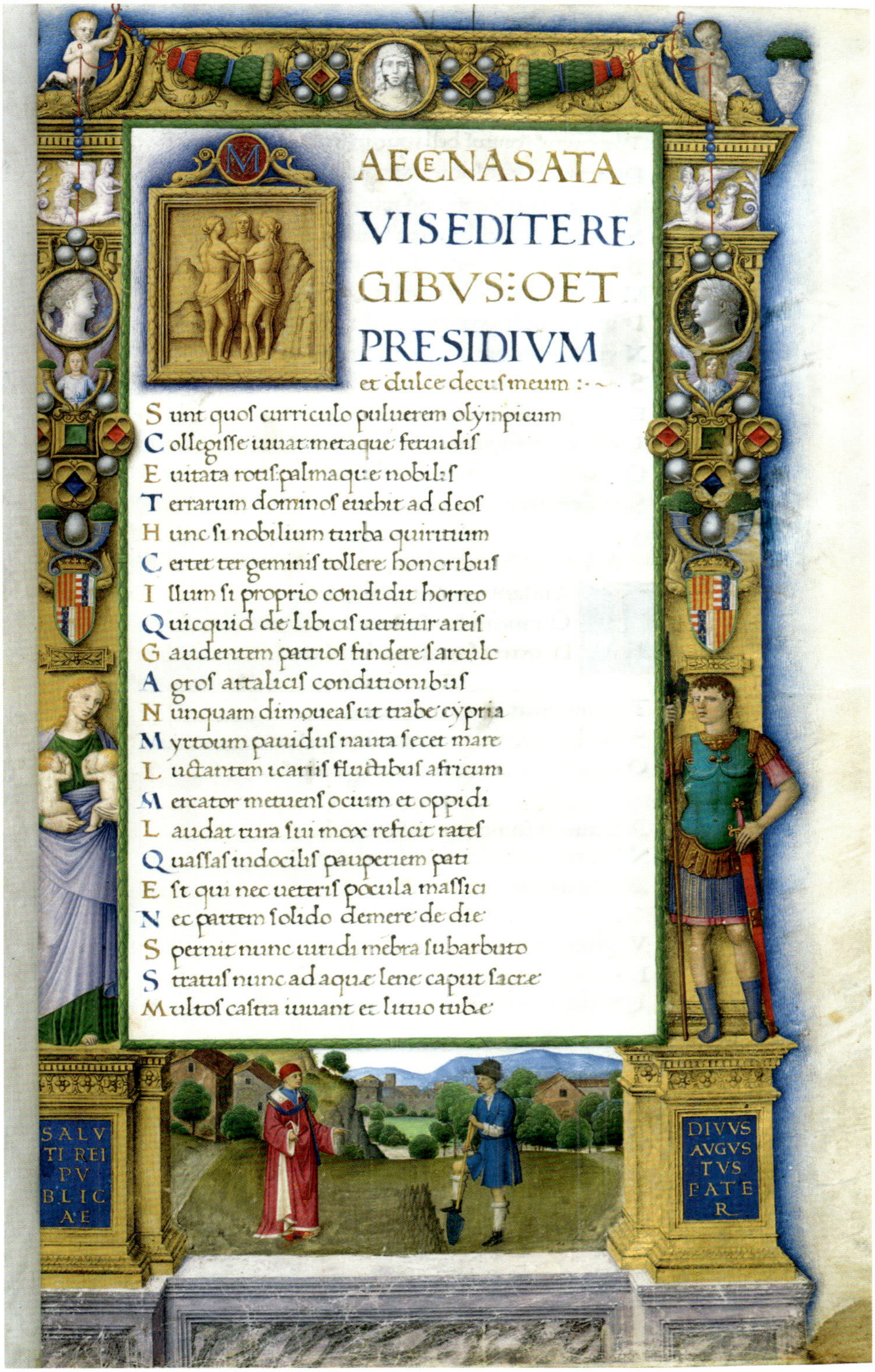
MAECENAS ATA
VIS EDITE RE
GIBVS: O ET
PRESIDIVM
et dulce decus meum :~
Sunt quos curriculo puluerem olympicum
Collegisse iuuat metaque feruidis
Euitata rotis palmaque nobilis
Terrarum dominos euehit ad deos
Hunc si nobilium turba quiritium
Certet tergeminis tollere honoribus
Illum si proprio condidit horreo
Quicquid de libicis uerritur areis
Gaudentem patrios findere sarculo
Agros attalicis conditionibus
Nunquam dimoueas ut trabe cypria
Myrtoum pauidus nauta secet mare
Luctantem icariis fluctibus africum
Mercator metuens ocium et oppidi
Laudat rura sui mox reficit rates
Quassas indocilis pauperiem pati
Est qui nec ueteris pocula massici
Nec partem solido demere de die
Spernit nunc uiridi mebra sub arbuto
Stratus nunc ad aquae lene caput sacrae
Multos castra iuuant et lituo tubae

Folio 2r

11

Eutropius, *Breviarium ab urbe condita*

Naples, last quarter of the 15th century

Manuscript on vellum, 10.9 × 6.3 cm; 73 leaves
French binding, brown calfskin, 11.5 × 7.1 × 1.3 cm

PROVENANCE Andrea Matteo Acquaviva of Aragon, Atri (Abruzzo); William Beckford collection, Fonthill/ Lansdown Tower, Bath (Ms. 692); from 1844 Hamilton Collection, Hamilton Palace (Ms. 241); acquired 1882 for the Kupferstichkabinett (78 B 23)

SELECT BIBLIOGRAPHY Hermann 1898, p. 150; Wescher 1931, p. 84; Boese 1966, p. 117; Concetta 1985, p. 172, note 60

The manuscript contains the *Breviarium ab urbe condita* (Short History of Rome from its Foundation), a work in ten books presenting a compendium of Roman history from the foundation of the city until the death of the Emperor Jovian in the year 364. Its author, Eutropius (d. after 387), held the office of *magister memoriae*, or 'secretary of state for general petitions', at the court of the Emperor Valens (364–78). It was the emperor himself who charged Eutropius with the task of writing a chronicle of the empire, in which the military exploits and vicissitudes of each imperial reign were to be related. In writing his text, Eutropius drew both on primary sources, including his own recollections, and such secondary sources as the *Histories* of Livy, for the chapters on the Roman Republic, and the *Lives* of Suetonius, for the reigns of Julius Caesar and Augustus, as well as other texts which are now lost. Eutropius's treatise is remarkable for the clarity and immediacy of its narration, qualities which made it well-known throughout the ancient world in a relatively short space of time; it was translated into Greek and even promoted as a 'school book' for teaching Latin. The fortunes of the *Breviarium* reached their height in the Middle Ages. In the eighth century, the work was taken up by the Lombard historian Paul the Deacon, who continued the historical narrative up to the reign of Justinian, renaming it *Historia Romana*, while in the eleventh century, another historian, Landolfus Sagax, added the events of the sixth to ninth centuries, completing the transformation of the original *Breviarium* into a new compendium entitled *Historia miscella*. Today we have numerous surviving manuscripts containing Eutropius's work. The Berlin manuscript is particularly important, having been made in the second half of the fifteenth century for the Calabrian prince Duke Andrea Matteo Acquaviva of Aragon (1458–1529). The Duke's name appears on the opening page of the codex, which shows a funerary monument bearing an inscription in Greek in honour of Matteo Acquaviva, composed by Angelo Durante da Messina. Significantly, the vellum is coloured purple and gold ink is used for the script, exactly replicating late antique and Carolingian codices. The choice of colours is deliberate, intended to testify to the nobility of the dedicatee. The Duke was not only a military leader, but also one of the most renowned humanists at the Aragonese court, a scholar of Greek and lover of ancient and mediaeval philosophy. He assembled a famous library in his castle in Atri and his love of books led him to found a printing press in Naples in 1525. The heraldic crest of the Acquaviva on the binding is mirrored in the *bas-de-page* on folio 1r, where two putti support the duke's coat of arms. In the centre of the folio, a portrait of Eutropius appears in the initial P, while a frieze of candelabra and plant motifs forms a border running round the page. The elegance of its overall appearance and the outstanding quality of its script make this little codex one of the most exquisite examples of fifteenth-century Neapolitan book illumination.

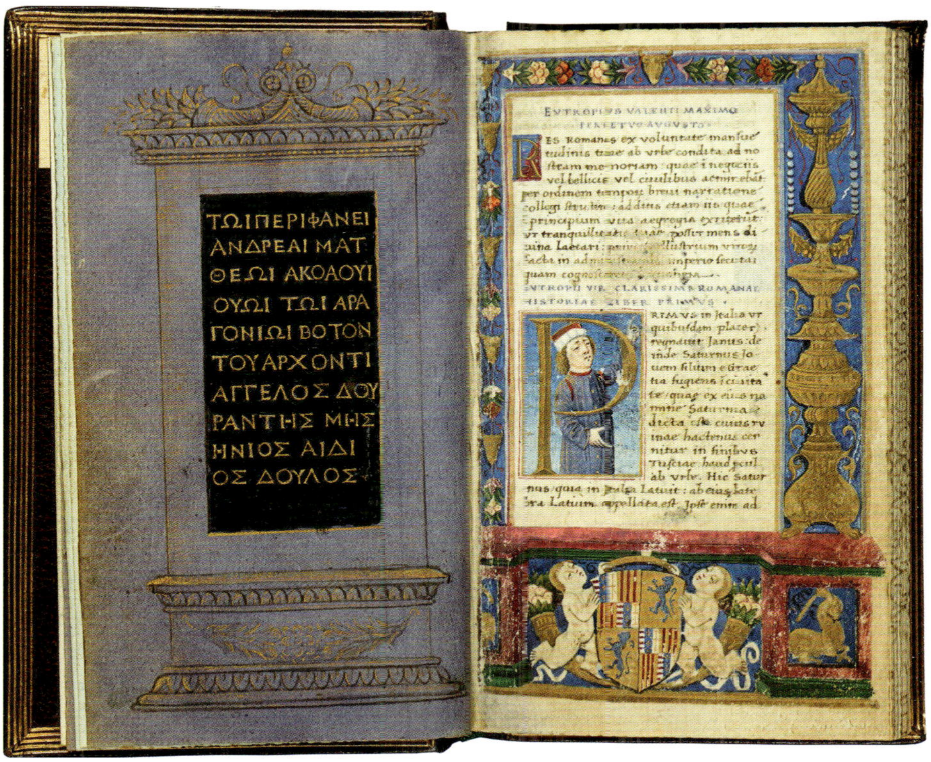

Flyleaf and folio 1r

12

Gaspare Ambrogio Visconti, *De Paulo e Daria amanti*

Milan, end 15th/beginning 16th century (after 1492), illuminated by Master B.F. (Francesco Binasco?)

Manuscript on vellum, 27.0 × 17.8 cm; 110 leaves
French binding, brown pigskin, 27.7 × 18.7 × 2.3 cm

PROVENANCE Duke Ludovico Sforza il Moro, Milan; Leonardo Murena; William Beckford collection, Fonthill/Lansdown Tower, Bath (Ms. 147); from 1844 Hamilton Collection, Hamilton Palace (Ms. 681); acquired 1882 for the Kupferstichkabinett (78 C 27)

SELECT BIBLIOGRAPHY Wescher 1931, p. 131–33; Milan 1958, no. 461, p. 146 (R. Cipriani); Berlin 1975, no. 140, pp. 201–02; Giordano 1991

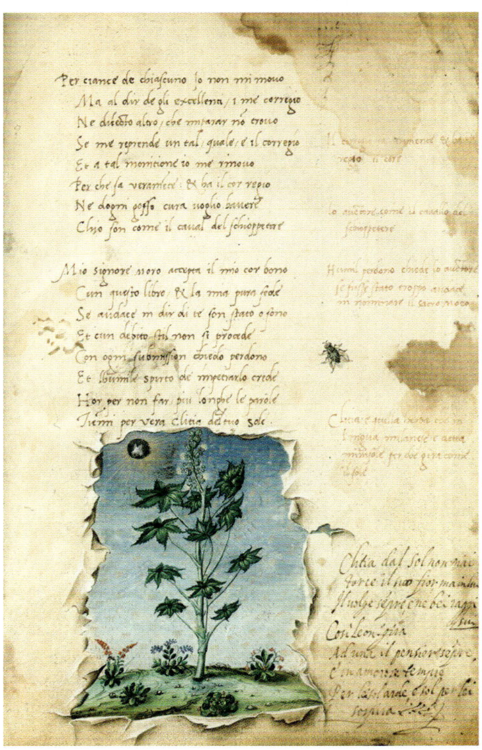

Folio 110r

This codex, containing the poem *De Paulo e Daria amanti* (On the Lovers, Paulo and Daria) by the Milanese humanist Gaspare Ambrogio Visconti (1461–1499), is in all probability the presentation copy made for the ruler of Milan, Ludovico Sforza, known as 'il Moro'. The opening lines address the prince as *Duca di Duci* (Duke of Dukes) of a *secul d'oro*, a golden age, while folio 69r bears the coat of arms of the Sforza family. The text tells the tragic tale of Paulo and Daria, lovers who die after many vicissitudes, their dream of love never having been fulfilled. The work, composed in the tradition of classical Greek and Latin tragedies on the theme of ill-fated love, is divided into eight books, each of which in turn contains eighty octaves. The lines of the text are written in elegant, humanistic cursive script, with a full-page miniature adorning the beginning of each book and an additional one at the end of the codex. The decoration is conceived according to a unified scheme: an architectural or landscape background in the trompe-l'œil manner frames the text, and into this small medallions are inserted, with vignettes showing episodes from each book. A very close relationship is thus created between text and image, as seen, for example, on folio 29r. This is the miniature which opens the third book of the poem. The frame consists of a ruinous wall, with vegetation growing out of holes, through which blue sky can be seen. At either side of the page are two medallions, apparently attached to the wall by nails or tree-branches, while a third medallion sits at the foot of the page. The medallion on the right shows Daria in her room, playing her viola; beside her is a peacock, sitting next to her sewing basket; the left-hand medallion shows the meeting of Paulo and Daria as children, under the eyes of Paulo's parents; in the medallion at the bottom we see Antonio Visconti secretly observing his son, who sits dejected and lost in thought after his separation from Daria. The artist depicts the surroundings and clothes of the figures in minute detail, but even more striking are the daring illusionistic devices, which he uses to great effect. The most striking appears in the miniature at the end of the poem, on folio 110r, where he paints a vellum which appears to be torn, with a fly sitting on it. Since the book mentions the restoration work on the Basilica of Sant'Ambrogio, which Ludovico il Moro commissioned from the architect Bramante in 1492, this provides a *terminus post quem* for the manuscript. The complex orchestration of the volume suggests the involvement of a scholarly overseer of the overall design, probably Gaspare Ambrogio Visconti himself, while there is almost universal agreement that the illuminations are by the Lombard master with the monogram B.F. (Francesco Binasco?). He was active at the court of Ludovico il Moro between approximately 1495 and 1545 and shows the influence of the painting of Leonardo da Vinci.

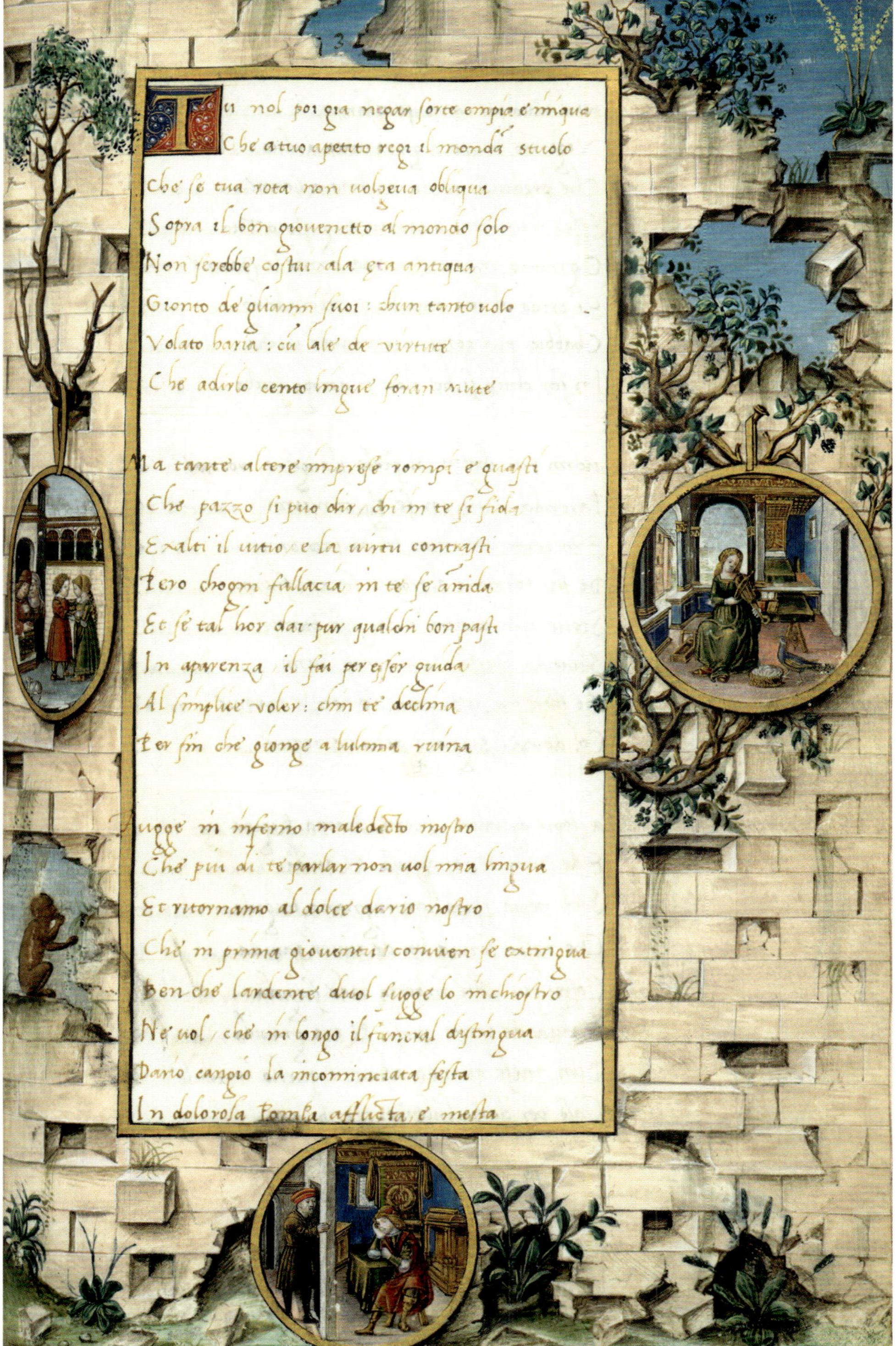
Tu nol poi gia negar sorte empia e' iniqua
Che a tuo apetito regi il mondo stuolo
Che' se tua rota non uolgeua obliqua
Sopra il bon giouenetto al mondo solo
Non serebbe' costui ala eta antiqua
Gionto de' gli anni suoi: ch'un tanto uolo
Volato haria: cu l'ale' de virtute
Che a dirlo cento lingue' foran mute'

Ma tante altere' imprese' rompi e' guasti
Che pazzo si puo dir, chi in te si fida
Exalti il uitio, e la uirtu contrasti
Pero ch'ogni fallacia in te se annida
Et se' tal hor dai pur qualch'i bon pasti
In aparenza il fai per esser guida
Al simplice' voler: ch'in te' declina
Per fin che' gionge a l'ultima ruina

Fugge' in inferno maledecto mostro
Che' piu di te' parlar non uol mia lingua
Et ritornamo al dolce' dario nostro
Che' in prima giouentu conuien se extingua
Ben che' l'ardente' duol fugge lo inchiostro
Ne' uol, che' in longo il funeral dystingua
Dario cangio la incomminciata festa
In dolorosa tomba afflicta, e' mesta

Folio 29r

13

Saint Jerome, *Epistolae*

Venice, last quarter 15th century, transcribed by Johannes Nydenna de Confluentia, illuminated by Giovanni Todeschino (?)

Manuscript on vellum, 29.7 × 19.5 cm; 344 leaves French binding, red morocco leather, 30.8 × 20.4 × 7.0 cm

PROVENANCE Mocenigo family, Venice (?); William Beckford collection, Fonthill/Lansdown Tower, Bath (Ms. 221); 1826 Harding & Co., London; comte Alexis de Golowkin (no. 39 in his catalogue of 1798); Hamilton Collection, Hamilton Palace (Ms. 297); acquired 1882 for the Kupferstichkabinett (78 D 13)

SELECT BIBLIOGRAPHY Wescher 1931, pp. 114–16; Boese 1966, pp. 148–50; Alexander 1969, pp. 17–20; Mariani Canova 1969, no. 74, p. 64; *Handbuch* 1994, no. 1.14, pp. 59–60 (Frauke Steenbock); London/New York 1994, no. 28, pp. 84–87 (Lilian Armstrong); D'Urso 2007, pp. 70, 317–18; Mariani Canova 2009, pp. 351–52

Not exhibited in London

This exceptional manuscript contains the letters of Saint Jerome (347–420 AD), one of the Fathers of the Church, who is best known for having translated the Bible into Latin. In terms of both literature and religion, his letters – also written in Latin – occupy a key place among Jerome's works, for in them he provides a personal account of his life as an ascetic and a Christian between East and West at the turn of the fifth century. Jerome himself is depicted in this full-page miniature at the beginning of the codex (folio 5r), dressed in a cardinal's red gown and accompanied by a lion, his iconographic attribute. The saint is seated on a *faldistorium*, a folding episcopal seat, and is in the act of greeting a group of people who stand before him, including two black-clad men and a dignitary of the Venetian Republic in a blue gown with a red hat and sash. The scene takes place in an arcade, with four putti playing among the columns. In the background, through an open door, the façade of a church can be glimpsed, and beyond it a landscape with a river. The illuminator demonstrates remarkable skill in his naturalistic handling of the scene. The play of light and shadow over the figures, the marble of the tondos in the spandrels and the glass in the small window above the door, typically Venetian in style, are all skilfully rendered. The artist also demonstrates his remarkable skills in the magnificent frieze which frames the page, into which he incorporates a series of gems and cameos *all'antica*. In the four corners are allegorical representations of the virtues (below left, Justice; below right, Fortitude; above right, Temperance; and at the upper left a figure with a cornucopia who may represent Prudence). At the bottom there is a punishment scene, in grisaille, framed by the winged bodies of two fantastical creatures. This may represent the story of Saint Jerome's dream, in which he was punished by angels, at the behest of a personification of Faith, seated on a globe, for devoting too much attention to classical authors. Standing out in golden capital letters against the arch above are the first words of Letter 52, addressed by Jerome to Nepotian, in which he explains the duties of the priesthood. The whole scene has recently been interpreted as portraying Saint Jerome instructing Nepotian (Mariani Canova 2009, pp. 351–52). Nonetheless, the two figures in dark, hooded tunics are reminiscent of the members of the Scuola or Fraternity of Saint Jerome who appear in the painting of the funeral of the saint by Lazzaro Bastiani (Venice, Gallerie dell'Accademia). The painting was specially commissioned for the building of the Scuola. It is probable, therefore, that there was some connection with this same fraternity and that the codex may originally have been intended for it. A further element worthy of notice is the coat of arms of the Venetian Mocenigo family, which can be seen on either side of the decorative border. Pietro Mocenigo was Doge of Venice from 1474 to 1476, but there is nothing to confirm that this work was commissioned by a doge. From its style, however, the miniature must have originated in the

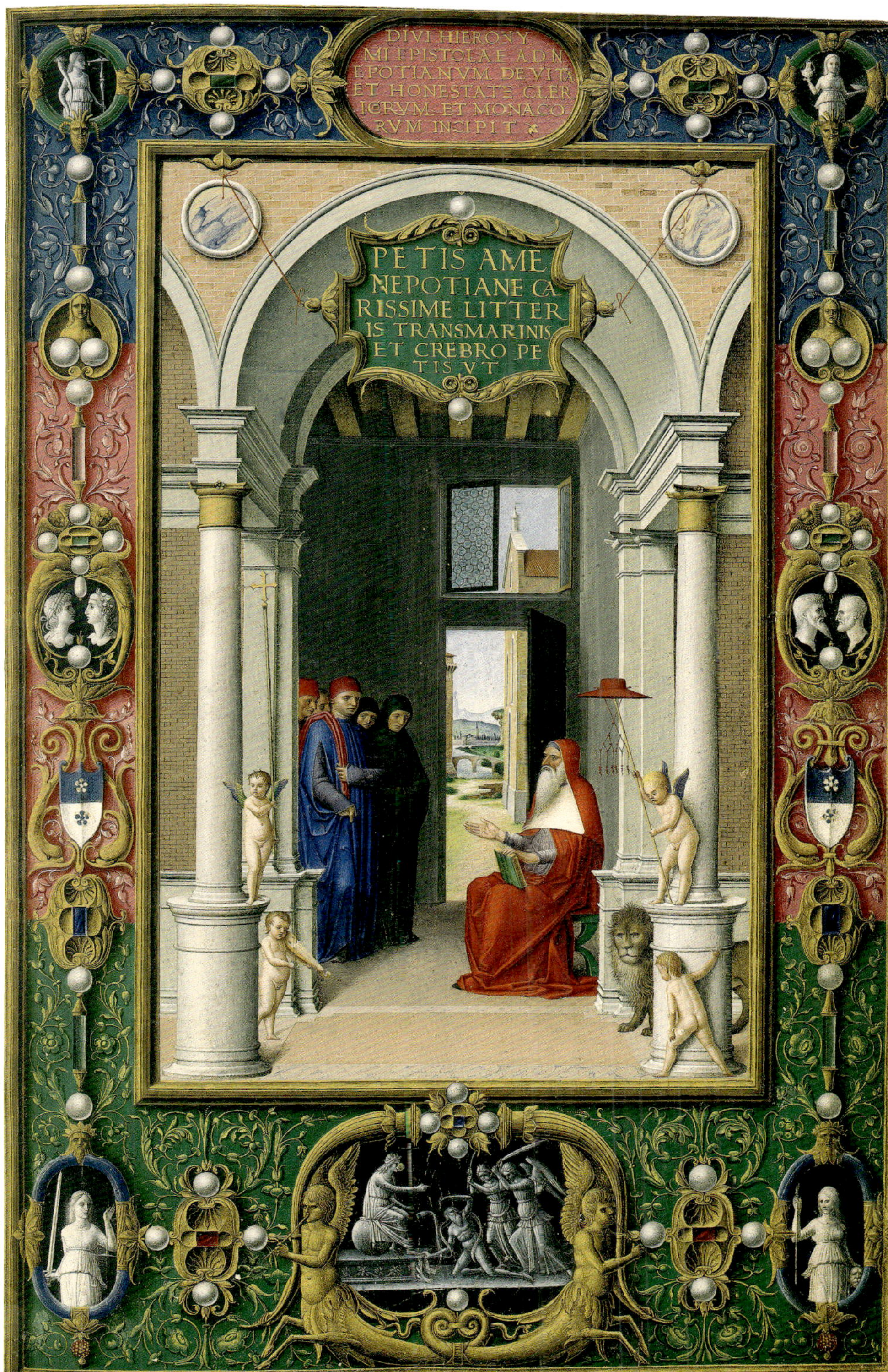
DIVI HIERONY
MI EPISTOLAE AD N
EPOTIANVM DE VITA
ET HONESTATE CLER
ICORVM ET MONACO
RVM INCIPIT
PETIS AME
NEPOTIANE CA
RISSIME LITTER
IS TRANSMARINIS
ET CREBRO PE
TIS VT

Folio 5r

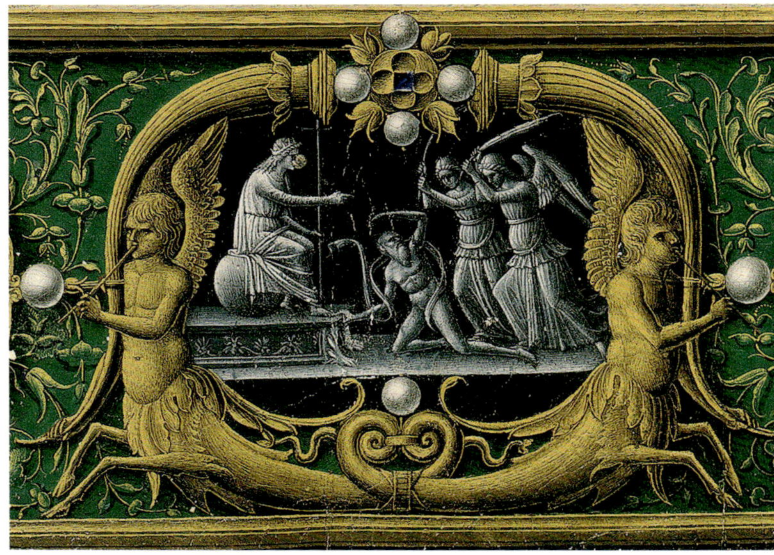

Detail of folio 5r

Veneto. Evidence for this lies in the classicising elements derived from Andrea Mantegna, the naturalistic handling reminiscent of the painter Antonello da Messina, active in Venice in the last quarter of the fifteenth century, and the evident familiarity of the artist with manuscripts of the Veneto-Paduan school, notably those painted *all'antica* in the second half of the fifteenth century by the Master of the London Pliny. It has been suggested that this anonymous master should be identified with Giovanni Todeschino (see cat. no. 10), to whom indeed the illuminations of these *Epistolae* have been attributed. The scribe of the present codex, Johannes Nydenna de Confluentia (Coblenz?), is also documented in Padua in the 1470s. It is a product of the last flowering of Venetian manuscript illumination.

14

Missale Romanorum

Rome, 16th century (1520–21), transcribed by Ludovico Arrighi da Vicenza, illuminated by Matteo da Milano

Manuscript on vellum, 38.0 × 27.0 cm; 411 leaves French binding, red morocco leather, 40.2 × 29.0 × 12.7 cm

PROVENANCE Cardinal Giulio de' Medici , Rome; before 1819 Hamilton Collection, Hamilton Palace (Ms. 443); acquired 1882 for the Kupferstichkabinett (78 D 17)

SELECT BIBLIOGRAPHY Wescher 1931, pp. 104–07; Boese 1966, pp. 213–14; Reiss 1991; Alexander 1992, pp. 34–38; Hermann 1994, pp. 166–71, 178–80 and *passim*; *Handbuch* 1994, no. 1.15, p. 60 (Frauke Steenbock); London/New York 1994, no. 128, pp. 239–42 (Jonathan J. G. Alexander)

This precious manuscript belongs to the category of liturgical books knows as missals; it contains all the texts required for the celebration of the Mass (prayers, readings and Psalms), as laid down in the liturgical calendar. According to an inscription on folio 404v, the missal was transcribed in the year 1520 by the copyist Ludovicus Vicentinus – who can be identified with the famous Ludovico Arrighi da Vicenza – at the behest of the Florentine cardinal Giulio de' Medici, the future Pope Clement VII (1523–34). Giulio's coat of arms often appears in the magnificent full-page miniatures. On folio 182v, for example, where Christ's crucifixion is depicted, the Medici coat of arms can be seen in the *bas-de-page*, surmounted by a cardinal's hat. In the upper border, the emblem of Lorenzo the Magnificent, the grandfather of Giulio, is shown – three coloured feathers encircled by a diamond ring, with a *cartello* bearing the motto *semper* (always). This *impresa* was later re-used by Giulio de' Medici, who introduced the new *cartello* with the words *card[inalis] iul[i]us Medices* which can be seen in the left-hand border of the page. The ornamental frieze is supremely elegant. The lower border shows the Instruments of the Passion, including the column where Christ was whipped, the ladder used for the Deposition and the lance which pierced Christ's side, together with his cloak and the dice used by the soldiers to cast lots for them. Above the head of the crucified Christ appears the image of a pelican, tearing open its own breast in order to feed its children, a symbol of God's sacrifice for the sake of mankind. Skilfully mingled amongst these learned iconographical references are brightly coloured birds, refined flowers in delicate colours and cameos in jewelled settings, all reflections of both the nobility and the reputation of the client, Cardinal Giulio, a patron and bibliophile of the

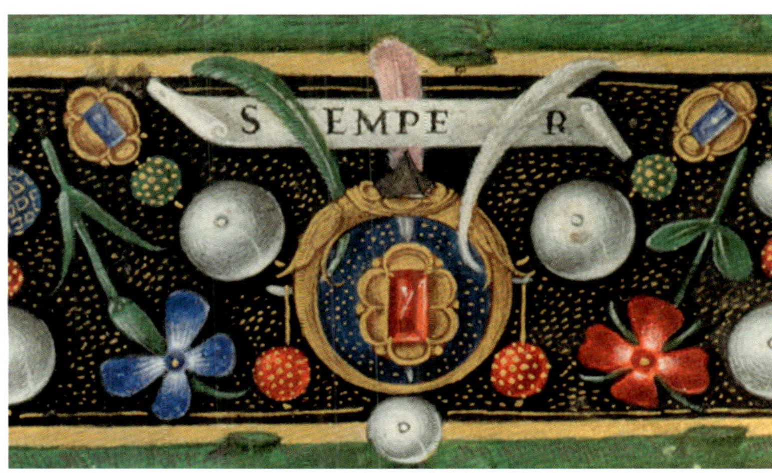

Detail of folio 182v

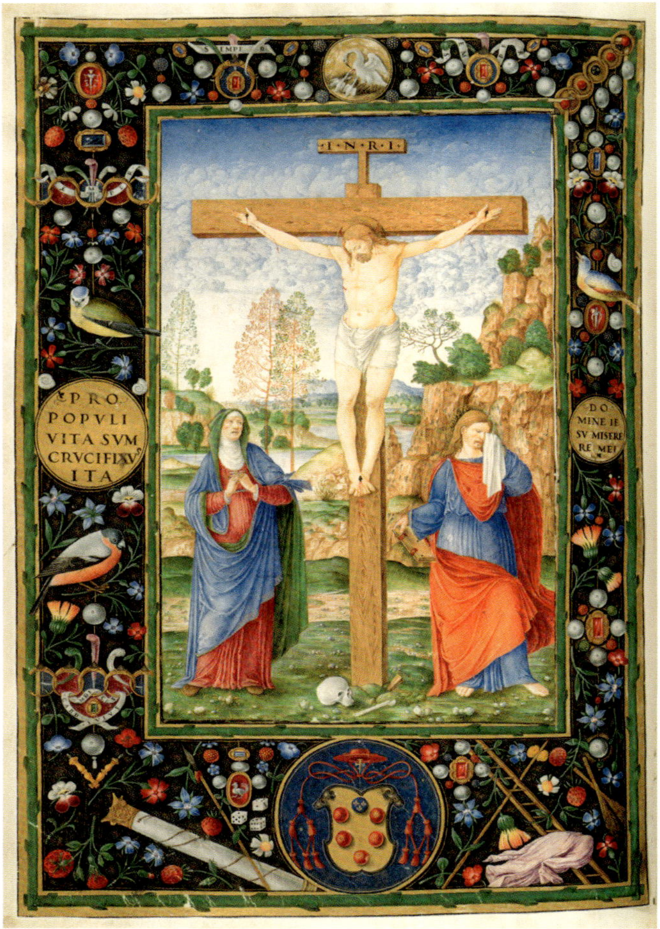

Folio 182v

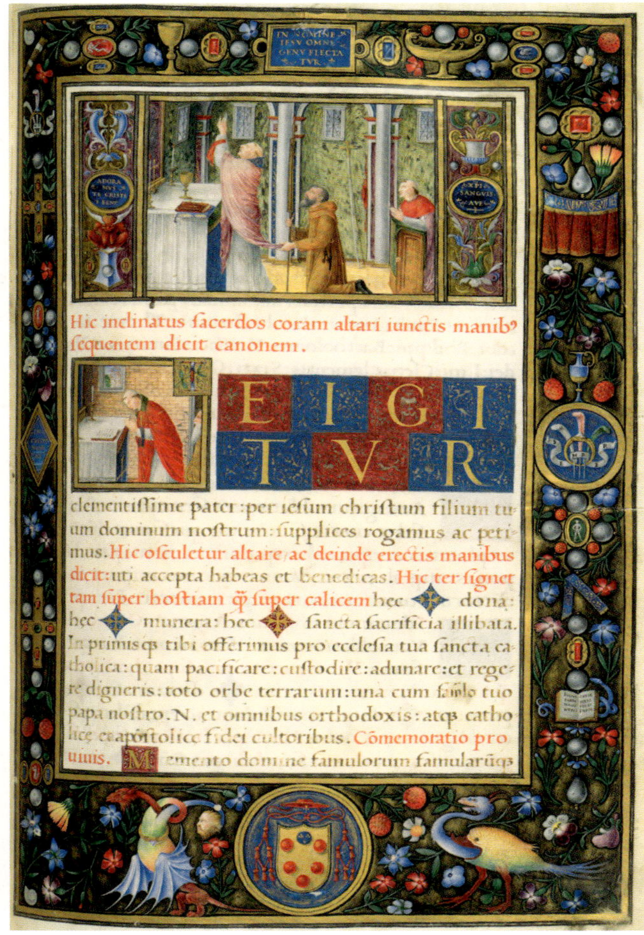

Folio 183r

first rank. The Cardinal's name is also highlighted on folio 183r in the inscription *Julius Cardinalis Medices me fieri fecit in urbe* (Cardinal Giulio Medici had me made in Rome) in an open book in the side margin. On this page, the Cardinal has himself depicted by the illuminator: Giulio kneels in a small chapel in which the Mass is being celebrated, while the upper part of the picture shows the Elevation of the Host. In this miniature, too, the use of colour is crucial: brilliant hues are juxtaposed by very delicate application of the brush. Matteo da Milano has been identified as the artist of this magnificent volume. The Lombard artist was a consummate master of illumination at the turn of the sixteenth century, serving as court illuminator to the greatest princes of Italy: he was active in Milan for Ludovico Sforza, in Ferrara for the Este – where he made the famous *breviarium* for Ercole I d'Este (Modena, Biblioteca

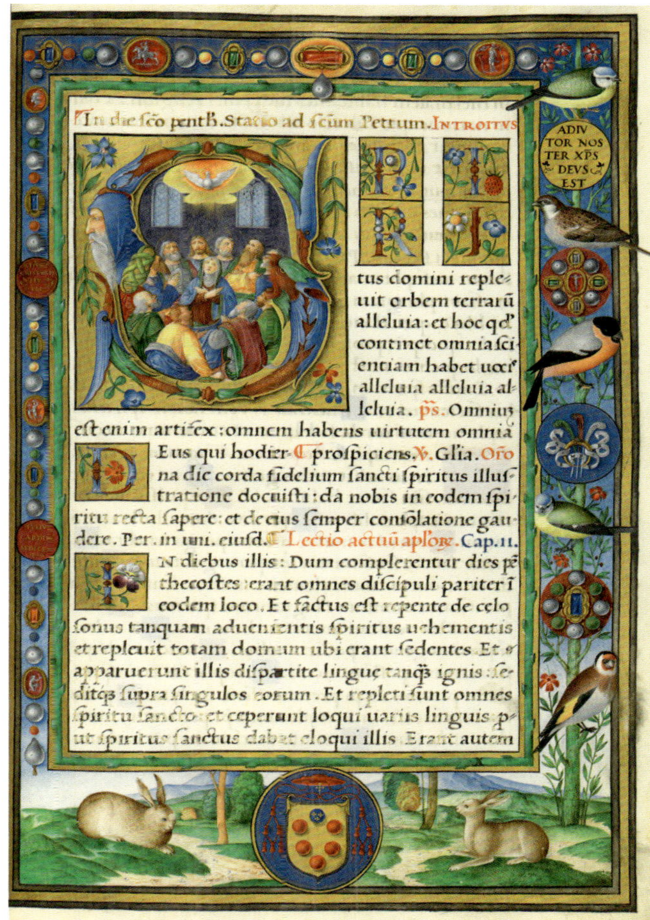

In die ſc̄o penth. Statio ad ſc̄um Petrum. INTROITVS
SPIRI
tus domini reple-
uit orbem terrarū
alleluia: et hoc qd'
continet omnia ſci-
entiam habet uocꝭ
alleluia alleluia al-
leluia. ps. Omniū
eſt enim artifex: omnem habens uirtutem omnia
DEus qui hodierꝛ prospiciens. ℣. Glia. Oro
na dic corda fidelium ſancti ſpiritus illuſ-
tratione docuiſti: da nobis in eodem ſpi-
ritu recta ſapere: et de eius ſemper conſolatione gau-
dere. Per. in uni. eiuſd. Lectio actuū aplorꝝ. Cap. II.
IN diebus illis: Dum complerentur dies pē
thecoſtes: erant omnes diſcipuli pariter ī
eodem loco. Et factus eſt repente de celo
ſonus tanquam aduenientis ſpiritus uehementis
et repleuit totam domum ubi erant ſedentes. Et
apparuerunt illis diſpartite lingue tanq̄ ignis: ſe-
ditq; ſupra ſingulos eorum. Et repleti ſunt omnes
ſpiritu ſancto: et ceperunt loqui uariis linguis: p-
ut ſpiritus ſanctus dabat eloqui illis. Erant autem

Folio 209r

Estense universitaria, D.V.G.11 = Lat. 424) – and finally in Rome, where he worked under Popes Leo X and Clement VII. He combines the motifs of pearls, grotesques and cameos typical of the tradition of the Veneto with a delight in an extremely naturalistic representation of plants and animals, inspired by Flemish models (folio 209r). The very human and expressive representation of figures and the precise and clear landscapes betray the influence of two of the most important artists of the period, Leonardo da Vinci and Albrecht Dürer. The sumptuousness of this manuscript made it an object of desire for collectors of book illuminations, who, probably at the beginning of the nineteenth century, cut out several pieces. Twenty of these fragments are now also to be found in the Kupferstichkabinett (Min. 2001–12; Min. 4627–34).

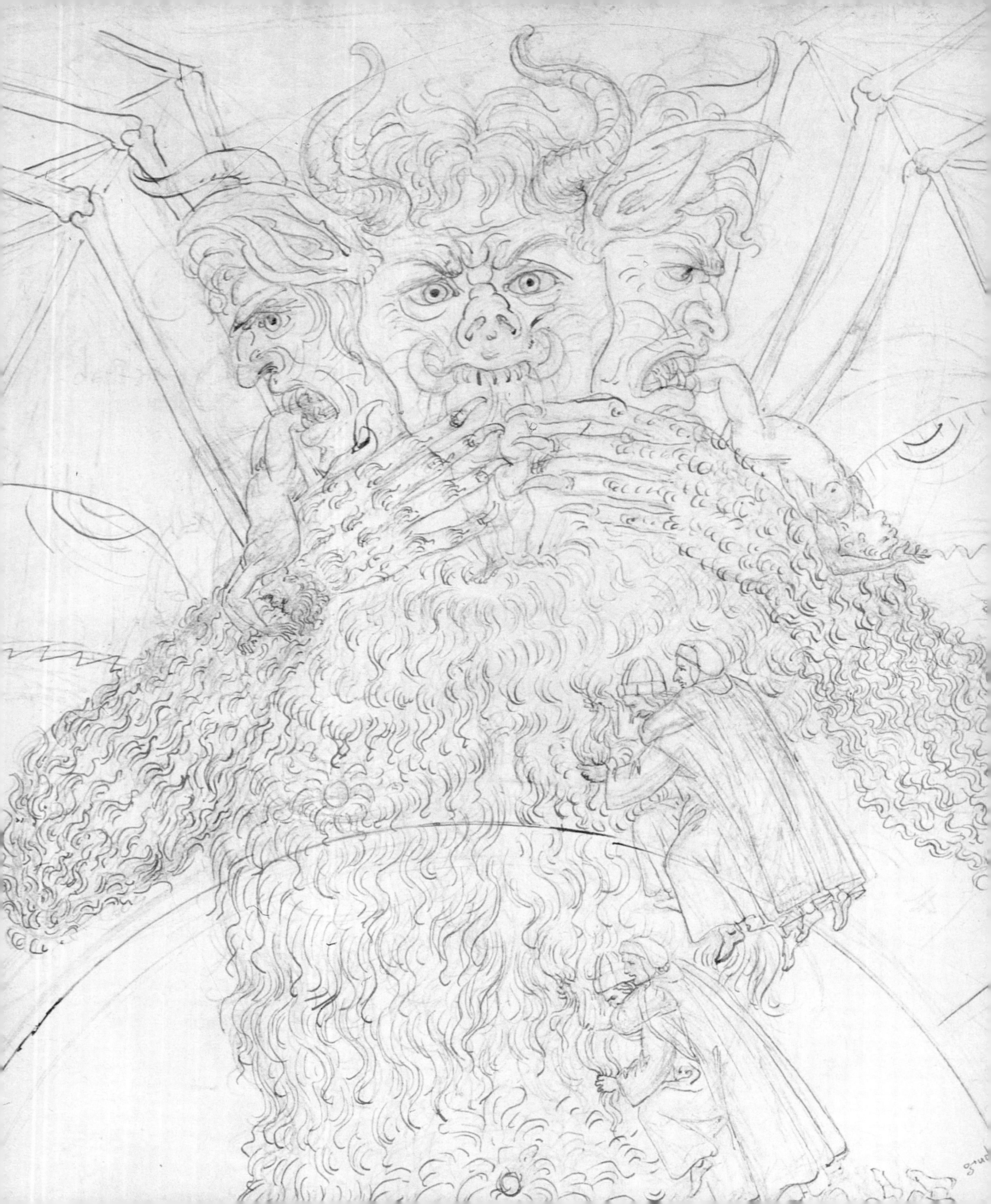

The Jewel of the Hamilton Collection: Sandro Botticelli's Drawings for Dante's Divine Comedy

"Of all the manuscripts which have ever occurred for sale this may without exaggeration be described as the most important, from an artistic point of view ... these marvellous works, which, for power of drawing, fertility of design and tenderness of feeling are unapproached and unapproachable."[1] This is how the catalogue written for the auction of the Hamilton Collection in 1882 describes under lot 201, the volume containing Botticelli's drawings for Dante's *Divine Comedy*. Since these masterpieces first became known thanks to the spectacular purchase of the Hamilton manuscripts by Berlin – a coup for which they were undoubtedly the major motivation – their reputation has remained undimmed. There is universal agreement that, in this truly monumental cycle of illustrations, Dante and Botticelli are ideally matched.

The *Commedia divina* or *Divine Comedy* by Dante Alighieri, written between around 1307 and the poet's death in 1321, is considered one of the most important and complex works of world literature. In one hundred cantos, it describes Dante's journey through the three realms of the afterlife, *Inferno* (Hell), *Purgatorio* (Purgatory) and *Paradiso* (Paradise). On his path of redemption, from sin and damnation through repentance and forgiveness to salvation, Dante is guided at first by Virgil, the poet of classical antiquity, a figure who personifies human reason. Finally, from Earthly Paradise onwards, beyond which human reason no longer serves, his guide is his youthful love, Beatrice. Here Beatrice is the celestially beautiful personification of Theology, whom Dante first glimpses at the end of *Purgatorio* and who now leads him through Paradise to God, the source of all things. In the *Commedia*, Dante develops an all-encompassing vision of the universe; the poem "was seen as a standard work of philosophy and summation of theology in one, surveying the whole of ancient mythology and drawing together everything which was known about the world at that time".[2]

The *Commedia* was always prized as a literary masterpiece, as is testified by over eight hundred early manuscripts of the work. None are fully illustrated; indeed only a few have any illustrations at all.[3] In the second half of the fifteenth century, however, a century and a half after it was written, the *Commedia* experienced a veritable renaissance in Dante's home town of Florence. The humanist-Neoplatonist commentary by Cristoforo Landino, which appeared in the first printed Florentine edition of the *Commedia* in 1481, exemplifies this phenomenon. In a fervent preface, presenting the poet as a fellow citizen of Florence, Landino declares that the great work must be freed from the barbarism of many foreign expressions introduced by non-Florentine commentators, so that Dante may be returned to his original, noble "*fiorentinità*" and thus, as it were, brought home from exile. (The historical Dante had died in exile.) This was the cultural context in which Sandro Botticelli, perhaps the most important Florentine artist of the day, undertook the task of providing the *Commedia* with a full set of illustrations. The result was a cycle of drawings, most of them executed in pen and brown ink over colourless tracing and metalpoint (lead and tin alloy) underdrawings on the softer, flesh side of what were originally one hundred and two sheets of vellum. Today, the Berlin Kupferstichkabinett holds the 85 sheets from codex 201 of the Hamilton Collection (seven further sheets are in the Biblioteca Apostolica Vaticana in Rome, while the remaining ten are presumed lost).[4] On the reverse, somewhat rougher, hair side of each vellum sheet, in landscape orientation, is the text of the previous canto, transcribed in four columns in a script known as *littera humanistica* by Niccolò Mangona (fig. 19).[5] Botticelli probably began work on the drawings after 1481/82, on his return from completing the frescoes of the Sistine Chapel in the Vatican in Rome. The engravings for the first nineteen cantos of the *Inferno* in the Landino Florentine edition, possibly executed by Baccio Baldini after Botticelli's designs, date from between 1481 and 1487 (see cat. no. 48). Some of the drawings are probably contemporary with these engravings, but Botticelli's work on his *Commedia* cycle

FACING Detail of cat. no. 25

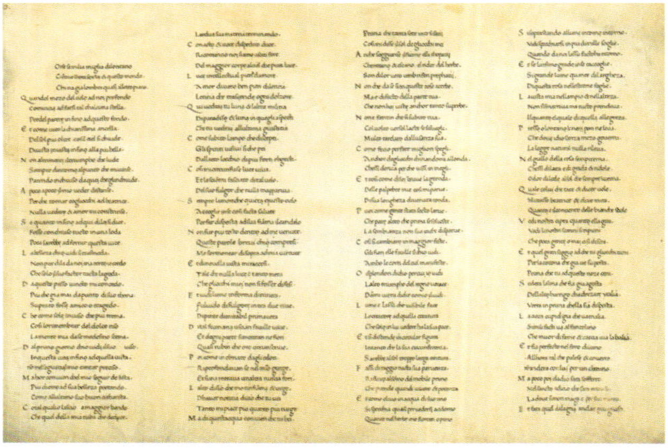

FIG. 19
Copyist Niccolò Mangona, text by Dante Alighieri, *Commedia*, *Paradiso* XXX (vellum sheet without drawing on the front), c. 1490–1500, Berlin, Kupferstichkabinett, Staatliche Museen zu Berlin, Botticelli *Paradiso* XXXI

lasted much longer, extending over some two decades. Any exact dating of individual sheets is difficult; although at first the artist probably worked through the drawings roughly in order, he obviously returned again and again to earlier pages, finishing, altering and adding details. However deep Botticelli's personal involvement may have been, there must have been a formal contract for a work such as this. Without doubt, it would have been made for an educated patron, and this was probably Lorenzo di Pierfrancesco de' Medici; the most concrete piece of evidence we have, associated with the drawings, is a report by the so-called Anonimo Magliabechiano,[6] stating that Botticelli "painted and devised a Dante on vellum for Lorenzo di Pierfranceso de' Medici, which was a wonderful thing".[7] A "wonderful thing" these drawings certainly are, yet their very uniqueness poses many unanswered questions, which it is not the intention of the exhibition, or of this catalogue, to explore in greater depth, or attempt to answer. The two most recent and comprehensive publications by the Kupferstichkabinett, Hein-Th. Schulze Altcappenberg's exhibition catalogue from the year 2000 and Peter Dreyer's commentary on the facsimile of 1989, were both based on rigorous research of the drawings and the codex and remain the most up-to-date reference works, even if there have since been one or two new findings and new focuses of research.[8]

In the Hamilton Collection sale catalogue and in all previous references to it, the volume containing the drawings was termed a 'manuscript', since at the time the drawings were bound into a late eighteenth-century binding (see cat. no. 47).[9] Accordingly, it was assigned to the library within the Duke of Hamilton's extensive art collection. Shortly after the drawings arrived at the museum, they were removed from their binding and mounted. This was a form of storage more in keeping with their presence in a public collection, since it was easier to exhibit the individual works and thus satisfy the public's desire to see them.[10] Botticelli himself probably never envisaged such publicity for the drawings; their delicacy requires concentrated viewing from close up. Today we should assume that they were not originally loose and certainly not framed, but bound into a codex in a manner probably somewhat similar to that proposed by Peter Dreyer in his reconstruction for the facsimile edition. His suggestion still seems the most convincing today, especially since the best way to keep a portfolio of this sort is indeed in book form. It is likely, then, that the artist did in fact envisage the drawings, not as preparatory works for a cycle of frescoes[11] or even as *tabulae*, that is, loose sheets for display, but as a series of illustrations intended to accompany the text.[12] However, this should not lead us to lose sight of the fact that Botticelli's work on the individual sheets must be understood within the tradition of drawing, with all the technical and conceptual aspects of that particular creative process. In other words, the drawings cannot necessarily be compared in every respect with manuscript illuminations, even though Botticelli's handling of the *Commedia* shows a level of engagement with the written text that was certainly a "real process of assimilation – in the sense of *imitatio* and *aemulatio*".[13] It is clear that the drawings are based on an intense, personal engagement on the part of the artist with the work of the poet, something which would definitely have been encouraged both by the patron himself, Lorenzo di Pierfrancesco de' Medici, and by the humanism of his circle. As a result, Botticelli, with his stylus or pen, is able to seek and find a language, a "*visibile parlare*",[14] which approaches the universality of Dante's perspective. Text and illustration are not combined on one page; each, equally important, occupies a page to itself. The text of a whole canto is accompanied by a single illustration, so that each of the one hundred cantos should have its own drawing. In the arrangement suggested in Dreyer's facsimile opening on the

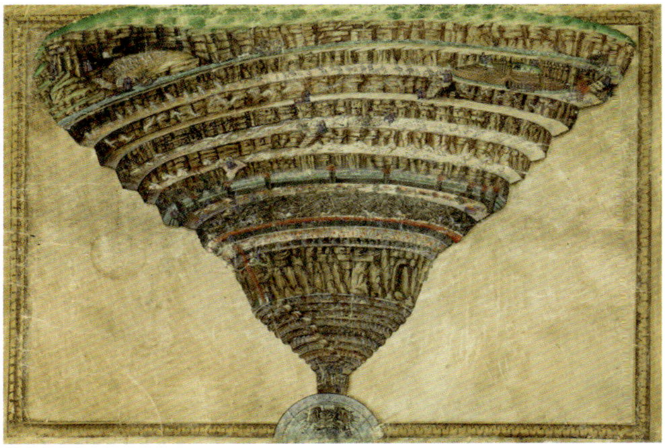

FIG. 20
Sandro Botticelli, *The Chart of Hell*, c. 1481–90, opaque watercolour over pen in brown ink, on vellum
Rome, Biblioteca Apostolica Vaticana, Codex Reg. Lat. 1896, fol. 101r

long side, as one looked at the volume, the text, inscribed on the verso of the next drawing, would be seen below the picture (see fig. 5, p. 29). There is much to be said for the theory that, as a rule, the drawing was set down first on the vellum, with the text added subsequently. One piece of evidence to support this is the leaf with the discarded sketch for the 31st canto of *Paradiso*, which was later re-used for the double folio at the end of the *Inferno*; it would have been impossible to reposition the leaf if it had already been inscribed with the text (see cat. no. 25). The drawings for each canto, unlike earlier illustrations of the *Commedia* by other artists, are not usually restricted to the representation of one or two individual episodes, but attempt to convey visually the content of the entire canto, giving a comprehensive account of all the events in their every detail. The eye of the viewer is thus led through a number of scenes illustrated simultaneously, in which the main figures, each appearing several times on one sheet, carry the viewer along with them from stage to stage. Elements from other cantos are also included to make it easier for us to get our bearings. Botticelli, a master of the fluid line, thus makes both the outer and the inner progress of the travellers through the afterlife comprehensible in every detail while keeping very close to the text of the *Commedia*.

Although the few hand-coloured sheets in the Dante cycle are more widely known than the others, thanks to their better reproducibility and greater 'wall power' (in particular the Vatican sheet depicting *The Chart of Hell*, which plays a major role in Dan Brown's bestseller *Inferno*),[15] the majority of the drawings remained uncoloured. It is impossible, in the end, to know for certain whether the colouring, mostly only partial, which has been added to four of the sheets (*The Chart of Hell*, *Inferno* X, XV, XVIII), was actually done by Botticelli, even in the case of the beautifully executed Berlin sheet (*Inferno* XVIII, cat. no. 17).[16] A plan to colour all the drawings must have existed at one stage, even if only temporarily, before being subsequently abandoned. The addition of colour would have hidden some noticeable erasures and *pentimenti* (evidence of revisions which give us an insight today into the creative process and the artist's struggle to translate word into image) – notably *Paradiso* V, cat. no. 40. Certain colourful descriptions in the *Commedia* could also have been even more faithfully reproduced (see *Purgatorio* VII, cat. no. 29). However, colour would no doubt also have concealed many of the details, including the tiny signature *sandro di mari ano* on a little panel held by an angel (*Paradiso* XXVIII, fig. 21). The fact that on some leaves inks of slightly different colours were used for drawing (ranging from light reddish-brown to dark brown)[17] is probably due, in most cases, to the drawing process being interrupted and resumed later; only in a few exceptional cases can it have been the expression of a conscious choice or motivated by the content of the text. Ultimately we can never know whether the death of Lorenzo di Pierfrancesco de' Medici in 1503 may have been a reason for the lack of colour on almost all the leaves. The third last and the (now missing) final leaves of *Paradiso* were left empty and in many places the metalpoint underdrawing was not 'fixed' with pen and ink, so, even as a cycle of drawings, the work must be seen as unfinished. There must have been broader and, probably, more pragmatic reasons for this than that the final cantos of *Paradiso* were beyond Botticelli's powers to draw, even if it is perhaps impossible to render the ineffable and the unfathomable in images.

The drawings selected for the exhibition comprise about one third of the sheets held in Berlin. They are intended to present the viewer with a representative group, in which the individual drawings give, on the one hand, a general idea of the journey through the afterlife related in the *Commedia*, and, on the other hand, demonstrate the unique nature and distinctive features of these works by Botticelli. The

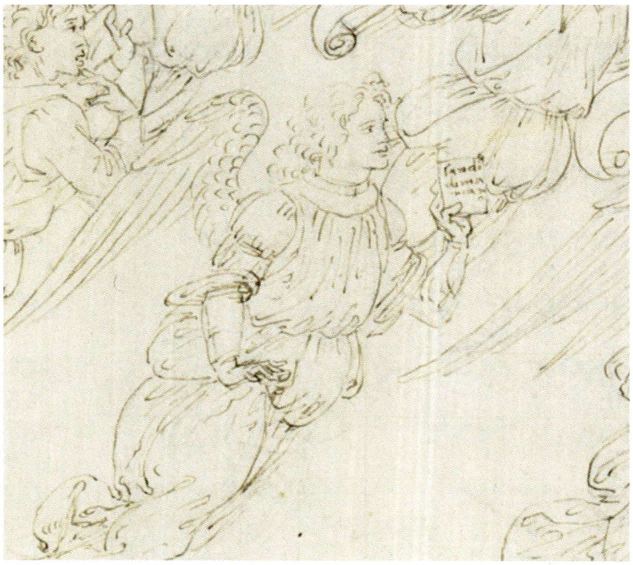

FIG. 21
Sandro Botticelli, angel bearing a plaque with Botticelli's name in the ninth sphere of Paradise, c. 1481–95, pen in brown ink over metalpoint on vellum, 32.5 × 47.0 cm (Berlin, Kupferstichkabinett, Staatliche Museen Berlin, Botticelli *Paradiso* XXVIII, detail)

selection is large enough to give an impression of their enormous variety and monumentality and to show why it is that in Botticelli's drawings for Dante's *Divine Comedy* we have a cultural treasure comparable with that other great highlight of the Staatliche Museen zu Berlin, the Pergamon Altar. As Peter-Klaus Schuster, former director-general of the Staatliche Museen zu Berlin, once put it, the drawings are a "Pergamon Altar on parchment".

Notes

1 Sale catalogue 1882, p. 31, lot 201: "Manuscript on Vellum by a Tuscan Scribe, written in the XVth century ... superbly ornamented with 88 exquisitely beautiful Designs by Sandro Botticelli, all except six the full size of the page (including a splendid Drawing of the Mouth of Hell in colours, and full-length portraits of Dante), half red morocco".

2 Dombrowski 1996, p. 47: "*... galt als philosophisches Standardwerk und theologische Summe in einem, überblickt die gesamte antike Mythologie, faßt das gesammelte Weltwissen ihrer Zeit zusammen*".

3 On the number of fourteenth- and fifteenth-century manuscripts of the *Commedia*, see www.danteonline.it – *Indice dei manoscritti* (accessed 24 July 2015).

4 The following drawings are presumed lost: *Inferno* II–VII, *Inferno* XI, *Inferno* XIV. In Berlin, at a time unknown, the empty leaf intended for the drawing for *Paradiso* XXXIII and the leaf containing *Paradiso* XXXIII disappeared. The disappearance may have been due to a lack of appreciation of the leaves without drawings; thanks to becoming part of a museum collection the works were valued for the first time as a cycle of illustrations, but the text was obviously seen as being of only secondary importance.

5 On the attribution to this copyist, see Dreyer 1986, pp. 39–40. Manuscripts associated with his name date roughly between 1482 and 1503.

6 See Stapleford 1995, p. 397.

7 Florence, Biblioteca Nazionale di Firenze, Cod. Magliabechiano, XVII, 17, fol. 84; as quoted in Stapleford 1995, p. 408.

8 Berlin/Rome/London 2000–01; Dreyer 1986. The following more recent literature can also be mentioned: Kilian 2014; Korbacher 2014; Meier 2013; Klettke 2010; Papillo 2007 a and b; Rehm 2007; Rubin 2007, pp. 339–40; Küpper 2006.

9 Clarke 1819; Waagen 1854 a, vol. 3, p. 307. In 1975 some individual sheets were shown in the exhibition *Zimelien. Abendländische Handschriften des Mittelalters*, where this context was at least notionally re-created (Berlin 1975, no. 137, pp. 199–200).

10 It is no longer museum practice to remove drawings from the context of an existing album. Today a solution is sought which will allow the works to be displayed individually, while at the same time allowing for better storage and also preserving the overall context of the volume. On this subject, see the diploma thesis entitled 'Der "Kleiner Klebeband" der Fürsten zu Waldburg-Wolfegg. Konzept zur Erhaltung von Altmeisterzeichnungen in einem Album' (2013), written by Svenja Heidenreich in collaboration with the Kupferstichkabinett as part of her diploma in the conservation and restoration of archive and library material and works of art on paper at the Staatliche Akademie der Bildenden Künste in Stuttgart.

11 Parronchi 1990, pp. 77–80.

12 See Schulze Altcappenberg 2000, pp. 28–31.

13 Meier 2013, p. 7.

14 Dante Alighieri, *Commedia*, *Purgatorio* X, v. 95.

15 This appeared 2013; in it, the author describes the drawing as a painting and does not mention that it is part of an extensive cycle. On this subject, see also Andreas Platthaus: '*Lasst allen Dante fahren*', *Frankfurter Allgemeine Zeitung*, http://www.faz.net/-gro-7946e (accessed 24 July 2015).

16 See Oltrogge/Fuchs/Hahn 2000, p. 388. An example of a similar case would be the *Triumph of Love*, an illustration for Petrarch's *Trionfi* in a vellum manuscript in the Biblioteca Classense in Rimini (Ms. 143), which is likewise not fully coloured. There is, however, some uncertainty about the attribution of this work to Botticelli. (see Berlin/Rome/London 2000–01, Appendix, no. 13, p. 361, Julia Schewski).

17 On the inks, see Oltrogge/Fuchs/Hahn 2000, p. 336.

FACING Detail of cat. no. 23

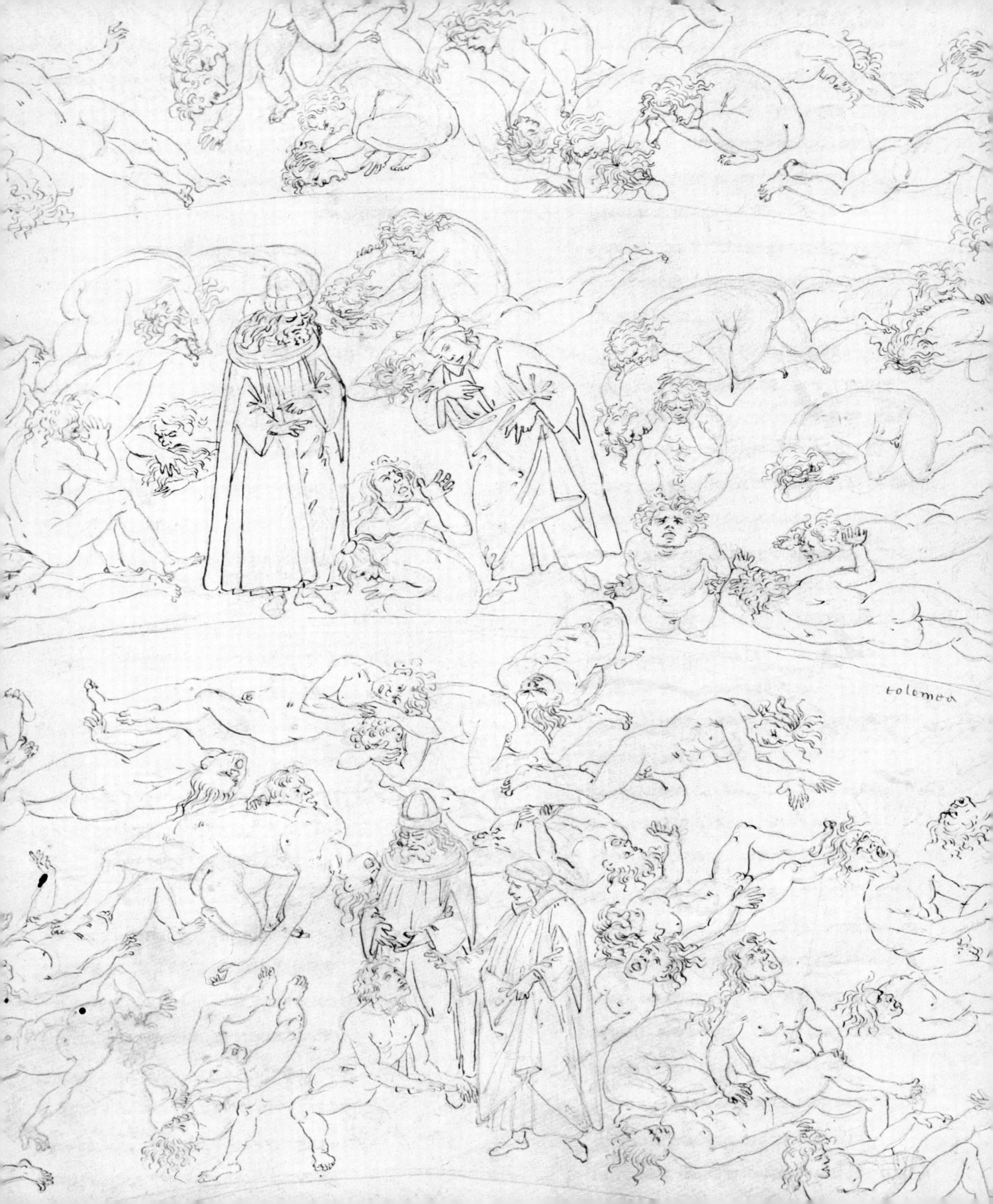
tolomea

15

Inferno VIII

Virgil and Dante in the fifth circle of Hell: the wrathful in the Styx; before the gates of the city of Dis

Pen and brown ink over metalpoint on vellum, 32.4 × 47.2 cm; text of *Inferno* VII in four columns on the verso (pen and brown ink)

SELECT BIBLIOGRAPHY Watts 1995 b passim

With this, the first Berlin drawing from Botticelli's *Commedia* series, we are already right in the middle of the action. Dante and Virgil have already traversed one section of Hell. They are entering the fifth circle of Hell in the top right corner through a rock crevice, and arrive at a swampy body of water, the river Styx. On the battlements of a tower, we see a devil waving two torches. Although Dante glimpses sources of light, he cannot make out their origin in the eternal darkness of Hell. The boatman Phlegyas approaches, in order to row Dante and Virgil across the river. In its muddy currents, the souls of the torpid (suffering from acedia) have sunk, while on the surface, those of the wrathful do battle. One of them, the soul of Filippo Argenti from Florence, clings to the poets' barge, but is berated by Dante, and shoved back by Virgil. Virgil embraces his charge and praises his disdain for evil. After Phlegyas has set down the travellers before the city of Dis, he turns back, while Virgil requests entry from the devils guarding the city – but to no avail. The figures of the poets here approximate the size of those of the devils, and, as such, are somewhat smaller than above: it is a stalemate, Dante and Virgil are unable to force their way through. However, the eyes of the viewer are able to wander on into the city of Hell with its fiery tombs, which do not appear in the *Commedia* until somewhat later. Through this visual anticipation, which refers beyond the confines of the current canto, Botticelli orients the viewer within the broader narrative. Within the drawing, the strong, vertical accents of the imposing towers provide a tripartite structure for the narrative progression in the picture. Presuming that the sheets were bound as a codex, a page of text was placed underneath the drawing, the four columns of which correspond precisely to the two towers and the position of the pairs on the left and the right (see Kilian 2014, p. 232). The events on the sheet also refer beyond the edges of the picture: the devils are concentrated in their gestures not just on Dante and Virgil, but rather, with their grotesque faces, they also grin provocatively at the viewer, who, just like the two poets, is a stranger in their realm.

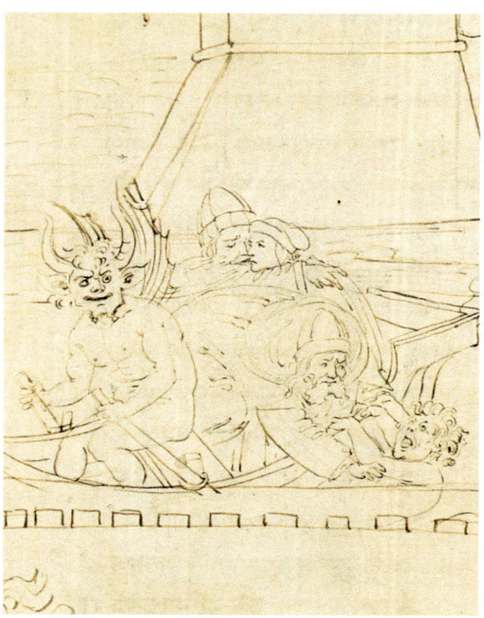

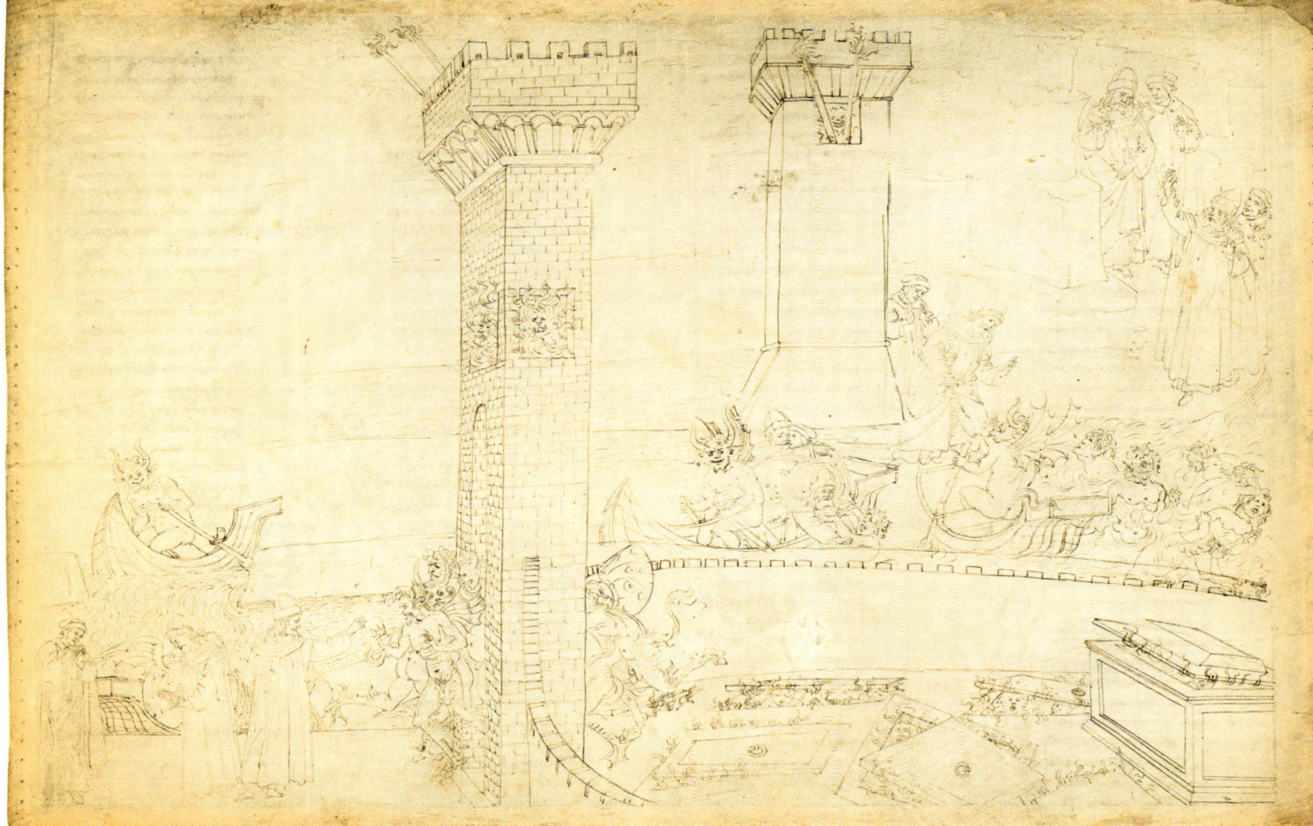

16

Inferno XVII

Virgil and Dante in the seventh circle of Hell: violators of the divine order; the punishment of usurers; descent into the abyss on the back of Geryon

Pen and brown ink over metalpoint on vellum, 32.3 × 47.2 cm; text of *Inferno* XVI in four columns on the verso (pen and brown ink)

SELECT BIBLIOGRAPHY Stuttgart 1980, no. 12, pp. 71–72

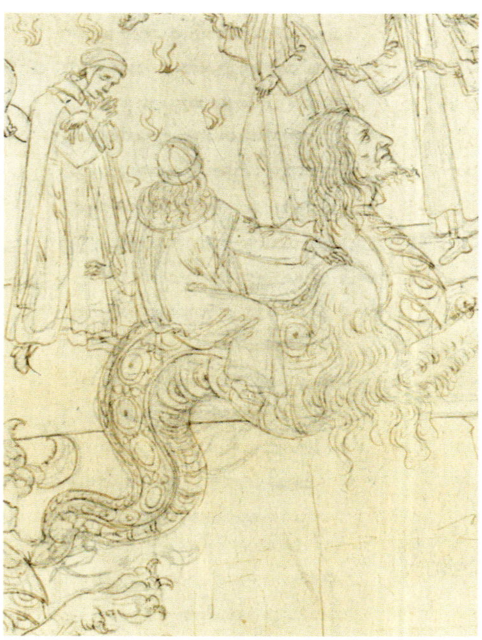

This sheet was described by Kenneth Clark as "one of the most beautiful drawings in the *Inferno*" (1976, p. 18). The viewer is struck by its highly detailed depiction, almost ornamental in its density, and by the animated gestures of the protagonists, which bear witness to their lively communication. Thanks to the densely arranged sequence of the figures – Dante can be seen eight times and Virgil six – we can easily trace the path of the travelling poets from our slightly elevated perspective, across the top from right to left, to the centre and then straight down. In the centre of the illustration, they encounter Geryon, a peculiar chimaera with the benevolent countenance of a righteous man, two hairy paws, and the body of a snake adorned with knots and circlets, which Botticelli renders in detail in the drawing, perhaps in part because Dante's use of the word *dipinto* (painted) – as we will often note – particularly inspired the artist. While Virgil speaks with Geryon, Dante continues on in order to converse with the tormented souls of usurers. They sit, tortured by the flames like dogs by flies, fleas and the heat of summer, wearing purses around their necks. The vibrant coats of arms on their little sacks are not rendered here by Botticelli, but perhaps these were to have been realised in the colouring stage. When Dante returns to Virgil, Virgil is sitting on Geryon's back and invites him to climb on as well. Dante is struck dumb with fear during this ride through Hell. He holds his shoulders tensely, even though he is held fast by Virgil, who sits between him and the poisonous spines of Geryon's scorpion-like tail. In concert with the circular form of Hell, Geryon flies downwards with the two of them on his back in sweeping loops, the drama amplified still more by his flowing locks and the Phlegethon, the river of Hell roaring down into the depths. In the middle of the circular abyss, minute and remote, the group is merely hinted at in metalpoint, before they vanish from our sight.

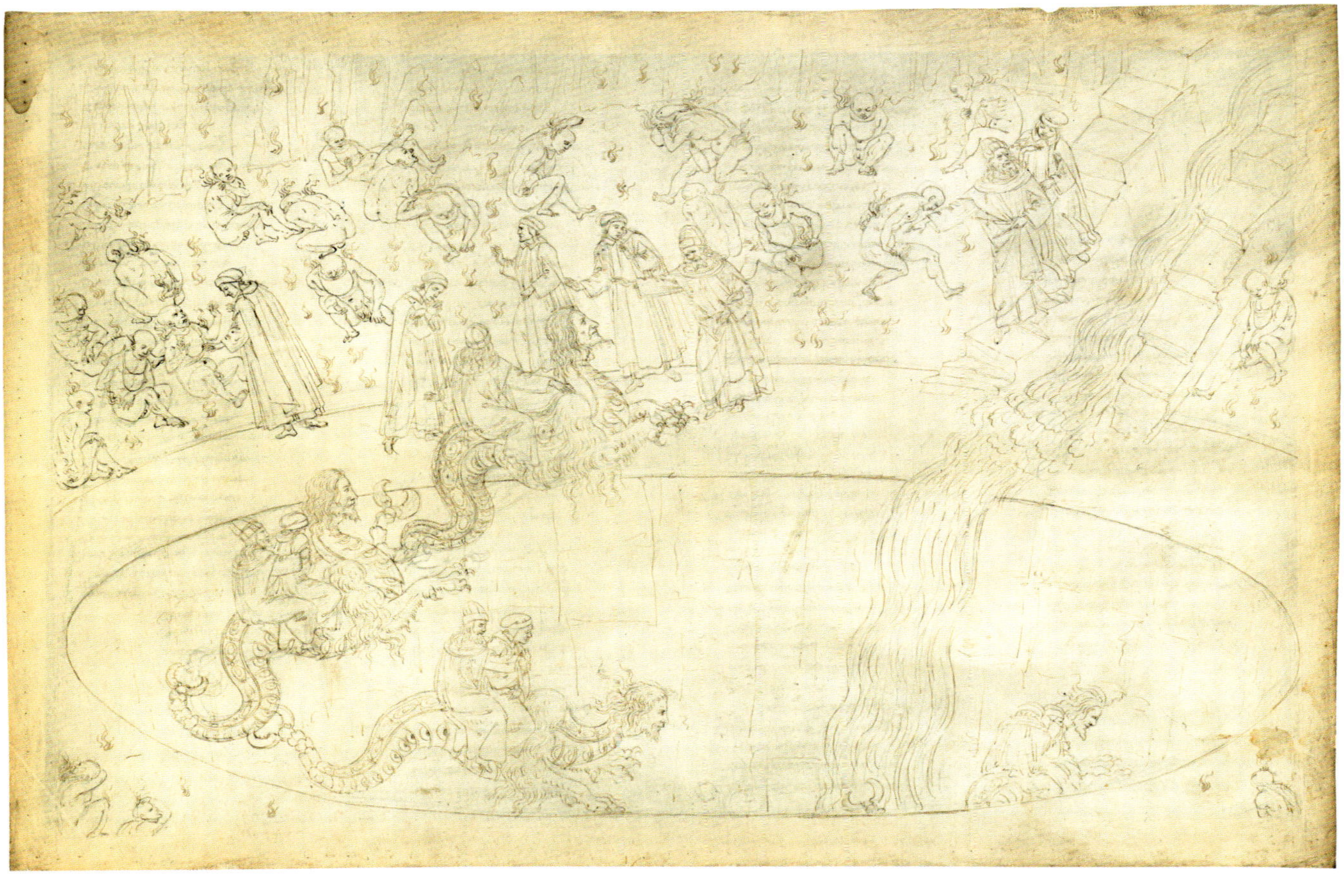

17

Inferno XVIII

Virgil and Dante in the eighth circle of Hell (*Malebolge*), 1st and 2nd *bolge*: punishment of panderers and seducers, flatterers and whores

Body colour, pen and brown ink over metalpoint on vellum, 32.4 × 47.2 cm; text of *Inferno* XVII in four columns on the verso (pen and brown ink)

Not exhibited in London

Only four of the drawings that have been preserved from Botticelli's *Commedia* series are entirely or partially hand-coloured – of these, this illustration of *Inferno* XVIII is one of the most complete. The two travellers are shown in bright colours, while Hell and its inhabitants and inmates are kept in dull brown and grey tones. The visual narrative begins in the top left corner of the image, where we see Geryon, who has brought Dante and Virgil to the "*malebolge*" (evil ditches). The half-human, half-snake guard at the crossing to this eighth circle of Hell is the only figure that remains uncoloured. This is even more remarkable since it is precisely this figure which Dante portrays in the most sumptuous colours, 'even more colourful than woven oriental fabrics'. "Botticelli evidently found no colouring which would have been able to distinguish Geryon from the coloured wanderers sufficiently, and at the same time connect him with the uncoloured or dark realm of the sinners" (Meier 2013, note 44). Initially, the two travellers move to the right, along the edge of the trench in which the souls of the panderers are whipped by horned devils and driven around in circles. Dante takes a few steps back because he has recognised one of the souls and wants to make certain. Afterwards, he and his guide pass over a stone bridge from which they can see the faces of the damned, who move towards them. Virgil points out Jason, who, here distinguished with a crown, atones for toying with Medea's love. From the next ditch the travellers are confronted by a terrible stench, from which Dante attempts to protect himself by flinging his hand in front of his face. Here, the flatterers and prostitutes serve out their eternal sentence in a swamp of excrement. Dante speaks with Alessio Interminei from Lucca, a flatterer of the most wicked kind during his life, who is made to stand out in the image, just like Thaïs, the hetaera, who is depicted frontally in the centre of the image. Dante and Virgil leave the scene at the bottom right corner and continue on to the third ditch, which is the subject of the following canto.

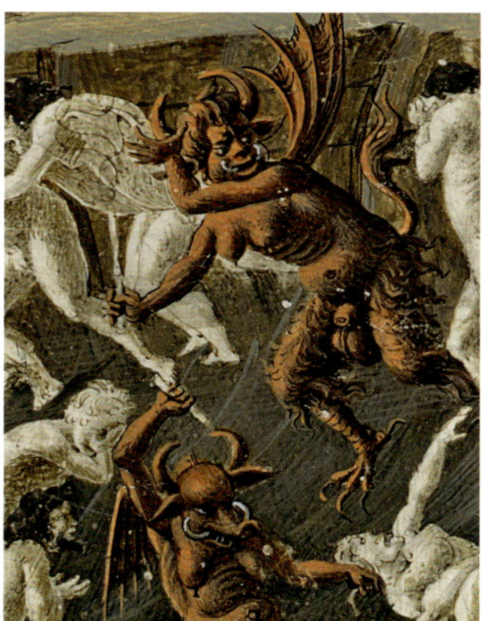

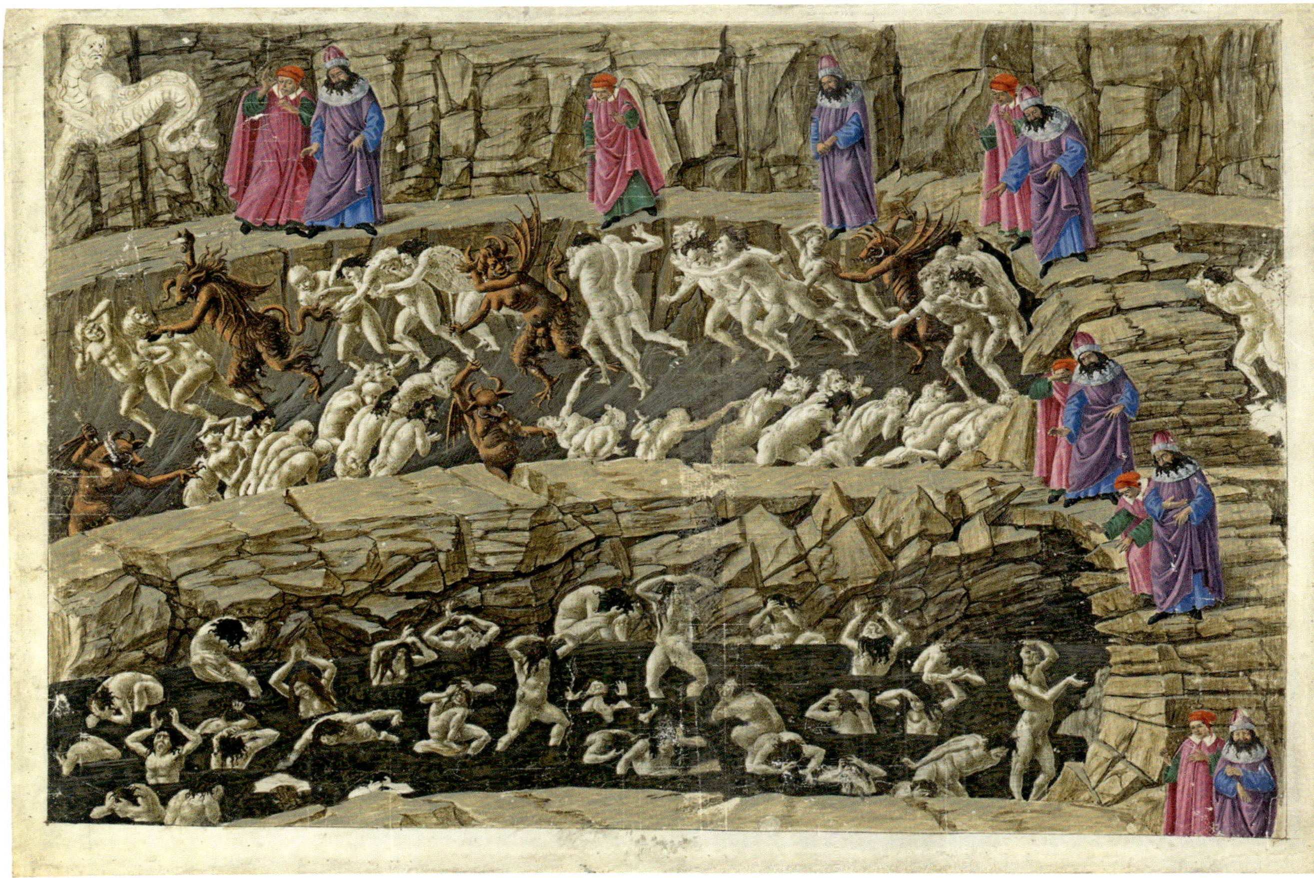

18

Inferno XIX

Virgil and Dante in the eighth circle of Hell (*Malebolge*), 3rd *bolgia*: corrupt clergy, the punishment of simonists

Pen and brown ink over metalpoint on vellum, 32.0 × 47.0 cm; text of *Inferno* XVIII in four columns on the verso (pen and brown ink)

With its elongated, deep ditches, arched over by stone bridges, we recognise the landscape of this drawing from the previous sheet. We are still located in the *malebolge*, which forms a structure all of its own within Hell. The ditch of the flatterers and whores from the Canto XVIII is repeated in this image for the sake of narrative continuity and the overall orientation of the viewer, although in the text of the *Commedia* it no longer plays a role at this point. From there, walking side by side the whole time, Dante and Virgil approach the third ditch, the site of punishment for simonists – Church dignitaries who during their lives had abused their office for their own material gain. They are stuck here head-first in circular holes in the bottom of the ditch, which paradoxically remind Dante of baptismal fonts. Their legs protrude, flailing, and flames blaze on the soles of their feet, faithfully visualised by Botticelli in an unforgettable "example of Dantesque precision" (Clark 1976, p. 12). From his elevated standpoint, Dante catches a glimpse of a sinner whose limbs twitch with particular violence under this enduring punishment. Virgil carries him a little bit further down, to a less steep point in the ditch, so that he can speak with this soul. Attentively, he bends down to the splayed legs and harkens to the words of the soul being punished. It is Pope Nicholas III (1277–80), who initially thinks that his successor in office has joined him, since both he, Nicholas, and his successor had allowed unbridled corruption to reign. After Dante has given a sermon to the sinful Pope, Virgil takes him back up to the next bridge.

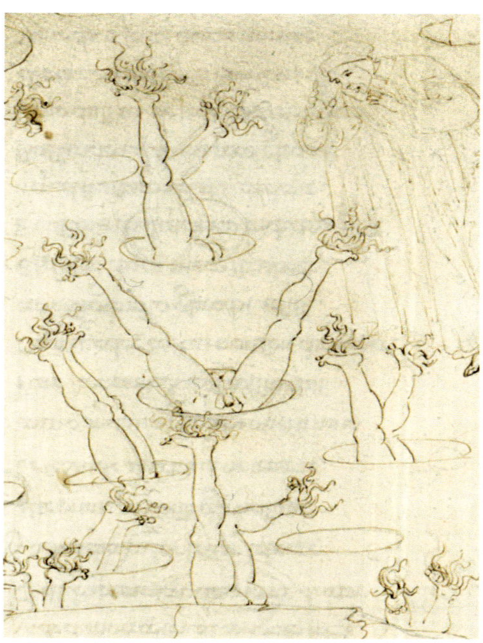

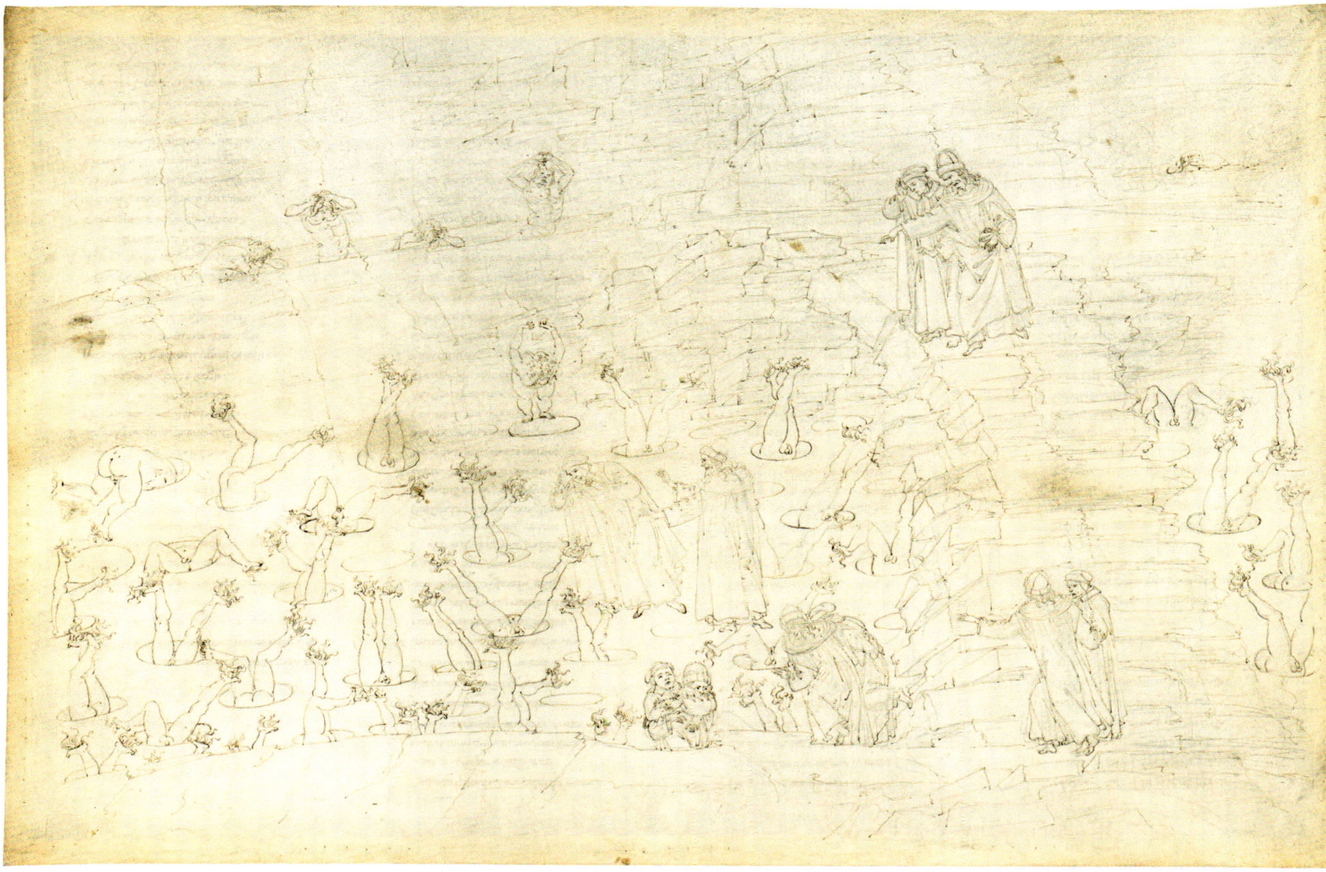

19

Inferno XX

Virgil and Dante in the eighth circle of Hell (*Malebolge*), 4th *bolgia*: punishment of seers; encounter with Manto

Pen and brown ink over metalpoint on vellum, 32.6 × 47.5 cm; text of *Inferno* XIX in four columns on the verso (pen and brown ink)

Not exhibited in Berlin

With the third ditch of the *malebolge* and its circular, though here empty, holes still visible towards the upper margin of the image, the two travellers approach the next *bolgia*. The figures of the sinners of the fourth ditch are oddly distorted: their heads are wrenched around, rotated at 180°, so that their faces are looking behind them. They are thus forced to walk backwards, because they cannot see forwards.

However, there is a certain ambivalence to this assertion, as Botticelli's visualisation shows, for judging from the legs and bodies, some souls certainly do seem to walk forwards, even if they feel their way with outstretched hands, since of course they cannot see in that direction. Others, meanwhile, appear to walk backwards, their heads bowed and hands clasped across their stomachs. The sight of these sinners moves Dante to tears of compassion, and he leans on the boulder jutting out of the ground at the crossing to this ditch. Virgil, however, shown here frowning in response to the inappropriate behaviour of his charge, admonishes him: compassion for those whom the judgment of God has damned to this realm for eternity is misplaced, because they arrogated the right to look into the future and twisted the truth. Amongst the soothsayers, Manto takes on a special role, since Virgil takes the encounter with her as an opportunity to explain in great detail the geographical particularities and the foundation of his home city of Mantua. In response to Dante's enquiry as to which soul Virgil still recognises and considers worth mentioning, he names the bearded Greek seer Eurypylus, who can be seen on the left of the drawing. In this sheet, the particularly daring perspective with which Botticelli stages the events stands out: the bridges that Dante and Virgil walk over are seen from a steeply elevated perspective, and the viewer can also see right down into the ditches, taking in their full width. The figures, on the other hand, are shown by Botticelli from the side, which allows him to depict in vivid detail their gestural and facial expressions, their postures and their relation to one another.

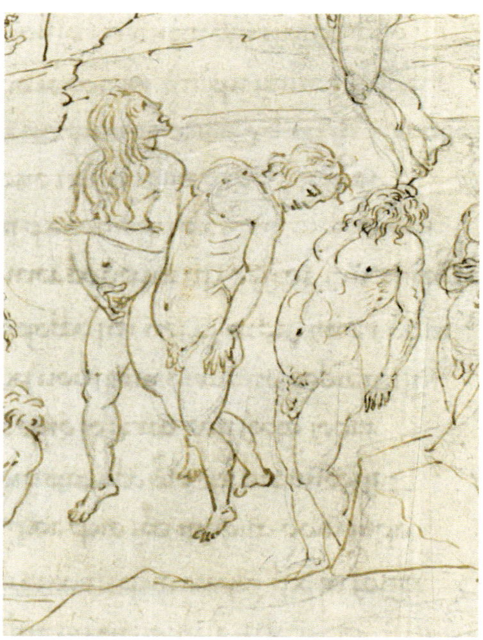

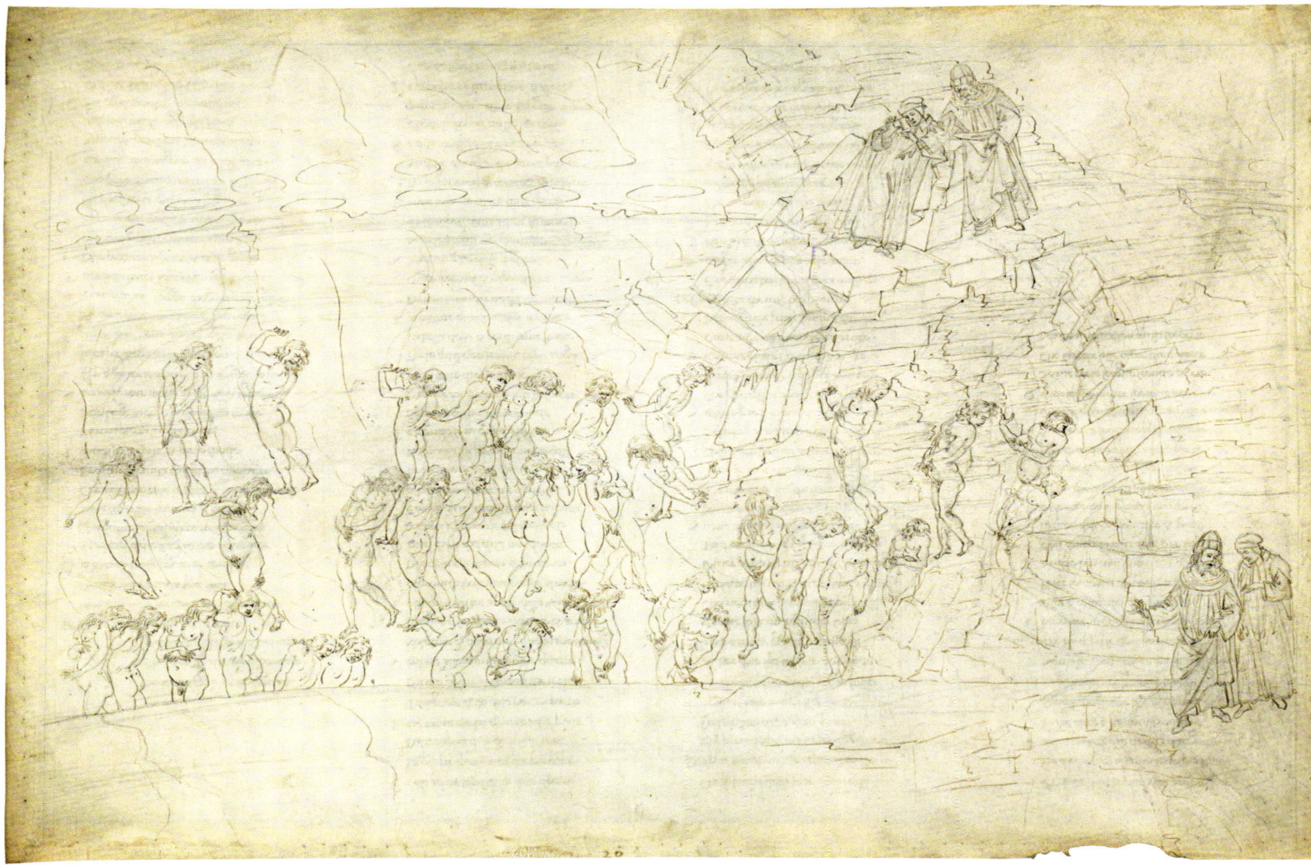

20

Inferno XXII

Virgil and Dante in the eighth circle of Hell (*Malebolge*), 5th *bolgia*: punishment of the corrupt; Ciampolo's escape

Pen and brown ink over metalpoint on vellum, 32.9 × 47.1 cm; text of *Inferno* XXI in four columns on the verso (pen and brown ink)

A quick glance back helps us to locate this episode in the manifold landscape of sins and eternal punishments of the pit of Hell. A narrow strip on the upper margin of the picture still shows the fortune tellers and diviners in the fourth *bolgia*. On this side of the dividing rock face, in the fifth *bolgia*, we see in the foreground the two travellers of the hereafter making their way from left to right. They are escorted by a hoard of hellish, spear-wielding guides. Dante takes this in with resignation. After all, he thinks, one goes to church with saints, with guzzlers in the tavern, so why not with devils into Hell? In the ditch behind them, the corrupt office bearers of secular power crouch in silken tar like frogs, with only their mouths to be seen. When, to alleviate their agony, they arch their backs out of the swamp like dolphins, the devils that guard them stab at them with their long spears. Upon seeing the wild hordes leading Dante and Virgil, they all dive under, except for one, who is immediately fished out and mistreated. It is Ciampolo, who was once in the service of King Thibaut II of Navarre. Through a ruse, he manages to escape, and jumps back into the boiling tar pit. A great skirmish ensues, in which a section of the savage hordes themselves fall in, during which time Dante and Virgil make their way to the next ditch.

This sheet has a special aesthetic appeal. The apparently random tangle of the spears structures the sheet and focuses the action on two points, first on the throng of devils coming from the left, amongst which Dante and Virgil appear very restrained, and secondly on the abuse of Ciampolo by the savage hordes, which Dante and Virgil experience as spectators. The isolation here of the fate of an individual sharpens the drama of the plot. Botticelli renders the devils – to whom Dante assigns expressive names such as Barbariccia (Bushy beard), Graffiacane (Dog scratcher), Malacoda (Evil tail) and so on – in an equally individual, almost caricatural fashion.

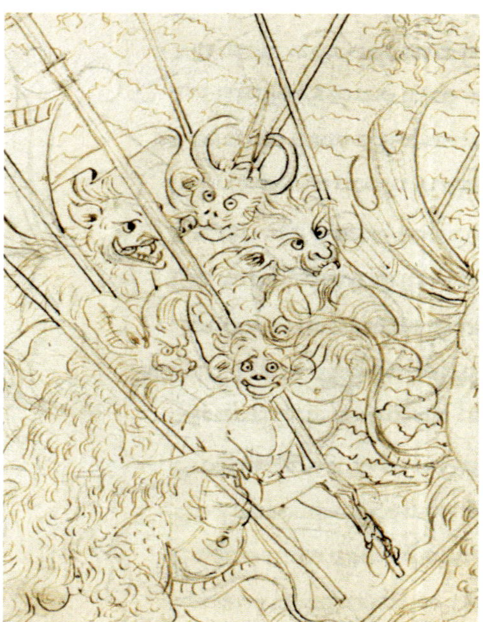

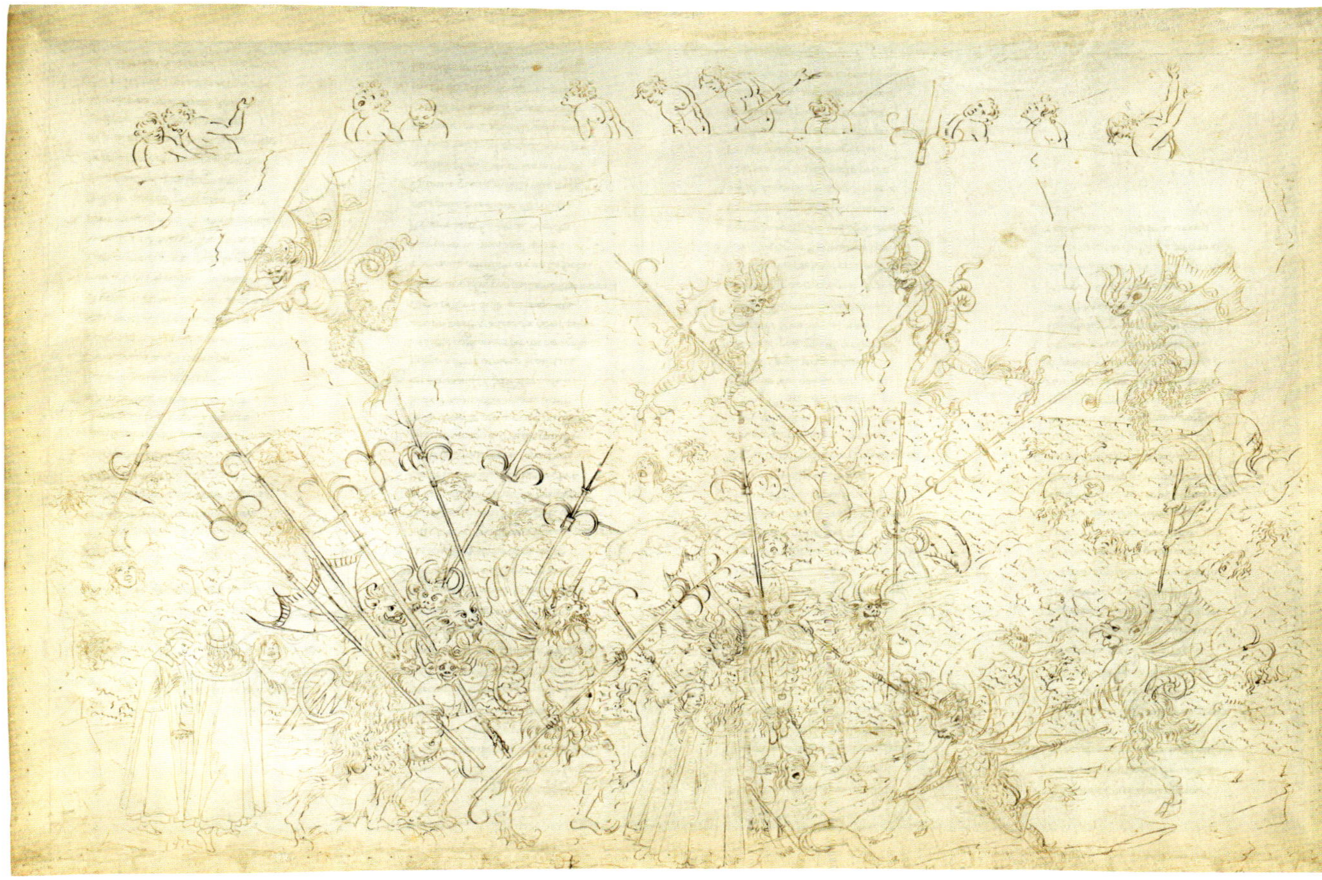

21

Inferno XXVII

Virgil and Dante in the eighth circle of Hell (*Malebolge*), 8th *bolgia*: punishment of evil counsellors; conversation with Guido da Montefeltro

Pen and brown ink over metalpoint on vellum, 32.5 × 47.2 cm; text of *Inferno* XXVI in four columns on the verso (pen and brown ink)

This sheet, only sparingly sketched out in metalpoint, exudes great confidence. Botticelli had evidently acquired assurance in drawing the characteristic landscape of the *Malebolge*, consisting of ditches, dams and bridges, such that he laid out this sheet relatively swiftly and without preliminary considerations of the composition and arrangement of the scene, and also without modifications or corrections. The particular clarity of the depiction – which is further emphasised by the strong, dark colour of the ink that Botticelli uses here – also corresponds to the concentration on a single scene, positioned in the centre of the picture, Dante's dialogue with Guido da Montefeltro. Guido appears – as do the other tormented souls in this ditch – not in human form, but rather veiled in a bundle of flames. The flames of the eighth circle of Hell, in the overall presentation of Botticelli's *Commedia* series, act as a kind of intimation of the flames that represent the "luminous spirits" (the souls of the blessed) in the heaven of the Fixed Stars in the eighth sphere of Paradise (Cantos XXIII–XXVI). In their ornamental abstraction and near decorative and even distribution in the *bolgia*, the larger flames on this sheet representing Canto XXVII of *Inferno* conceal the agony of the souls as well as the once human forms of the false counsellors. From some bundles of fire, a face emerges with a gaping mouth, enabling them to articulate themselves in a human language which Dante can comprehend. Botticelli limits himself to depicting the situation; there is no hint of the complex content of the conversation between Dante and the *condottiere* Guido da Montefeltro, of his fate or of that of the Romagna and the political situation.

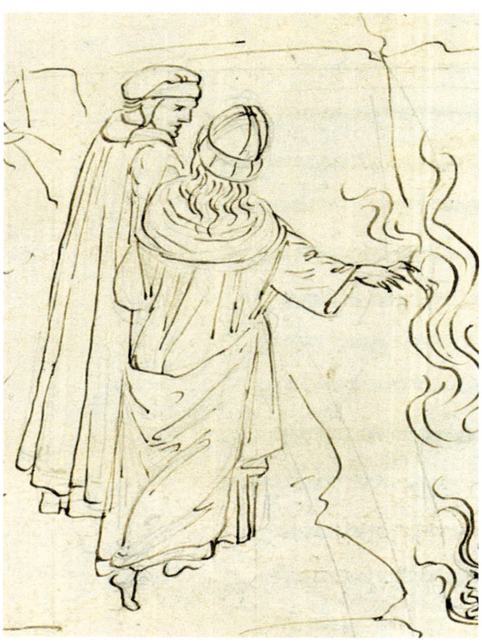

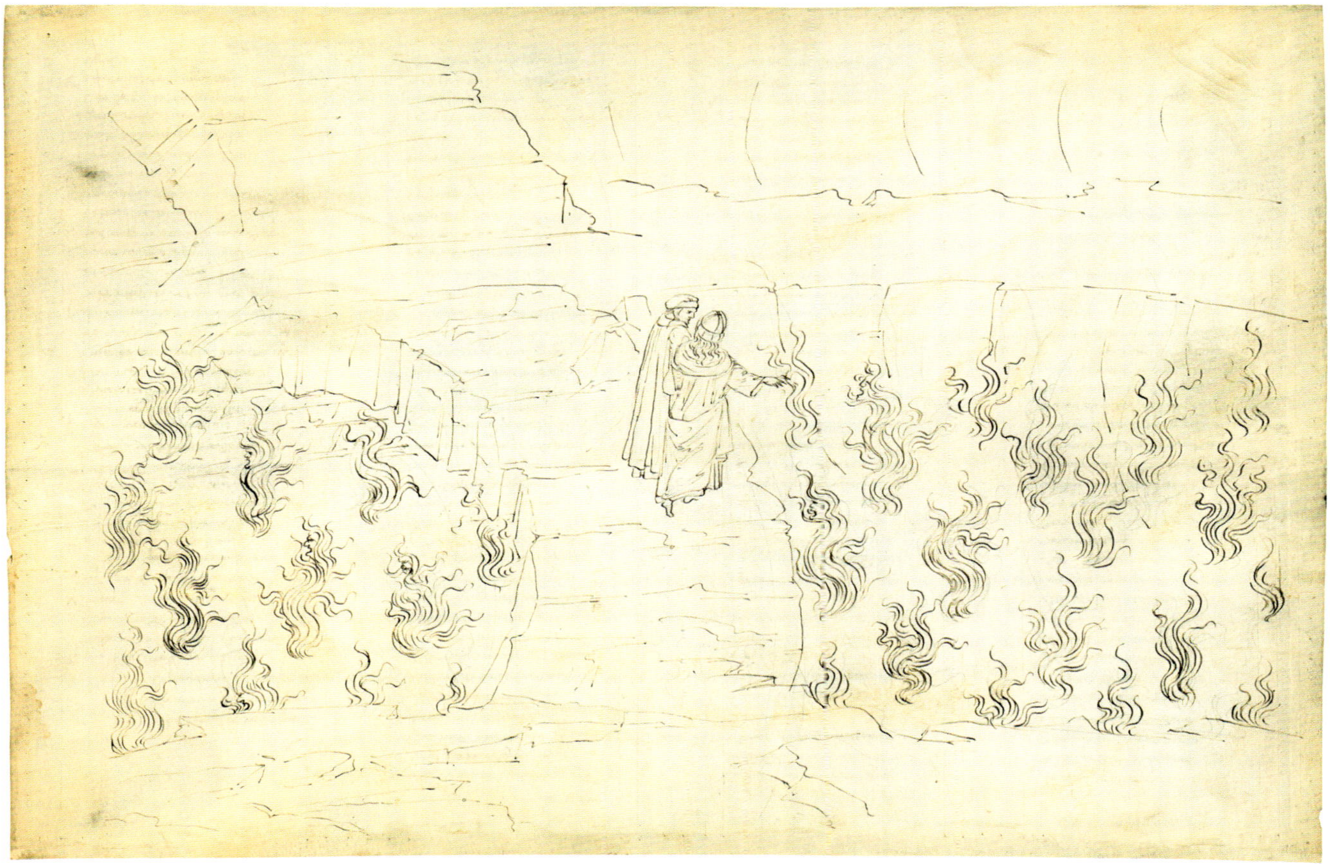

22

Inferno XXIX

Virgil and Dante in the eighth circle of Hell (*Malebolge*), 10th *bolgia*: punishment of falsifiers and alchemists

Pen and brown ink over metalpoint on vellum, 32.6 × 47.2 cm; text of *Inferno* XXVIII in four columns on the verso (pen and brown ink)

The retrospective glance into the ninth *bolgia* is here more than an orientation aid offered to the viewer by the artist, for it takes up a great deal of space on the sheet, the entire upper half: in the text of the *Commedia* as well, this landscape – in which the breakers of faith and sowers of discord are punished for their sins – also plays a role at the beginning of this canto, since Dante pauses here, causing a delay. The reason he lags behind is that he believes his relative Geri del Bello to be in this ditch. It is only as they come to the end of the bridge that spans the ditch that Virgil points out Geri's likeness, which at that moment is stretching its finger menacingly into the air. It turns out that Dante had overlooked him until then because he was so fascinated by the strange appearance of the troubadour Bertran de Born, who must carry around his decapitated head in front of him like a lantern, as punishment for having sown discord in the family of King Henry II of England. Botticelli had initially sketched out Bertran's figure intact – that is, with a head – only then to delineate the final form with the decapitated head later in ink. In addition to this correction, numerous others on this sheet attest to a struggle to achieve a convincing narrative thrust. The view under the bridge – which Botticelli had previously avoided – here appears particularly audacious. Eventually, Dante and Virgil arrive at the next ditch, in which the falsifiers and alchemists attempt to scratch putrescent leprous sores and scurf from their bodies. The travellers turn to the left (from our perspective to the right) in order to see better, and encounter two male figures who are leaning their backs against each other. One was an alchemist in Arezzo, the other a falsifier of metals. In this ditch, through the example of the two figures on the far right, it becomes evident that this series of drawings by Botticelli also represents a "self-referential atlas of motifs from his painted works" (Schulze Altcappenberg 2000, p. 28): this group calls to mind the pursuit of Flora by Zephyr in the *Primavera* (Florence, Galleria degli Uffizi), which is likewise depicted on the far right of the picture space.

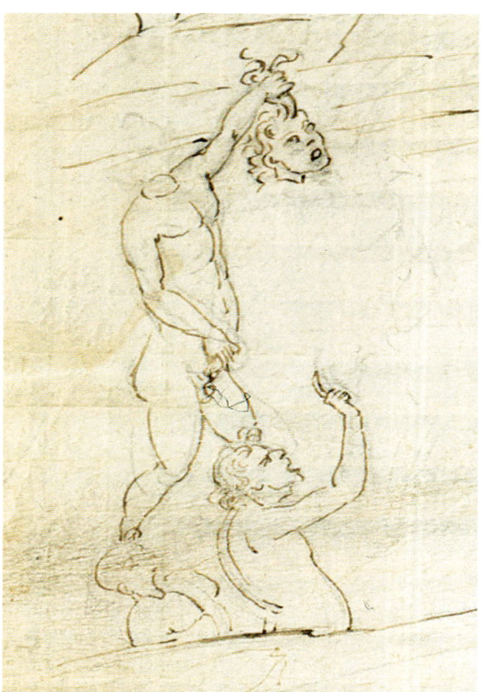

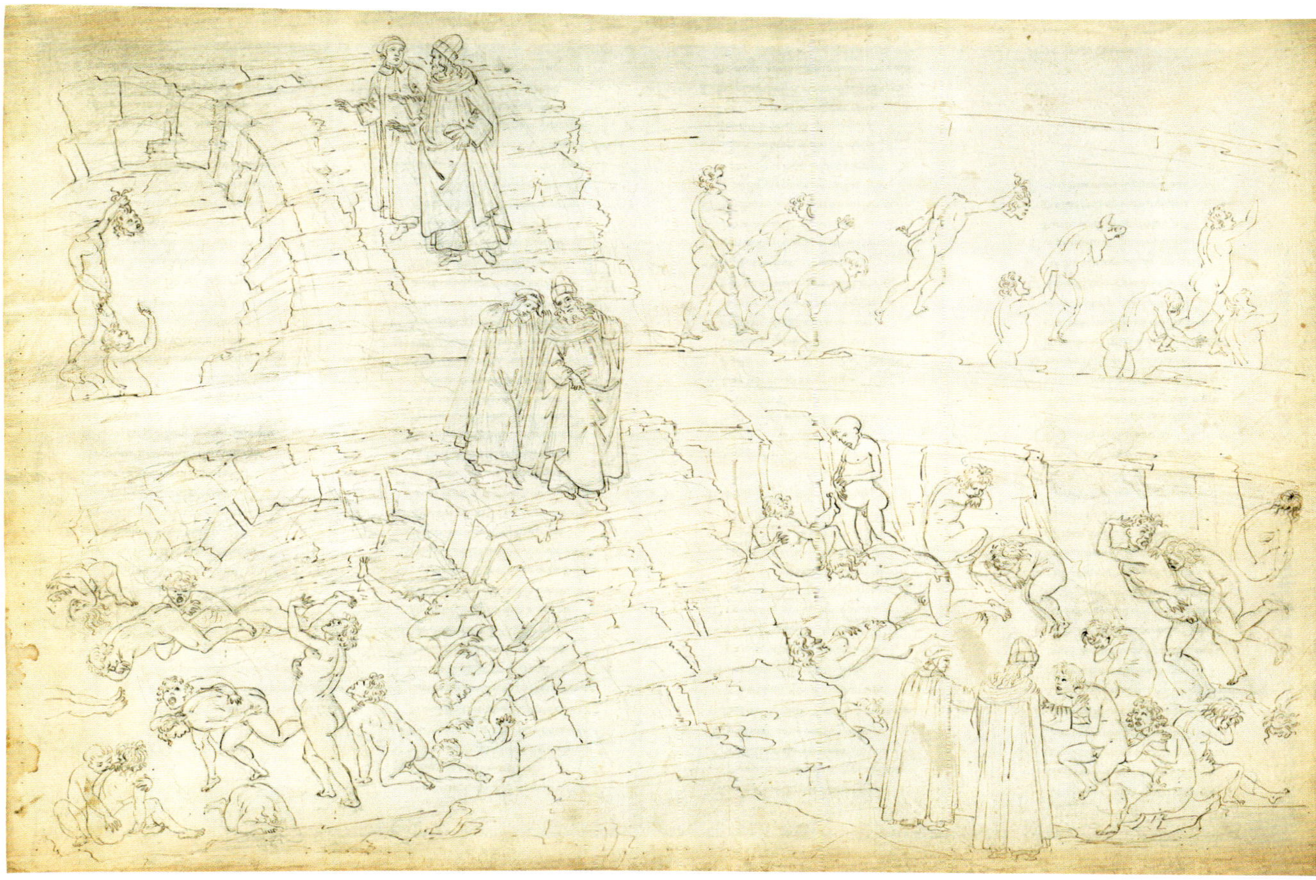

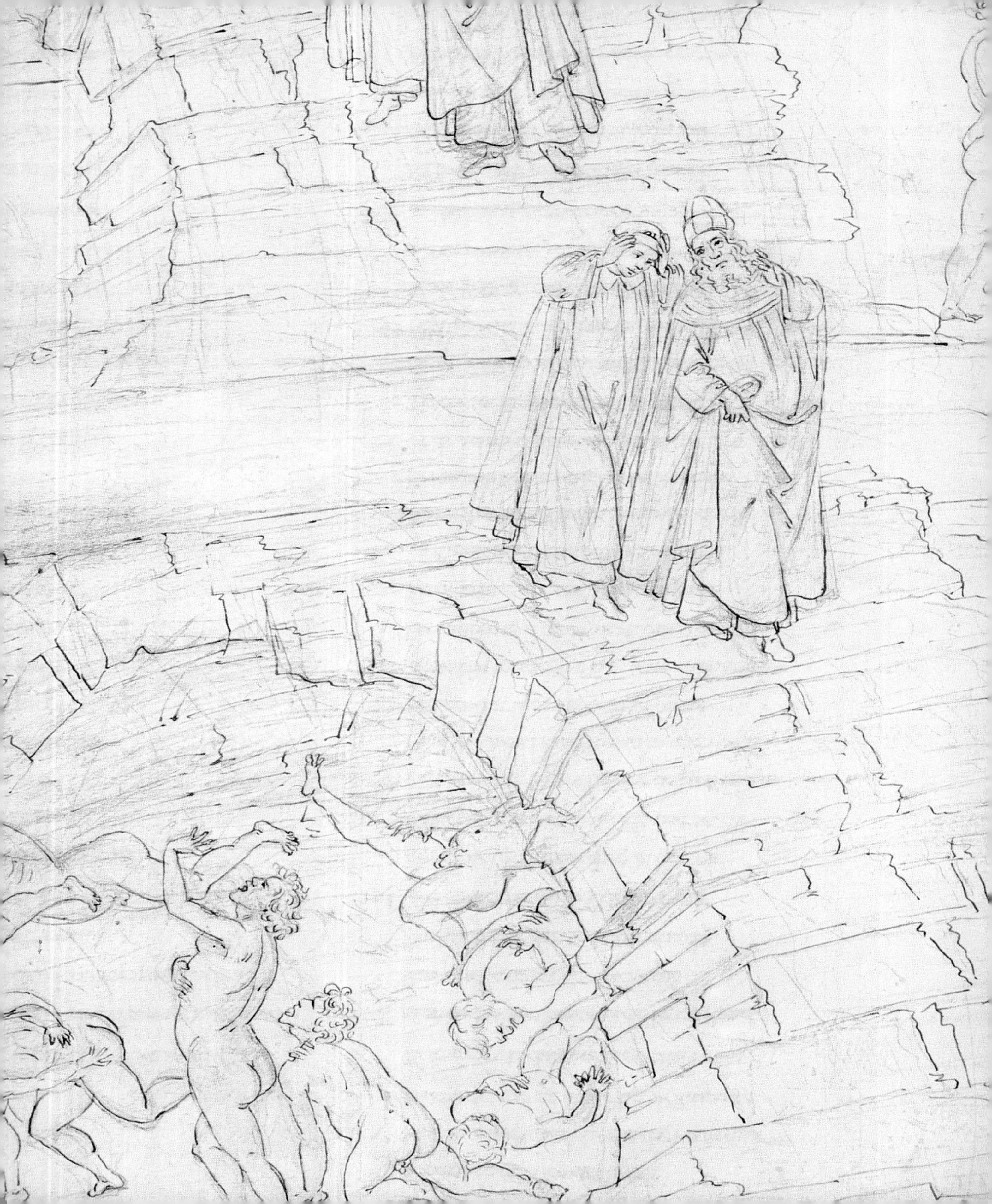

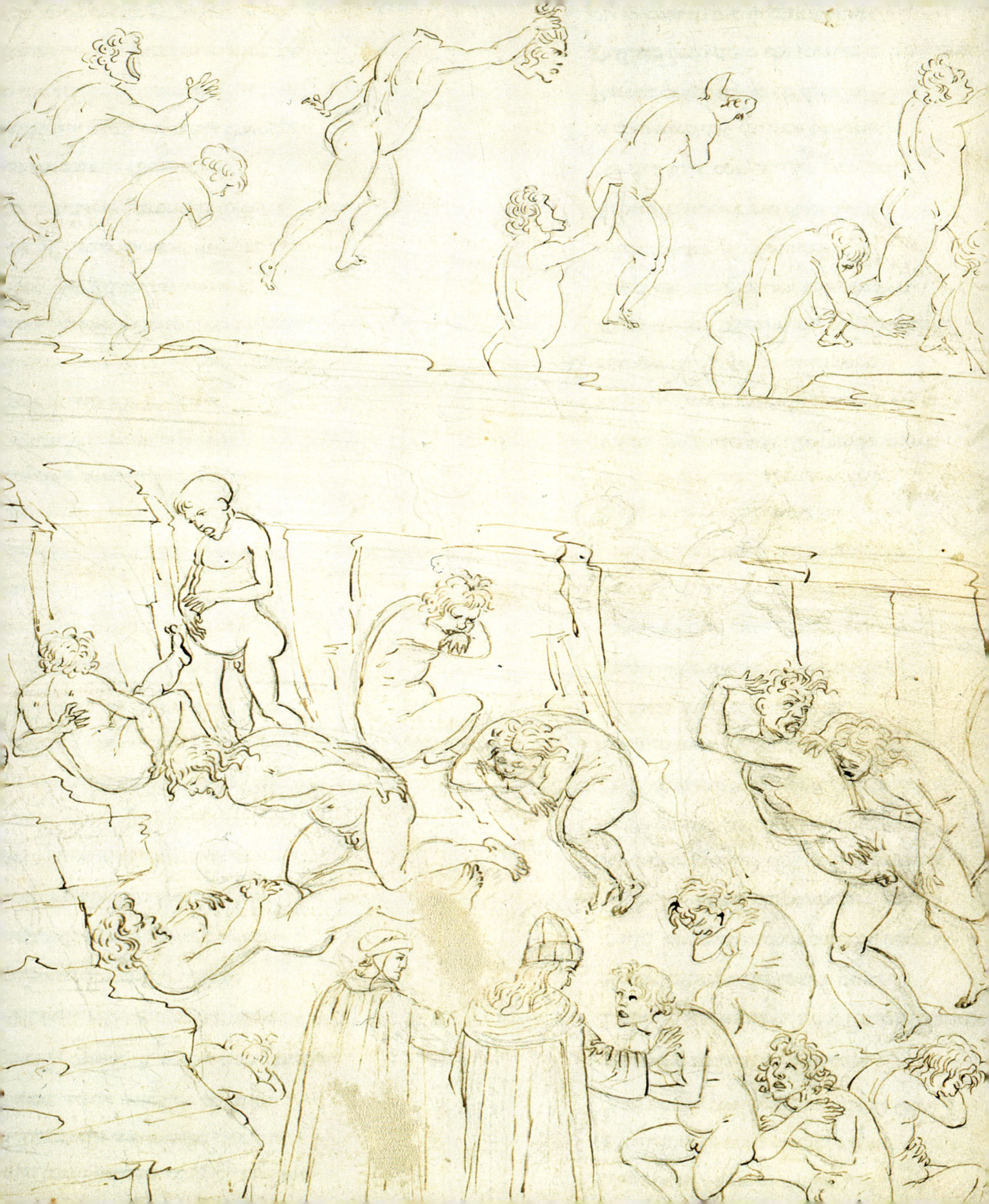

23
Inferno XXXIII

Virgil and Dante in the ninth circle of Hell (*Cocytus*), 3rd ring: Ugolino's account of his death; punishment of traitors in the ice of Tolomea

Pen and brown ink over metalpoint on vellum, 32.7 × 47.0 cm; text of *Inferno* XXXII in four columns on the verso (pen and brown ink)

The ninth circle of Hell is the lowest region of the funnel-shaped pit of Hell, eternally frozen over with ice, in which the treacherous are encased. Botticelli's renderings of their bodies is as curious as it is haunting, suggesting that we can see their agonised poses through the crystal-clear ice, in which the sinners remain for all eternity. With more than one hundred figures, this sheet is one of the most striking of the *Inferno*. The deepest circle of Hell, Cocytus, is divided into separate rings. On the right-hand side, Botticelli has furnished them with precise assignations. In the process, though, he initially made an error, for on the upper ring the erased title *Giudecca* can be found, which has been corrected to *Caina*, named after the biblical fratricide Cain. Here those who betrayed their own kin pay for their sins. Dante and Virgil had already crossed this ring in the preceding canto, which is why it can only be seen here on the upper margin. Meanwhile, they have already arrived in the *Antenora* (after the Trojan Antenor, who supposedly opened the gates of Troy to the Greeks), where those who have betrayed their country are punished. There they encounter Ugolino della Gherardesca, who starved to death as a prisoner together with his children. Now he is seen gnawing away at the head of his tormentor, Archbishop Ruggieri, and only briefly lets up in order to tell Dante his story. In the following ring, *Tolomea* (named after Ptolemy of Jericho, who murdered his guests), those who have betrayed their guests are punished for their misdeeds. There, they speak with one soul, which purports to be Frate Albergio. Dante is stunned, since, to the best of his knowledge, Albergio is still alive. The sinner explains to him that the soul of a traitor is sometimes separated from their body during their own lifetime, and banished to this place in Hell, while a demon takes possession of the still-living body of the traitor. The faces of the sinners are here strained upward, which prevents their tears from being able to flow, freezing them directly in their eye sockets. On the left-hand side, we see a group of figures which is reminiscent of a *Pietà*. Not yet in the picture, only hinted at by the designation *Giudecca*, is the lowest realm of Hell, named after Judas. It is not entered until the next canto. The use of somewhat darker ink in the centre and towards the bottom highlights the increasing profundity and darkness which Dante and Virgil are entering.

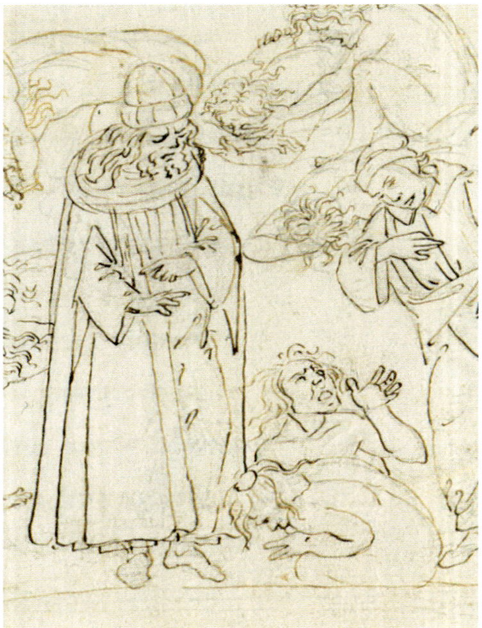

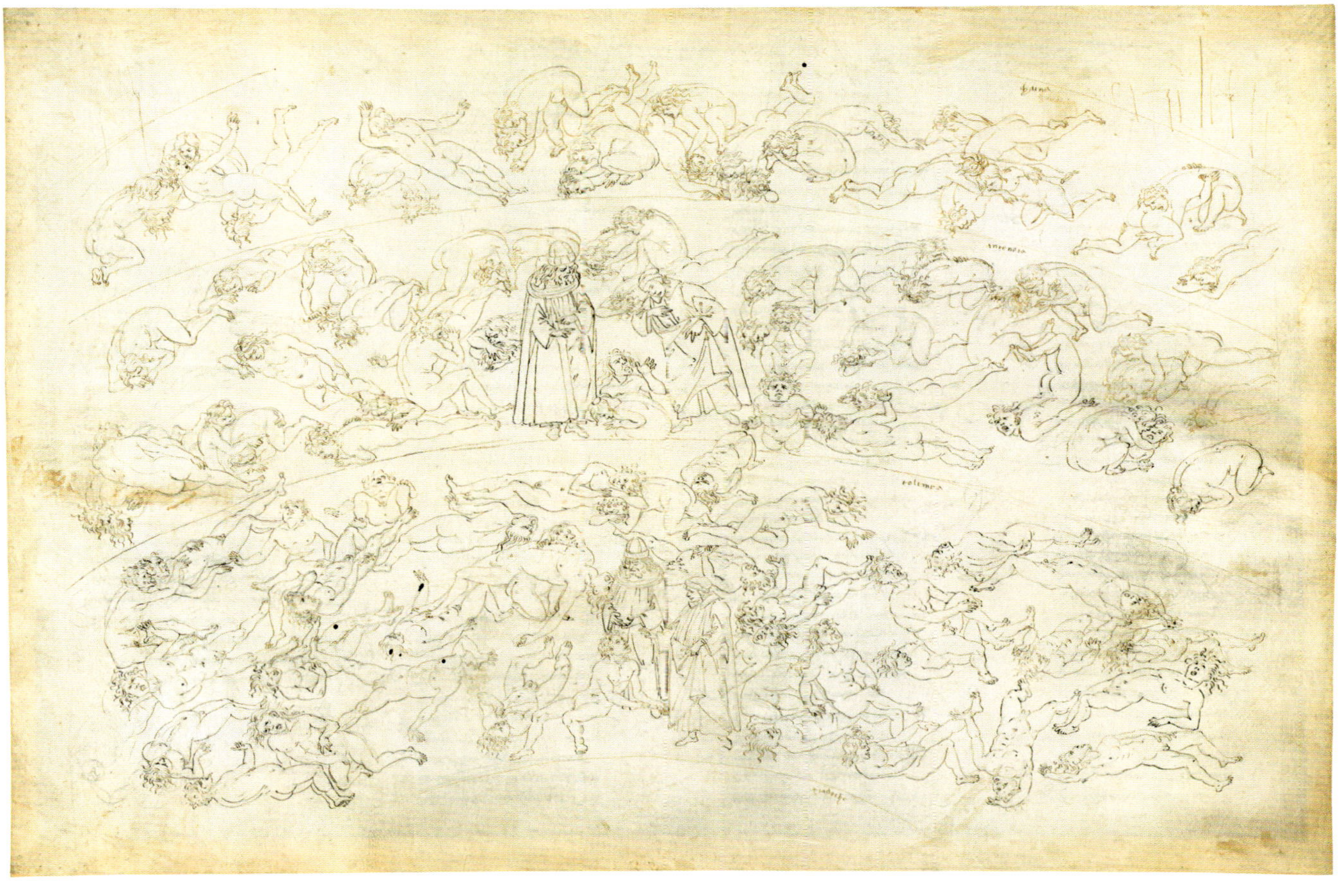

24

Inferno XXXIV, 1

The centre of Hell: Lucifer in the ice of Giudecca, mauling Judas, Brutus and Cassius

Pen and brown ink over metalpoint on vellum, 32.5 × 47.0 cm; text of *Inferno* XXXIII in four columns on the verso (pen and brown ink)

Having arrived right at the bottom of Hell, Dante initially believes he has seen an enormous building in the frosty fog. However, as they step nearer, the two travellers of the netherworld are confronted by the gigantic figure of Lucifer, half-protruding from the ice sea. The powerful ruler of Hell boasts six bat wings, which Botticelli renders here with their membranes, bones, joints and claws in near-zoological exactitude. The continual beating of Lucifer's wings creates the icy wind that causes the ice sea to freeze over. Of his three heads, Botticelli depicts one frontally and two in profile. These are also rendered in great detail and are reminiscent of masks. The horror lies not so much in Lucifer's appearance, but much more in his actions, as he crushes the souls of the three arch-traitors in his jaws. In the middle, Judas's head is bitten off, while left and right, Brutus and Cassius, the betrayers of Caesar, are mauled feet-first. Interestingly, though this drawing was extensively laid out in metalpoint, it was only partially inked in. Although Botticelli also dedicates the following drawing to this canto, where he even depicts the events on a double sheet, this sheet of vellum remained part of the series, primarily because the text of Canto XXXIII of *Inferno* is written on the reverse side.

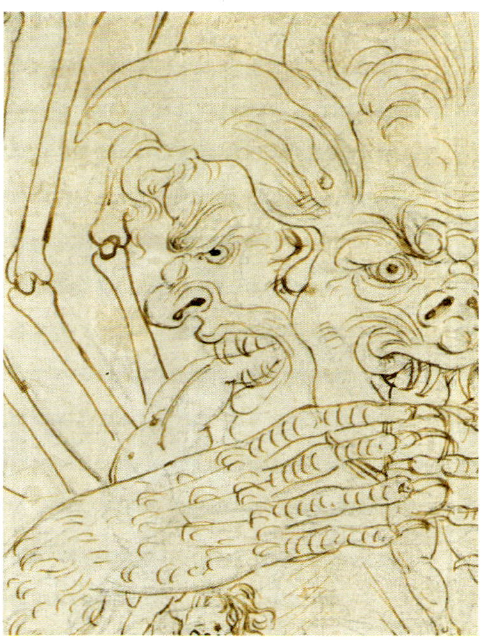

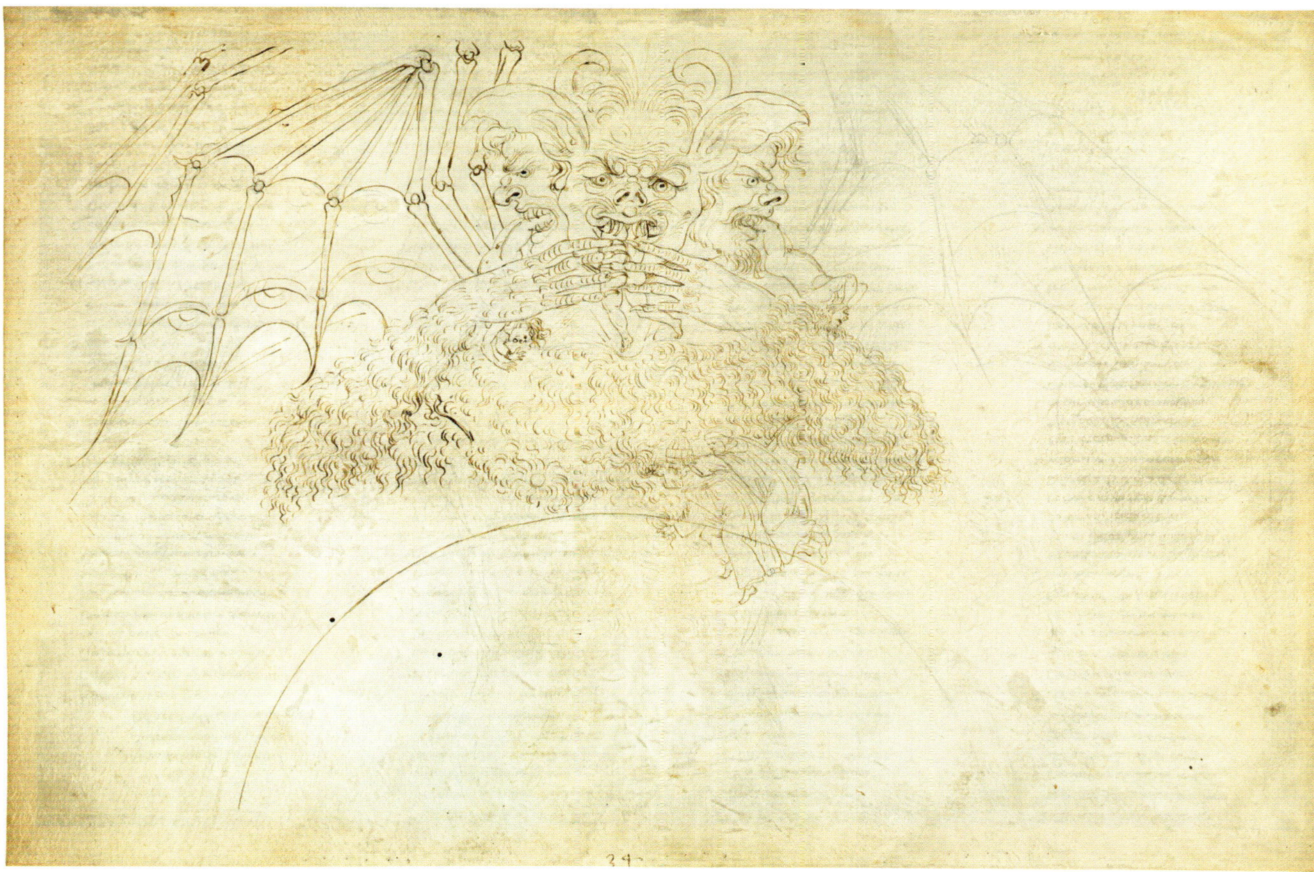

25

Inferno XXXIV, 2

The centre of Hell: the full figure of Lucifer (The Great Satan); departure from *Inferno*

Pen and brown ink over metalpoint on vellum, 63.2 × 46.3 cm (in the detail visible in the passepartout); text of *Inferno* XXXIV in four columns on the verso (pen and brown ink)

But for a few differences in detail, Botticelli here carries on from the previous drawing, though he now depicts the entire figure of Lucifer. The spreading of the illustration – entirely unique in the series – on to two sheets of vellum, stuck together, enables the artist not just to show the path that Dante and Virgil traverse, but also to represent this moment in the narrative as a turning point and as a transition. It is a turning point in a physical sense, too, a turning from the *vita bestiale* (the bestial life) to the *vita humana* (human life), as described in Landino's commentary (see Dombrowski 1996, p. 61). Having arrived at Lucifer, Virgil urges Dante to hurry, upon which Dante wraps his arms around the shoulders of his guide. The two poets swing down in this fashion from tuft to tuft on Lucifer's ice-encrusted pelt until they reach the middle, the spot where the thigh merges into the swelling of the haunch. There, Virgil turns around and climbs back up in the opposite direction. From this perspective Dante sees Lucifer's feet and body, which to him now appears to be hanging upside down. For us viewers, Botticelli's drawing would now need to be rotated 180° in order to experience this altered perspective. Eventually, Dante and Virgil creep through a round opening in the rock and climb up out of Hell in this way, to see the stars once more. On the lower margin, we can already make out the belt of reeds which surrounds the island of Purgatory, on which the two travellers will continue their journey. This illustration was obviously not originally intended to occupy a double sheet, because Botticelli had used a vellum that was actually intended for Canto XXXI of *Paradiso*, as we can deduce from the largely erased inscription with the opening words and the number of this canto between Lucifer's feet. This allows us to make inferences about Botticelli's procedure in the illustration of the entire *Commedia*, and to speculate that he did not just draw one canto after the other, but in the course of his critical confrontation with the content also returned to sheets that had already been drawn in order to continue working on them.

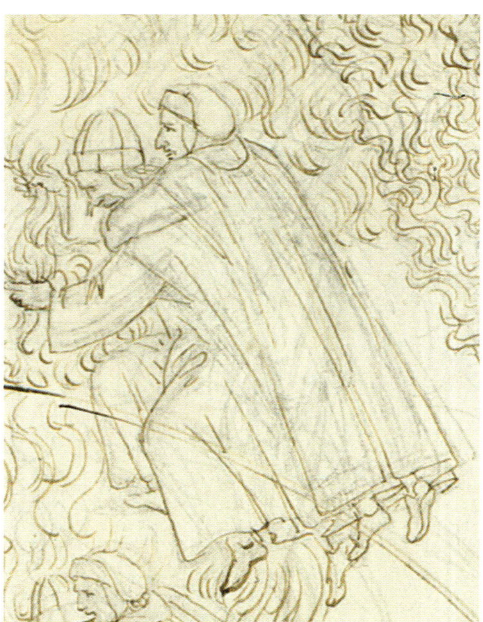

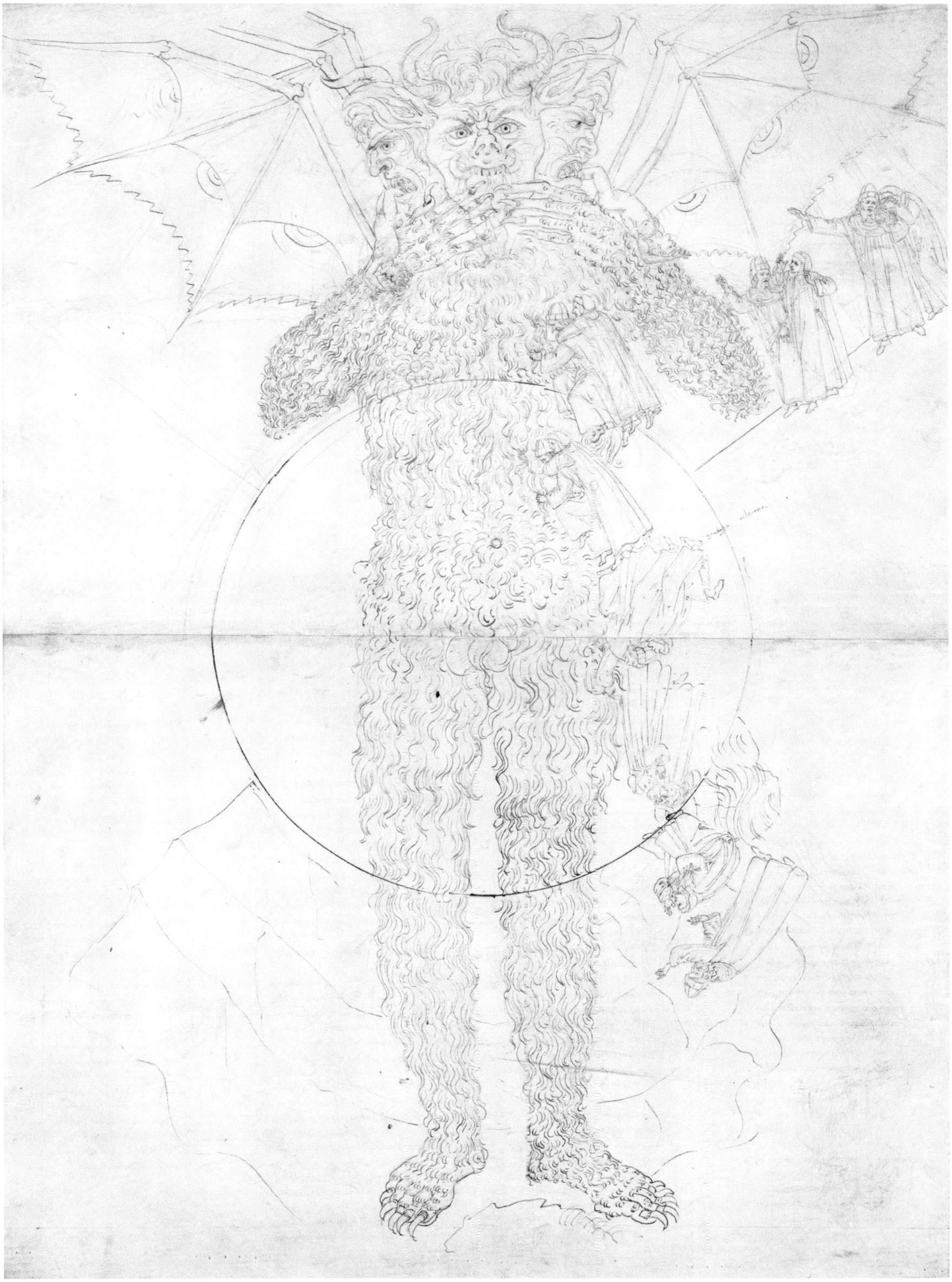

26

Purgatorio I

The island plain: mount of Purgatory; encounter with Cato of Utica

Pen and brown ink over metalpoint on vellum, 32.4 × 47.6 cm; the verso is ruled, but remained without text

SELECT BIBLIOGRAPHY Morrison 2012, p. 78

Not exhibited in London

Dante and Virgil have left Hell behind them and have now arrived in Purgatory. In the centre of the illustration, they step out from a cleft in the rock into the clear morning air and on to the foot of the mountain. They meet the bearded old man Cato of Utica, whose appearance makes a strong impression on Dante. Botticelli renders this effect by depicting him somewhat larger than the two poets. Cato, once a Roman senator and opponent of Caesar, here embodies moral integrity and freedom of conscience, and presents himself to them as the custodian of Purgatory. At Virgil's behest, Dante kneels before him. Since Dante's journey is occurring on behalf of a lady of Heaven, Beatrice, Cato permits them to continue. He instructs Virgil to prepare his charge accordingly. In the foreground we see how he takes morning dew from the grass in order to clean Dante's face of the grime of Hell, and how he girds him with rushes from the ocean shore as a symbol of humility. The intoning souls depicted on the left disembarking on to the island are a kind of preview, as the two travellers will not be able to observe them until Canto II. In addition to the depiction of the arrival of Dante and Virgil in the second realm of the hereafter, in this drawing Botticelli offers us a highly detailed schematic diagram of Purgatory. Here, souls are cleansed by doing penitence while they ascend higher and higher, in order ultimately to be worthy of obtaining entrance and eternal residence in Paradise. The mount of Purgatory is located in the southern hemisphere, set on an island in an ocean. It is subdivided into a base section, a middle section, in which the heart-shaped Valley of the Rulers is clearly recognisable, and Purgatory proper, which is accessed through a gate. Seven ring-shaped terraces lead up toward the summit, a plateau on which the shining Divine Forest of Earthly Paradise is located. The circular motif, with which we are already familiar from the composition of Hell, is here inverted into its positive form – a cone-shaped mountain instead of a funnel-shaped pit.

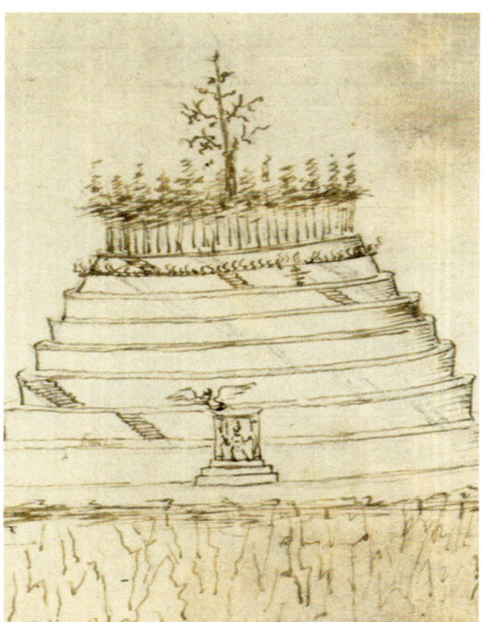

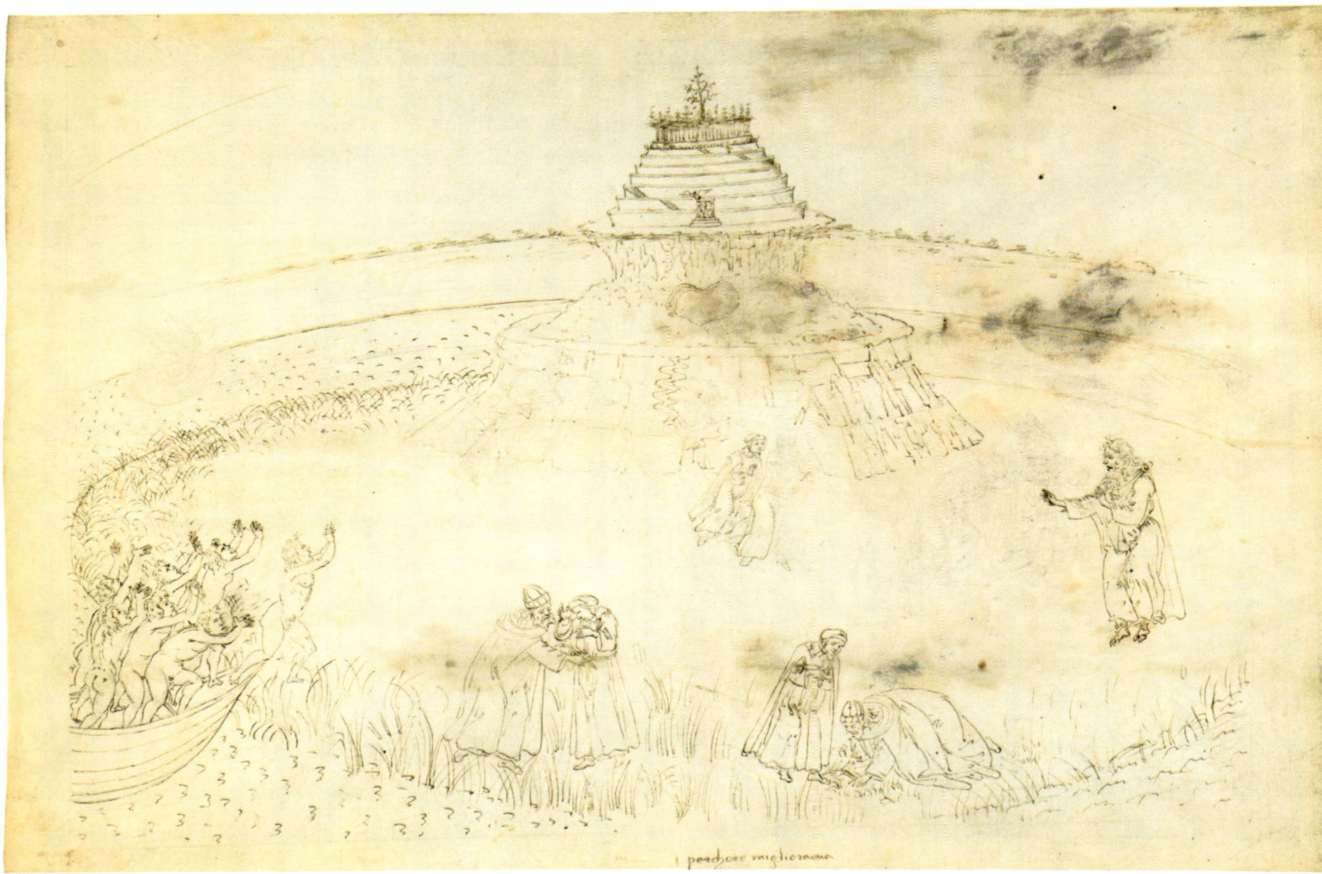

27

Purgatorio III

The island plain: penance of excommunicates; conversation with Manfred of Sicily

Pen and brown ink over metalpoint on vellum, 32.4 × 47.7 cm; text of *Purgatorio* II in four columns on the verso (pen and brown ink)

An angel has brought happy souls on to the island and sets back out to sea in his boat. Dante and Virgil leave the group of new arrivals and turn towards the mount of Purgatory. On the far left, the sun hangs like a ball over the curved horizon. For the first time in their journey, it shines directly on the travellers, and this is the only time that Botticelli depicts it. The sun plays a central role here, because it reveals that in this realm only living humans cast a shadow. Because Dante sees his own shadow but not that of his companion, he believes he has been abandoned. Terrified, he turns around to Virgil, who chides him for his mistrust, a sin, and for his failure of faith, given his limited human capacity to grasp the wonders of divine Providence. Seeking out a place where they can risk climbing on to the steep rocky slope, they encounter the souls of those who have died excommunicate. These souls cluster towards the rock face on the right like a herd of sheep. From amongst them, a particularly noble-looking soul parts from the group and reveals himself to be King Manfred of Sicily. He instructs Dante to ask his daughter Constance to pray for him, and thus to shorten his waiting time at the foot of the mountain. What is conspicuous in this drawing is the use of a lighter and a darker ink. This probably has to do in part with the working process, in which the artist first laid out forms with a lighter ink, in order then to render them more precisely with a darker ink in a second stage. What is remarkable, however, is that the parts that are left lighter also bring out the spots lit up by the sunshine. Perhaps this differentiation served as an indicator for a later colouring, beneath which it would have then disappeared. Body colour would have probably conveyed Dante's descriptions of the reddish glows of the morning sun, but above all the hard shadow that Dante casts, which is lacking here.

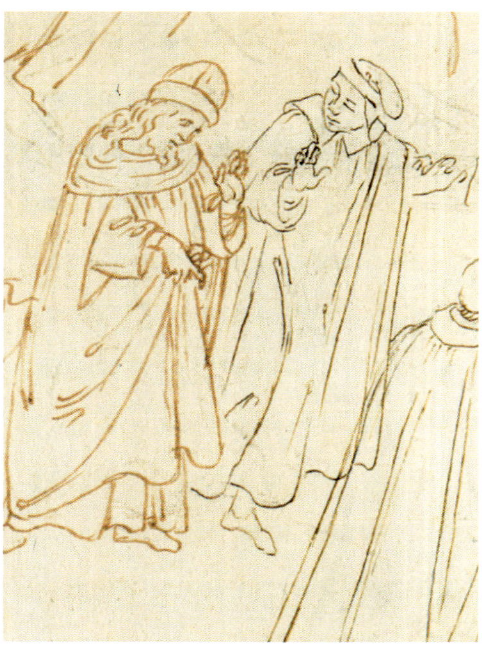

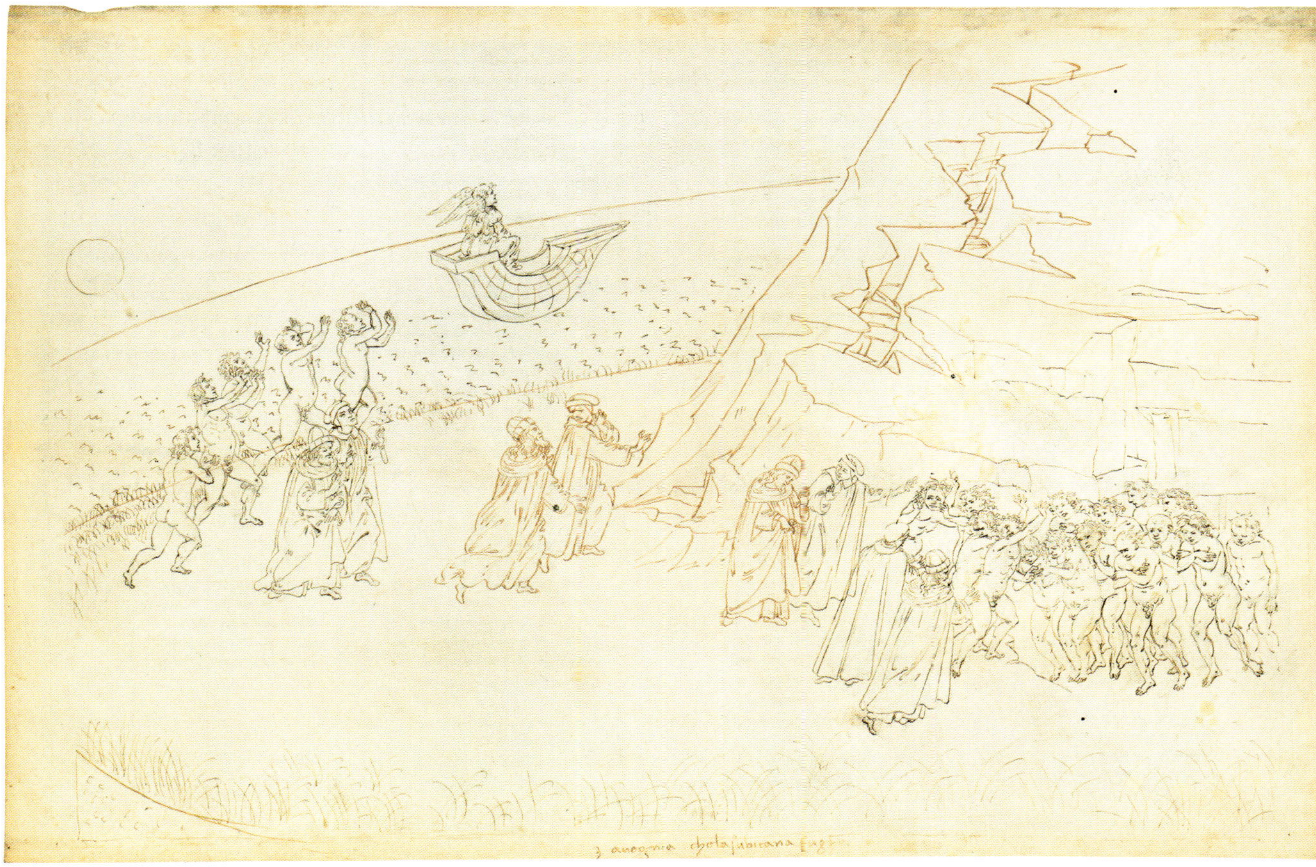

28

Purgatorio V

Ante-purgatory (middle section): late repentants who met their end in violence

Pen and brown ink over metalpoint on vellum, 32.4 × 47.4 cm; text of *Purgatorio* IV in four columns on the verso (pen and brown ink)

SELECT BIBLIOGRAPHY Papillo 2007 a, pp. 96–104

The intersecting diagonals of this composition present a particular attraction for the eye of the viewer. While Dante and Virgil wander diagonally from the bottom left to the top right, on both sides of their path groups of souls are distributed amongst niches in the rocks, where they await the beginning of the process of their penance. They attempt to hold up the progress of the travellers as they hurry past. They do this in the bottom left by crying out to them, upon which Virgil admonishes Dante not to allow himself to be distracted, and to resist such disruptions as steadfastly as a tower – a metaphor which Botticelli reflects in his illustration by lending Dante's robe a stark solidity, with heavily falling folds in the fabric. Somewhat further up, in the centre of the scene, two scouts head towards the travellers: they have been sent forth from a larger group of penitents to enquire whether it really is a living person who strolls in this realm, which is exclusively populated by souls. They return to their cohort, and upon hearing that Dante is indeed a man of flesh and blood, who upon his return to the land of the living could make intercessions for them and so shorten the duration of their atonement, the souls lose all timidity and flock towards him. They tell, individually and in great detail, of their respective origins and fates, and beg the poet to make these known in the world of the living, that people might pray for them. They all died a violent death, but, shortly beforehand, were able to beg forgiveness for their sins and thus, at the last moment, their souls were able to find peace. In contrast to the isolated lingering in the eternal agony of Hell, in Purgatory the souls form groups and communities, a social behaviour that foreshadows the completion of their humanity that will occur through their penitence (see Dombrowski 1996, pp. 61–62). Here as well, the features of the individuals are laid out in markedly more portrait-like fashion than in the first, dark realm of the afterlife, another indication of their proximity to humanity, and evidence of the artist's outstanding ability to bring the complexity of Dante's text to life in drawings.

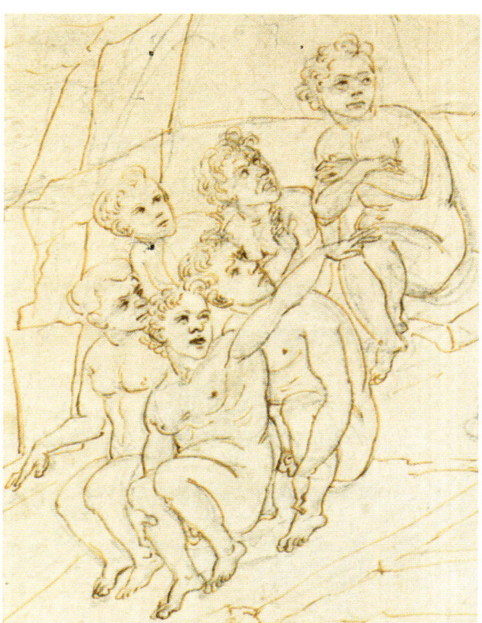

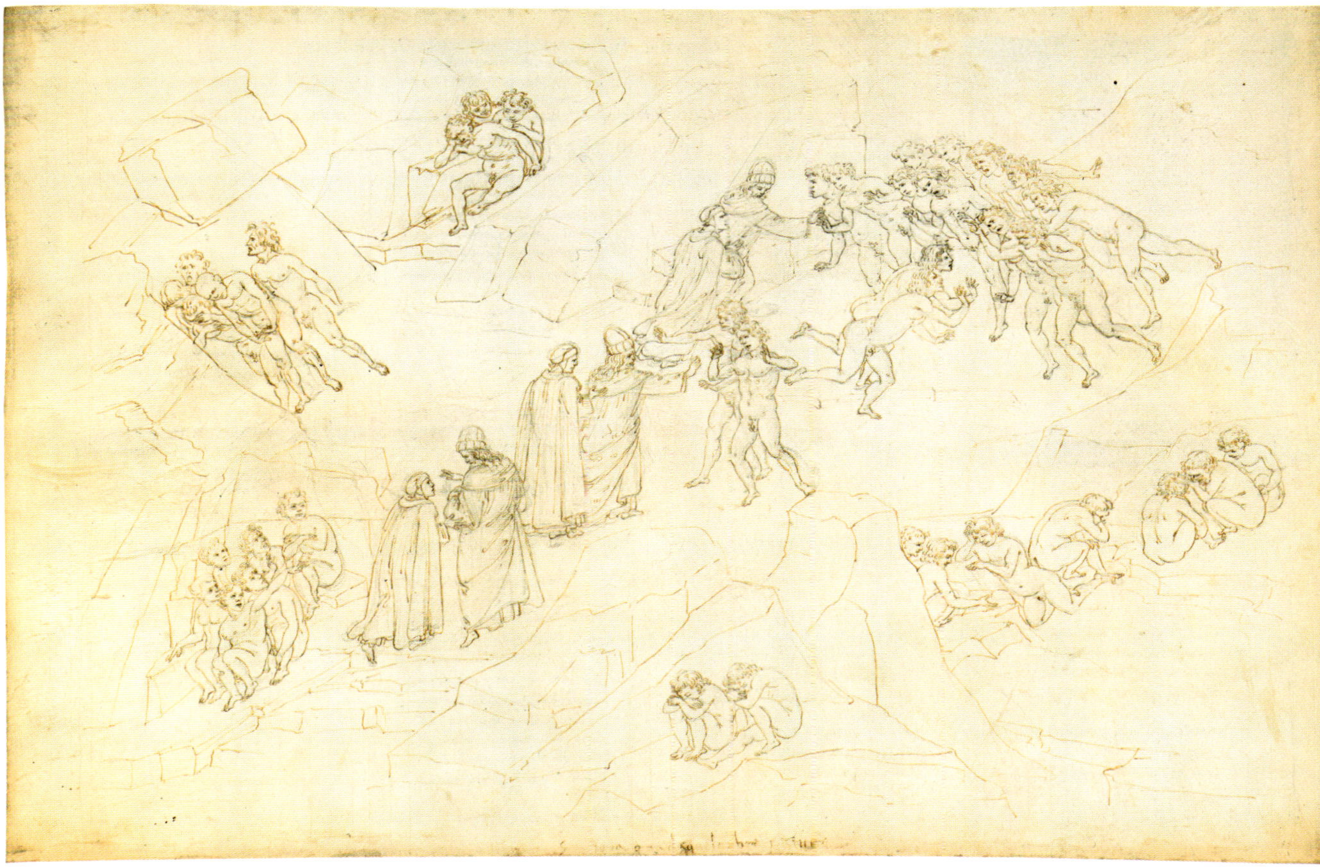

29

Purgatorio VII

Ante-Purgatory (middle section): valley of the negligent rulers

Pen and brown ink over metalpoint on vellum, 32.5 × 47.6 cm; text of *Purgatorio* VI in four columns on the verso (pen and brown ink)

The scene begins in the bottom left corner with the joyous meeting of three poets. The troubadour Sordello recognises with amazement and awe his Mantuan countryman, the great classical poet Virgil, and embraces him on his knees, as befits Sordello's lower status. Since evening is approaching, and it seems inadvisable for the travellers to carry on, Sordello offers to lead his two colleagues a little further, until a view on to a swale opens up. We recognise once more the winding path that they trace as the heart-shaped edge of the Valley of the Rulers from the schematic diagram that accompanied the first canto of *Purgatory*. From their elevated standpoint, Dante and Virgil, guided by Sordello, gain a sound overview of this location, as do we, the viewers, who occupy an equally elevated position in relation to them. We can make out some of the rulers sitting here, a number of whom are only rendered in metalpoint, perhaps because Botticelli was uncertain about their exact spatial arrangement. Because they have not attended to their salvation during their lives, they must wait here until they are able to begin their ultimate passage of atonement and ascent. In the front, Rudolf of Habsburg is sitting on a raised patch of ground in a pensive posture, with a crown on his head. With him stands his erstwhile opponent, Ottokar II, King of Bohemia, offering him words of consolation. Reclining behind them, his head on his hand, and in this posture reminiscent of representations of the sleeping Adam, is Henry of Navarre. Propped up behind him are Philip the Bold and, somewhat set apart, Henry II of England. The Valley of the Rulers is a veritable *locus amoenus*, an almost paradisiacal place, in which flowers blaze in the most beautiful colours and sweet scents stream, and, in the evening, the souls sing the *Salve Regina,* a Marian hymn. While aromas and melodies cannot be depicted in the picture, a later colouring would presumably have reproduced the abundance of colours, particularly as Dante described them in the *Commedia* in an extremely pictorial fashion, with similes from the material world of the workshops of painters, goldsmiths and sculptors.

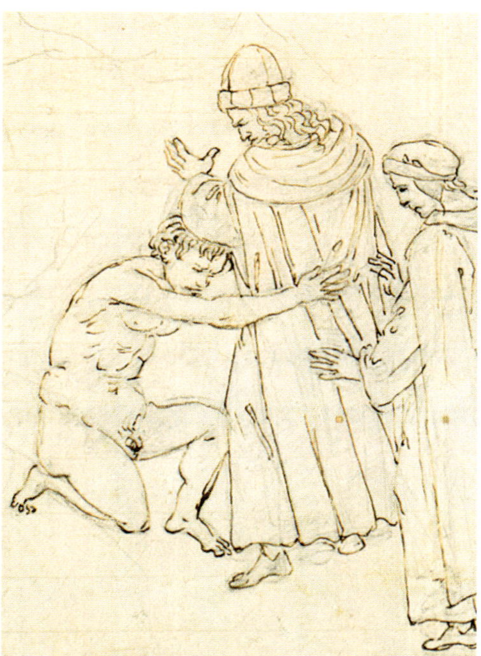

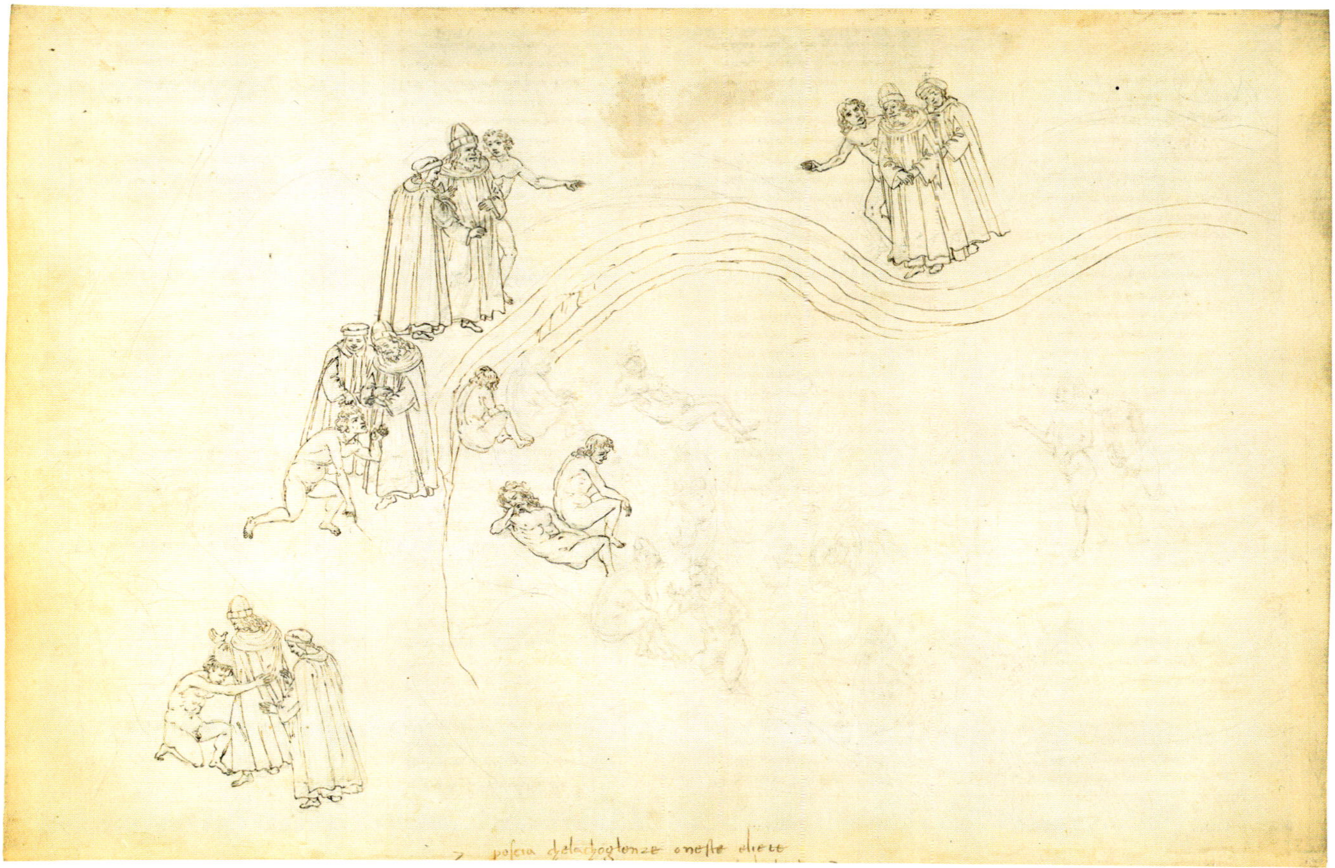

30

Purgatorio X

First terrace of Purgatory: the marble reliefs; penance of the proud

Pen and brown ink over metalpoint on vellum, 32.4 × 47.5 cm; text of *Purgatorio* IX in four columns on the verso (pen and brown ink)

SELECT BIBLIOGRAPHY Baskins 1993, p. 117; Rehm 2007, pp. 309–17; Rubin 2007, pp. 144–46, 340–41; Morrison 2012, p. 80; Meier 2013, pp. 19–20

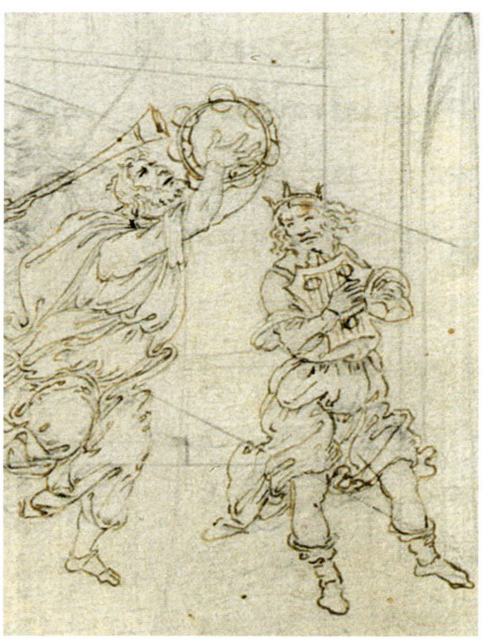

Without a doubt, Canto X of *Purgatorio* must be considered one of the most important for Botticelli's engagement with the *Commedia.* Its theme, the fine arts, their illusory force and the limits of these, are central for the artist and his entire artistic practice. This theme is developed here in the snow-white marble reliefs that are carved directly into the rockface in the first ring-shaped terrace of the mount of Purgatory, which Dante and Virgil reach here through a narrow crack in the rock. In the *Commedia,* Dante appears to be particularly impressed by the vividness of the depictions, which managed to bring the past to life and make it appear contemporary and real. From the left, Virgil and Dante inspect God's artworks, which are to serve the penitents as examples, and which all depict images of modesty and humility, as in a museum. Common to all of them is a kind of threshold which separates the space of the image from the viewing space of the travellers. On the far left, the Annunciation is depicted, in the centre, David's dance before the Ark. In both cases, an architectural perspective is only faintly sketched out, against which the central image stands out. The many-figured image on the far right, which depicts the Justice of Trajan, is fitted with an illusionistic frame, a veritable image within an image. In front of this, the first penitents, the proud, come crawling along on all fours with stones on their backs. The relief character of the works here tends to recede into the background, while a wealth of detail unfurls which would have been overshadowed by the colouring. The virtuoso graphic realisation of the works, described by Dante and created by God, the great artist, broadens the horizon of the concept of *disegno,* which was so central to the art theory of the Italian Renaissance. This term referred not only to the rendering of a figure or scene through drawing, but also to the internal image, the underlying idea. As such, *disegno* is closely tied to the invention of the image (*invenzione*). This raises the question of whether the 'divine' art form might ultimately be neither relief sculpture nor painting but the art of drawing.

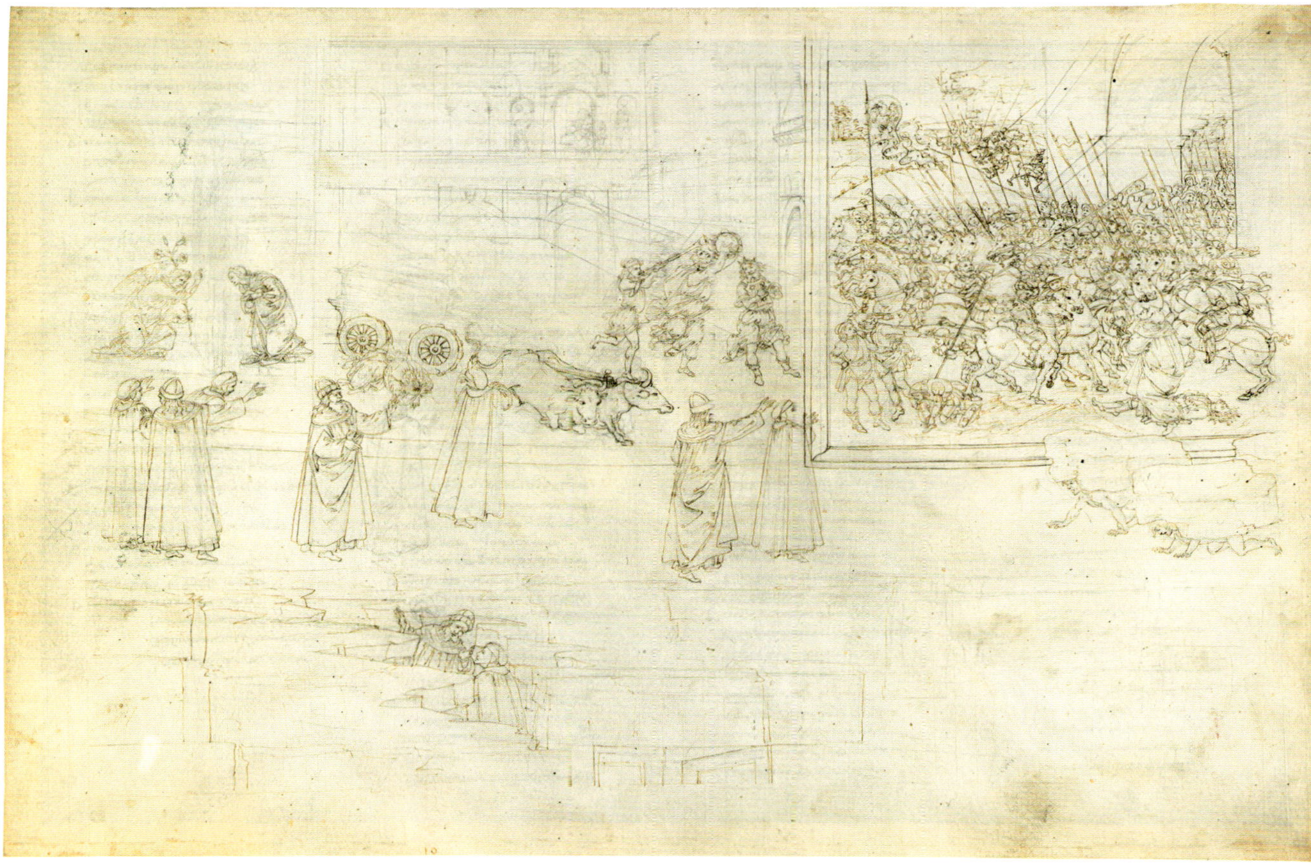

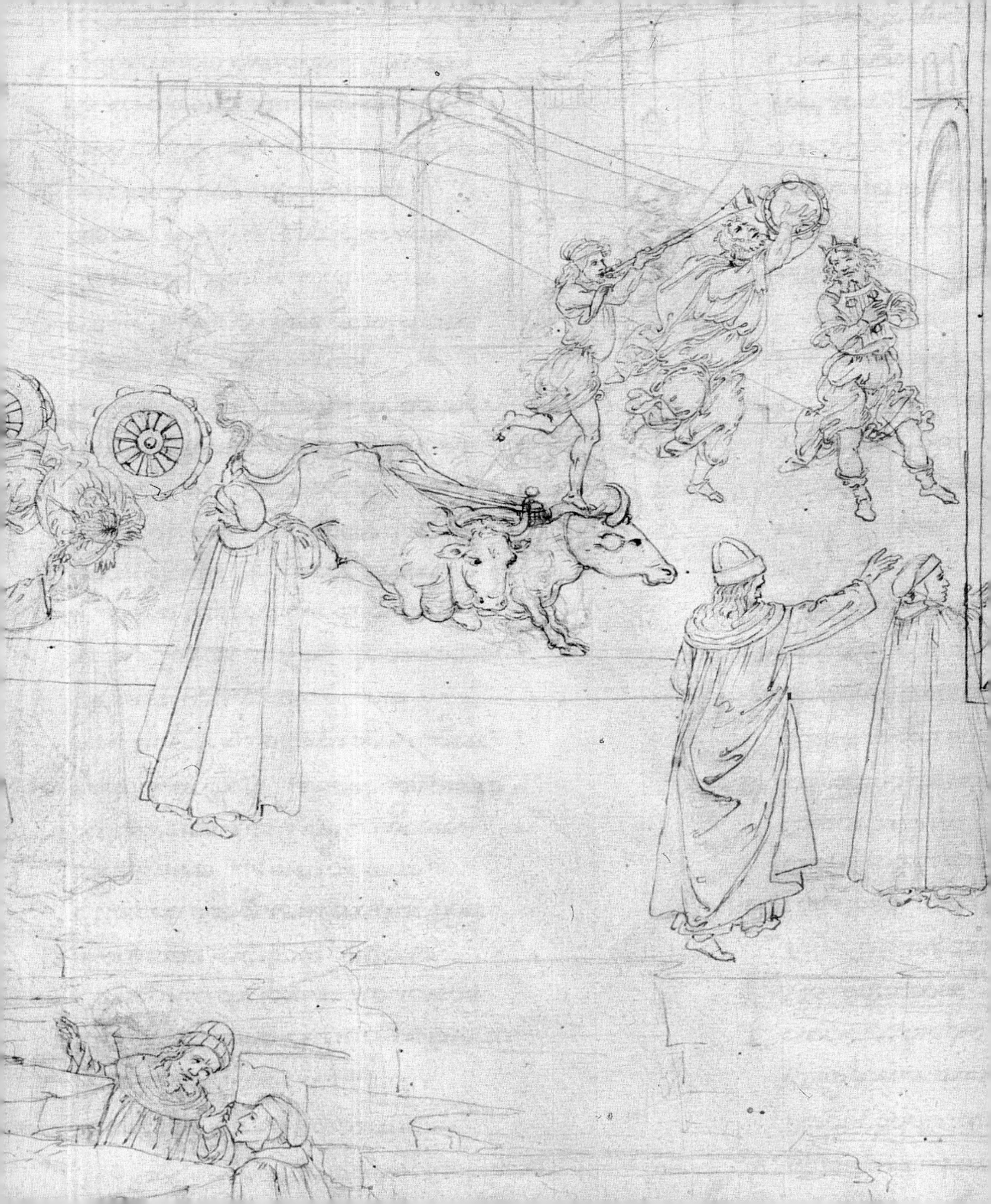

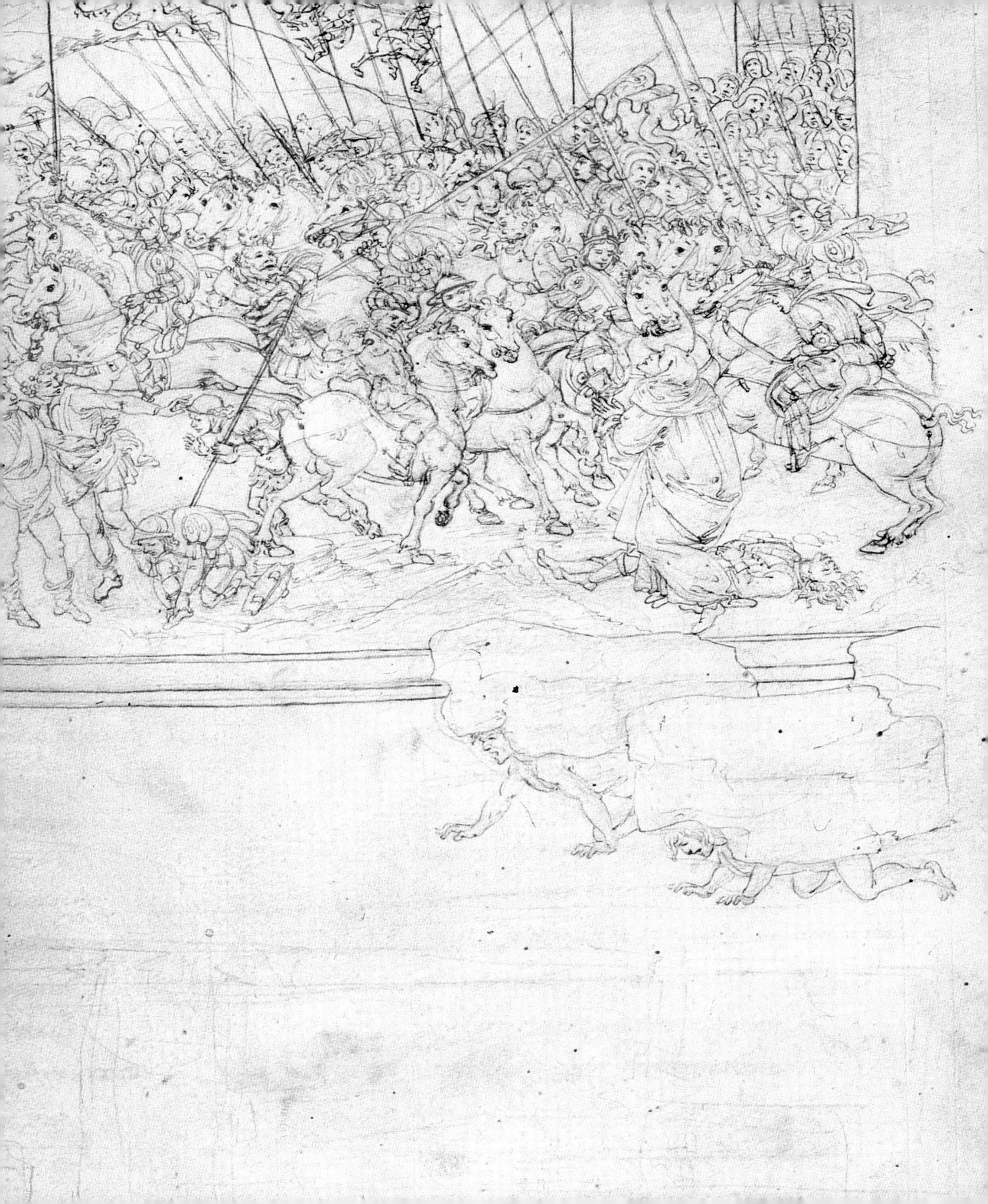

31
Purgatorio XI

First terrace of Purgatory: penance of glory-seeking knights and artists

Pen and brown ink over metalpoint on vellum, 32.5 × 47.7 cm; text of *Purgatorio* X in four columns on the verso (pen and brown ink)

Dante and Virgil continue on along the terrace that forms the first ring of Purgatory on the side of the mountain. Compared with the previous illustration, they have changed their direction here, and in accordance with the *Commedia,* which states that the cliff face is located to their right, they are no longer walking to the right, but to the left. The focus of this illustration lies entirely on the proud souls, which are being purified by remaining in a posture which is opposed to that of their sins. They must walk forward bowed in humility or even on all fours, because a weighty stone on their back does not allow them to stand proudly as they once did or raise their heads. This canto appears to have made a particular impression on Botticelli, too – not just because, like the preceding canto, it concerns the general nature of an artist's work, but because, more importantly, it concerns book illumination and thus addresses the specific activity of the engagement with a literary work. Here, Dante meets the once famous book illuminator Oderisi da Gubbio, whose own guild believed him to be the best of all time. However, his fame was soon outshone by a successor, just as Cimabue, as Dante says elsewhere in this canto, was overshadowed by Giotto. Botticelli may have taken these words of admonition so deeply to heart that he gave the penitents, once proud artists and illuminators, his own visage, in the humble awareness of the impermanence of his own fame (see Berlin/Rome/London 2000–01, p. 160). The face of the central penitent, turned toward the viewer, is reminiscent of Botticelli's self-portrait from the painting *The Adoration of the Magi* (fig. 22). On this drawing, he has rendered only a relatively narrow strip in pen and ink towards the bottom of the sheet in which the events are played out. This underscores Dante's reflex to bow to the penitents and to continue for a while with them in this position, until Virgil exhorts him to stand up straight again in order to travel on.

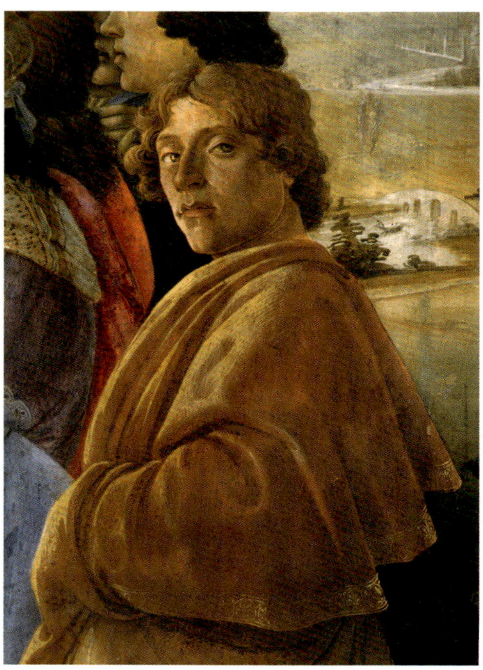

FIG. 22
Sandro Botticelli, *The Adoration of the Magi* (detail), c. 1475, tempera on panel, 111 × 134 cm, Florence, Galleria degli Uffizi

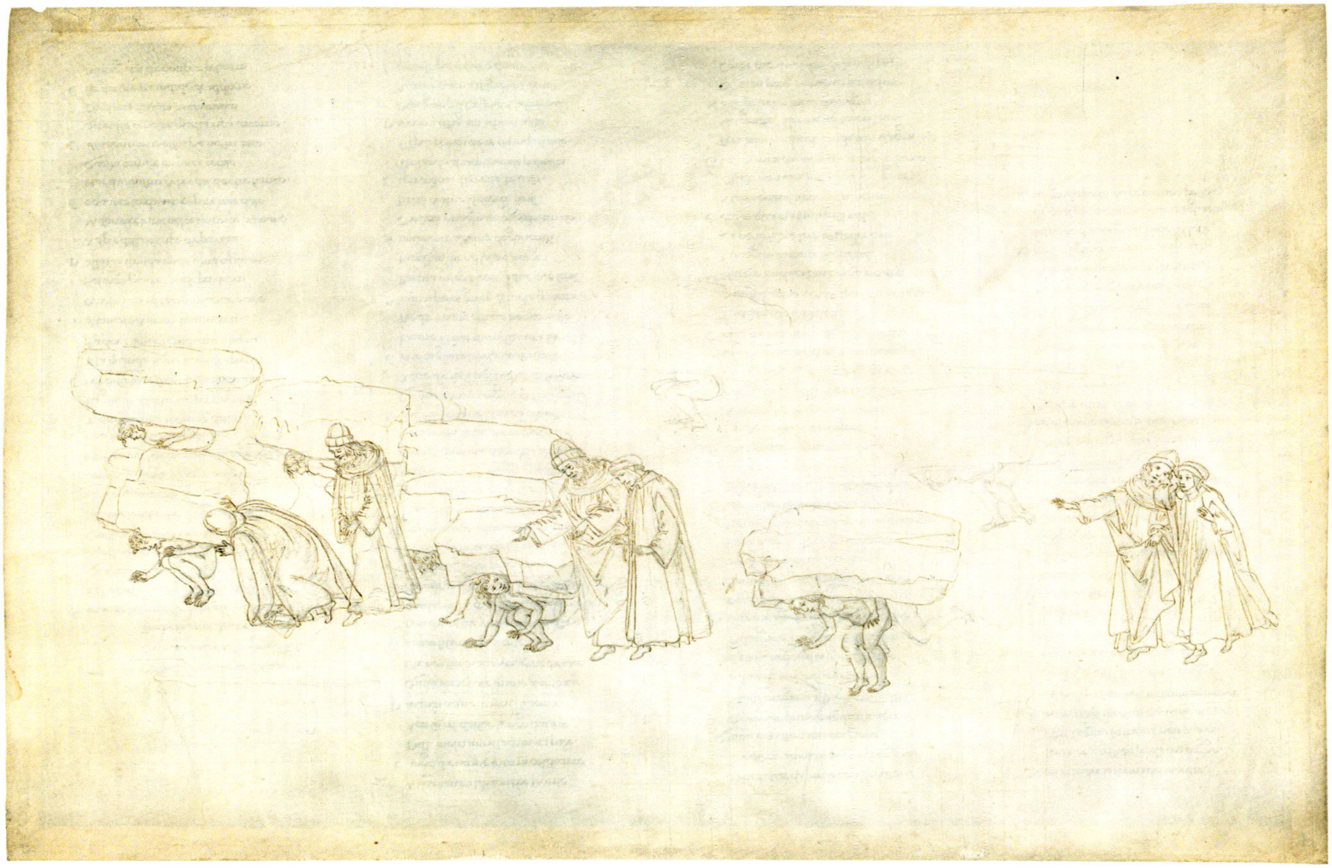

32

Purgatorio XII

First terrace of Purgatory: images of pride punished; the angel before the steps to the second terrace

Pen and brown ink over metalpoint on vellum, 32.6 × 47.6 cm; text of *Purgatorio* XI in four columns on the verso (pen and brown ink)

SELECT BIBLIOGRAPHY Papillo 2007 a, p. 104; Meier 2013, p. 21

In Canto XII, the two poets once again encounter works of art which are intended to serve as examples for penitents. In contrast to the images of Canto X, they are not designed to incite emulation, but rather to act as deterrents. Their subject is the great fall which follows pride. We recognise, for instance, the fall of Lucifer, who takes the form here of an almost doll-like version of the terrifying figure depicted on the monumental double sheet at the end of *Inferno* (cat. no. 25). Images follow of the fates of other proud figures who have fallen – the dismembered bodies of slain giants encircled by their conquerors, Nimrod at the base of the tower of Babel, the suicide of Saul, Niobe surrounded by her slain children, and the destruction of Troy; and on the other side, closer to the cliff face, the flight of the Assyrians after Judith's beheading of Holofernes and the dead giant Briareus. In parts, these depictions are only laid out very delicately in metalpoint, but all together they are, as images within the image, reproduced on a considerably smaller scale. Unlike the drawing of Canto X, here they are part of the space which the two viewers inhabit, giving the impression that Dante and Virgil were wandering through a miniature wonderland comprised of tiny architectural models populated by figurines. The realism of the images that is praised by Dante is embodied here particularly impressively. The power of art to evoke an illusion of reality has always fascinated artists, and was also a theme for Botticelli. Though the two travellers, coming from the right, pause near the image of the fallen Lucifer, they hurry between the other examples to the left, where an angel approaches them. The angel spreads its arms and wings and leads them to a stairwell, and there embraces Dante's head with its wings. In stepping on to the stairs, Dante feels how moving forward has grown easier. Still on the steps, he runs his fingers across his brow. One of the signs of the Seven Sins, which were marked on him upon entering Purgatory (Canto IX), that of pride, has been effaced.

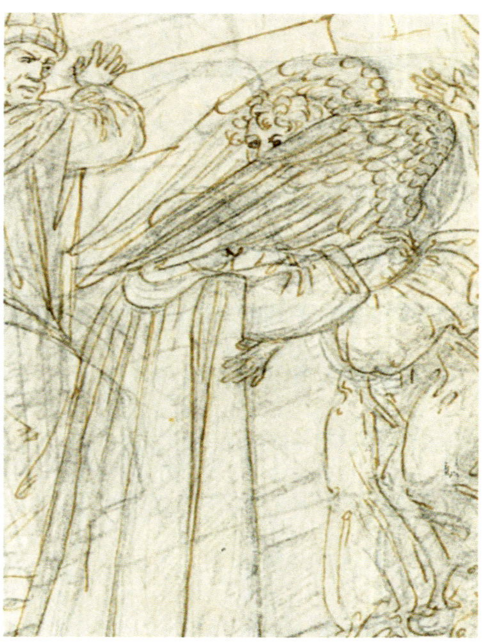

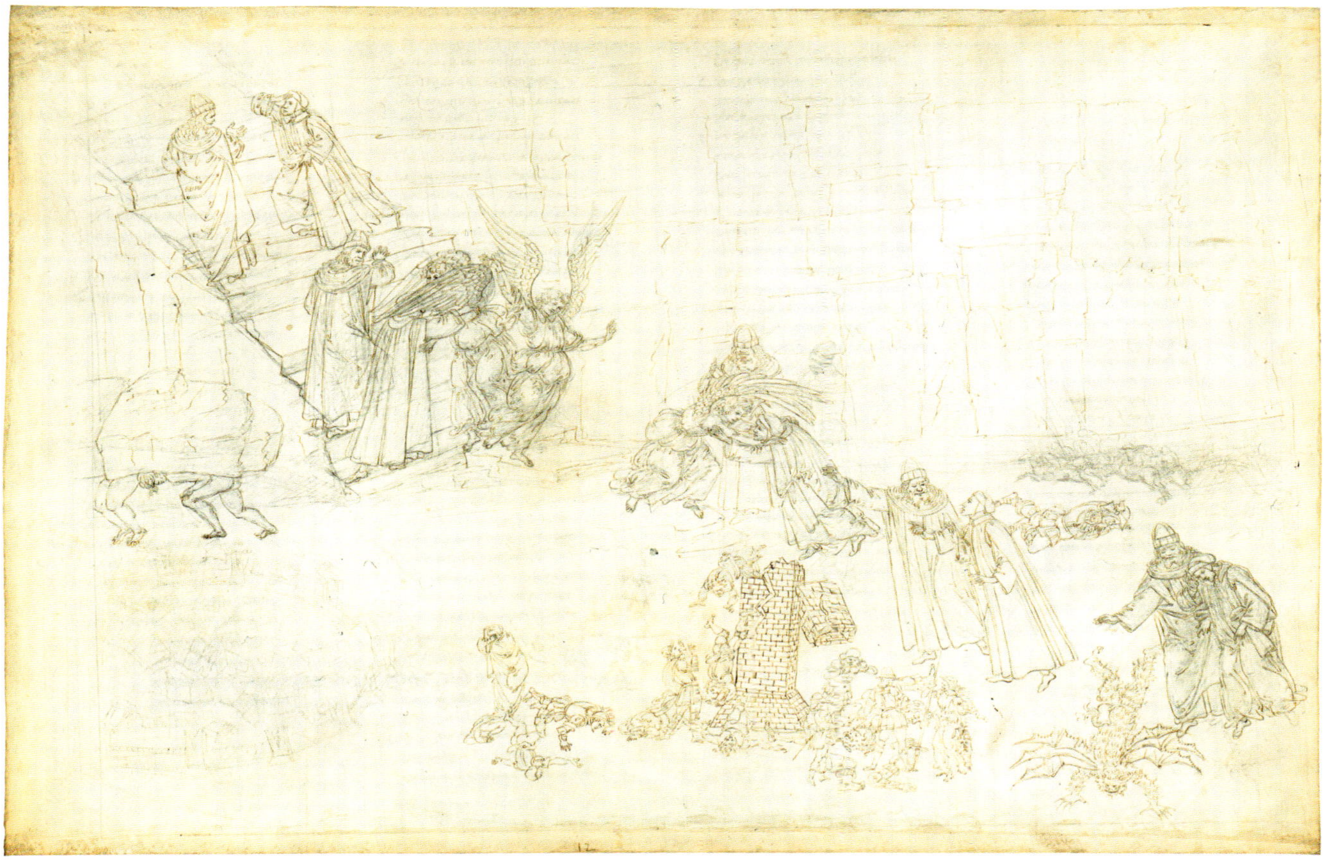

33

Purgatorio XV

Ascent to the third terrace of Purgatory: the angel before the steps, Dante's visions of meekness

Pen and brown ink over metalpoint on vellum, 32.0 × 47.2 cm; text of *Purgatorio* X in four columns on the verso (pen and brown ink)

Dante and Virgil find themselves on the second terrace of Purgatory, where souls atone for their erstwhile envy and malice. During their lifetimes, they had been blind with envy, and for this reason everything is colourless here; the robes that cover their naked bodies match the colour of the rock face against which they cower motionlessly. They lean on each other like blind people, their eyelids sewn together with wire. Dante and Virgil have already traversed the better part of this section, and from the right are now approaching the spot from which they can ascend to the next terrace via a staircase. Here, suddenly, the late afternoon sun shines in Dante's face. The natural sunlight is amplified by an intensive, heavenly lustre. Dante is startled by the blinding glare and shades his eyes with his right hand: this is precisely how it is described in the text, and it is faithfully visualised by Botticelli. Dante also raises his left hand in order to shield his face from the blazing light. The light is emanating from the angel that is inviting them to continue their ascent. Virgil has explained to his charge the difference between earthly and heavenly goods, heavenly goods being infinite, thus making envy utterly irrelevant. Upon hearing this, Dante sees images of meekness before his inner eye. His legs begin to wobble. Botticelli represents him prostrate on the ground, which may reflect further discussion with Virgil about eyes that become blind when the body without a soul lies on the ground. This canto posed a particular challenge for Botticelli, for, despite the central theme of sight and blindness, it consists primarily of Dante's abstract thoughts and inner visions. The artist shows primarily the spatial progression of the two poets, and in the process, through lively gestures, lends expression to Dante's inner sense of commotion. The difficulties that Botticelli had with the composition of this sheet can be seen in the top left corner, in an abandoned underdrawing of Dante and Virgil, depicted encountering cowering souls. This leads to the assumption that he completely reconceived the arrangement of the scene at a second stage, and placed it somewhat lower on the sheet.

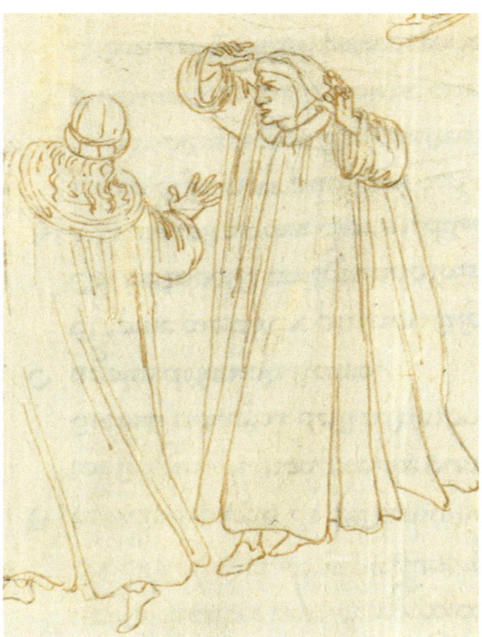

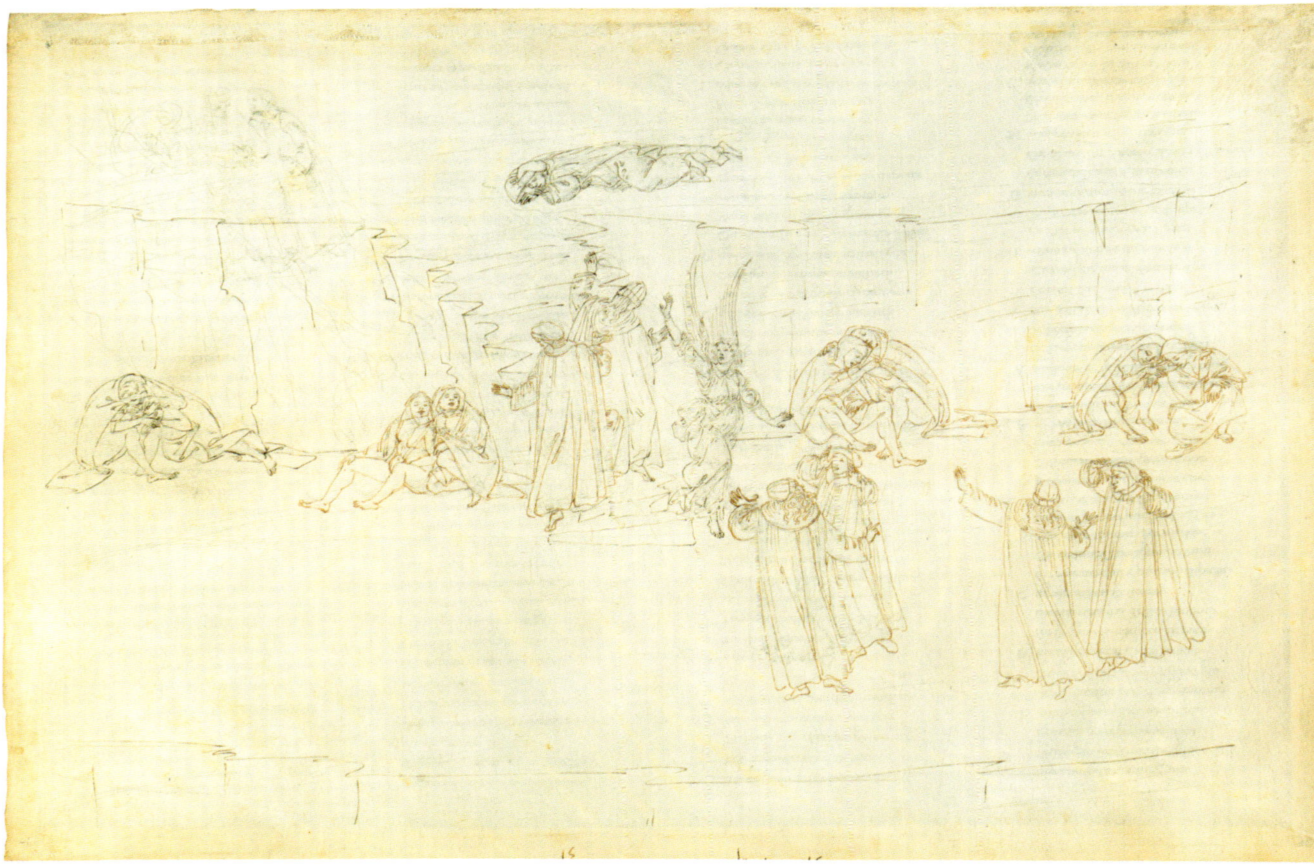

34

Purgatorio XVIII

Fourth terrace of Purgatory: Virgil expounds the principle of love and the role of free will; penance of the slothful

Pen and brown ink over metalpoint on vellum, 32.3 × 47.5 cm; text of *Purgatorio* XVII in four columns on the verso (pen and brown ink)

Not exhibited in Berlin

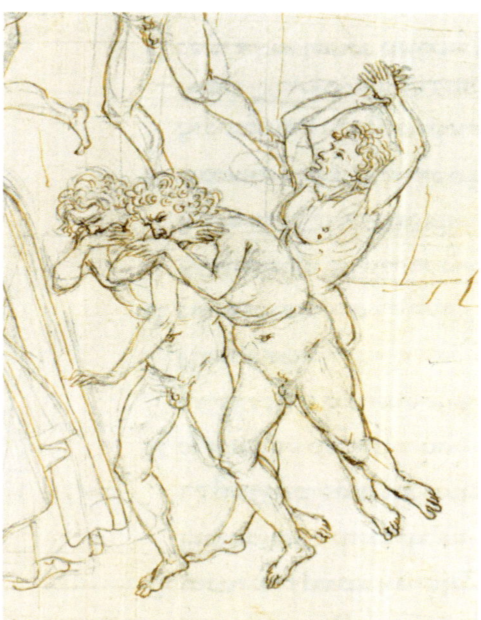

As in the text of Canto XVIII of *Purgatorio*, which it accompanies, this is a sheet of two very different parts – a scene of concentrated dialogue, and two figures in an almost ecstatically charged mêlée. To begin with, depicted here on the far right, somewhat isolated, we see Virgil, who at Dante's request continues with his explanation of the principle of love that he had begun in the preceding canto, which, as he explains, can motivate both good and bad deeds. Dante is portrayed in profile, full of the thirst for knowledge, stepping towards his guide and directing on him "the sharp eye of [his] intellect" (v. 16). Virgil responds to Dante's probing address – indicated by his raised hand – with a gesture; however, in doing so, Virgil does not look at his charge, but at the viewer, as if to incorporate us into his homily as well. As they continue towards the left, the calm and concentrated mood which characterises this theoretical episode is abruptly disrupted from behind by a group of penitent souls rushing toward them. They are the souls of the slothful and the negligent. Their penitence – in perfect accordance with the Dantean principle of *contrapasso* (the atonement of a sin through an activity or posture which is diametrically opposed to it) – consists in their constantly rushing around. They also cannot stop to speak with the two travellers, as is made clear at the left margin, where the scene comes to a dramatic climax, as Dante and Virgil, evidently by accident, have ended up in the path of these rushing souls, and are almost trampled by two of them. The penitents wring their hands frantically and throw their arms over their heads ecstatically; the allusion in the *Commedia* to Bacchic and bacchanalian scenes is here made visually as well. A particularly haunting detail can be seen in some of the penitents biting their own hands in order to punish themselves for their erstwhile slothfulness (v. 132).

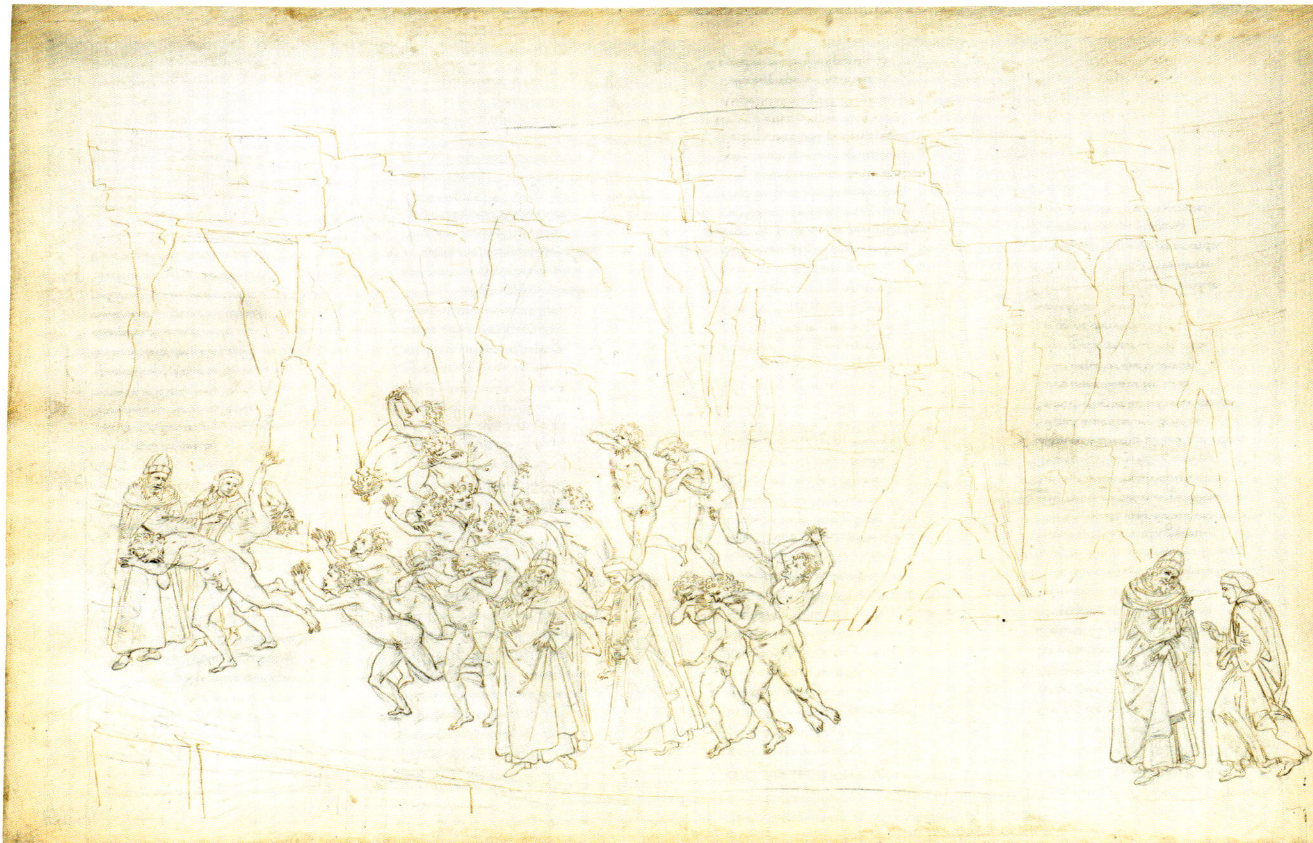

35
Purgatorio XXIII

Sixth terrace of Purgatory: penance of gluttons; encounter with Forese Donati

Pen and brown ink over metalpoint on vellum, 32.4 × 47.6 cm; text of *Purgatorio* XXII in four columns on the verso (pen and brown ink)

On the sixth terrace of the mount of Purgatory, both Dante and the viewer are captivated by a strange tree, the trunk and branches of which grow from top to bottom, entirely in opposition to the laws of nature. It hangs full of apples, and from above a clear spring flows over its foliage and licks like flames along the length of the trunk. While Dante, on the far right, pauses and marvels at this apparition, Virgil turns to him and urges him to hurry. Here, the litany of repentance, '*Labia mea Domine*' (Lord, open my lips) rings out, intoned by a host of emaciated souls, whose bodies and faces are sunken from hunger. With his pen, Botticelli strikingly outlines the contours and features of their cadaverous physiognomy, using clear and hard, at times angular lines. One of the members of the host of hollow-eyed souls addresses Dante, and it is only upon hearing his voice that Dante recognises his friend from youth, Forese Donati. Donati explains to him that the former gluttons atone for their sin by resisting the temptation of the aromatic fruit and fresh water, because during their lifetime they had indulged with excessive greed. Between the two Florentines, a longer conversation unfolds, and Dante falls somewhat behind his guide as they progress towards the left. Virgil, meanwhile, has been joined by Statius, another Roman poet. The bony, meagre souls rush around between them and the rock face of the mount of Purgatory.

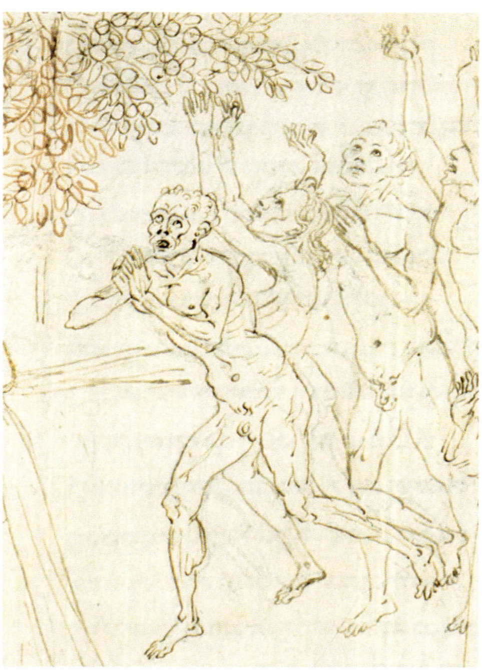

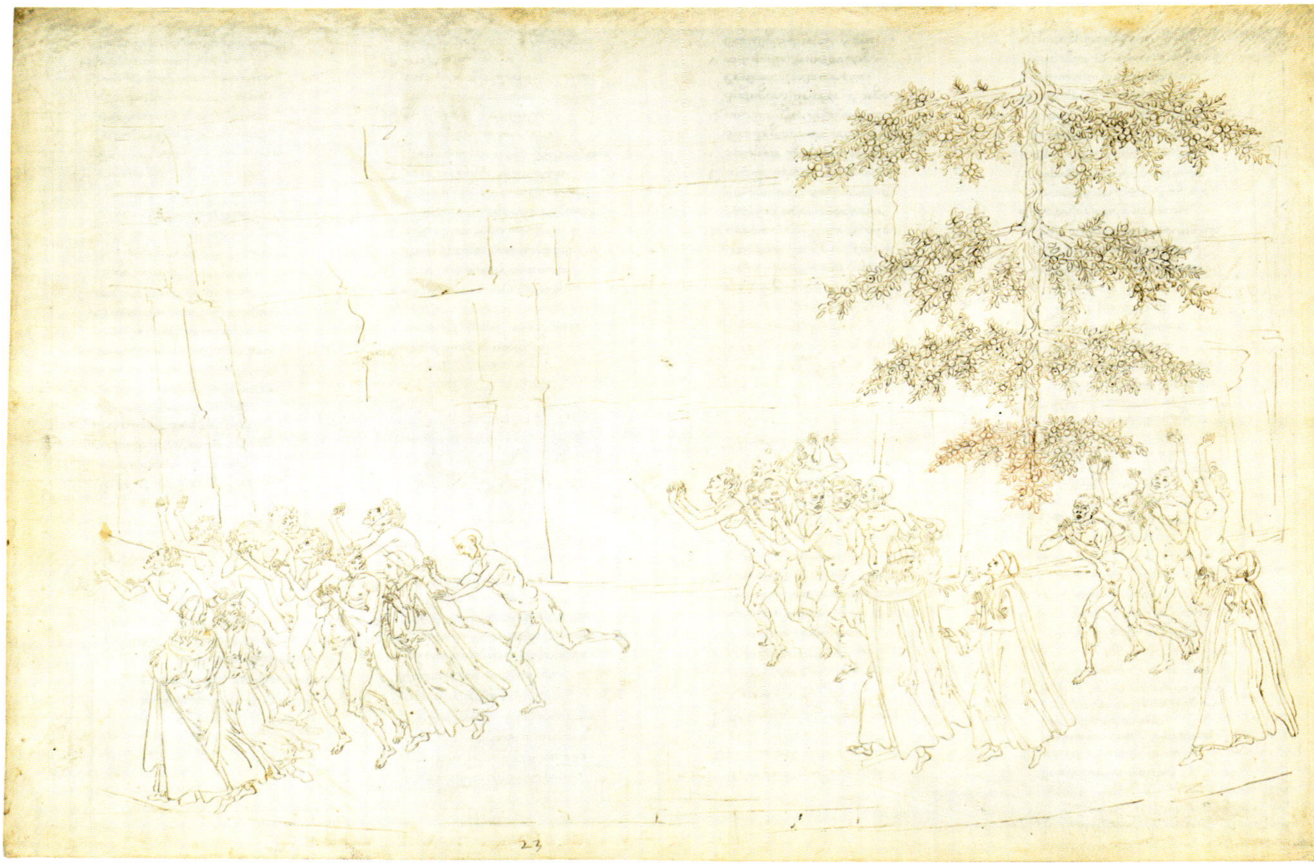

36

Purgatorio XXXII

The Earthly Paradise: the Tree of Knowledge and the fate of the Church

Pen and brown ink over metalpoint on vellum, 32.3 × 47.5 cm; text of *Purgatorio* XXXI in four columns on the verso (pen and brown ink)

SELECT BIBLIOGRAPHY Papillo 2007 b, pp. 425–28

By now, Dante has scaled the mount of Purgatory and finds himself in the Earthly Paradise. His guide up till now, the classical poet Virgil, is sent back to his proper place, the "*nobile castello*" in limbo. Since he is a heathen, his passage is refused, and the human reason that he embodies no longer holds sway. In their density, symbolic force and historical and moral allusions, the highly complex events of this canto set themselves apart from those of the others, and must have presented the artist with a special challenge. The balanced and highly detailed composition is well thought through, sketched out in metalpoint in detail and completely reworked in ink. Approaching from the left and accompanied by Statius and Matelda, the guardian of the Earthly Paradise, Dante is transfixed by the sight of Beatrice, the love of his youth who had died ten years earlier, and he loses himself in the vision of her. Beatrice is enthroned as a heavenly apparition on a chariot, which is pulled by a griffin, and accompanied by the Evangelical symbols of the Bull, Eagle, Angel and Lion (not visible here). Botticelli's illustration brings to mind depictions of secular triumph, such as the charioted Triumph of Love in illustrations for Petrarch's *Trionfi* (see cat. no. 9). On the far right, the procession surrounding Beatrice passes the Tree of Knowledge, which flourishes in contact with the griffin carriage, and symbolises the renewal of Christendom through the fruitful union of religious and secular power. While Beatrice now sits under the tree and is surrounded by allegories of virtues, Dante witnesses an eagle (the Roman Empire during the persecution of Christ) and a fox (heresy) swooping on to the car and spreading on it the feathers of the bird, out of which the heads of a beast grow. A whore is now enthroned on top (representing the Roman Curia) with her suitor (Philip the Fair of France, 1268–1314), who ultimately pulls the entire monster out of Dante's field of vision (representing the exile of the papacy in Avignon, 1309–77). The attendants of Beatrice's procession that ascend in quick succession into the heavenly spheres anticipate at this point the transition to the third realm, Paradise, which now imminently awaits Dante.

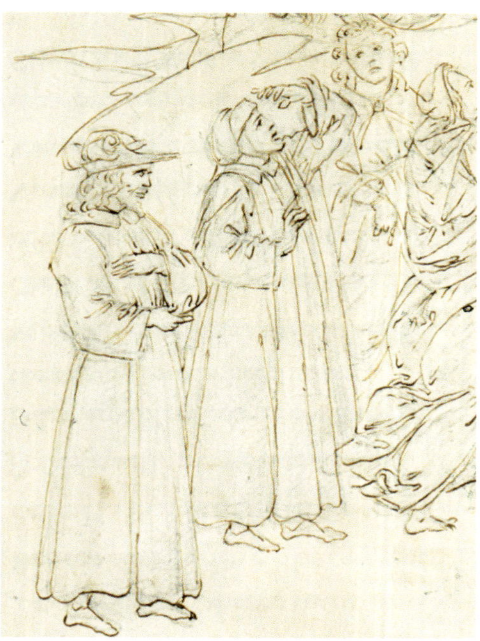

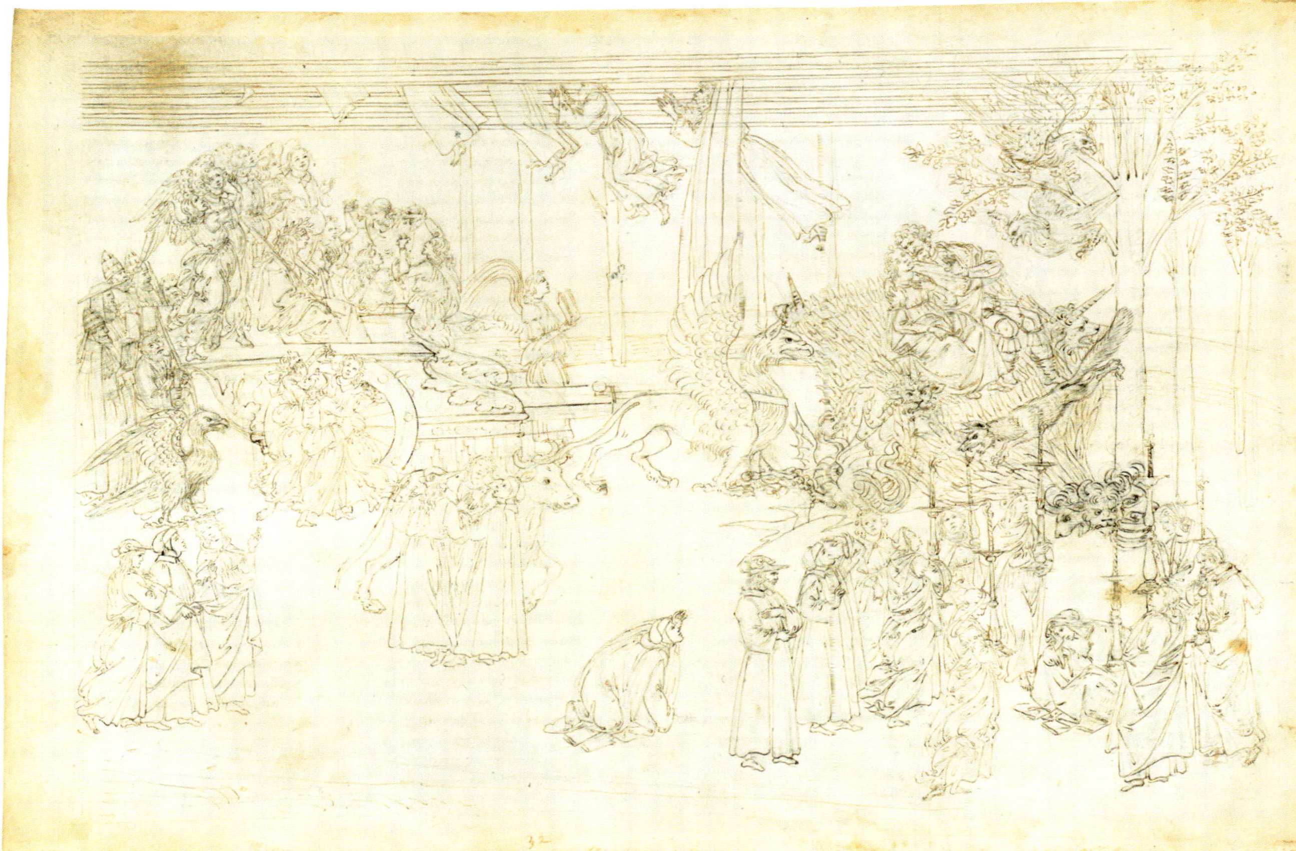

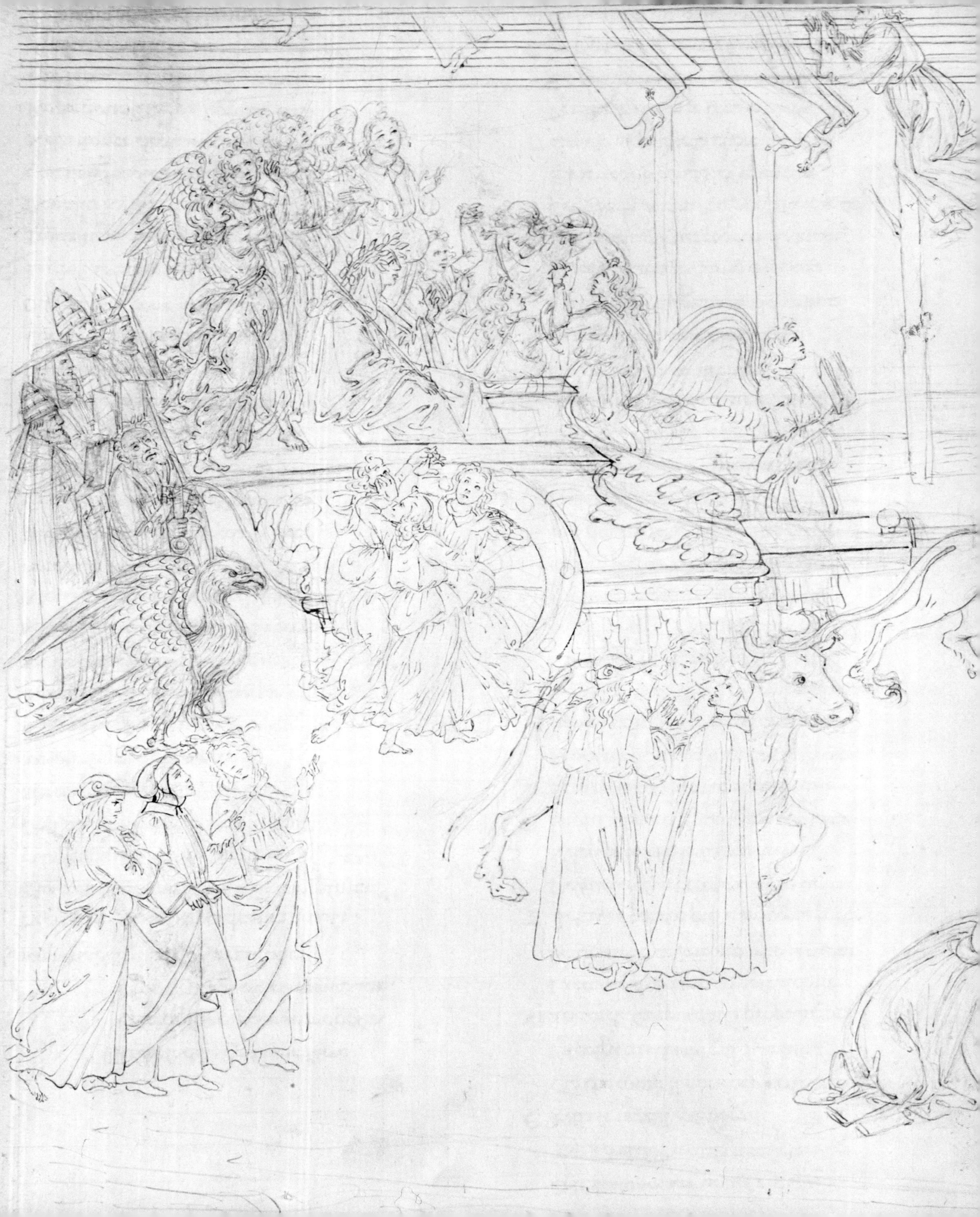

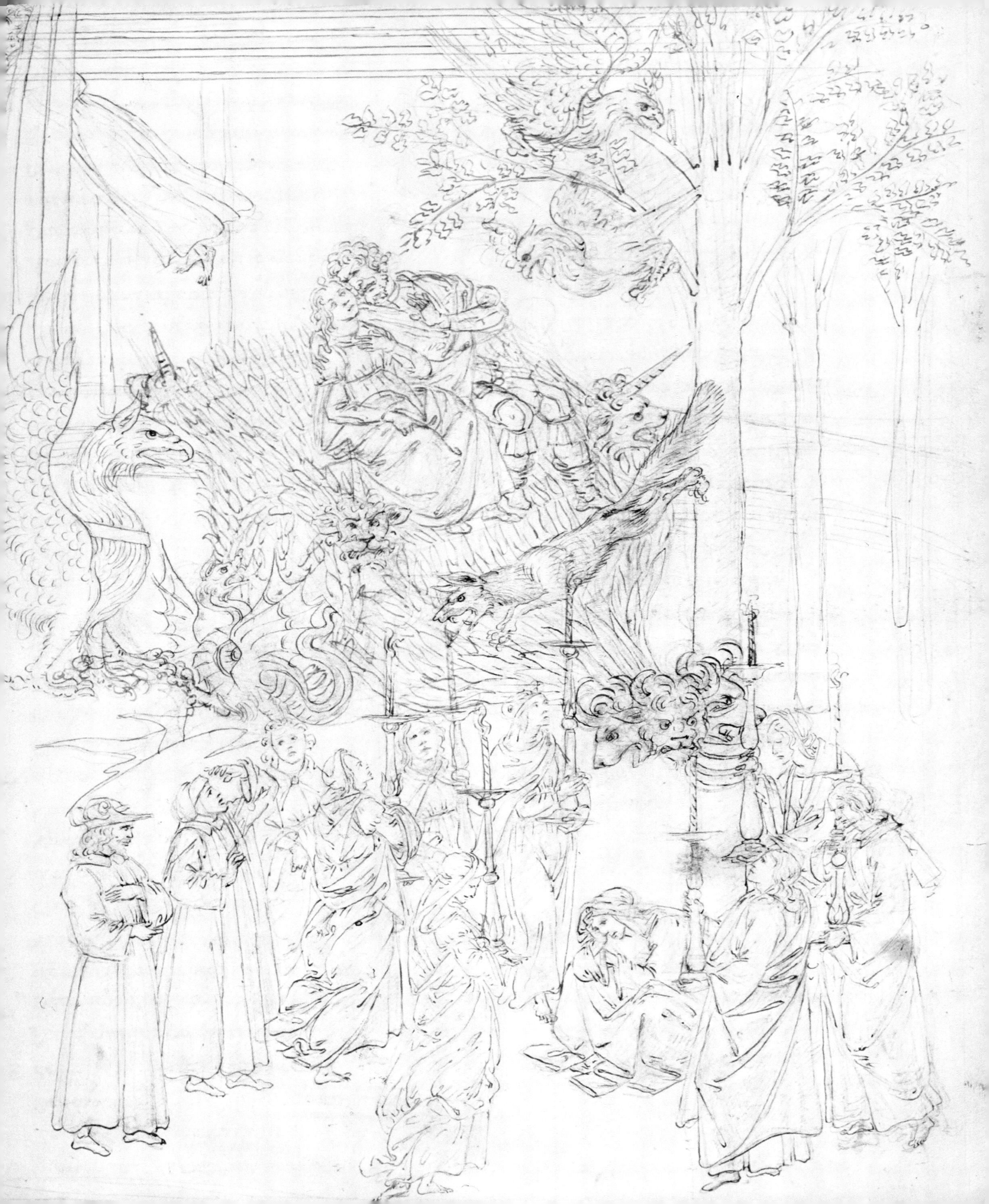

37

Paradiso I

The ascent to the heaven of Fire: Beatrice explains the forces of Universal Order

Pen and brown ink over metalpoint on vellum, 32.4 × 47.6 cm; text of *Purgatorio* XXXIII in four columns on the verso (pen and brown ink)

Guided by Beatrice, Dante now leaves the earthly realm behind him and ascends to Paradise. The Sacred Wood of Earthly Paradise on the summit of the mount of Purgatory, surrounded by the circular confluence of the rivers Lethe and Eunoe, does not actually appear in this canto. It is depicted here in order to denote Dante's shift in location. Beatrice sets her gaze firmly on the sun to the left. The poet, by contrast, is unable to look into the blinding light and instead keeps his eyes on his guide. He stares at her so intensely, internalising her aspect in his imagination, that he even comes to resemble her in the drawing. And in this manner, through the fixity of a stare, he is transported to the heaven of Fire, the first section of Paradise. Botticelli underlines the importance of Dante's gaze by making his eyes the first part of his face to cross its arc. In Dante, this transition is marked by the figures' transfiguration into new, non-human forms. Botticelli shows Dante still as a man. From now on, though, he and Beatrice are represented much larger than before, with Beatrice always towering above him. Here Botticelli decides against using the one-point perspective popular in his day, and instead opts for a hierarchical arrangement for the figures. This apparently antiquated technique was better suited to depicting the increasingly abstract action that unfolds in this section of the *Commedia*, beyond the logic of space and time. At the beginning of the third section of the *Commedia*, Dante invokes Apollo, asking the god to enable him to give adequate expression to the scenes he sees, in the hope that he will prove himself worthy of the laurel wreath that, in this drawing, we see adorns his head and that of his companion. An initial sketch in metalpoint shows the two figures outlined at the exact opposite angle, heading towards the ground. It would seem Botticelli was unhappy with that arrangment and turned the sheet around before drawing the final scene in ink. This shows that the drawing must have been rendered on the sheet first and the text on the verso second, since the text is in keeping with the other cantos and is not inverted. Kenneth Clark was especially moved by this sheet, primarily for its "delicate and economical beauty, unequalled in Western art" (1976, p. 22).

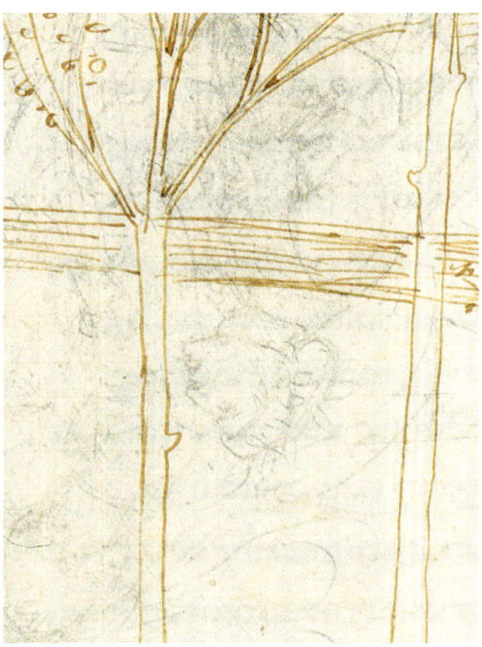

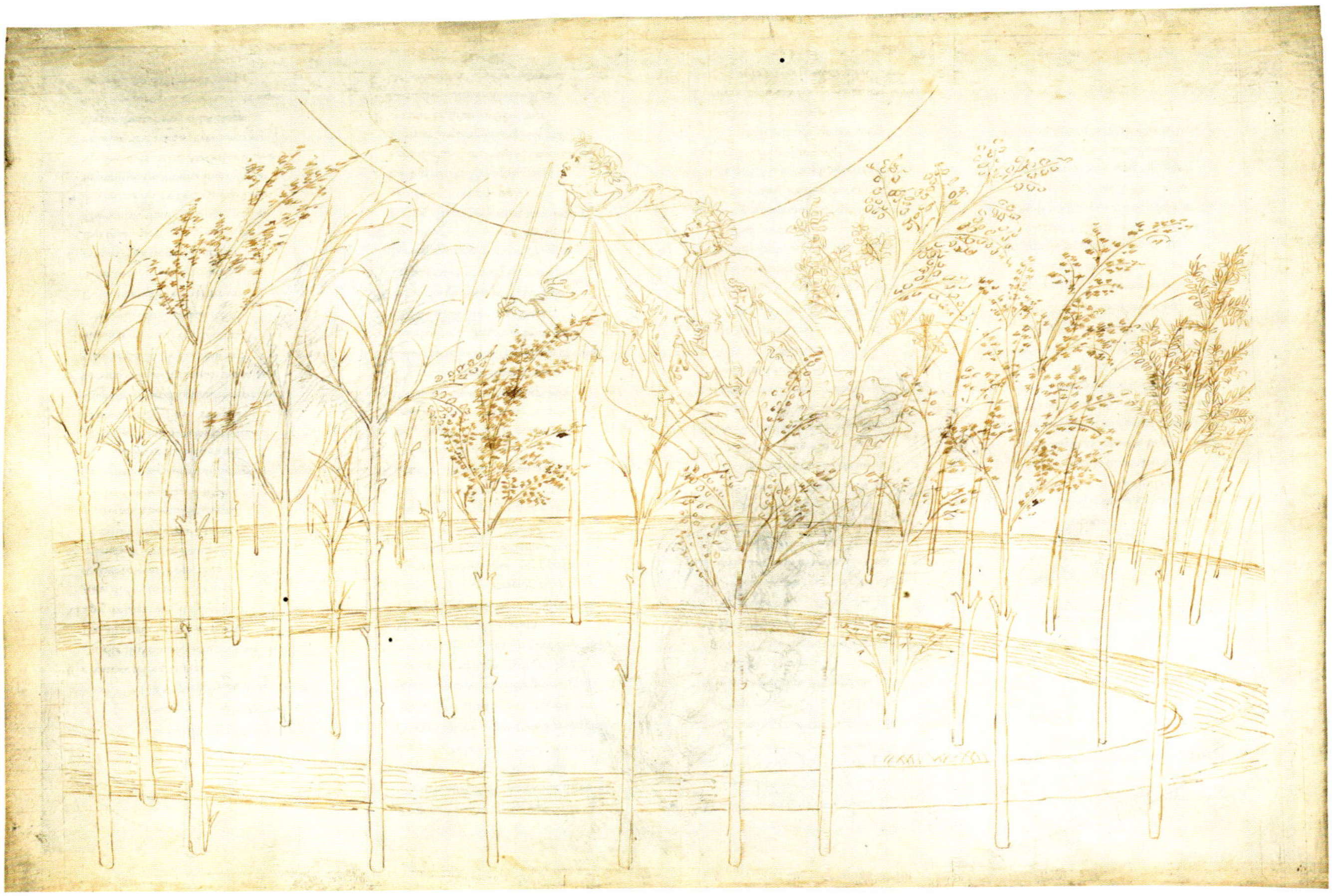

38

Paradiso II

First planetary sphere (heaven of the Moon): Beatrice explains the origin of lunar spots and the order of the cosmos

Pen and brown ink over metalpoint on vellum, 32.4 × 47.4 cm; text of *Paradiso* I in four columns on the verso (pen and brown ink)

In defiance of the natural laws of gravity, Dante, so Beatrice tells him, will rise with her through the spheres of Paradise all the way to the origin of all being. This sheet provides the viewer with a topographical overview of this third realm for orientation purposes – similar to those at the beginning of *Inferno* (*The Chart of Hell* in the Vatican, fig. 20, p. 75) and *Purgatorio* (*Purgatorio* I, cat. no. 26). Paradise consists of concentric spheres, each corresponding to one of the planets. The Earth (*tera* [sic]) stands at the centre, in keeping with the geocentric Ptolemaic worldview that held sway in Dante's lifetime. Around it are the Earth's atmosphere (*aria*) and the zone of fire (*fuocho*), after which come the seven celestial spheres, with the Sun and Moon distinguished by their separate symbols. On the outer edges are the Fixed Stars and, at the outermost reaches, the Primum Mobile. The core motif of Paradise is the circle, and most of the sheets show traces of an arc sketched with a compass. In contrast to the circles of Hell and the rings of Purgatory, the spheres of Paradise are in the main not imbued with spatial or physical qualities, but rather by an abstract flatness, which corresponds to the increasingly abstract nature of action and theme. Dante and Beatrice are seen here in one such sphere, the heaven of the Moon, with Beatrice explaining the lunar spots. She is about to reveal to him how Paradise is ordered. She points upwards, while touching the poet gently on the lips with the other hand. Dante is shown here with a strikingly harder mien and older in appearance than before, perhaps as a way to signal the great change he has experienced during the ascent. Beatrice's figure is drawn in a lighter ink, possibly to denote her divine nature as opposed to that of the human traveller by her side.

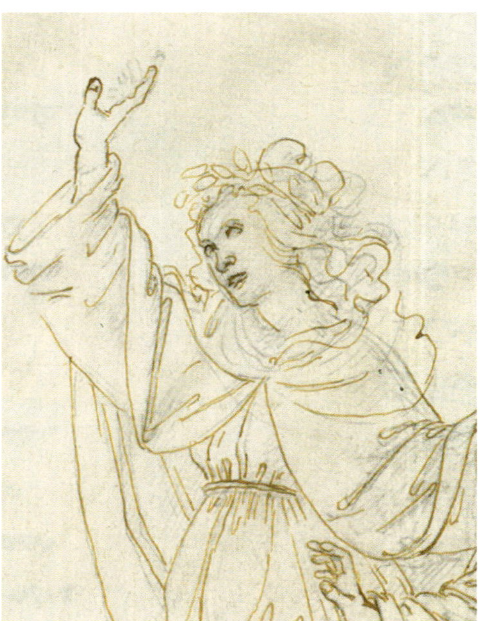

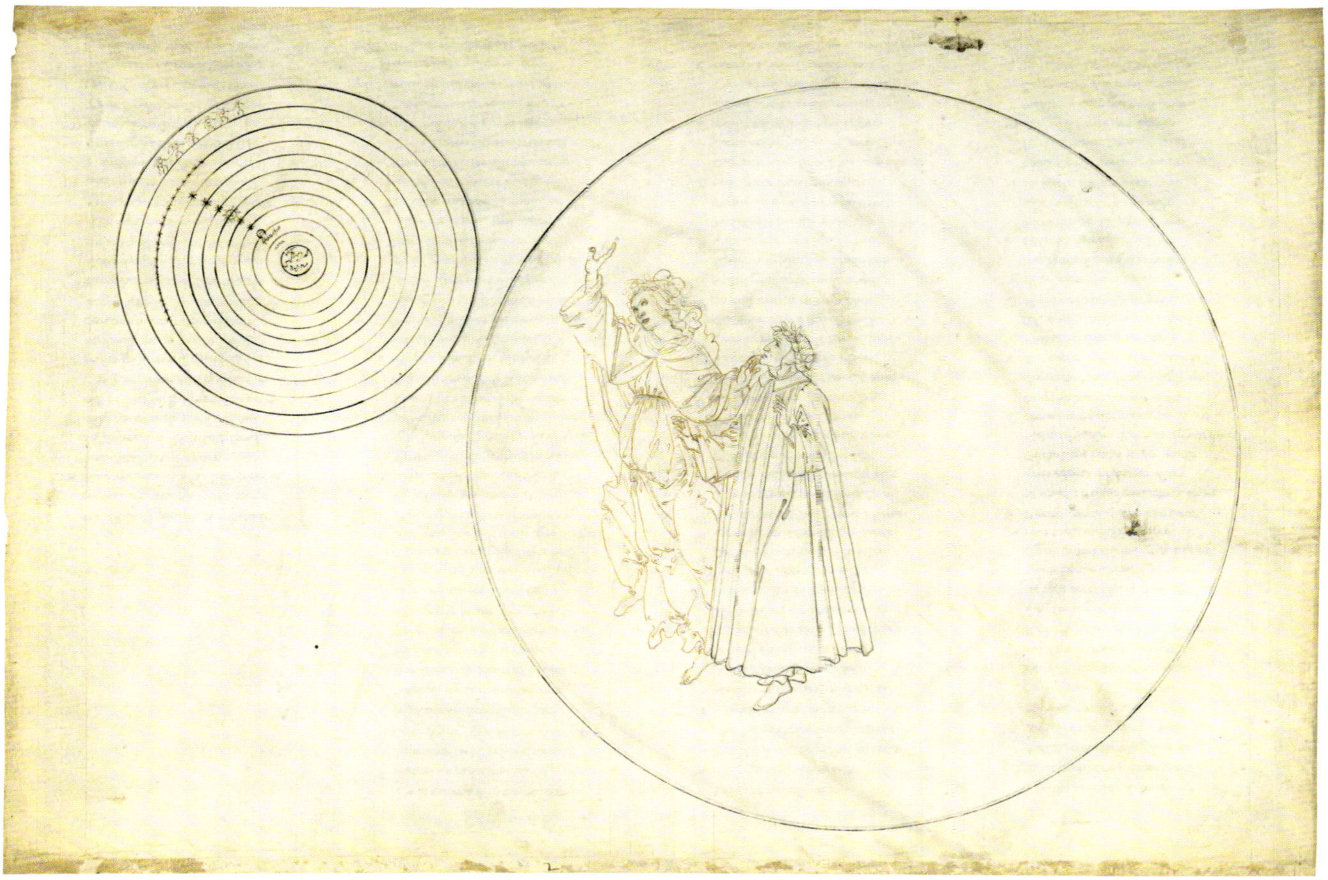

39

Paradiso III

First planetary sphere (heaven of the Moon): the souls of those prevented from keeping their religious vows; Dante converses with Piccarda Donati

Pen and brown ink over metalpoint on vellum, 32.7 × 47.7 cm; text of *Paradiso* II in four columns on the verso (pen and brown ink)

The cantos of the *Commedia,* and consequently also the drawings for *Paradiso*, are notable for the way in which the narrative is starkly pared down, to a greater or lesser extent, to a series of key interactions. Here, Dante is still travelling with Beatrice through the heaven of the Moon. Figures suddenly emerge from the light and form a semi-circle around the pair. In the poem, Dante turns round to see where these spectres are coming from; in the drawing, he only turns his head, a movement the artist suggests by drawing the poet's head in both positions, looking backwards and forwards, thus creating the impression that he has two faces, like the mythical Janus. Behind him, he sees only emptiness. However, when he turns back, Beatrice explains that the spectres are not mere reflections, but true beings. Dante begins to talk with the blessed spirits. This first celestial sphere is inhabited by souls who, though not through any fault of their own, broke or were unable to fulfil their vows. Despite the fact that they must remain in the circle farthest from Paradise, they feel no desire to ascend any further; such an aspiration would not be reconcilable with the essence of salvation. Among them is the former nun Piccarda Donati, the sister of Forese Donati (*Purgatorio* XXIII), who was forced into matrimony against her will, thus breaking her vow of chastity. Behind her, a fellow nun appears who suffered a similar fate and was abducted from a convent to be married. She addresses Dante, too, with a welcoming gesture. She is Constance, wife of the Holy Roman Emperor of the Hohenstaufen line, Henry VI, and mother of Frederick II. A relatively large number of the blessed depicted here are dressed as nuns or monks. In contrast to the lost souls trapped in Hell or atoning for sins in Purgatory, all the beings here are fully clothed and depicted very individually, distinguished by different clothing, head coverings, hairstyles and physiognomies. It was this sheet that Lippmann chose as an example of Botticelli's *Commedia* cycle in an early publication of 1883. Printed as a collotype, it was the first ever reproduction of one of these drawings (see Lippmann 1883, p. 72).

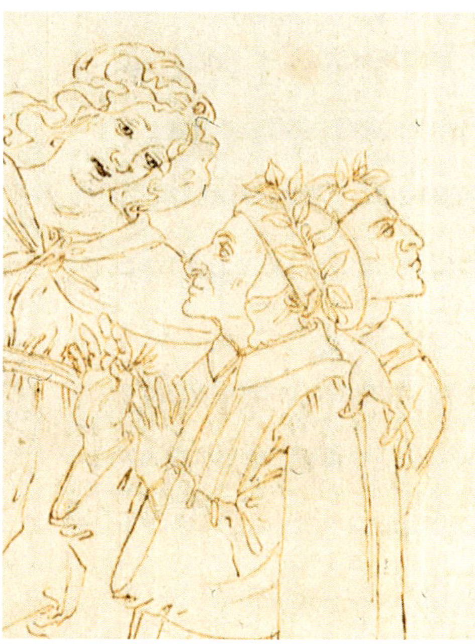

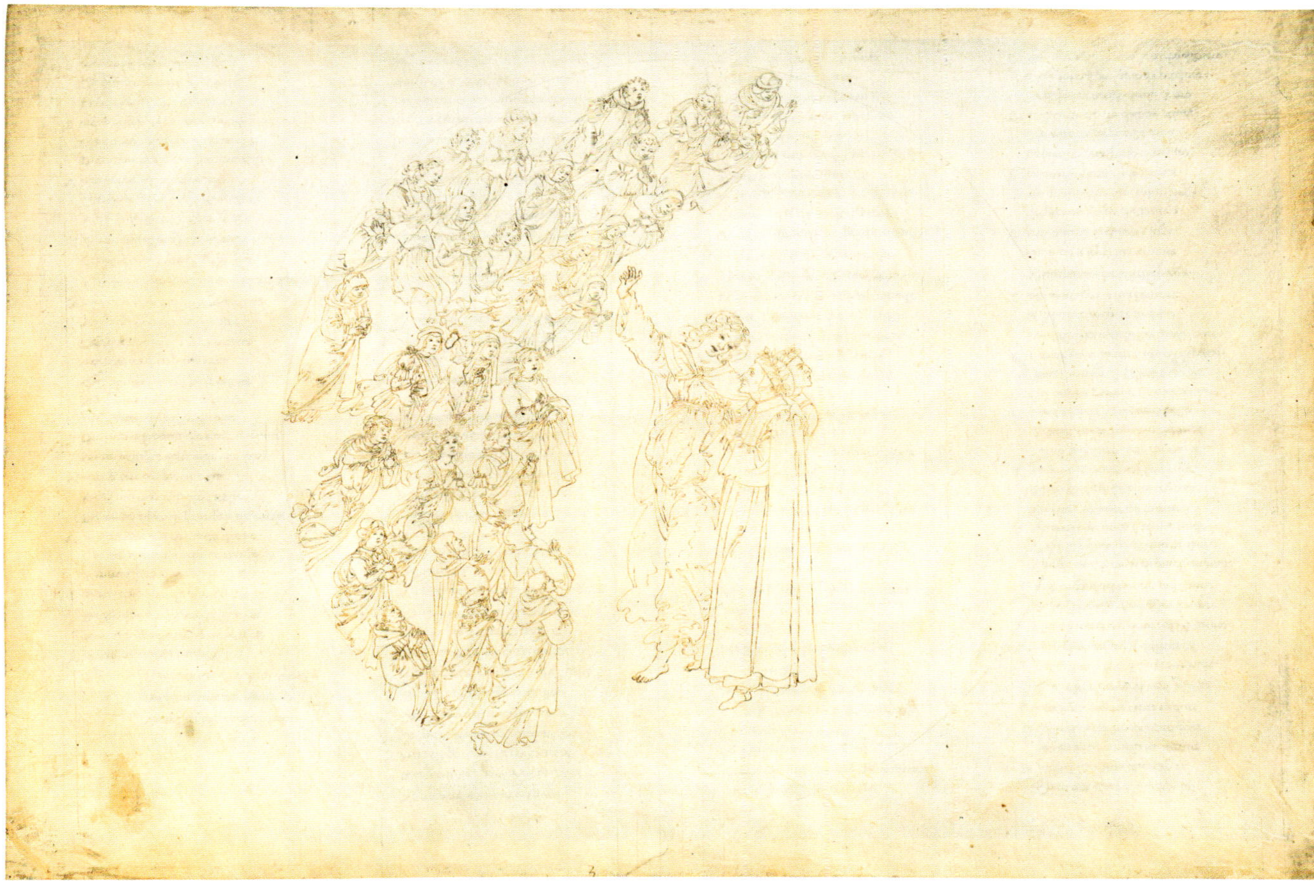

40

Paradiso V

First planetary sphere (heaven of the Moon): Beatrice explains the principles of vows and dispensations; ascent to the sphere of Mercury

Pen and brown ink over metalpoint on vellum, 32.5 × 47.5 cm; text of *Paradiso* IV in four columns on the verso (pen and brown ink)

Certain drawings of *Inferno* and *Purgatorio* make it clear that, for Botticelli, the visualisation of Dante's journey and the universe of the *Commedia* sometimes involved a struggle to find the ideal position of figures in the picture space to suit Dante's words. This drawing from *Paradiso*, focused on the two figures of Dante and Beatrice, is a good illustration of the way the artist also subjected the posture of individual figures, and with it the precise moment of the narrative, to intense deliberation, often enacted with the metal stylus. Here the figure of Beatrice shows a strikingly dense underdrawing. The pair are still in the heaven of the Moon. Beatrice's gaze originally pointed upwards, her head inclined, as is still clearly visible in the metalpoint sketch. This would have related to the moment when she turned to "where the world is most alive" (v. 87), namely to the higher spheres. This upward orientation remains evident in Beatrice's gesturing hands and in the way she floats, already announcing the ascent to the second planetary sphere, that of Mercury. This may be why in the end Botticelli decided to depict Beatrice with head downcast, emphasising a different aspect of the canto – the figures' conversation, sustained through the eye contact between them. He ultimately chose to ink in this posture, after trying out several possibilities with the metal stylus. However, the elaboration of Beatrice's gown, worked out in many little strokes, curves and hatches, remained as an underdrawing. Botticelli may have sought, in the gown's powerful fluttering movements, a visual correspondence to Beatrice's flaming love for Dante ("in the heat of love I flame upon thee", v. 1).

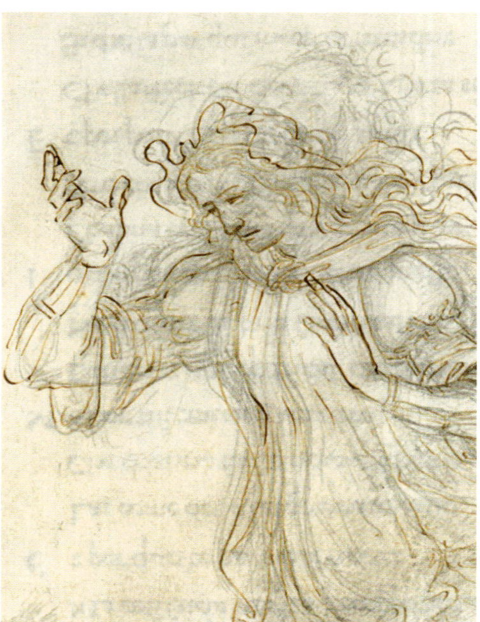

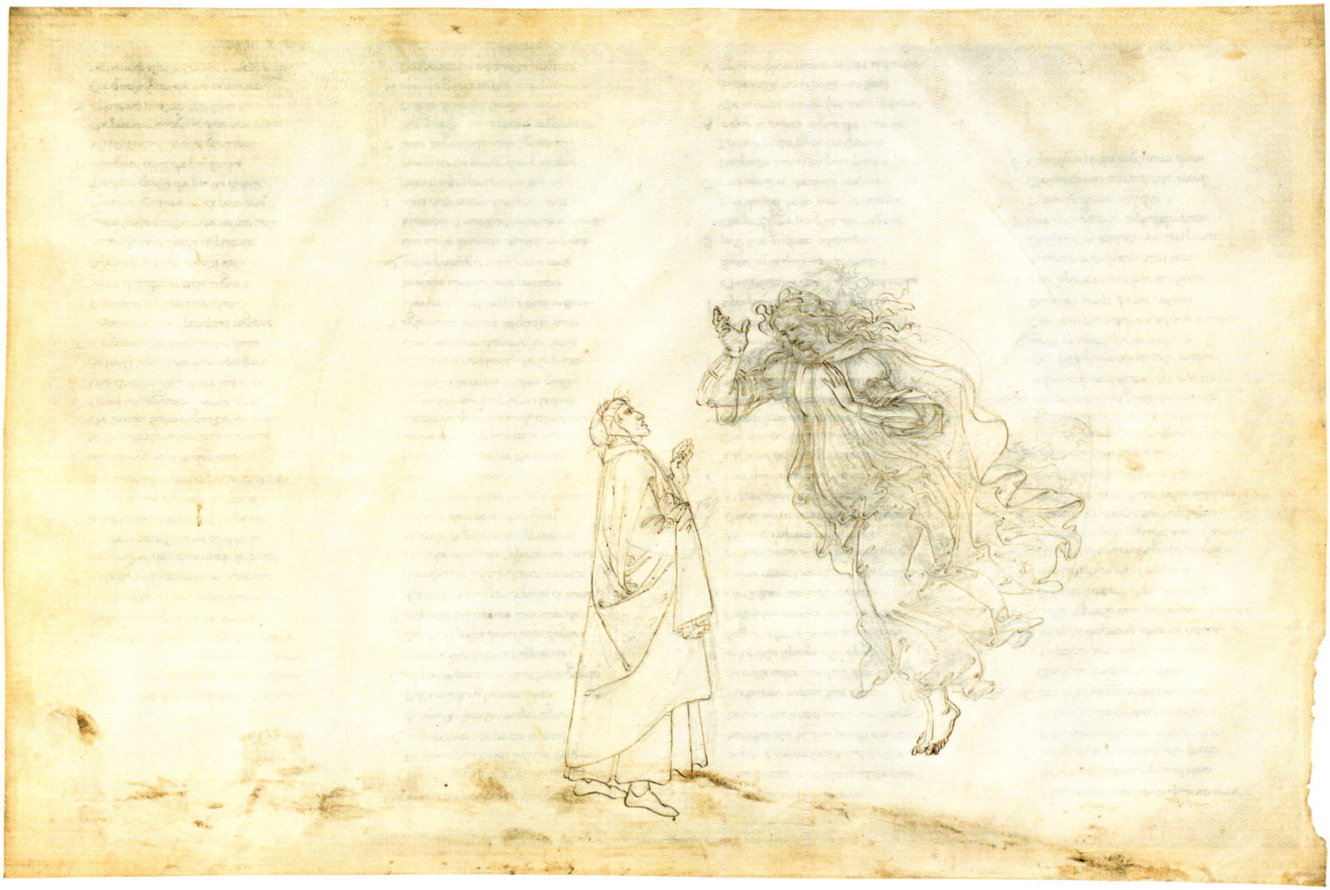

41

Paradiso VI

Second planetary sphere (heaven of Mercury): Justinian recounts the history of the Roman Empire and tells him of the souls of the just in Mercury

Pen and brown ink over metalpoint on vellum, 32.5 × 47.6 cm; text of *Paradiso* V in four columns on the verso (pen and brown ink)

There is a radiant brilliance in the second celestial sphere. The blessed glitter in rings around Dante like a thousand small fish in water, little flames spread out evenly across the circular surface of the heaven of Mercury. Gathered here are the souls of the just. One flares up brightly and praises Dante for having been allowed to see Paradise even though still alive. Dante speaks to the flame, which is that of the Roman emperor Justinian. A long conversation follows regarding Justinian's achievements as a reformer of the law and on the history of the Roman Empire. We recognise again in this drawing a clear *pentimento*, a 'repentance' (as the Italian word suggests) that allows the viewer to see a change in the composition between the underdrawing and the final ink version. Apparently Botticelli had originally planned to place Dante somewhat higher in the circle, allowing him to look down on one of the little flames, the soul of Justinian. Yet this would have disrupted the clear orientation towards higher spheres, expressed through Beatrice's gesture (also corrected, so as to be somewhat more steeply placed) and the direction of her gaze, as well as the way all the flames point upwards (reflecting their rectitude) and Dante, too, looks up. Friedrich Lippmann professed to being fascinated by these drawings of the cantos of Paradise. Dante and Beatrice alone are visible in nearly half the drawings, joined in conversation either with one another or with the blessed. As Lippmann remarked, "these groups are not uniform at all, but rather varied in ever new ways, and represent in their sublime simplicity one of the greatest glories of the whole" (Lippmann 1883, p. 67).

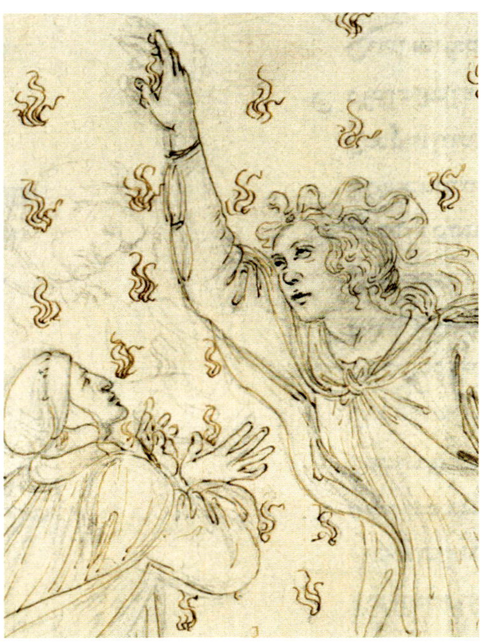

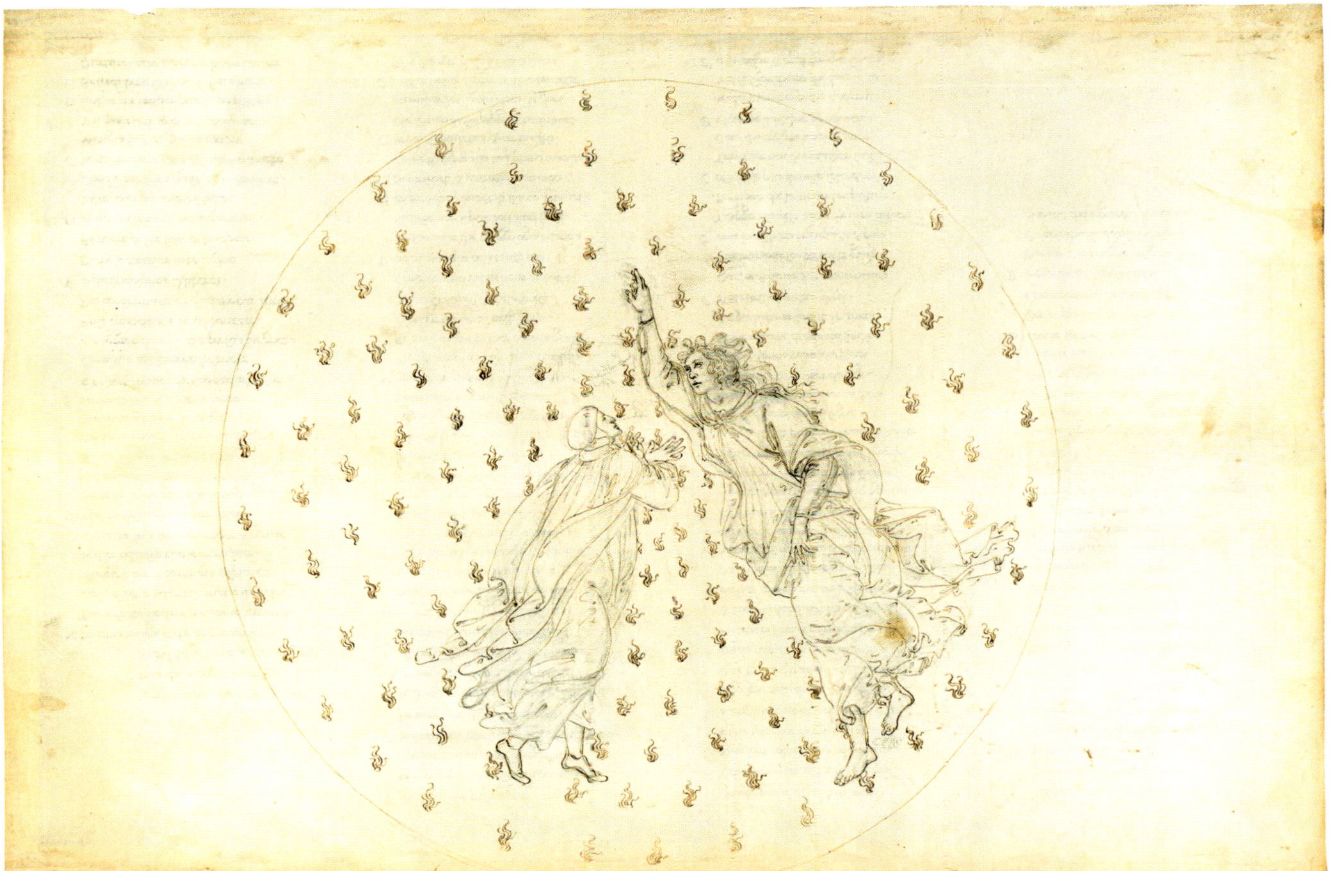

42

Paradiso XX

Sixth planetary sphere (heaven of Jupiter): the eagle names the individual souls that make up its eye, among them two pagans, whereupon Dante's doubts are momentarily reinforced and ultimately dispelled

Pen and brown ink over metalpoint on vellum, 32.4 × 47.4 cm; text of *Paradiso* XIX on verso (pen and brown ink)

This sheet is dedicated to Canto XX of *Paradiso*, as shown by the inscription bearing the first two words of the canto "*Quando colui*" (When he ...) and the number 20 on the lower edge of the sheet. It focuses solely on the two figures of Dante and Beatrice in the sphere of Jupiter. The dramatic image that Dante conjures – an eagle composed of the shining souls of the blessed – is not rendered here at all. Botticelli possibly originally intended this light-filled apparition to be included to the left of the two figures. Beatrice not only delights Dante but also the viewer with the hint of a tender smile (v. 13). In her unusually ethereal appearance, we can recognise the complexity of character that Botticelli liked to lend such figures, wholly in keeping with the Dantean model. Beatrice not only resembles the Madonna-like Venus from his famous painting *Primavera* (Florence, Galleria degli Uffizi), but also the figure of John the Baptist in the painting *The Trinity with Saints* (London, Courtauld Gallery), which was probably made around the same time as this work (fig. 23). In XXIV of his *Vita Nuova* (*The New Life*), Dante explains that Beatrice has a precursor who foretells her arrival. She is 'Primavera' (spring), because, he states, she "will come first" ("*prima verrà*"). For this reason, she is named Giovanna, for she foresees Beatrice's arrival, just as John the Baptist (Italian: Giovanni Battista) foresaw the coming of Christ. As the guide leading the traveller through the paradise of the *Commedia*, Beatrice takes on a new significance as prophesier of greater things to come and thus assumes a role similar to that of John the Baptist. The text of the *Commedia* in this canto also evokes the baptism of Christ (vv. 127–29) by Saint John.

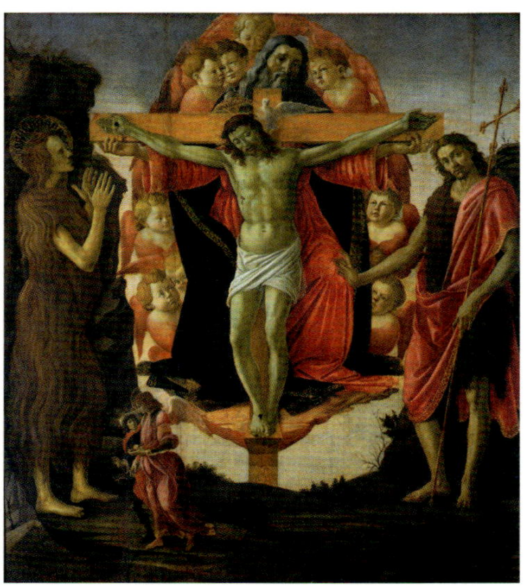

FIG. 23
Sandro Botticelli, *The Trinity with Saints Mary Magdalene and John the Baptist, the Archangel Raphael and Tobias*, 1491–94, tempera and oil(?) on panel, 256 × 192.4 cm, London, The Courtauld Gallery

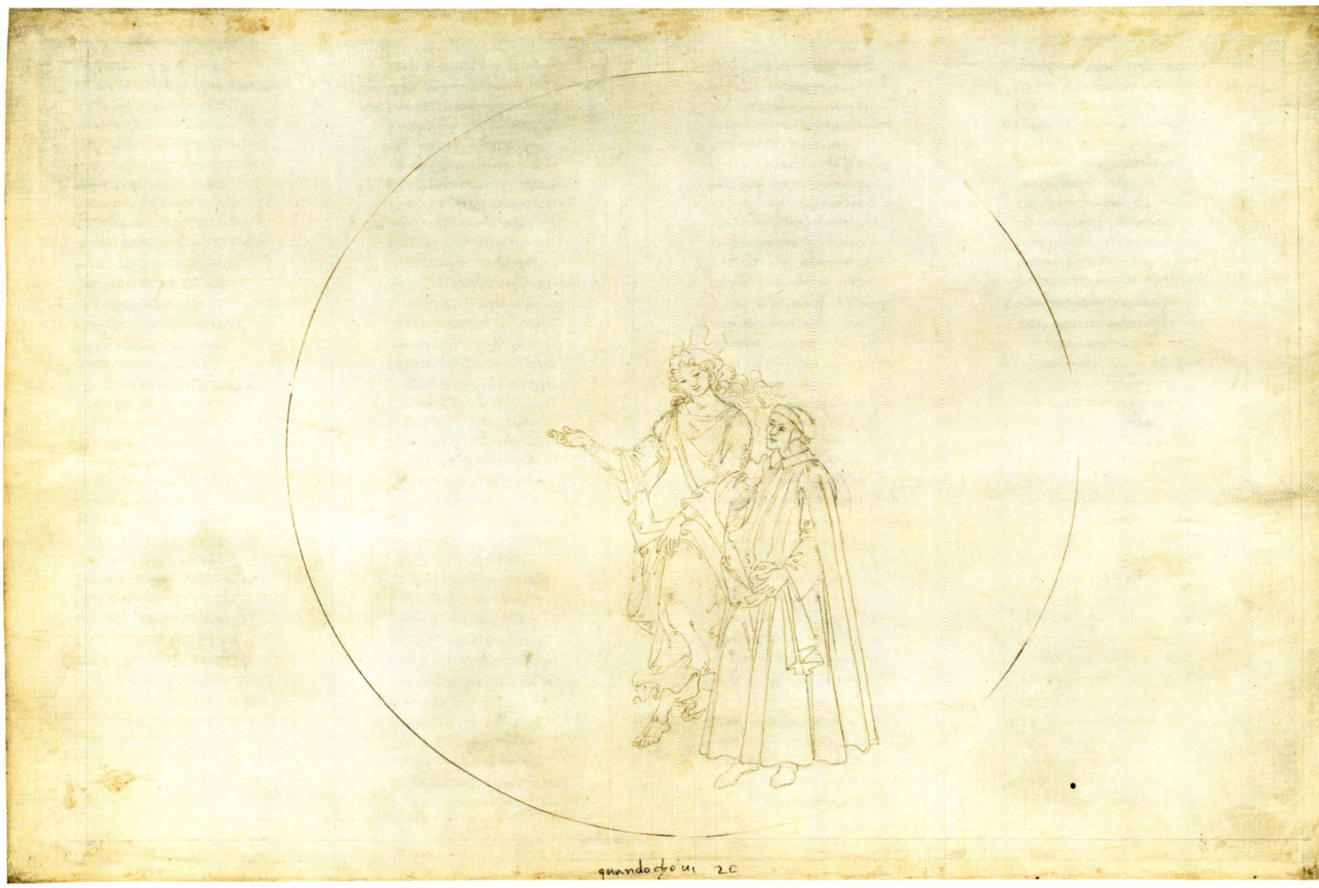

43
Paradiso XXI

Ascent to the seventh planetary sphere (heaven of Saturn): Jacob's ladder and the light of the blessed who excelled in the contemplative life; speech of Peter Damian

Pen and brown ink over metalpoint on vellum, 32.5 × 47.5 cm; text of *Paradiso* XX in four columns on the verso (pen and brown ink)

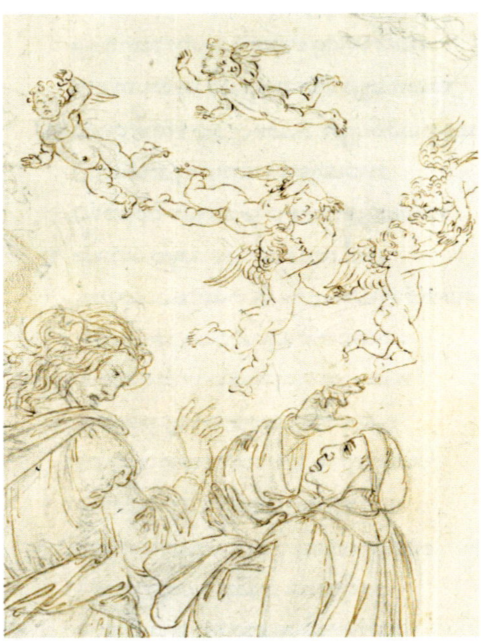

Above the seventh celestial sphere stands a flaming lion, sketched in metalpoint on the upper left, above the circle. Dante and Beatrice are in the heaven of Saturn, reflecting the legendary Golden Age, the age of Saturn, when only love and goodness reigned among humanity and there was nothing bad in the world. Beatrice's austere facial expression derives from the fact that she – in contrast to the preceding canto – explicitly does not smile when looking at Dante. He would burn, she explains to him, if she were to confront him now in the glory of her true, transcendent beauty, which has grown even more radiant through the ascent into this sphere. Looking and seeing increasingly become a central theme of interpretation, of such complexity that it is virtually impossible to convey graphically. To be able to continue seeing, Dante must follow Beatrice's eyes in spirit only. Her eyes serve as a mirror for the images to be seen. Thus he spies a radiant golden ladder, the top of which evades his gaze. The sparkling lights of souls circle the ladder, moving up and down. Although Dante goes on to speak of "little flames", Botticelli depicts them in the form of tiny, putti-like little angels, distributed loosely on the ladder and in space, as though in cheerful play. The drawing shows the biblical ladder to Heaven in the dream of Jacob, which appeared to him full of angels. A faint outline of the figures of Dante and Beatrice can be made out a second time on the ladder. Apparently the artist first wanted to show their ascent into the sphere above, the heaven of the Fixed Stars. He then decided against it, neatly scratched out the lines of ink and illustrated the ascent in the next drawing. With this erasure he decided against rendering the figures' accelerated progress through simultaneous action in favour of a greater clarity of vision, which the text explores through the concept of *contemplatio*, the inner beholding of God (vv. 89–90).

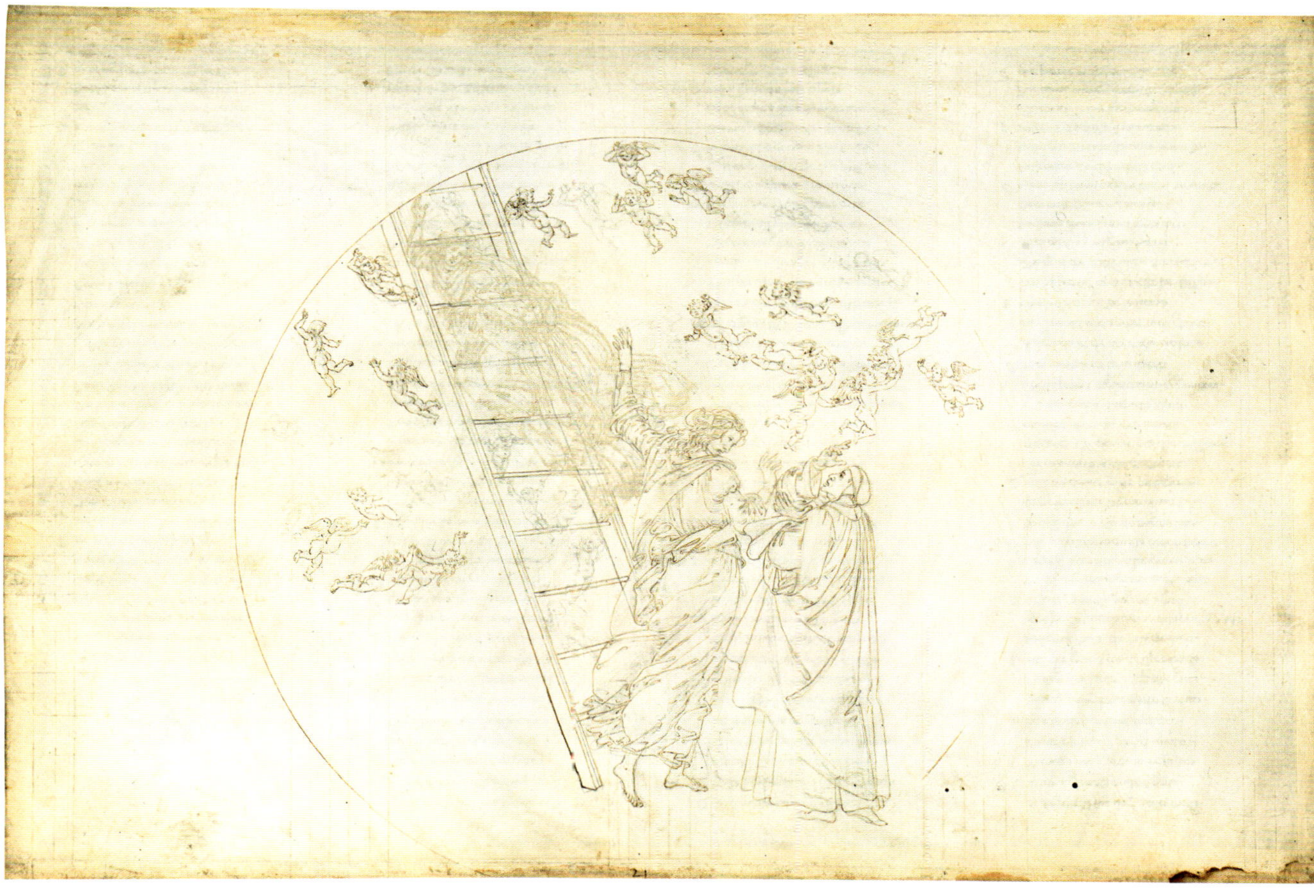

44

Paradiso XXVI

Eighth sphere (heaven of Fixed Stars): John questions Dante on the third theological virtue, love; Dante's power of vision returns to him, stronger than before; the light of Adam shines

Pen and brown ink over metalpoint on vellum, 32.7 × 47.7 cm; text of *Paradiso* XXV in four columns on the verso (pen and brown ink)

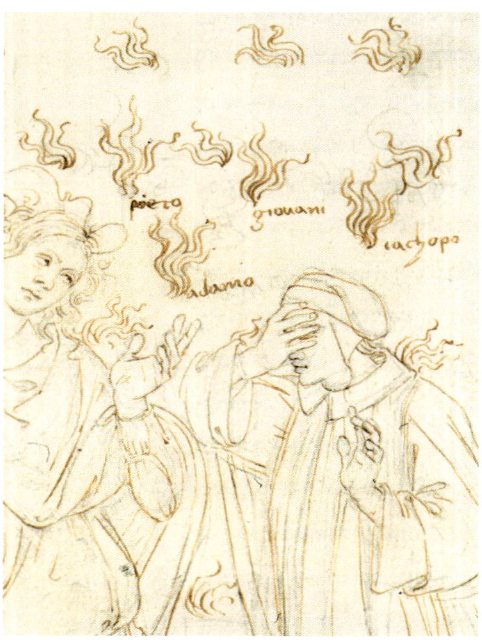

Dante and Beatrice have climbed Jacob's ladder into the heaven of the Fixed Stars, where the hosts of the heavenly armies are seated. The heaven of the Fixed Stars opens above them – allowing Botticelli to introduce a new quality of perspective. The abstract circular space through which Dante and Beatrice had been moving among the celestial spheres undergoes a further unbounding now that they have reached the uppermost sphere. The little flames of souls are in concentric circles, arching upward and surrounding the centre in which appears the visage of Christ, garlanded with dense beams of light. Unlike in the lower spheres of Paradise, in which the individual flames of souls were not distinguished from one another, Botticelli seems to place value here on the correct identification of Dante's interlocutors and permits himself recourse to the written word. The souls of Peter, Adam, John and Jacob are shown as little flames, in keeping with their purely spiritual nature, but also have their names inscribed. When John the Evangelist flares up, Dante is rendered temporarily unable to see owing to the dazzling glare. Botticelli reflects this by depicting the poet for the first time covering his eyes entirely with his hands, thus showing the light's intensity, although by this point Dante has already been blinded by strong light many times since leaving Purgatory. Beatrice opens Dante's eyes again with the radiance of her own. He can now perceive everything with a much greater clarity and, after an extensive discussion with John and Adam, is ready to ascend further.

The incorrect numbering of the canto (25 instead of 26) inscribed on the lower edge, a consequence of the incorrect numbering that runs from the preceding drawing throughout the remaining ones, may be regarded as another indication that the drawings were made first and only later, in a second stage, were the texts of the respective preceding cantos written on the reverse side of the leaf, rotated by 180°. At the same time, writing the text of individual cantos on each piece of vellum meant a definitive determination of the order of the sheets, which was apparently still relatively variable at certain points while Botticelli was drawing. Here the artist's increasingly universal, concentrated and abstract visualisation incorporates references to other cantos as well, making a clear association difficult.

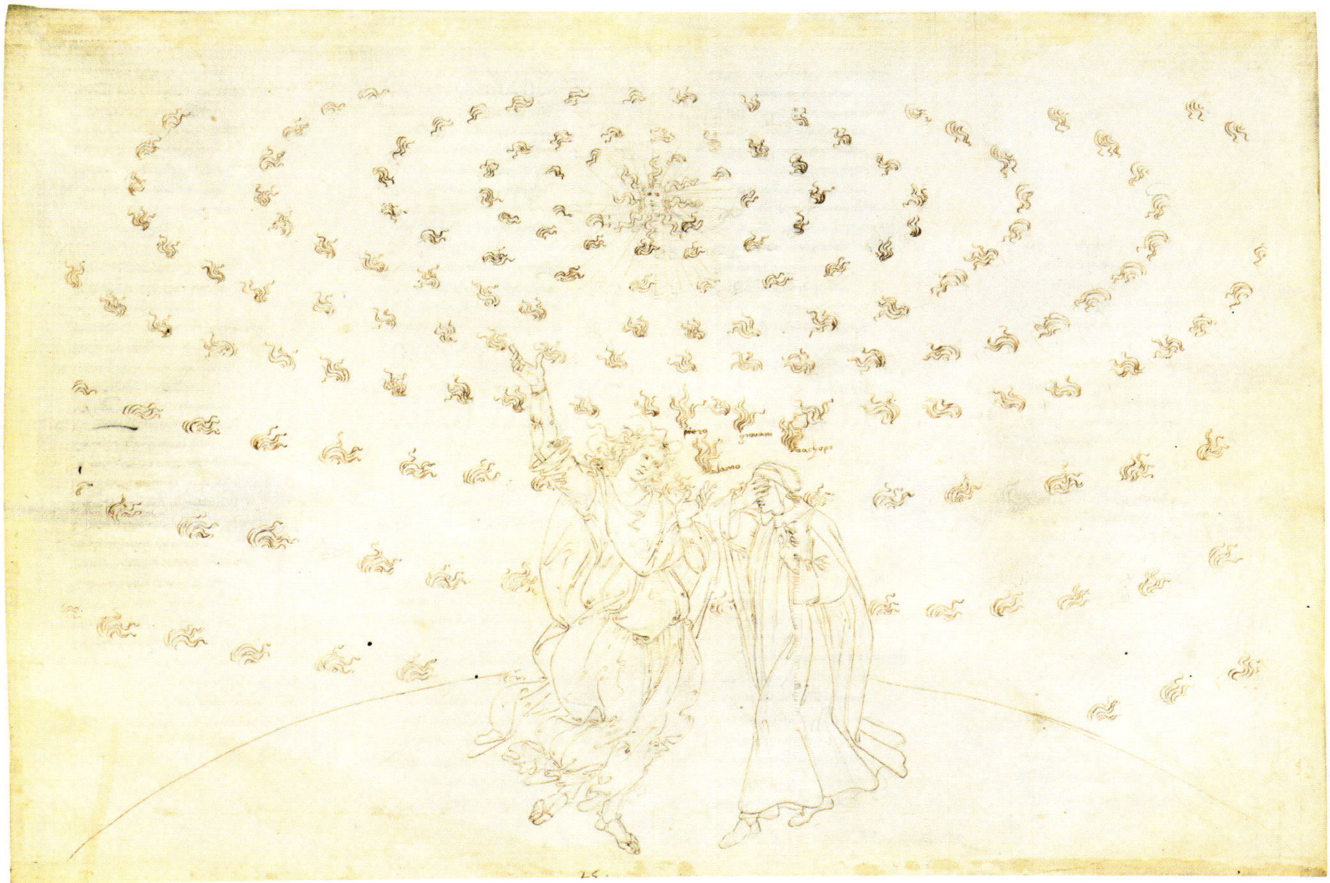

45

Paradiso XXX

The path to the Empyrean: Dante and Beatrice in the river of light

Pen and brown ink over metalpoint on vellum, 32.2 × 47.2 cm; text of *Paradiso* XXIX in four columns on the verso (pen and brown ink)

SELECT BIBLIOGRAPHY Klettke 2010, passim

This drawing shows the *Commedia's* "last image still perceptible in time and space" (Berlin/Rome/London 2000–01, p. 282) and at the same time its last *locus amoenus*. Having arrived at the entrance to the Empyrean, Dante turns his eyes again to Beatrice and must confess that his art of poetry, which previously had been able to do justice to her beauty, now surrenders in the face of it. Perhaps there is an analogous surrender by Botticelli's art of drawing, which does not depict the supernatural grace of her visage. Botticelli employs the artifice of showing the heavenly Beatrice from behind, her head in profile, half-covered by her hair, turned to her charge. Equipped again with a renewed, transcendent power of vision, Dante now sees a river of pure light, the "light intellectual replete with love" (v. 40), its banks wondrously "depicted with an admirable Spring" (v. 63). This adjective *dipinte* (painted) surely held a particular appeal for Botticelli the artist, and he presents this spring through an immense diversity of flowers and plants, shown with a wealth of detail and distributed decoratively in space (on the left in pen and ink over the metalpoint underdrawing, on the right only the latter). Living sparks move in the river and on the shore. Botticelli shows them, in a manner similar to his depiction of souls in the drawing of *Paradiso* XXI, as putti-like little angels, some surrounded by a corona of light. They dip into the river with childlike joy, swim, and crawl into the flowers and out again. The figural representation of the souls' sparks, in opposition to the text, allows the artist to show their lively activity and their carefree, happy mood with greater clarity than was the case in their depiction as abstract little flames. The small child as a symbol of the incorporeal soul was an established medieval convention. Whereas in the previous cantos the space was still roughly round and concentrically defined, here the circular form no longer plays any part, since the sphere is so broad that it surpasses the circumference of the sun (vv. 103–05), and is thus incapable of representation on vellum.

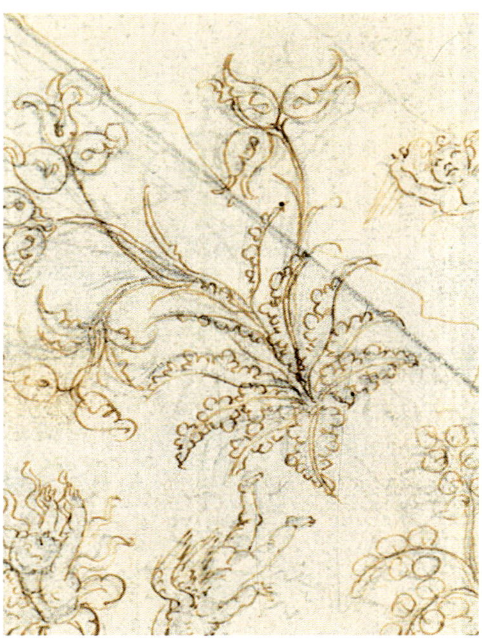

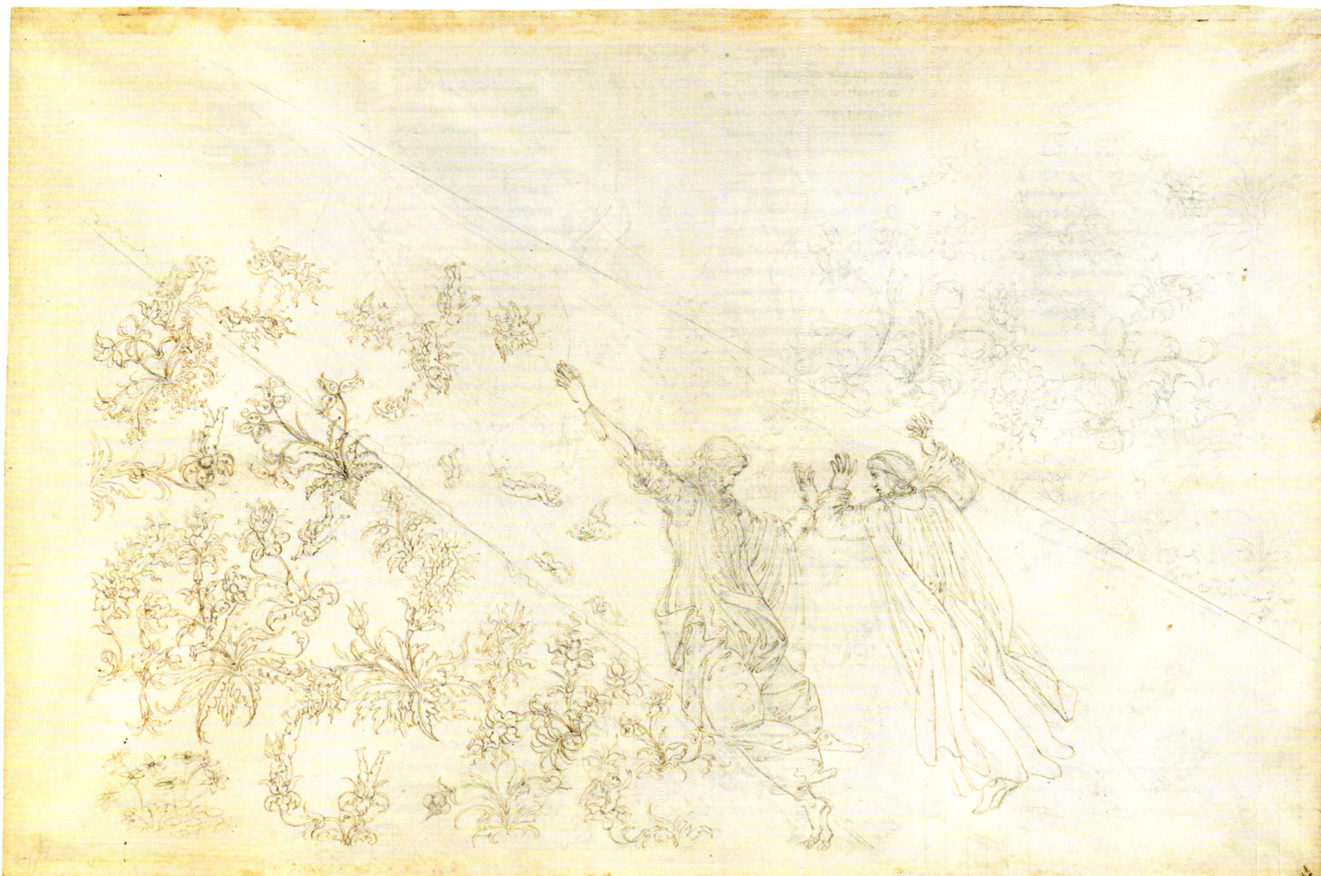

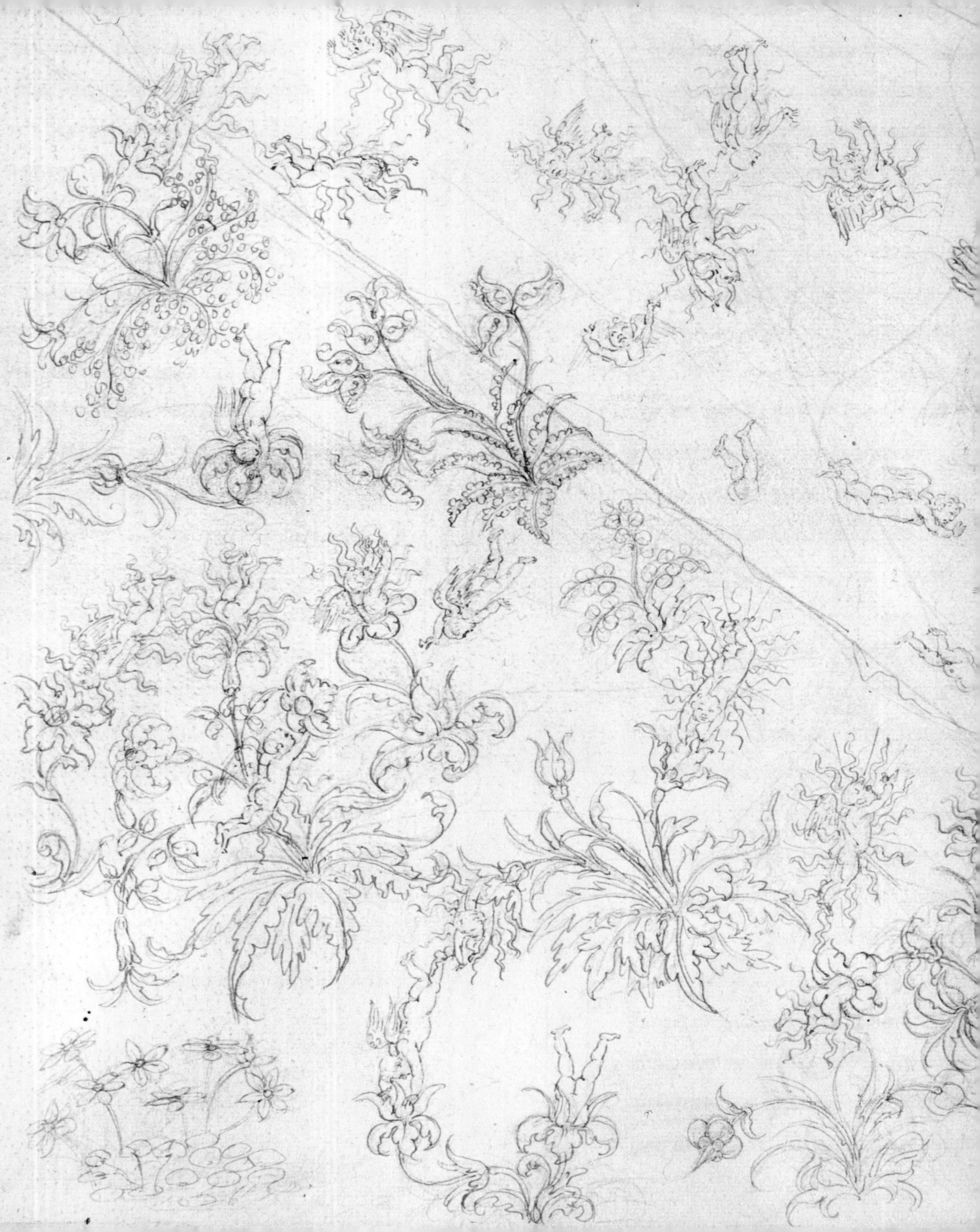

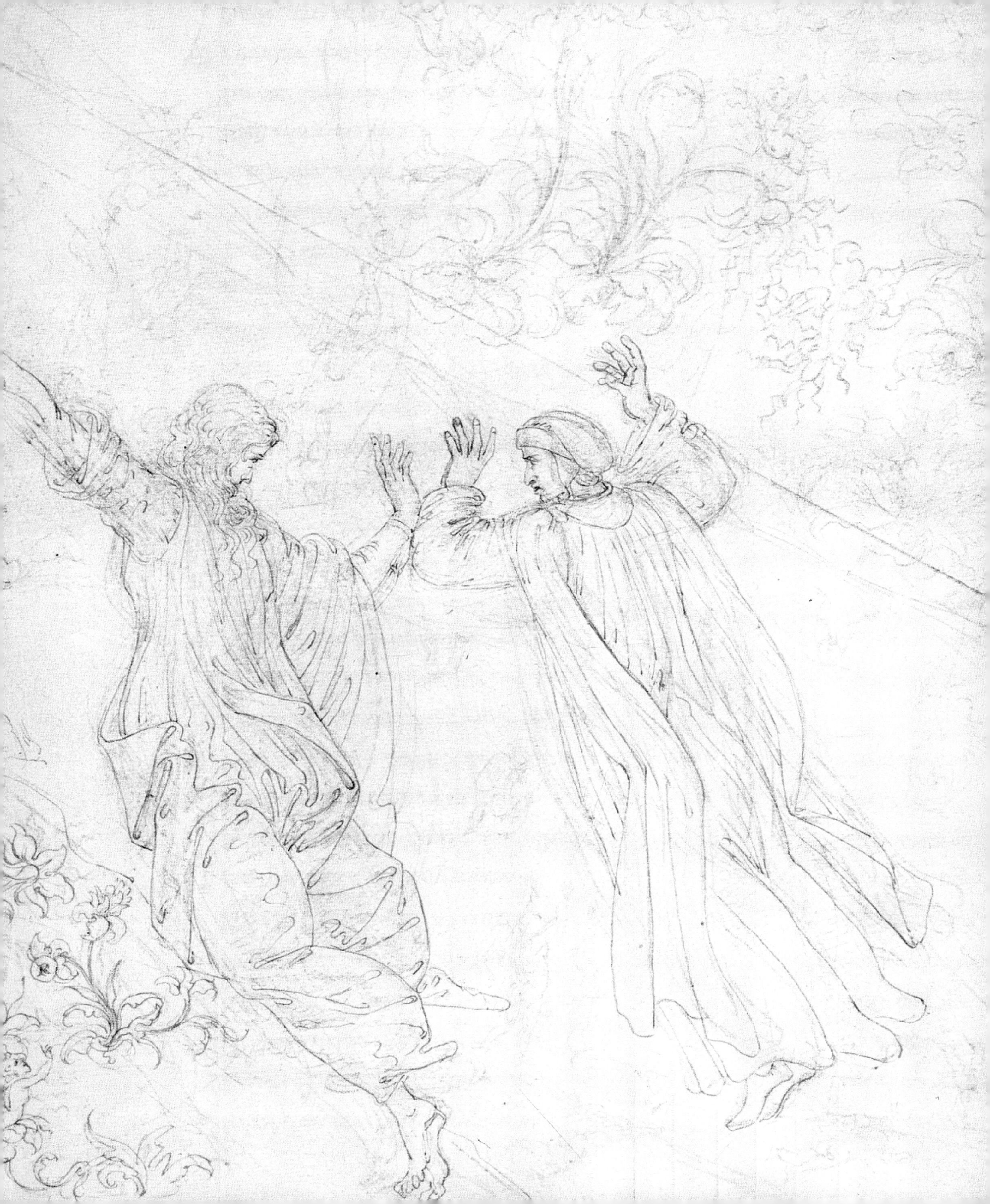

46

Paradiso XXXII

The Empyrean: Bernard of Clairvaux explains the Mystic Rose; Dante's vision of the Virgin Mary

Pen and brown ink over metalpoint on vellum, 32.4 × 47.0 cm; text of *Paradiso* XXXI in four columns on the verso (pen and brown ink)

SELECT BIBLIOGRAPHY Morrison 2012, p. 80

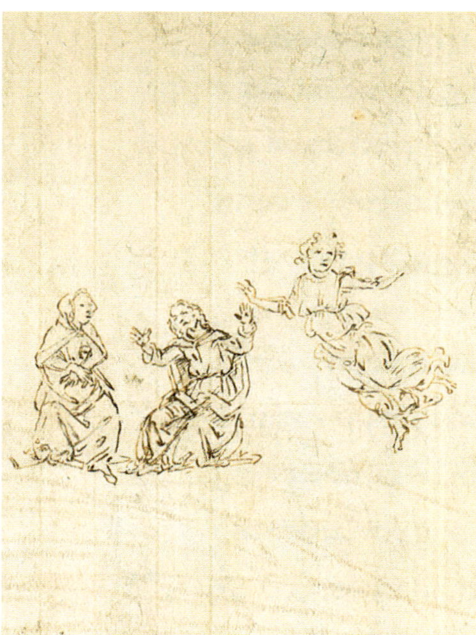

The last drawn sheet of the cycle contains only a tiny scene. This may be surprising, since the text of the *Commedia* in this canto sets forth a picture, rich in forms and figures, of the white Mystic Rose in which the saints of the Old and New Testament have their place in the utmost proximity to God. The remnants of the scratched out metalpoint underdrawing, parts of which can still be made out despite the erasure, show that the artist did not simply reduce or condense the canto down to a small three-figure scene from the outset, but instead struggled to find an adequate visual representation of the Empyrean. The great arc on which the scene is placed could have been intended as a petal of the Mystic Rose. It would seem that a dance of angels was initially intended for the space to the right of the small executed scene. The scene shown, drawn in pen and ink, corresponds to Dante's vision of Mary and the Archangel Gabriel, flanking the risen Christ, who bears the stigmata, and alludes visually to depictions of the Annunciation, the Crowning with Thorns, the Transfiguration and the Last Judgement. The minuscule dimensions in relation to the size of the sheet suggest that the viewer is infinitely far away, even as the distinct details suggest an extreme clarity of vision. Here, in contrast to the preceding drawings of *Paradiso*, Dante and Beatrice are not shown. Whether this is because the drawing is unfinished or because, perhaps, the artist intended to give the viewer Dante's perspective (see Meier 2013, p. 17) must ultimately remain a matter for speculation. The sheet that was originally supposed to show the preceding canto was used for the double folio at the end of *Inferno*, and its replacement was left empty. The leaf (now lost) on the following canto was likewise unmarked. In this canto, Dante's journey ends, beyond all images capable of imagination or representation, with a prayer and the vision of the "love which moves the sun and the other stars".

47

The Binding of Hamilton Codex 201

France (Paris?), 1780–1803

Half-bound in red morocco leather, 49.4 × 36.0 × 5.1 cm; 85 vellum guards on to which the illustrations were glued, one sheet with the text of *Paradiso* XXX still attached to a guard

At the time of its acquisition by Berlin in 1882, the 87 leaves of vellum with the manuscript text of the *Commedia* and the 84 drawings by Botticelli were bound together in a codex. They were enclosed in a half-leather binding with seven raised bands. The spine and corners were bound in red morocco leather and the front and back boards were covered with pink coloured paper. The compartments between the bands and the ribs themselves were decorated with geometric patterns in gold while the second compartment contained the inscription: *DANTE/ MANOSCRITTO*. In the centre of the front cover, turned 90° to the left, is a title label of red morocco leather with an inscription stamped in gold: *LA COMEDIA/ DI/ DANTE ALIGHIERI/ MANOSCRITTO SU PERGAMENA/ DELL ANNO 1400 AL 1450/ CON DISEGNI ORIGINALI/ FATTI DA SANDRO BOTIREL/ LI* [sic]/ *OD ALTRO DI QUEL TEMPO/ DELLA SEUOLA* [sic] *FIORENTINA*. The orientation of the label shows that the volume was meant to have an oblong format and be read with the spine pointing upwards. The inner sides of the front and back boards were covered with marbled endpapers. They were adjoined to sheets of writing paper that served as flyleaves: these were produced by the French paper manufacturers Buges Cie. Between these leaves, there were 85 vellum guards on to which the sheets of vellum were once affixed, as can be seen from the last remaining leaf in this binding with the text of *Paradiso* XXX. Thus, when perusing the book, the illustration corresponding to each canto would have been seen on the verso of the next recto. To protect from abrasion, each sheet of vellum was separated by a layer of thin paper also sewn into the binding. Two different types of paper were used for these dividers: a very thin laid paper (known as 'Post' paper) from James Whatman, and an ultra-thin wove paper specially manufactured for copying letters by James Watt & Company. A folded sheet of letter paper with a description of the codex was stuck to the inside of the front cover; this was written by the antiquarian Giovanni Claudio Molini on 27 April 1803 in Paris, perhaps as a record of the contents in the event of a transfer of ownership. On the same piece of paper, Friedrich Lippmann added his own summary of the contents of the codex in 1882.

It has generally been thought that the binding was made in England between 1803 and 1819 (Berlin/Rome/London 2000–01, p. 356). A more recent analysis, however, suggests that it was probably made in France at the end of the eighteenth century. The remnants of a printed text can still be seen on one of the first vellum guards. They would have come

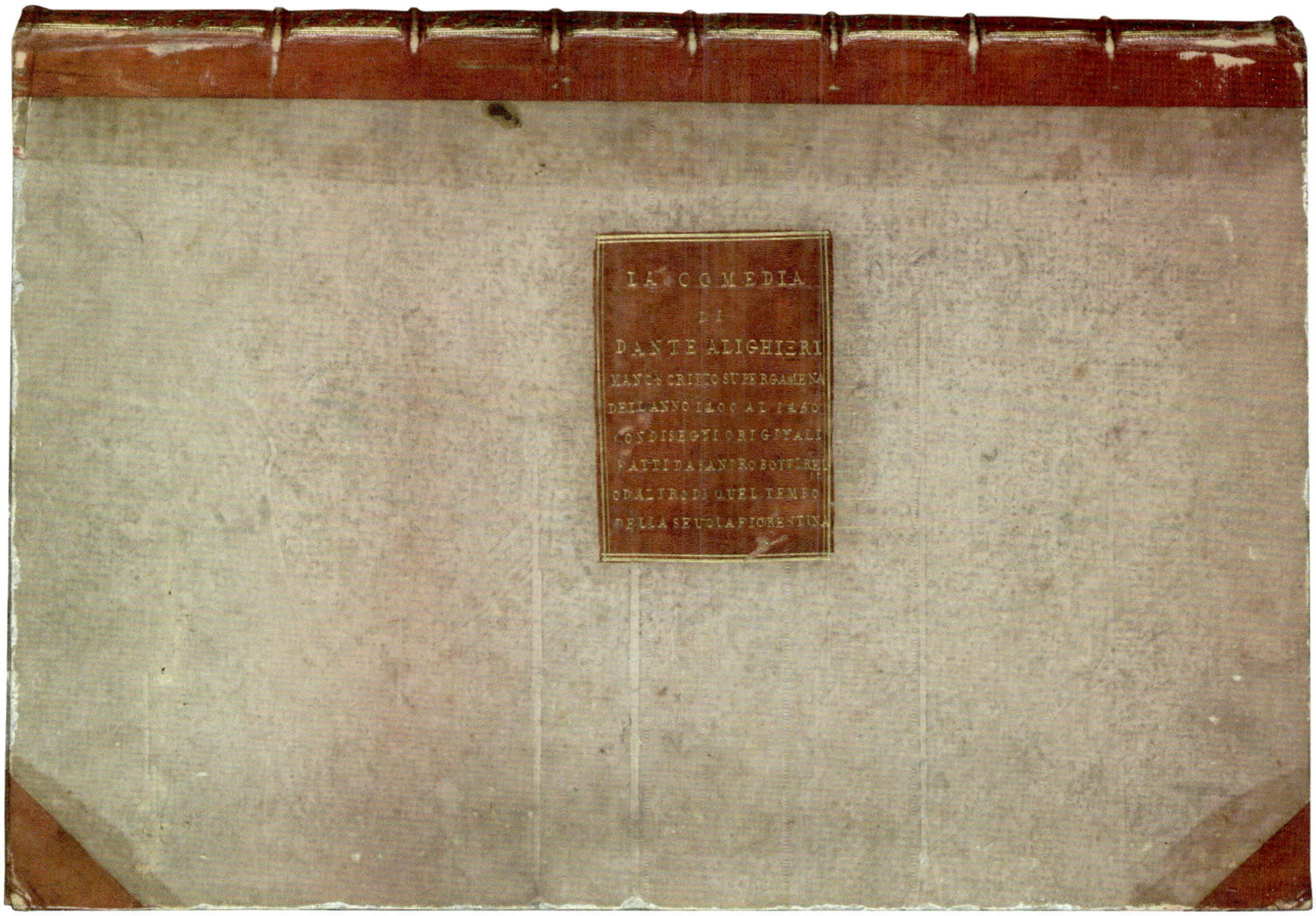
LA COMEDIA
DI
DANTE ALIGHIERI
MANOSCRITTO SU PERGAMENA
DELL'ANNO 1400 AL 1450
CON DISEGNI ORIGINALI
FATTI DA SANDRO BOTTICELLI
O DA ALTRO DI QUEL TEMPO
DELLA SCUOLA FIORENTINA

from waste paper that was placed on the leaves of the manuscript when they were mounted to aid drying, and pieces of this evidently got stuck to the guard. The word *réguliè*[*re*] can be deciphered in one section which makes it seem likely that it was produced in a French workshop. The protective dividing sheets were manufactured in English paper mills; however, the fact that their watermarks do not include the year of production indicates that they were manufactured before 1794, as, from that time on, it was stipulated by law that watermarks had to display the year. The special paper for copying letters, on the other hand, cannot have been made earlier than 1780, as that was the year when James Watt patented his copying press for creating duplicates of letters. Of course, we cannot know how long the paper was in storage between its manufacture and use. It does not prove that the binding was made in England as Watt's letter copying presses were also sold at a branch in Rouen in France, which would have most likely supplied the special paper required, too.

The binding enclosed the Berlin Botticelli drawings for barely one hundred years. It seems that just a short time after the treasures from the Hamilton Collection arrived in Berlin, work began on taking the codex apart, apparently for conservation reasons. As the codex would be viewed more often at the museum, it was felt that the turning of the pages necessitated by the bound book form would pose too much of a risk. Lippmann reports in 1883 that the vellum sheets had already been removed from the binding and stretch-mounted in passepartouts that allowed both sides of the sheets to be seen, i.e. the text and the illustrations. The vellum sheets were first separated from the guards attached to the binding, dampened and mounted in the double-sided passepartouts by applying adhesive along all four edges of each sheet. The report does not mention who was responsible for carrying out this delicate operation in such a short space of time. A letter from Alfred Lichtwark, director of the Hamburg Kunsthalle, to the painter Max Liebermann of 2 May 1894 discussing an order for two large-format portraits in pastels on vellum provides an interesting clue, however: "The mounting [of the vellum] can be difficult and must be undertaken by a specialist, in Berlin most reliably by the conservator at the Kupferstichkabinett Hauser II, previously called Haubenreißer" (Braun 2011, p. 353). This comment raises the question how a restorer could have become so well known outside of the confines of his own museum for mounting vellum, if not by working on such a large and famous cycle as the *Commedia*. The account books of the general administration of the Königliche Museen of Berlin attest that one "Herr Haubenreißer" was permanently employed at the museum from 1 April 1881 as a "restorer" and received a "bonus payment" of 150 marks on 2 April 1883 for the period from 1882 to 1883. The reason for this bonus is not recorded but it is likely that it was connected to the transfer of the Botticelli drawings to their new mounts, in which most of them have remained to the present day.

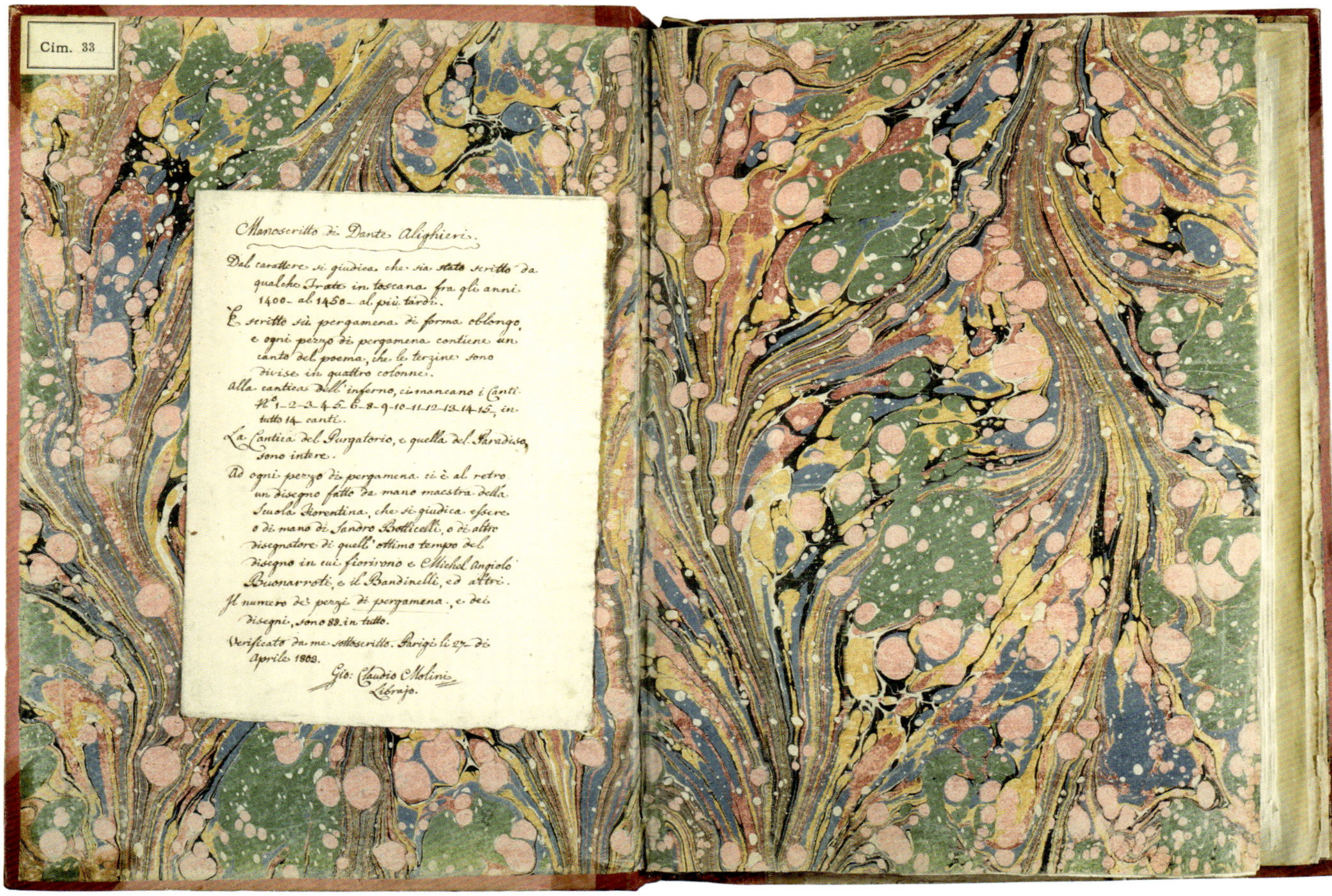
Cim. 33
Manoscritto di Dante Alighieri.
Dal carattere si giudica che sia stato scritto da
qualche Frate in toscana fra gli anni
1400 al 1450 al più tardi.
È scritto sù pergamena di forma oblongo,
e ogni pezzo di pergamena contiene un
canto del poema, che le terzine sono
divise in quattro colonne.
Alla cantica dell' inferno, ci mancano i Canti
N.o 1-2-3-4-5-6-8-9-10-11-12-13-14-15, in
tutto 14 canti.
La Cantica del Purgatorio, e quella del Paradiso,
sono intere.
Ad ogni pezzo di pergamena ci è al retro
un disegno fatto da mano maestra della
Scuola Fiorentina, che si giudica essere
o di mano di Sandro Botticelli, o di altro
disegnatore di quell' ottimo tempo del
disegno in cui fiorirono e Michel Angiolo
Buonarroti, e il Bandinelli, ed altri.
Il numero dei pezzi di pergamena, e dei
disegni, sono 88 in tutto.
Verificato da me sottoscritto. Parigi li 27 di
Aprile 1803.
Gio: Claudio Molini
Librajo.

to muouersi/se prima non si muoue la ragione. Entrai per lo camino alto: cioe profondo/chome diciamo alto mare et alto fiume: perche el primo camino fu per linferno cioe per la cognitione de uitii: equali sono infimi: perche sempre consistono circa le chose terrene. ET SILuestro: perche chome dicemo nel principio epeccati nascono dalla selua cioe dalla materia che e/elcorpo.

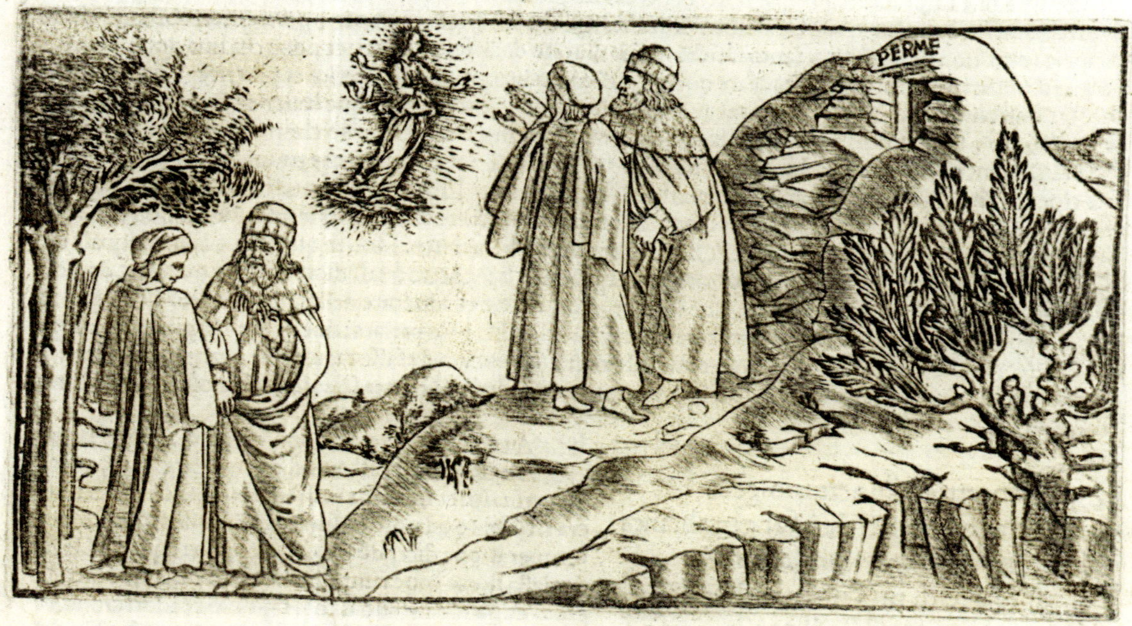

CANTO TERTIO DELLA PRIMA CANTICA

p Er me si ua nella citta dolente
per me si ua nelletherno dolore
per me si ua tra laperduta gente
Iustitia mosse el mio alto factore
fecemi la diuina potestate
la somma sapientia el primo amore
Dinanzi a me nonfur chose create
se non etherne et io etherno duro
lasciate ogni speranza uoi chentrate
Queste parole di colore obscuro
uidio scripte al sommo duna porta
perchio maestro el senso lor me duro.

s Ono alchuni equali credonoche edue primi capitoli sieno stati inluoghi di proemio: et questo terzo sia el principio della narratione. Ma se considerremo chon diligentia tutta la materia/facilmente si puo prouare che la narratione comincia nel primo capitolo: et nel uerso Io non ui so ben dire chomio uentrai. Imperoche Danthe narra in questa sua peregrinatione essersi ritrouato nella selua: et hauere smarrito la uia Essersi condocto appie del monte. Et dipoi essersi addirizato uerso el sole per erto camino elquale lo conduceua asaluamento se le tre fiere non lauessino ripincto al basso. Et finalmente ridocto quasi al fondo hauere hauuto el soccorso di Virgilio et dalle tre donne. Et p lesue parole esser psuaso lasciãdo el corto ãdare del mõte seguitarlo per linferno et purgatorio; laqual uia sanza sinistro intoppo lo puo conducere al cielo. Ilche significa quello che gia disopra habbiamo dimostro. Et se alchuno dicessi che in amendue questi canti molte chose scriue conle quali capta beniuolẽtia et attẽtione et docilita: Enon si uieta che ĩ ogni pte del poema non si possi fare questo. Anzi maximamẽte sirichiede allo scriptore che le capti douũque truoua occasione di poterlo fare Hora perche siamo gia al puncto chel poeta descende nellinferno. Giudico sia utile exprimere che chosa sia inferno: et in quanti modi si dica alchuno scendere allinferno. Inferno adunque e/linfima: et bassa parte del mondo/decto inferno da questa dictione infra che significa disocto: Ne solamente dal popolo di dio e/posto lonferno: Ma anchora da molti poeti: et maxime da Homero da Virgilio. Ouidio. Statio: et Claudiano: Et molto piu egregiamente dal principe de philosophi Platone/Costui incritone nel qual libro induce Socrate disputante della immortalita dellanimo/dimostra che lanime humane dopo la morte sono giudicate secondo le loro colpe: et nellonferno tormentate insino atanto che si purghino/se epeccati non sono stati molto graui. Ma quelle che hanno commesso scelerateze enorme: et sono impurgabili secondo lui/sono mandate in luogho piu profondo decto tartaro et quiui sono afflicte inetherno con grauissimi supplicii. La quale oppinione e/molto simile alla christiana fede: et abbraccia lonferno el purgatorio: Et la maggior pte

The Divine Comedy: Early Illustrations in Printed Editions

Until the discovery of Botticelli's drawings for Dante's *Divine Comedy* in the Hamilton Collection, the illustrations engraved for the 1481 Florentine printed edition of the *Commedia*, universally accepted as being based on Botticelli's designs, were considered to be amongst the most important works of Italian art: "Botticelli's designs, engraved for the Dante of 1481, have always been esteemed among the most precious monuments of Italian Art."[1] Various British collectors, including the Duke of Hamilton, possessed copies of this incunabulum.[2] The execution of the altogether nineteen engravings for the *Inferno* was ascribed to Baccio Baldini (see cat. no. 48). Since, in Vasari's estimation, Baldini was not a particularly gifted draughtsman and based everything he created on ideas and preliminary drawings by Sandro Botticelli, an attribution of the original designs to Botticelli was made at an early date, and has always since been maintained.[3] Although the existence of the drawings was forgotten, these works have always been known. In the nineteenth century, in particular, when interest in Botticelli revived,[4] they were seen as visual evidence of the significant relationship between the Florentine artist and his fellow countryman, the great poet. For a long time it remained the only link between them, for, although Walter Pater concluded, from another of Vasari's remarks – "*... comentò una parte di Dante, e figurò lo Inferno e lo mise in stampa*" (he made a commentary on a part of Dante, illustrated the *Inferno* and had it printed) – that the artist must have composed a written commentary on Dante, no such commentary was known.[5] The two British art critics, Walter Pater[6] and John Ruskin,[7] saw Botticelli as a deeply Dantean artist. While Pater tended to see the harmony between them in terms of shared aesthetic and poetic qualities, for Ruskin it was the theological and moral content of the works of poet and artist that were crucial.[8] Both agreed, however, that Dante and Botticelli were linked on a uniquely spiritual artistic plane. Against this background, when the existence of the drawings for the *Commedia* became known as a result of their imminent sale to Berlin, they must have appeared the pinnacle and the heart of Botticelli's entire artistic endeavour. And, from an art-historical perspective, the engravings receded from the limelight accordingly.

Three early printed Dante editions are discussed here to illustrate the context of the Botticelli drawings. Besides a copy of the Landino edition of 1481, with Baldini's engravings after Botticelli, two other illustrated editions of the *Commedia* have been selected whose imagery derives from it. Each is reproduced at the page with the illustration to the first canto of the *Inferno*, with which the *Commedia* begins. Remarkably, the Kupferstichkabinett, or its then director, Friedrich Lippmann, bought both books in 1881 from Ellis & White, the same London book dealer who one year later handled the sale of the Hamilton library to Berlin.

NOTES

1 Sale catalogue 1882, p. 31, lot 201. Although William Clarke mentioned the volume with the drawings in 1819, Gustav Friedrich Waagen was the first to make the link with the engravings: "... he is known to have studied Dante with great zeal, and to have furnished the drawings for Baldini's engravings in the Landino edition": Waagen 1854 a, vol. 3, p. 307.

2 See Havely 2014, p. 245, note 243: probably the Duke originally possessed one of the more common copies, with two or three engravings, before acquiring a copy with nineteen illustrations in 1848 (this copy is now in the Morgan Library, New York).

3 Vasari (1550/1568) 1987, vol. 5, p. 3; on the engravings, see Dresden 2013, pp. 72–74; Keller 2000; Bellini 1990, esp. pp. 47–48.

4 See Berlin/London 2015–16 passim.

5 See Vasari (1550/1568) 1987, vol. 3, pp. 516–17, and Vasari (1550/1568) 2010, p. 29; Pater (1870) 1986, p. 34. Today it is thought more likely that the remark refers to these engravings.

6 Pater (1870) 1986, passim.

7 John Ruskin, 'Design in the Florentine School of Engraving (Sandro Botticelli)', in Ruskin 1903–1912, vol. 22, pp. 422–62; see also Weinberg 1987.

8 See Watts 1995 a, pp. 81, 87; Watts 1993, p. 61; Ruskin 1903–12, vol. 27, letter 22, 19 September 1872, pp. 371–72.

FACING *La Comedia di Danthe,* Florence 1481, cat. no. 48, *Inferno* III

48

La Comedia di Danthe Alighieri poeta fiorentino

The *Comedy* of Dante Alighieri with a commentary by Cristoforo Landino

Florence, Niccolò della Magna, 30 August 1481

Letterpress print on paper, 41.8 × 30.1 cm; 372 leaves, with three additional engravings inserted (*Inferno* I and two impressions of *Inferno* by Baccio Baldini [?]), c. 1481–87
Half-bound in leather, brown sheepskin, 'kibitz' spatter paper, 41.2 × 29.1 × 9.1 cm

PROVENANCE Sammlung Karl Ferdinand Friedrich von Nagler, Ansbach/Berlin (Lugt 2529); acquired for the Kupferstichkabinett in 1835

SHELF NUMBER 2541 (no. 148)

SELECT BIBLIOGRAPHY Berlin/Rome/London 2000–01, appendix, no. 5, p. 350–51 (Peter Keller), with earlier references

This is the first Florentine edition of Dante's *Commedia* and is a testimony of the excitement surrounding Dante's work in Florence towards the end of the fifteenth century. It is a product of the cultural climate in the milieu surrounding Lorenzo de' Medici il Magnifico, and established Florence's claim to the great poet. In accordance with the lofty ambitions of the project, one of the most important Florentine artists of the time, Sandro Botticelli, was to provide the designs for the engravings. The engraving was, it seems, assigned to Baccio Baldini. Furthermore, it was in this edition that the commentary by the humanist Cristoforo Landino was published for the first time, which attempted to return the text of the *Commedia* to the original purity and simplicity of the Florentine language. Remarkably, it is precisely the quality of the text in this edition which leaves much to be desired, as there are a great many gaps and discrepancies between the commentary and the text that it discusses. The illustration of the edition was an ambitious and complex undertaking, and was thus perhaps doomed to failure from the start. While the text itself was prepared in letterpress, the images were intended to be placed on the same page in the form of engravings, that is, by means of intaglio printing, requiring two separate and quite distinct work phases. This immediately led to mishaps. For example, the typesetter forgot to leave space for the illustration of *Inferno* I, meaning that it had to be placed beneath the text, where it was subsequently truncated by the bookbinder. What is more, in this copy, the engraving for *Inferno* II was accidentally printed a second time where the illustration of *Inferno* III was supposed to be. However, over several years, a total of nineteen engravings (*Inferno* I–XIX) were eventually produced. Most of the editions that have been preserved – like this one – contain only two or three of them. The connection with Botticelli and his *Commedia* drawings is not entirely clear. However, Botticelli's series can by no means be regarded as preparatory drawings for the engravings; they were an independent project entirely. In part, the similarities between the drawings (for example, that of *Inferno* I in the Vatican) and the corresponding engraving are indeed very close, but then certain differences suggest that the engraver at the very least took liberties with the master's original. Nevertheless, these engravings provide valuable points of reference for what the lost illustrations of *Inferno* (II–VII, XI, XIV) may, more or less, have looked like.

CANTO PRIMO DELLA PRIMA CANTICA O VERO COMEDIA DEL DIVINO POETA FIORENTINO DANTHE ALEGHIERI : CAPITOLO PRIMO :

EL
ME
ZO
DEL
CA
MI
NO
DI
NO
S T
RA
VI
TA

Mi ritrouai peruna selua obscura
che la diricta uia era smarrita
Et quanto adire quale era e/ cosa dura
esta selua seluaggia et aspra et forte
che nel pensier rinuoua lapaura
Tanto era amara che pocho e piu morte
ma per tractar del ben chio ui trouai
diro dellaltre cose chio uho scorte
I non so ben ridire chomio uentrai
tantera pien disonno insu quel puncto
che lauerace uia abbandonai
Ma poi chio fui appie dun colle giunto
la oue terminaua quella ualle
che mhauea dipaur elcor compuncto
Guardai inalto et uidi lesue spalle
coperte gia deraggi delpianeta
che mena dricto altrui per ogni calle
Allhor fu lapaura un pocho queta
che nellago del chuor mera durata
lanocte chio passai con tanta pieta

h abbiamo narrato non solamente lauita del poeta et eltitolo dellibro et che cosa sia poeta Ma etiam quãto sia uetusta et anticha quãto nobile et uaria quanto utile et ioconda tal doctrina. Quanto sia efficace a muouere lhumane mẽti; et quãto dilecti ogni liberale ĩgegno. Ne giudicammo da tacere quanto in si diuina disciplina sia stata la excellentia dello ingegno del nostro poeta. Inche sisono stato piu brieue che forse non si conuerebbe; consideri chi legge che lanumerosa et quasi infinita copia dellecose delle quali e necessario tractare missforza non uolẽdo chel uolume cresca sopra modo; a inculcare et inuiluppare piutosto che explicare; et distẽdere moltecose et maxime quelle lequali quãdo ben tacessi non pero ne resterra obscura la expositione del testo. Verremo adunque aquella. Ma perche stimo non esser lectore alcuno ne di si basso ingegno; ne di si pocho giudicio; che hauendo inteso quanto sia et laprofondita et uarieta della doctrina; et la excellentia et diuinita dello ingegno delnostro toscano; et fiorentino poeta; non si persuada che questo principio delprimo canto debba per sublimita et grandeza esser pari alla stupenda doctrina dellechose che seguitano; pero con ogni industria in uestigheremo che allegoricho senso arechi seco questo mezo delcamino; et che cosa sia selua Dicheueggio non piccola differentia essere stata tra glinterpreti et expositori diquesta cantica. Impero che alchuni dicono; che il mezo della uita humana e el sonno mossi; credo dalla sententia daristotele dicendo lui nellethica nessuna differentia essere tra felici; et miseri nella meta della uita per che lenocti che sono lameta del tempo cinducono sonno; et daquello nasce che ne bene nemale sentir possiamo. Ilperche uogliono questi; che el poeta pongha el mezo della uita per la nocte; et lanocte pelsonno; ad notare che questo poema non sia altro che una uisione che gliapparue dormẽdo per laquale hebbe cognitiõe delle cose dallui descripte ĩ queste tre comedie. Dicono adũque che lui imita Ioanni euangelista el quale dormẽdo sopra elpecto di christo redemptore hebbe uisione delle chose celeste; ouerамẽte ponghi lanocte dimostrando lui hauere cominciato elsuo poema dinocte nella quale raccoglẽdosi lanimo insemedesimo et absoluendosi et liberandosi da ogni cura meglo intenda. Ma benche tale sententia quadri al poeta; nientedimeno leparole non la dimostrono senon cõ tanto obscura ambiguita; che non pare degna della elẽgantia ditanto poeta Prima perche nonseguita che benche nelle reuolutioni deltempo tanto spatio occupin lenocti quanto e di; perquesto dicendo io scripsi dinocte sintenda io scripsi nel mezo della mia eta; perche et nel principio et nelfine della eta humana sono lenocti chome nel mezo et similmente e di. Il perche per lamedesima ragione si potrebbe fare tale interpretatione pel di chome per lanocte. Altridicono che uolle pelmezo del camino intendere che nelmezo delleta dette principio alsuo poema. Ma non e unamedsima opinione deltermine della nostra eta; per che diuersi scriptori diuersamente sentono. Aristotile nel suo de republica

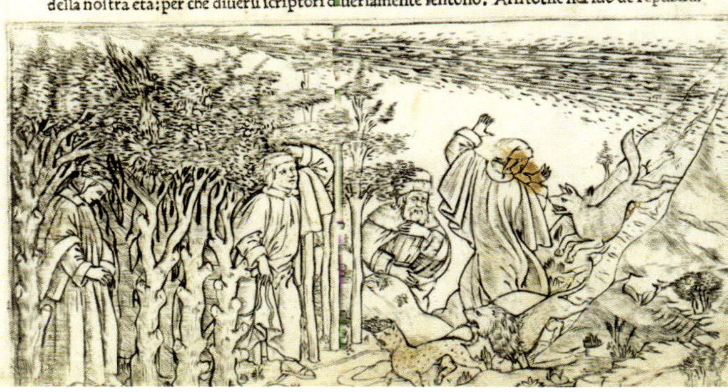

49

La Comedia di Danthe Alighieri Poeta Fiorentino

The *Comedy* of Dante Alighieri with a commentary by Cristoforo Landino

Brescia, Bonino de' Bonini, 31 March 1487

Letterpress print on paper, 34.6 × 24.2 cm; 310 leaves, with 68 partially coloured woodcuts by various artists
Half-bound in leather, brown sheepskin, marbled, 34.4 × 23.5 × 6.2 cm

PROVENANCE Ellis & White, London; acquired for the Kupferstichkabinett in 1881

SHELF NUMBER 2513 (no. 143)

SELECT BIBLIOGRAPHY Berlin/Rome/London 2000–01, appendix, no. 6, p. 352–53 (Peter Keller) with earlier references; Petrella 2012, passim

Not exhibited in London

This 1487 edition of the *Commedia* is one of the masterworks of fifteenth-century Brescian book printing. After the Florence edition of 1481 (cat. no. 48), this was the second illustrated edition of the work, and, in terms of the illustrations, a considerably more successful endeavour. In total, 68 full-page woodcuts adorn the cantos of *Inferno* and *Purgatorio,* right up to the first canto of *Paradiso*. The illustrations, however, are taken from just 60 woodblocks, since some were used multiple times. Such a pragmatic decision is hardly surprising given the scope of the project, although of course it caused discrepancies between text and image. The lack of images for *Paradiso* II can perhaps be explained by the fact that the increasingly abstract material was difficult to illustrate. However, it appears to have been a conscious decision, since from this point on in the text there were no empty pages designated for illustrations. Evidently, for these heavenly events, invisible to the human eye, trust was placed in the pure power of the written word.

This corresponds to the layout of various illuminated manuscripts of the *Commedia*, which, if they included illustrations at all, often confined themselves to *Inferno* and *Purgatorio* (see Malke 2003, p. 128). The borders around the illustrations, which display classical motifs such as candelabra, masks and ornamental scrollwork in white on a black background, were probably already in stock in the printing workshop, since they also appear in other books from this period. The woodcut illustrations themselves are the work of various individuals, although the first nineteen of *Inferno* were clearly modelled on the engravings from the Florence edition of 1481, with a number of differences. In particular, the portrait format necessitated some compositional alterations to the landscape format of the original images. With the illustration of the first canto of *Inferno*, the arrangement of the narrative progression is thus more vertical than horizontal. From the right, Dante exits the forest, walking drowsily and melancholically, his cheek rested on his hand. He glances upwards to the summit of the mountain and is blinded by sunlight, and in the end is frightened – now viewed from the front and not depicted from behind – by the three savage animals, while Virgil walks towards him from the foreground.

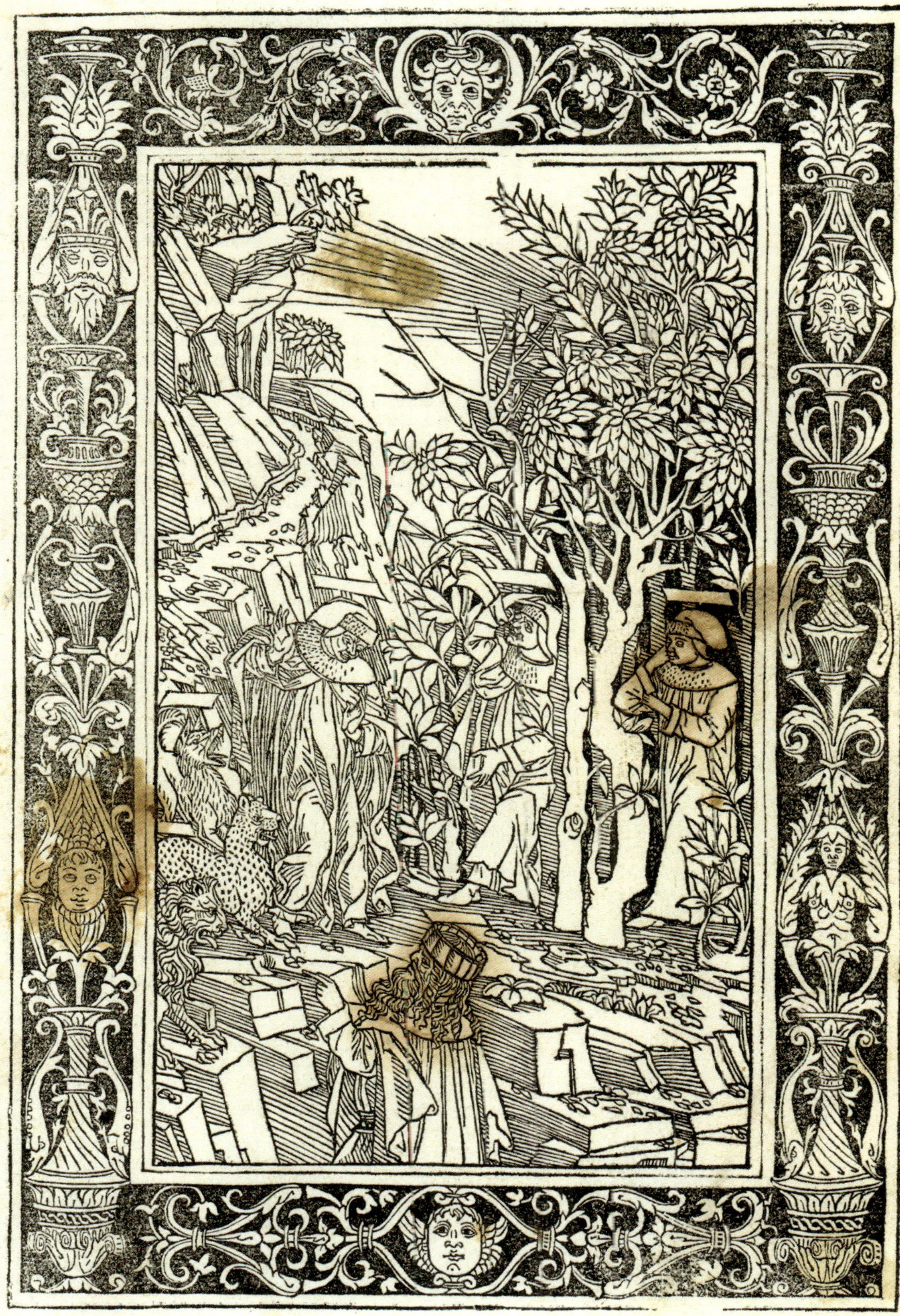

50

La comedia di Danthe alighieri poeta fiorentino

The *Comedy* of Dante Alighieri with a commentary by Cristoforo Landino

Venice, Pietro de' Plasii il Cremonese, 18 November 1491

Letterpress print on paper, 31.3 × 22.5 cm; 324 leaves, with 100 woodcuts by Giovanni Pico della Mirandola
Full-bound in red Morocco leather, 31.2 × 22.3 × 5.0 cm

PROVENANCE Ellis & White, London; Friedrich Lippmann collection; acquired in 1881 for the Kupferstichkabinett

SHELF NUMBER 2754 (no. 194)

SELECT BIBLIOGRAPHY Berlin/Rome/London 2000–01, appendix, no. 7, pp. 354–55 (Peter Keller), with earlier references

Not exhibited in London

It was only in two Venetian editions of 1491 (in addition to this edition, the one by Bernardo Benali and Matteo da Parma from 3 March 1491) that a complete illustration of the *Commedia* was achieved – after the only partially successful attempts in Florentine and Brescian editions (see cat. no. 48, 49) – both of which include the commentary by Cristoforo Landino. For the woodcut illustrations, the strategies that were employed in the two preceding projects – at least for *Inferno* and *Purgatorio* – were used as a model, but again they were modified. Here, the reason for the success of the project becomes apparent: assuming that an image will be added to all one hundred cantos, then a complete illustration of the *Commedia* could only ever be achieved if certain reductions were made in scale, for without them the project would exceed the viable timeframe and labour costs customary for a printed book. This is reflected here in the notably smaller format of the woodcuts and the more extreme simplification of the composition and illustration. In addition, the pictures also reveal a number of changes in content which serve to make their meaning clearer. A prime example of this can be seen in the illustration of *Inferno* I, where Dante's drowsiness is conveyed in his sitting down, and not, as in the illustrations of the previous editions, walking through the dark forest like a sleepwalker. Despite the differing media and demands, looking at these three projects in illustration printing, it becomes clear just how difficult and complex an endeavour Botticelli had set himself in attempting to produce a complete series of illustrations of the *Commedia*.

CANTO PRIMO DE LA PRIma cantica o uero comedia del diuino Poeta Fiorentino Dante Aleghieri. Capitulo. I.

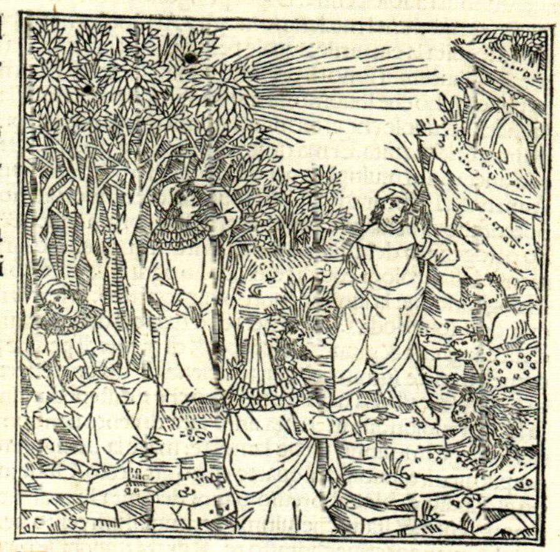

NEL Mezo del camin di noſtra uita
Mi ritrouai p una ſelua obſcura
Che la diricta uia era ſmarrita
Ah quanto adir quale era coſa dura
qſta ſelua ſeluaggia aſpra & forte
che nel penſier rinuoua la paura
Tãto era amara che poco e piu morte
ma per tractar del bẽ chio ui trouai
diro dellaltre coſe chio uo ſcorte
I non ſo ben ridir chomio uentrai
tãtera piẽ di ſonno inſu quel pũcto
che la uerace uia abbandonai
Ma poi chio fui appie dũ colle giũto
la oue terminaua quella ualle
che mhauea di paura el cor cõpũcto
Guardai in alto & uidi le ſue ſpalle
ueſtite gia de raggi del pianeta
che mena diricto altrui p ogni calle
Alhor fu la paura un pocho queta
che nellago del cuor mera durata
la nocte chio paſſai con tanta pieta

hAbbiamo narrato non ſolamente la uita del poeta & el titulo del libro & che coſa ſia poeta: ma etiã quãto ſia uetuſta & anticha: quãto nobile & uaria: quãto utile & ioconda tal doctrina. Quãto ſia efficace a muouere lhumane menti: & quãto dilecti ogni liberale ingegno. Ne giudicammo da tacere quãto ĩ ſi diuina diſciplina ſia ſtata la excellẽtia dello ĩgegno del noſtro poeta. Inche ſi ſono ſtato piu brieue che forſe non ſi conuerebbe: cõſideri chi legge che lanumeroſa & quaſi infinita copia delle choſe dellequali e neceſſario tractare mi fforza non uolẽdo chel uolume creſca ſopra modo: a inculcare & inuiluppare piu toſto che explicare: & diſtendere molte choſe & maxime quelle lequali quãdo bẽ taceſſi non pero ne reſtera obſcura la expoſitione del teſto. Verremo adunque a quella Ma perche ſtimo non eſſer lectore alcuno ne di ſi baſſo ĩgegno: ne di ſi pocho giudicio: che hauẽdo ĩteſo: quãto ſia & la profondita & uarieta della doctrina: & la excellentia & diuinita dello ingegno del noſtro toſcano: & fiorẽtino poeta: non ſi perſuada che queſto principio del primo cãto debba per ſublimita & grandezza eſſer pari alla ſtupẽda doctrina delle choſe che ſeguitano: pero con ogni ĩduſtria inueſtigheremo che allegoricho ſenſo arechi ſeco queſto mezo del camĩo: & che choſa ſia ſelua. Diche ueggio non piccola differentia eſſere ſtata tra glinterpreti & expoſitori di queſta cãtica. Impero che alchuni dicono: che il mezo della uita humana e el ſonno moſſi: credo dalla ſententia daristotile dicẽdo lui nellethica neſſunna differentia eſſere tra felici: & miſeri nella meta della uita perche le nocti che ſono lameta del tempo cinducono ſonno: & da quello naſce che ne bene ne male ſentir poſſiamo. Il perche uogliono queſti: che el poeta pongha el mezo della uita per la nocte: & la nocte pel ſonno: ad notare che queſto poema non ſia altro che una uiſione che gliapparue dormendo per laquale hebbe cognitione delle choſe da lui deſcripte ĩ queſte tre comedie. Dicono adũque che lui imita Ioanni euãgeliſta el quale dormendo ſopra el pecto di chriſto redemptore hebbe uiſione delle choſe celeſte: oueramẽte ponghi la nocte dimoſtrãdo lui hauere comĩciato el ſuo poema di nocte nella quale raccoglẽdoſi lanimo in ſe medeſimo & abſoluendoſi & liberãdoſi da ogni cura meglio ĩtẽda. Ma ben che tale ſententia quadri al poeta: niẽtedimeno le parole non la dimoſtrono ſe non con tanta obſcura ambiguita: che non pare degna della elegãtia di tãto poeta prima perche non ſeguita che benche nelle reuolutioni del tẽpo tãto ſpatio occupin le nocti quãto e di: per queſto dicẽdo io ſcripſi di nocte ſintenda io ſcripſi nel mezo della mia eta: perche & nel prĩcipio & nel fine della eta humana ſonno le nocti chome nel mezo & ſimilmẽte e di. Il perche per la medeſima ragione ſi potrebbe fare tale ĩterpretatiõe pel di come per la nocte
Altri dicono che uole pel mezo del camĩo ĩtẽdere che nel mezo deleta dette prĩcipio al ſuo poema. ma. A
non e una medeſima opinione del termĩe dela noſtra eta: perche diuerſi ſcriptori diuerſamẽte ſentono

Bibliography

Aceto 1992
Francesco Aceto, 'Pittori e documenti della Napoli angioina: aggiunte ed espunzioni', *Prospettiva*, LXVII, 1992, pp. 53–65

Agnoletto 2005
Sara Agnoletto, 'La Calunnia di Apelle: recupero e riconversione ecfrastica del trattatello di Luciano in Occidente', *Engramma. Rivista on line del Seminario di tradizione Classica del Dipartimento di Storia dell'Architettura all'Università IUAV di Venezia*, XLII, 2005; http://www.engramma.it/engramma_v4/rivista/saggio/42/42_saggiogalleria.html

Alexander 1969
Jonathan J.G. Alexander, 'Notes on some Veneto-Paduan Illuminated Books of the Renaissance', *Arte Veneta*, XXVIII, 1969, pp. 9–20

Alexander 1992
Jonathan J.G. Alexander, 'Matteo da Milano, Illuminator', *Pantheon*, L, 1992, pp. 32–45

Augustyn 1989
Wolfgang Augustyn, 'Zu Herkunft und Stil des lateinischen Hamilton-Psalters im Berliner Kupferstichkabinett (78 A 5)', *Jahrbuch der Berliner Museen*, vol. 31, 1989, pp. 107–26

Augustyn 1996
Wolfgang Augustyn, 'Der lateinische Hamilton-Psalter im Berliner Kupferstichkabinett (78 A 5)', *Spolia Berolinensia: Beiträge zur Literatur- und Kulturgeschichte des Mittelalters und der Neuzeit*, Hildesheim etc. 1996

Avril/Reynaud/Cordellier 2011
François Avril, Nicole Reynaud and Dominique Cordellier, *Les Enluminures du Louvre: Moyen Âge et Renaissance*, Paris 2011

Barkan 1999
Leonard Barkan, *Unearthing the Past: Archaeology and Aesthetics in the Making of Renaissance Culture*, New Haven / London 1999

Barolsky 1983
Paul Barolsky, 'Botticelli's Primavera and the tradition of Dante', in *Konsthistorisk tidskrift*, 52, 1983, pp. 1–6

Bartsch 1866
Adam Bartsch, *Le peintre-graveur*, 13 vols., Leipzig 1866

Bashir-Hecht 1985
Herma Bashir-Hecht, 'Die Paradieslandschaft bei Dante und Botticelli', *Die Kunst und das schöne Heim*, vol. 97, 1985, pp. 1031–34

Baskins 1993
Cristelle L. Baskins, 'Donatello's Bronze "David": Grillanda, Goliath, Groom?', *Studies in Iconography*, vol. 15, 1993, pp. 113–34

Batard 1952
Yvonne Batard, *Les dessins de Sandro Botticelli pour la Divine Comédie* (Collection Jeu savant, 2), Paris 1952

Bellini 1990
Paolo Bellini, 'Le due serie di disegni del Botticelli per la Commedia', in *Botticelli e Dante*, exh. cat. ed. Corrado Gizzi, Torre de' Passeri, Pescara / Casa di Dante in Abruzzo, Castello Gizzi, Milan 1990, pp. 41–50

Berenson 1938
Bernard Berenson, *The Drawings of the Florentine Painters, classified, criticised and studied as documents in the history and appreciation of Tuscan art; with a copious catalogue raisonné*, Chicago 1938

Berlin 1975
Zimelien. Abendländische Handschriften des Mittelalters aus den Sammlungen der Stiftung Preußischer Kulturbesitz, exh. cat. ed. Tilo Brandis, Staatliche Museen zu Berlin, Wiesbaden 1975

Berlin/London 2015–16
The Botticelli Renaissance. Botticelli 1445–2015, exh. cat. ed. Stefan Weppelmann und Mark Evans, Berlin, Gemäldegalerie, Staatliche Museen zu Berlin / London, Victoria and Albert Museum, Munich 2015

Berlin/Rome/London 2000–01
Sandro Botticelli. The Drawings for Dante's Divine Comedy, exh. cat. ed. Hein-Th. Schulze Altcappenberg, Berlin, Kupferstichkabinett, StaatlicheMuseen zu Berlin / Rome, Scuderie Papali al Quirinale / London, Royal Academy of Arts, Berlin 2000

Bertam 1950
Anthony Bertram, 'The English Discovery of Botticelli', *Journal of the Society of Arts*, vol. 98, no. 4819, 1950, pp. 468–84

Bessi 1987
Rossella Bessi, 'Il commento di Francesco Filelfo ai "Rerum vulgarium fragmenta"', *Quaderni petrarcheschi*, IV, 1987, pp. 229–70

Biadene 1887
Leandro Biadene, 'Manoscritti italiani della collezione Hamilton nel R. Museo e nella R. Biblioteca di Berlino', *Giornale storico della letteratura italiana*, X, 1887, pp. 313–55

Bjurström 2001
Per Bjurström, *Italian Drawings from the Collection of Giorgio Vasari, National Museum Stockholm*, Stockholm 2001

Bode 1903
Wilhelm Bode, 'Friedrich Lippmann, Direktor des Berliner Kupferstichkabinetts, gestorben am 2. Oktober 1903', *Kunstchronik. Wochenschrift für Kunst und Kunstgewerbe*, N.F. XV, no. 5, 20 November 1903, pp. 81–88

Bode 1930
Wilhelm von Bode, *Mein Leben*, 2 vols., Berlin 1930

Boese 1966
Helmut Boese, *Die lateinischen Handschriften der Sammlung Hamilton zu Berlin*, Wiesbaden 1966

Bologna 1969
Ferdinando Bologna, *I pittori alla corte angioina di Napoli 1266–1414*, Rome 1969

Bräm 2007
Andreas Bräm, *Neapolitanische Bilderbibeln des Trecento: Anjou-Buchmalerei von Robert dem Weisen bis zu Johanna I.*, Wiesbaden 2007

Braun 2011
Ernst Braun (ed.), *Max Liebermann: Briefe 1869–1895* (Schriftenreihe der Max-Liebermann-Gesellschaft Berlin, ed. Martin Faass, Band I), Baden-Baden 2011

Breslau 2003
Ralf Breslau, 'Die Provenienzen bis 1945. Die Erwerbung deutscher mittelalterlicher Handschriften und Inkunabeln 1661–1945', in *Aderlass und Seelentrost*, exh. cat. ed. Peter Jörg Becker and Eef Overgaauw, Berlin, Staatsbibliothek Berlin / Nuremberg, Germanisches Nationalmuseum), Mainz 2003, pp. 1–10

Brunner 1999
Michael Brunner, *Die Illustrierung von Dantes Divina Commedia in der Zeit der Dante-Debatte (1570–1600)*, Munich etc. 1999

Büttner 2006
Frank Büttner, 'John Flaxmans Illustrationen zu Dantes Divina Commedia. Die ersten Skizzen und die Herausbildung des "Umrißlinienstils"', in *Italiensehnsucht. Kunsthistorische: Aspekte eines Topos*, ed. Hildegard Wiegel, Munich / Berlin 2006, pp. 95–109

Carminati 1995
Marco Carminati, *Codici miniati del maestro B.F. a Casorate Primo*, Pavia 1995

Clark 1976
Kenneth Clark, *The Drawings by Sandro Botticelli for Dante's Divine Commedy after the Originals in the Berlin Museums and the Vatican*, London 1976

Clarke 1819
William Clarke, *Repertorium Bibliographicum; or, Some account of the most celebrated British libraries*, London 1819

C.D. 1904
C.D., 'The Late Dr. Lippmann', *The Burlington Magazine for Connoisseurs*, IV, no. 10, January 1904, pp. 7–8

Cogliati Arano 1985
Luisa Cogliati Arano, 'L'Acerba di Cecco D'Ascoli alla Biblioteca Laurenziana: datazione', in *La miniatura italiana tra gotico e rinascimento, in Atti del II congresso di storia della miniatura italiana (Cortona, 24.–26. September 1982)*, ed. E. Sesti, Florence 1985, pp. 243–53

Cologne 2011–12
Vor dem Gesetz. Skulpturen der Nachkriegszeit und Räume der Gegenwartskunst, exh. cat. ed. Kasper König et al., Cologne, Museum Ludwig, Cologne 2012

Concetta 1985
Bianca Concetta, 'La biblioteca di Andrea Matteo Acquaviva', in *Gli Acquaviva d'Aragona: duchi di Atri e conti di S. Flaviano, Atti del VI Convegno, Teramo, Morrodoro, Atri, Giulianova, 13–15 October 1983)*, Teramo 1985, pp. 159–73

Cox-Rearick 1994
Janet Cox-Rearick, 'Sacred to Profane: Diplomatic Gifts of the Medici to Francis I', *Journal of Medieval and Renaissance Studies*, vol. 24, 1994, pp. 239–58

D'Ancona 1920
Paolo D'Ancona, 'Un codice dell'Acerba di Cecco D'Ascoli illustrato da un ignoto lombardo del secolo XV', *L'Arte*, XXIII, 1920, pp. 120–24

D'Urso 2007
Teresa D'Urso, 'Giovanni Todeschino. La miniatura "all'antica" tra Venezia, Napoli e Tours', *Memorie dell'Accademia di archeologia, lettere e belle arti di Napoli*, XVI, Naples 2007

Dante, *Commedia*
Dante Alighieri, *La Commedia*, ed. Giorgio Petrocchi, Milan 1966

Dante, *Vita Nuova*
Dante Alighieri, *La Vita Nuova di Dante Alighieri*, ed. Michele Barbi, Florence 1932

Delaborde 1882
Henri Delaborde, *La Gravure: précis élémentaire de ses origines, de ses procédés et de son histoire*, Paris 1882

Dombrowski 1992
Damian Dombrowski, 'Die Divina Commedia als Stätte der Ganzheit. Sandro Botticellis Dante-Visionen', typescript, Magister-Arbeit, Westfälische Wilhelms-Universität, Münster 1992

Dombrowski 1996
Damian Dombrowski, 'Beobachtungen zu Botticellis Dante-Illustrationen', *Deutsches Dante-Jahrbuch*, vol. 71, 1996, pp. 45–75

Dombrowski 2013
Damian Dombrowksi, 'Botticelli, Dante and Space in Portraiture', in *Inventing Faces. Rhetorics of Portraiture between Renaissance and Modernism*, ed. Mona Körte et al., Berlin / Munich 2013, pp. 44–66

Dresden 2013
Ars nova: frühe Kupferstiche aus Italien; Katalog der italienischen Kupferstiche von den Anfängen bis um 1530 in der Sammlung des Dresdener Kupferstich-Kabinetts, exh. cat. ed. Gudula Metze, Dresden, Kupferstich-Kabinett, Petersberg 2013

Dreyer 1984
Peter Dreyer, 'Botticelli's series of engravings of 1481', *Print Quarterly*, I, no. 2, 1984, pp. 111–15

Dreyer 1986
Peter Dreyer, *Dantes Divina Commedia mit den Illustrationen von Sandro Botticelli. Codex Reg. Lat. 1896. Codex Ham. 201 (Cim. 33)*, Kommentarband zum Faksimile, Zurich 1986

Duplessis 1869
Georges Duplessis, *Les Merveilles de la gravure*, Paris 1869

Duplessis 1880
Georges Duplessis, *Histoire de la gravure en Italie, en Espagne, en Allemagne, dans les Pays-Bas, en Angleterre et en France*, Paris 1880

Eichberg 1998
Barbara Bruderer Eichberg, *Les neuf choeurs angéliques. Origine et evolution du theme dans l'art du Moyen Âge*, Civilisation Médiévale, VI, Poitiers 1998

Elbern 1990
Victor Elbern, *Wie im Himmel so auf Erden. Der christliche Bilderkreis in 150 Kunstwerken*, Berlin 1990

Elen 1995
Albert Jan Elen, *Italian Late-Medieval and Renaissance Drawing-Books from Giovannino de' Grassi to Palma Giovane: A Codicological Approach*, Leiden 1995

Engel 1882
Eduard Engel, 'Aus Anlass der Erwerbung der Hamilton-Sammlung für die königliche Bibliothek zu Berlin', *Zeitschrift für die Literatur des In- und Auslandes*, 23 December 1882, pp. 736–39

Engel 2006
Henrik Engel, *Dantes Inferno: zur Geschichte der Höllenvermessung und des Höllentrichtermotivs* (Kunstwissenschaftliche Studien 133), Munich etc. 2006

'Engraving' 1853
'Engraving and Printing on Copper', *The Illustrated Magazine of Art*, vol. 1, no. 5, 1853, pp. 292–97

Erbach-Fürstenau 1905
Adalbert zu Erbach-Fürstenau, 'Pittura e miniatura a Napoli nel secolo XIV', *L'Arte*, VIII, 1905, pp. 1–17

Evans 2005
Mark Evans, 'The Politicized Page: the Sforza Succession and Humanist Book Decoration in Milan', in *Manuscripts in Transition, Tagungsband (Brüssel, 5–9 Nov. 2002)*, ed. B. Dekeyzer and J. van der Stock, Leuven 2005, pp. 347–55

Festschrift 1880
Zur Geschichte der Königlichen Museen in Berlin. Festschrift zur Feier ihres fünfzigjährigen Bestehens am 3. August 1880, Berlin 1880

Fowler 1883
M.B.O. Fowler, 'Theory and Practice of Pen-Drawing', *The Art Amateur*, vol. 9, no. 2, July 1883, pp. 26–35

Frew/Lowrey 1991
John Frew / John Lowrey, 'Richard Payne Knight and Alexander, Future 10th Duke of Hamilton: A Rediscovered Correspondence, 1812–1815', *The Burlington Magazine*, CXXXIII, no. 1061, August 1991, pp. 541–43

Frey 1892
Carl Frey, *Il Codice Magliabechiano,* Berlin 1892

Fulford 1981
Roger Fulford (ed.), *Beloved Mama: Private Correspondence of Queen Victoria and the German Crown Princess 1878–1885,* London 1981

Garzelli 1985
Annarosa Garzelli, *Miniatura fiorentina del Rinascimento. Un primo censimento 1440–1525,* vol. 1, Florence 1985

Giordano 1991
L. Giordano (ed.), *B.F. e il Maestro di Paolo e Daria: un codice e un problema di miniatura lombarda*, Pavia 1991

Girolami Cheney 1988
Liana de Girolami Cheney, 'I disegni di Botticelli per la Divina Commedia di Dante', in *Letteratura italiana e arti figurative*, ed. A. Franceschetti, vol. 1, Florence, pp. 261–67

Gothein 1915
Eberhard Gothein, *Il Rinascimento nell'Italia meridionale,* Florence 1915

Greco 1990
Luigi Greco, 'Un libraire italien à Paris: Gian Claudio Molini (1724–1812)', *Mélanges de la Bibliothèque de la Sorbonne*, vol. 10, 1990, pp. 103–21

Handbuch 1994
Das Berliner Kupferstichkabinett. Ein Handbuch zur Sammlung, ed. Alexander Dückers, Berlin 1994

Havely 2014
Nicholas Havely, *Dante's British Public. Readers and Texts from the Fourteenth Century to the Present,* Oxford 2014

Hayes 2008
Kevin J. Hayes, *The Road to Monticello: The Life and Mind of Thomas Jefferson,* Oxford / New York 2008

Heinecken 1771
Karl Heinrich von Heinecken, *Idée générale d'une collection complette d'estampes, avec une dissertation sur l'origine de la gravure et sur les premiers livres d'images,* Leipzig / Vienna 1771

Heinecken 1778–90
Karl Heinrich von Heinecken, *Dictionnaire des artistes, dont nous avons des estampes,* Leipzig 1778–90

Hermann 1898
Julius Hermann, 'Miniaturhandschriften aus der Bibliothek des Herzogs Andrea Matteo III: Acquaviva', *Jahrbuch der kunsthistorischen Sammlungen des allerhöchsten Kaiserhauses,* XIX, 1898, pp. 147–216

Hermann 1994
H.J. Hermann, *La miniatura estense,* ed. Federica Toniolo, Modena 1994

Hind 1935
Arthur M. Hind, *An Introduction to a History of Woodcut* (London 1935), New York 1963

Holtus/Wunderli 2005
Günther Holtus / Peter Wunderli, *Franco-italien et épopée franco-italienne,* Grundriss der romanischen Literaturen des Mittelalters (GRLMA) III.1/2.10, Heidelberg 2005

Hutson 1986
James H. Hutson (ed.), *Supplement to Max Farrand's The Records of the Federal Convention of 1787,* New Haven 1986, p. XXIII

Jacoby 2014
Joachim Jacoby, *Raffael bis Tizian. Italienische Zeichnungen aus dem Städel Museum,* Petersberg 2014

Kablitz 1998
Andreas Kablitz, 'Jenseitige Kunst oder Gott als Bildhauer. Die Reliefs in Dantes Purgatorio (Purg. X–XII)', in *Mimesis und Simulation*, ed. Andreas Kablitz and Gerhard Neumann, Freiburg im Breisgau 1998, pp. 309–56

Keller 2000
Peter Keller, 'Die Kupferstiche zur Ausgabe der Göttlichen Komödie von 1481', in *Sandro Botticelli. Der Bilderzyklus zu Dantes Göttlicher Komödie*, exh. cat. ed. Hein-Th. Schulze Altcappenberg, Berlin, Kupferstichkabinett / Rome, Scuderie Papali al Quirinale / London, Royal Academy of Arts, Berlin 2000, pp. 326–33

Kilian 2014
Sven Thorsten Kilian, '"Non sanza prima far grande aggirata" – Turning the Pages in Dante and Botticelli', in *Dante e L'Arte, 1, Dante e il teatro*, 2014, pp. 227–40; http://revistes.uab.cat/dea/article/view/v1-kilian

Klemm 2009
David Klemm, *Italienische Zeichnungen 1450–1800 (Die Sammlungen der Hamburger Kunsthalle), Kupferstichkabinett,* 3 vols., Cologne / Weimar / Vienna 2009

Klettke 2010
Cornelia Klettke, 'Paradiesmystik im Grenzbereich des Nicht-Darstellbaren. Par. XXX: Dantes Wortgemälde und Botticellis Zeichnung. Analyse eines Medienwechsels', in*Letteratura & Arte*, 8 (*Immaginazione-Evocazione-Immagine. Dimensioni Teorico-Estetiche del rapporto Testo-Immagine nella Letteratura Italiana. Atti del Convegno di Berlino)* (Humboldt-Universität zu Berlin, 8–10 May 2008), ed. Michèle Mattusch und Sylvia Setzkorn, Pisa / Rome 2010, pp. 55–83

Korbacher 2014
Dagmar Korbacher, 'Paradiso Terrestre su pergamena: il canto XXVIII del Purgatorio disegnato da Sandro Botticelli', in *Dante e L'Arte, 1, Dante e il teatro*, 2014, pp. 207–26; http://revistes.uab.cat/dea/article/view/v1-korbacher

Kristeller 1913
Paul Kristeller, *Die Lombardische Graphik der Renaissance,* Berlin 1913

Küpper 2006
Joachim Küpper, 'Bilder der Sünde: Dante und Botticelli', *Deutsches Dante-Jahrbuch*, vol. 81, 2006, pp. 155–73

de La Chapelle 2015
Ariane de La Chapelle, 'Raphael: The Price of Success, or how to make several drawings from one', in *Raffael als Zeichner / Raphael as Draughtsman. Die Beiträge des Frankfurter Kolloquiums*, ed. Joachim Jacoby und Martin Sonnabend, Frankfurt am Main 2015, pp. 35–48

Leone de Castris 1986
Pierluigi Leone de Castris, *Arte di corte nella Napoli angioina,* Florence 1986

Levey 1960
Michael Levey, 'Botticelli and Nineteenth Century England', *Journal of the Warburg and Courtauld Institutes*, XXIII, 1960, pp. 291–306

Lightbown 1978
Ronald W. Lightbown, *Sandro Botticelli. Complete Catalogue,* London 1978

Lippmann 1882
Friedrich Lippmann, 'Der italienische Holzschnitt im XV. Jahrhundert (Fortsetzung)', *Jahrbuch der Königlich Preußischen Kunstsammlungen*, III, 1882, pp. 167–89

Lippmann 1883
Friedrich Lippmann, 'Die Zeichnungen des Sandro Botticelli zur Göttlichen Komödie', *Jahrbuch der Königlich Preußischen Kunstsammlungen*, IV, 1883, pp. 63–72

Lippmann 1884
Friedrich Lippmann, 'Der italienische Holzschnitt im XV. Jahrhundert (Fortsetzung)', *Jahrbuch der Königlich Preußischen Kunstsammlungen*, V, 1884, pp. 3 –26

Lippmann 1887
Friedrich Lippmann, *Zeichnungen von Sandro Botticelli zu Dante's Göttlicher Komödie nach den Originalen im K. Kupferstichkabinett zu Berlin*, 2 vols., Berlin 1887

Lippmann 1888
Friedrich Lippmann, *The Art of Wood Engraving in Italy in the Fifteenth Century*, London 1888

Lippmann 1921
Friedrich Lippmann, *Zeichnungen von Sandro Botticelli zu Dantes Göttlicher Komödie. Verkleinerte Nachbildungen der Originale im Kupferstichkabinett zu Berlin und in der Bibliothek des Vatikans, mit einer Einleitung und der Erklärung der Darstellungen*, Berlin (2nd edn) 1921

London/Florence 2010–11
Fra Angelico to Leonardo. Italian Renaissance Drawings, exh. cat. ed. Hugo Chapman and Marzia Faietti, London, The British Museum / Florence, Gabinetto disegni e stampe degli Uffizi, London 2010

London/Los Angeles 2003
Illuminating the Renaissance. The Triumph of Flemish Manuscript Painting in Europe, exh. cat. ed. Thomas Kren und Scot McKendrick, London, Royal Academy of Arts / Los Angeles, The Getty Museum, Los Angeles 2003

London/New York 1994–95
The Painted Page. Italian Renaissance Book Illumination 1450 –1550, exh. cat. ed. Jonathan J.G. Alexander, London, Royal Academy of Arts / New York, Pierpont Morgan Library, Munich 1994

Los Angeles 2010–11
Imagining the Past in France: History in Manuscript Painting 1250–1500, exh. cat. ed. Elizabeth Morrison and Anne D. Hedeman, Los Angeles, The Getty Museum, Los Angeles 2010

Milan 1958
Arte Lombarda dai Visconti agli Sforza, exh. cat. ed. Roberto Longhi, Milan, Palazzo Reale, Milan 1958

Malke 2003
Lutz S. Malke, 'Zur Entwicklung der Commedia-Illustration', *Deutsches Dante-Jahrbuch*, vol. 78, 2003, pp. 123–52

Mariani Canova 1969
Giordana Mariani Canova, *La miniatura veneta del Rinascimento, 1450 –1500*, Venice 1969

Mariani Canova 1998
Giordana Mariani Canova, 'La miniatura a Ferrara', in *La miniatura a Ferrara. Dal tempo di Cosmè Tura all'eredità di Ercole de' Roberti*, exh. cat. ed. Federica Toniolo, Ferrara, Palazzo Schifanoia, Modena 1998, pp. 15–38

Mariani Canova 2009
Giordana Mariani Canova, 'La miniatura in Veneto', in *La miniatura in Italia*, II, *Dal Tardogotico al manierismo*, ed. A. Putaturo Donati Murano and A. Perriccioli Saggese, Naples 2009

Marmor 2003
Max C. Marmor, 'From Purgatory to the "Primavera": Some Observations on Botticelli and Dante', *Artibus et Historiae*, vol. 24, no. 48, 2003, pp. 199–212

Masséna 1907–14
Victor Massena, Prince d'Essling, *Les livres à figures vénitiens de la fin du XVe siècle et du commencement du XVIe*, Florence / Paris 1907–14

Massing 1990
Jean Michel Massing, *Du texte à l'image. La Calomnie d'Apelle et son iconographie*, Strasbourg 1990

Mauro 2006
Walter Mauro, *Il doppio segno. Visioni di artisti che hanno illustrato la Divina Commedia: Signorelli, Botticelli, Michelangelo, Raffaello, Stradano, Zuccari, Füssli, Blake, Koch, Scaramuzza, Martini, Dalì, Sassu*, San Cesareo 2006

Medica 1998
Massimo Medica, 'Da Leonello a Borso: il protorinascimento a Ferrara e i suoi esiti', in *La miniatura a Ferrara. Dal tempo di Cosmè Tura all'eredità di Ercole de' Roberti*, exh. cat. ed. Federica Toniolo, Ferrara, Palazzo Schifanoia, Modena 1998, pp. 75–78

Mendelsohn 1982
Leatrice Mendelsohn, *Paragoni: Benedetto Varchi's Due Lezzioni and Cinquecento Art Theory*, Ann Arbor 1982

Meier 2013
Franziska Meier, *Renaissance des Mittelalters? Zu den Dante-Illustrationen von Sandro Botticelli*, Texte zur Diskussion, Kunstgeschichte. Open Peer Reviewed Journal, 2013; urn:nbn:de:bvb:355-kuge-331-9

Möhle 1963
Hans Möhle, *Das Berliner Kupferstichkabinett*, Berlin 1963

Molini 1774
Catalogo di libri italiani, edizioni antiche e moderne. Che trovansi presso Gio: Claudio Molini, libraio, rue de la Harpe, vis-à-vis celle de la Parcheminerie. Esteso per ordine alfabetico, e per nome degli autori, Paris 1774

Molini 1785
Catalogo di libri italiani di autori antichi, esteso per ordine alfabetico delle opere e degli autori, e di edizioni a tutto il passato secolo, che trovansi presso G. C. Molini, libraio, rue Mignon, quartier S. André-des-Arcs, vis-à-vis l'Imprimeur du Parlement, Paris 1785

Monbeig Goguel 1987
Catherine Monbeig Goguel, 'Le dessin encadré', *Revue de l'Art*, vol. 76, 1987, pp. 25–31

Morgan 2003
Leslie Zarker Morgan, 'The Passion of Ynide: Ynide's Defense in Huon d'Auvergne (Berlin, Staatsbibliothek, Hamilton 337)', *Medioevo Romanzo*, XXVII, 2003

Morgan 2008
Leslie Zarker Morgan, '(Mis)-quoting Dante: Early epic intertextuality in Huon d'Auvergne', *Neophilologus*, XCII, 2008, pp. 577–99

Morrison 2012
Karl F. Morrison, 'Moving Pictures: Dante and Botticelli (Purgatorio 10, 12, 28–33) and the Millenial Celebration of St Romuald's Martyrdom (Malines 1775)', in *Envisioning Experience in Late Antiquity and the Middle Ages. Dynamic Patterns in Texts and Images*, ed. Giselle de Nie und Thomas F.X. Noble, Farnham / Burlington 2012, pp. 47– 91

New York 2005–06
The Splendor of the Word: Medieval and Renaissance Illuminated Manuscripts at the New York Public Library, exh. cat. ed. Jonathan J.G. Alexander, James H. Marrow and Lucy Freeman Sandler, New York, Public Library, London 2005

Oltrogge/Fuchs/Hahn 2000
Doris Oltrogge / Robert Fuchs / Oliver Hahn, 'Finito und Nonfinito. Zur Technik von Zeichnung und Malerei in Botticellis *Divina Commedia*', in *Sandro Botticelli. Der Bilderzyklus zu Dantes Göttlicher Komödie*, exh. cat. ed. Hein-Th. Schulze Altcappenberg, Berlin, Kupferstichkabinett / Rome, Scuderie Papali al Quirinale / London, Royal Academy of Arts, Berlin 2000, pp. 334–41

Ottley 1816
William Young Ottley, *An Inquiry into the Origin and Early History of Engraving upon Copper and in Wood with an Account of Engravers and their Works from the Invention of Chalcography by Maso Finiguerra to the time of Marc'Antonio Raimondi*, vol. 1, London 1816

Pallat 1959
Ludwig Pallat, *Richard Schöne. Generaldirektor der Königlichen Museen zu Berlin. Ein Beitrag zur Geschichte der preußischen Kunstverwaltung 1872–1905*, Berlin 1959

Papillo 2007 a
Paul J. Papillo, 'Sandro Botticelli, Morgan's M676, and Pictorial Narrative: Gothic Antecedents to a Renaissance Dante', *Word and Image*, vol. 23, no. 1, 2007, pp. 89–115

Papillo 2007 b
Paul J. Papillo, 'Rogue Images in Manuscripts of the Divine Comedy', *Word and Image*, vol. 23, no. 4, 2007, pp. 421–38

Parronchi 1990
Alessandro Parronchi, 'Le illustrazioni del Botticelli per la "Commedia" e il progetto di un "Pantheon" fiorentino', in *Botticelli e Dante*, exh. cat. ed. Corrado Gizzi, Torre de' Passeri, Pescara / Casa di Dante in Abruzzo, Castello Gizzi, Milan 1990, pp. 77–80

Pater (1870) 1986
Walter Pater, 'Sandro Botticelli', in *The Renaissance*, ed. Adam Phillips, Oxford 1986

Perriccioli Saggese 2002
Alessandra Perriccioli Saggese, 'Modelli giotteschi nella miniatura napoletana del Trecento, in Medioevo: i modelli', in *Atti del Convegno Internazionale di Studi (Parma, 27 settembre – 1 ottobre 1999)*, ed. A. Quintavalle, Parma 2002, pp. 661–67

Perriccioli Saggese 2010
Alessandra Perriccioli Saggese, 'Cristophoro Orimina. An Illuminator at the Angevin Court of Naples', in *The Anjou Bible. A Royal Manuscript Revealed. Naples 1340*, ed. Lieve Watteeuw and Jan van der Stock, Paris / Leuven 2010, pp. 113–25

Pescara 1985
Füssli e Dante, exh. cat. ed. Corrado Gizzi, Torre de' Passeri, Pescara / Casa di Dante in Abruzzo, Castello Gizzi, Milan 1985

Pescara 1990
Botticelli e Dante, exh. cat. ed. Corrado Gizzi, Torre de' Passeri, Pescara / Casa di Dante in Abruzzo, Castello Gizzi, Milan 1990

Petrella 2012
Giancarlo Petrella, *Dante Alighieri, Commedia, Brescia, Bonino Bonini, 1487. Repertorio iconografico delle silografie*, C.R.E.L.E.B. – Università Cattolica, Milano, Milan 2012

Popham/Pouncey 1950
A.E. Popham / Philip Pouncey, *Italian Drawings in the Department of Prints and Drawings in the British Museum*, London 1950

Ragghianti Collobi 1996
Licia Ragghianti Collobi, *Il Libro de' Disegni del Vasari*, Florence 1996

Rao 2007
Ida Giovanna Rao, 'Il cosmo illustrato. L'Acerba di Cecco D'Ascoli', *Alumina*, V, 2007, pp. 46–51

Reggio Emilia 2000–01
Disegno antico: i disegni della collezione Villani donati ai Musei civici di Reggio Emilia, exh. cat. ed. Mario Di Giampaolo et al., Reggio Emilia, Musei Civici, Bologna 2000

Rehm 2007
Ulrich Rehm, '"Richte Deinen Geist nicht nur auf einen Ort!" – Spuren der Zeitlichkeit in Sandro Botticellis *Divina Commedia*', in *Zeitlichkeit in Text und Bild*, ed. Franziska Sick and Christof Schöch, Heidelberg 2007, pp. 303–18

Reiss 1991
Sheryl Reiss, 'Cardinal Giulio de' Medici's 1520 Berlin Missal and other works by Matteo da Milano', *Jahrbuch der Berliner Museen*, XXXIII, 1991, pp. 107–28

Ricci (1930) 1960
Seymour de Ricci, *English Collectors of Books and Manuscripts 1530–1930* (1930), Bloomington 1960

Rieger 2002
Angelica Rieger, *L'Ystoire du bon roi Alexandre: der Berliner Alexanderroman; Handschrift 78 C 1 des Kupferstichkabinetts Preußischer Kulturbesitz Berlin. Begleitband zur Faksimile-Ausgabe*, Stuttgart / Lachen am Zürichsee 2002

Rieger 2006
Angelica Rieger, *Der Alexanderroman: ein Ritterroman über Alexander den Großen. Handschrift 78 C 1 des Kupferstichkabinetts, Preußischer Kulturbesitz Berlin*, Wiesbaden 2006

Risset 2008
Jacqueline Risset, 'De Botticelli à Dante. Naissance de Beatrice', in *La Divine Comédie. Dante Alighieri. Illustrations. Sandro Botticelli*, ed. Diane de Selliers, Florence, pp. 11–25

Röthlisberger 1956
Marcel Röthlisberger, 'Notes on the Drawing Books of Jacopo Bellini', *The Burlington Magazine*, XCVIII, 1956, pp. 358–64

Rubin 2007
Patricia Rubin, *Images and Identity in Fifteenth Century Florence*, New Haven / London 2007

Ruskin 1903–12
The works of John Ruskin, ed. E.T. Cook / Alexander Wedderburn, London 1903–12

Sale catalogue 1882
The Hamilton Palace Libraries. The Hamilton Collection of Manuscripts, Sotheby, Wilkinson & Hodge, London 1882

Sale catalogue 1889
Catalogue of Ninety-one Manuscripts on Vellum, illuminated by English (Anglo-Saxon), Byzantine, French, Flemish, Dutch, Burgundian, German, Italian and Spanish Artists, of the VIIth to the XVIIth Century, chiefly from the Famous Hamilton Collection, and till lately in the possession of The Royal Museum of Berlin, Sotheby, Wilkinson & Hodge, London, 23 May 1889

Scattolini 2012
Michela Scattolini, 'Berlin, Kupferstichkabinett 78 D 8', *Repertorio Informatizzato Antica Letteratura Franco-Italiana* (entered 14 November 2012); www.rialfri.eu/rialfriWP/manoscritti/berlin-kupferstichkabinett-78-d-8

Schöne 1904
Richard Schöne, 'Zur Erinnerung an Friedrich Lippmann', *Jahrbuch der Königlich Preußischen Kunstsammlungen*, XXV, no. 1, 1904, pp. III–VIII

Schulze Altcappenberg 2000
Hein-Th. Schulze Altcappenberg, 'Per essere persona sofistica. Botticellis Bilderzyklus zur Göttlichen Komödie', in *Sandro Botticelli. Der Bilderzyklus zu Dantes Göttlicher Komödie*, exh. cat. ed. Hein-Th. Schulze Altcappenberg, Berlin, Kupferstichkabinett / Rome, Scuderie Papali al Quirinale / London, Royal Academy of Arts, Berlin 2000, pp. 14–35

Seidlitz 1883–85
Woldemar von Seidlitz, 'Die illustrirten Handschriften der Hamilton-Sammlung zu Berlin', *Repertorium für Kunstwissenschaft*, VI, 1883, pp. 256–73; VII, 1884, pp. 78–79, 295–306; VIII, 1885, pp. 94–110

Sottili 1974
Agostino Sottili, 'Codici del Petrarca nella Germania Occidentale, VII', *Italia Medioevale e Umanistica*, XVIII, 1974

Stapleford 1995
Richard Stapleford, 'Vasari and Botticelli', *Mitteilungen des Kunsthistorischen Institutes in Florenz*, XLIX, nos. 2/3, 1993, pp. 397–408

Steenbock 1998
Frauke Steenbock, 'Zur Überlieferungs-geschichte des Stundenbuchs der Maria von Burgund und Kaiser Maximilians', in *Das Berliner Stundenbuch der Maria von Burgund und Kaiser Maximilians. Handschrift 78 B 12 im Kupferstichkabinett derStaatlichen Museen zu Berlin*, ed. Eberhard König mit Beiträgen von Fedja Anzelewsky, Bodo Brinkmann und Frauke Steenbock, Lachen am Zürichsee 1998, pp. 155–64

Stoltz 2011
Barbara Stoltz, *Gesetz der Welt – Ordo der Kunst. Federico Zuccaris Dante-Zeichnungen*, Hildesheim 2011

Strzygowski 1885–86
Josef Strzygowski, 'Neuentdeckte Handzeichnungen Botticelli's zum Inferno', *Kunstchronik, Beiblatt zur Zeitschrift für Bildende Kunst und zum Kunstgewerbeblatt*, vol. 21, no. 28, 1885–86, cols. 465–72

Strzygowski 1887
Josef Strzygowski, *Die acht Handzeichnungen des Sandro Botticelli zu Dante's Göttlicher Komödie im Vatikan. Ein Supplement zu dem Codex im Kgl. Kupferstichkabinett zu Berlin*, 2 vols., *Faksimile der Illustrationen und erklärende Beschreibung*, Berlin 1887

Stuttgart 1980
Dante, Vergil, Geryon: der 17. Höllengesang der Göttlichen Komödie in der bildenden Kunst, exh. cat. ed. Christian von Holst, Stuttgart, Staatsgalerie, Stuttgart 1980

Swinburne (1868) 1901
Algernon Charles Swinburne, 'Notes on Designs of the Old Masters at Florence', in *Essays and Studies, 1837–1909*, 5th edn, pp. 314–57

Tait 1983
A.A. Tait, 'The Duke of Hamilton's Palace', *The Burlington Magazine*, CXXV, no. 964, July 1983, pp. 394–402

Thoss 1987
Dagmar Thoss, *Flämische Buchmalerei. Handschriftenschätze aus dem Burgunderreich*, exh. cat., Österreichische Nationalbibliothek, Vienna, Vienna / Graz 1987

Titus et al. 2006
Sonja Titus, Regina Schneller, Gerhard Banik, Enke Huhsmann und Ulrike Hähner, *The Copying Press Process: History and Technology, Part 1*, Restaurator 27, 2006, pp. 90–102

Toesca 1912
Pietro Toesca, *La pittura e la miniatura nella Lombardia dai più antichi monumenti alla metà del Quattrocento*, Milan 1912

Toesca 1922
Pietro Toesca, 'Sandro Botticelli e Dante', *La Bibliofilia. Rivista di Storia del libro e delle arti grafiche*, XXIV, 1922, pp. 1–19

Tomei/Paone 2010
Alessandro Tomei / Stefania Paone, 'Paintings and Miniatures in Naples: Cavallini, Giotto and the Portraits of Robert', in *The Anjou Bible. A Royal Manuscript Revealed. Naples 1340*, ed. Lieve Watteeuw and Jan van der Stock, Paris / Leuven 2010, pp. 53–71

Toscano 1993
Gennaro Toscano, 'La librairie des rois d'Aragon à Naples', *Bulletin du Bibliophile*, II, 1993, pp. 265–83

Vasari (1550/1568) 1987
Giorgio Vasari, *Le vite de' più eccellenti pittori, scultori e architettori: nelle redazioni del 1550 e 1568*, ed. Rosanna Bettarini und Paola Barocchi, Florence, 1987

Vasari (1550/1568) 2010
Giorgio Vasari, *Das Leben des Sandro Botticelli, Filippino Lippi, Cosimo Rosselli und Alesso Baldovinetti*, trans. Victoria Lorini, ed. Damian Dombrowski et al., Berlin 2010

Venturi 1921
Adolfo Venturi, *Il Botticelli interprete di Dante*, Florence 1921

Voigt 2014
'Alte Meister, von neuem geliebt, interview mit Jorinde Voigt, aufgezeichnet von Boris Pofalla', *Monopol*, vol. 01, 2014, p. 32

Waagen 1854 a
Gustav Friedrich Waagen, *Treasures of Art in Great Britain*, 3 vols., London 1854

Waagen 1854 b
Gustav Friedrich Waagen, 'On the Importance of Manuscripts with Miniatures in the History of Art', *Bibliographical and Historical Miscellanies of the Philobiblon Society*, vol. 1, 1854, pp. 3–11

Watts 1993
Barbara J. Watts, 'Dante's Role in the Nineteenth Century Rediscovery of Botticelli', *Italian Culture*, XI, 1993, pp. 59–76

Watts 1995 a
Barbara J. Watts, The Pre-Raphaelite Movement and the International Competition for Sandro Botticelli's Dante Drawings Manuscript', in *Pre-Raphaelite Art in its European Context*, ed. Susan P. Casteras und Alicia Craig Faxon, Madison NJ / London 1995, pp. 81–99

Watts 1995 b
Barbara J. Watts, 'Sandro Botticelli's illustrations for Inferno VIII and IX: narrative revision and the role of manuscript tradition', *Word and Image*, II, no. 2, 1995, pp. 149–73

Watts 1996
Barbara J. Watts, 'Artistic Competition, Hybris and Humility: Sandro Botticelli's Response to "Visibile Parlare"', *Dante Studies, with the Annual Report of the Dante Society*, vol. 114 (1996), pp. 41–78

Wehry 2013
Katrin Wehry, 'Kaiser Friedrich III. (1831–1888) als Protektor der Königlichen Museen: Skizze einer neuen Kulturpolitik', *Jahrbuch der Berliner Museen*, N.F. 54, 2012, Beiheft, Berlin 2013

Weinberg 1987
Gail S. Weinberg, 'Ruskin, Pater, and the Rediscovery of Botticelli', *The Burlington Magazine*, CXXIX, 1987, pp. 25–27

Wescher 1931
Paul Wescher, *Beschreibendes Verzeichnis der Miniaturen, Handschriften und Einzelblätter des Kupferstichkabinetts der Staatlichen Museen Berlin*, Leipzig 1931

Wierda 2009
Bouk Wierda, 'The true identity of the Anonimo Magliabechiano', *Mitteilungen des Kunsthistorischen Institutes in Florenz*, LIII, 2009, pp. 157–68

Williams 1997
Robert Williams, *Art, Theory and Culture in Sixteenth-Century Italy. From Techne to Metatechne,* Cambridge 1997

Wittlin 1983
Curt Wittlin, *De Sant Miquel Arcàngel. El quint tractat de "libre dels àngels" per Francesc Eiximenis,* Barcelona 1983

Woronowa/Sterligow 1996
Tamara Woronowa / Andrei Sterligow, *Westeuropäische illuminierte Handschriften vom 8. bis 16. Jahrhundert in der Russischen Nationalbibliothek Sankt Petersburg: Frankreich, Spanien, England, Deutschland, Italien, Niederlande,* Bournemouth 1996

Zanichelli 2008
Giuseppa Z. Zanichelli, 'Le Ore di Cecilia Gonzaga', in *Storie di artisti, storie di libri: l'editore che inseguiva la bellezza: scritti in onore di Franco Cosimo Panini*, Rome 2008, pp. 327–43

Zgraja 2015
Karolina Zgraja, 'Mischwesen und Ungeheuer in Federico Zuccaris "Dante Historiato"', in *Monster. Fantastische Bilderwelten zwischen Grauen und Komik*, exh. cat. ed. Peggy Große, G. Ulrich Großmann and Johannes Pommeranz, Nuremberg, Germanisches Nationalmuseum, Nuremberg 2015, pp. 429–37

Zöllner 1997
Frank Zöllner, 'Zu den Quellen und zur Ikonographie von Sandro Botticellis Primavera', *Wiener Jahrbuch für Kunstgeschichte*, 50, 1997, pp. 131–58, 357–66

PHOTOGRAPHIC CREDITS